The American
Immigration Collection

The Immigrant's Day in Court

KATE HOLLADAY CLAGHORN

Arno Press and The New York Times

NEW YORK 1969

THE IMMIGRANT'S DAY IN COURT

AMERICANIZATION STUDIES
ALLEN T. BURNS, DIRECTOR

THE IMMIGRANT'S DAY IN COURT

BY

KATE HOLLADAY CLAGHORN

HARPER & BROTHERS PUBLISHERS
NEW YORK AND LONDON
1923

PUBLISHER'S NOTE

THE material in this volume was gathered by the Division of Legal Protection and Correction of Studies in Methods of Americanization.

Americanization in this study has been considered as the union of native and foreign born in all the most fundamental relationships and activities of our national life. For Americanization is the uniting of new with native-born Americans in fuller common understanding and appreciation to secure by means of self-government the highest welfare of all. Such Americanization should perpetuate no unchangeable political, domestic, and economic régime delivered once for all to the fathers, but a growing and broadening national life, inclusive of the best wherever found. With all our rich heritages, Americanism will develop best through a mutual giving and taking of contributions from both newer and older Americans in the interest of the commonweal. This study has followed such an understanding of Americanization.

FOREWORD

THIS volume is the result of studies in methods of Americanization prepared through funds furnished by the Carnegie Corporation of New York. It arose out of the fact that constant applications were being made to the Corporation for contributions to the work of numerous agencies engaged in various forms of social activity intended to extend among the people of the United States the knowledge of their government and their obligations to it. The trustees felt that a study which should set forth, not theories of social betterment, but a description of the methods of the various agencies engaged in such work, would be of distinct value to the cause itself and to the public.

The outcome of the study is contained in eleven volumes on the following subjects: Schooling of the Immigrant; The Press; Adjustment of Homes and Family Life; Legal Protection and Correction; Health Standards and Care; Naturalization and Political Life; Industrial and Economic Amalgamation; Treatment of Immigrant Heritages; Neighborhood Agencies and Organization; Rural Developments; and Summary. The entire study has been carried out under the general direction of Mr. Allen T. Burns. Each volume appears in the name of the author who had immediate charge of the particular field it is intended to cover.

Upon the invitation of the Carnegie Corporation a committee consisting of the late Theodore Roosevelt, Prof. John Graham Brooks, Dr. John M. Glenn, and Mr. John A. Voll has acted in an advisory capacity to the director. An editorial committee consisting of Dr. Talcott Williams, Dr. Raymond B. Fosdick, and Dr. Edwin F. Gay has read and criticized the manuscripts. To both of these committees the trustees of the Carnegie Corporation are much indebted.

The purpose of the report is to give as clear a notion as possible of the methods of the agencies actually at work in this field and not to propose theories for dealing with the complicated questions involved.

TABLE OF CONTENTS

CONTENTS

CONTENTS

CONTENTS

CONTENTS

CONTENTS

INTRODUCTION

AMONG the relations which make up the network of influences operating to help or hinder the assimilation of the foreign-born residents of this country into our American life, none can be more important, none involves more directly the general relation of confidence, mutual trust, and mutual loyalty than the relation with the law, and its administration.

The immigrant comes here, to a strange country, the ways of which he does not understand. Each new experience affords him a lesson in what is established as justice in this country, and adds its weight toward establishing the degree to which his allegiance and respect for the country will rise.

It is the purpose of this study to follow the immigrant from the port of entry, through some of the troubles that call for the intervention of the law, to see to what extent the law reaches his troubles, how far the administration of law secures for him the substantial justice aimed at in any legal system, what is done by various agencies to adjust him to our laws and legal procedure, and what are his reactions in the way of satisfaction with the country and friendliness to it.

We are not, of course, to suppose that every immigrant who comes to this country gets into all or perhaps any of the forms of trouble described in these pages, or has had some direct encounter with the law through court procedure. Many an immigrant, like many a native of the country, has never been in a difficulty requiring the intervention of the court, has never appeared before a court. Just how great a proportion of the incoming thousands have needed, or have had the attention of, the law it is impossible to say. There is reason to think, however, that in general the immigrant needs the protection of the law more than does the native born. And whatever the number of immigrants who actually come into relation with the law, for every one of these there will be a hundred other immigrants who will know about the case and will be influenced by his impression of what has happened to his friend, or acquaintance, or dweller in his neighborhood, in his own feeling about our laws and our country.

In making this study, it was impossible to gather all cases of difficulty in all parts of the country, for all immigrants, or to view all of the courts at their work through a period of time. The method followed was to make observations and to secure case records in leading cities and towns, mainly in the Eastern and Middle Western states, where the foreign population is large. No claim is made that the data gathered are complete, or that they are valid for other places and times; but it is the belief of the writer that the experiences given are typical; and it is the hope of the writer that what is written here will be an incentive to the reader in any community to take an interest in finding out just what the immigrant is experiencing there, and to take a hand in removing some of the stumbling blocks in his way.

For assistance in this study the writer wishes to thank the court officials, the representatives of social agencies, and other busy people who were so kind as to make the valuable contribution of their own experience and opinions by filling out questionnaires, by giving access to records, and by giving generously of their time in talking over the matters under discussion.

She also wishes to thank the investigators who

INTRODUCTION

gathered a considerable part of the material here presented—Mrs. Margaret D. Laing, Mrs. Florian Znaniecki, Miss Helen Fisher, Mr. Elmo T. Hohman, Miss Jeannette Munro, Mr. Philip A. Greenberg, and Mr. S. M. Auerbach. For friendly and valuable criticism of certain parts of the study the writer wishes especially to thank Dr. George W. Kirchwey and Mr. John A. Fitch, of the New York School of Social Work, and Mr. Robert Ferrari of the New York Bar.

KATE HOLLADAY CLAGHORN

NEW YORK SCHOOL OF SOCIAL
WORK
October, 1922.

THE IMMIGRANT'S DAY IN COURT

THE IMMIGRANT'S DAY IN COURT

I

MONEY TROUBLES

FROM the very moment that the immigrant, who is generally a peasant, decides to start on the long journey to the new country the economic customs and habits that have served him throughout his life so far, and have served his fathers before him, are rudely broken into, and after he reaches here they are found inadequate to meet the new situations he encounters in his daily life.

The European peasant, speaking generally, and in especial the peasant from southern and eastern Europe, has been reared in an economic system in which production is carried on primarily for domestic consumption, and only incidentally for profit through sale in an open market. In such a system money transactions are comparatively few, and money values are by no means a complete measure of economic welfare.

In this system, a business relation is a friendly relation, safeguarded by respect for the relation of friend to friend and for community opinion regarding it.

But just as soon as the peasant emerges from his village he is plunged into a world where business is impersonal, where economic values are measured in money, where general friendly understandings are displaced by written guaranties which will hold in a court of law.

And as there is always some one standing ready to take advantage of ignorance and inexperience, occasions for the immigrant to be cheated out of his money arise

1

even before he has left his own country, continue throughout his journey, and present themselves at every turn for many years after his arrival in the new land.

To begin at the very beginning, in many country villages of Europe agents of steamship lines or of industrial concerns in the United States have found it possible, notwithstanding legal prohibitions against the improper stimulation of immigration, to mislead the peasant, by extravagant promises of large wages, into making a change which his circumstances do not warrant. He does not realize that the wages, which seem so large expressed in terms of dollars, will be considerably reduced by the higher prices of the new country, and by the fact that while at home the peasant usually is able to supply himself with some articles of food and clothing directly from the soil, without money expenditure, in the new country every article of consumption has to be paid for in money.

Having decided to make the journey, he may be cheated in the purchase of steamship tickets, in the provision of the legal papers necessary for leaving the country. Within the past few years a considerable number of immigrants have been debarred from landing at our ports because it was found that their passports, provided by some agent on the other side, had been forged.

PERILS OF THE JOURNEY

On the way, other swindlers will be found to rob the immigrant of money and baggage. In cases recently reported, one woman whose husband lives in Chicago arrived at the port of New York with only one dollar. Another with her five children had only $7.50 when she reached Ellis Island. Another with two children had been robbed of all her money and had lost three hundred pounds of baggage.

On landing in the new country, unless special protection is afforded him, the immigrant will find lying in wait for him, at the very moment of leaving the ship, a swarm of persons ready to relieve him of all the cash he has left after the draining process of the first part of the journey. At the port of New York, in former times, each need of the immigrant had been made the occasion of the most ruthless spoliation. If he wanted his money changed some swindler might give him counterfeit money in exchange for his foreign currency, or might take him to a bank a couple of blocks away, and charge a fee of twenty dollars for the "service." To transport his baggage to a boat or train, or to some city address not far off, some baggage-man or porter might charge eight or ten dollars for what should have cost no more than two, at the most. Not knowing his way around, he might be persuaded to take a cab to his destination. If this was only a block or two away, the cabman might drive him around and around in a circle until time enough was spent to make a basis for a heavy charge. He might also be taken to the wrong destination and turned out in the street, lost and helpless.

This sort of treatment is bad enough in the case of a man, but a woman subjected to it may fall into the worst hands and suffer the worst evils.

At a port of entry through which such masses of immigrants pour as at New York, instances of hard-ship and loss pile up to such an extent that they force themselves on public attention and demand a remedy. Consequently, at this port, measures have been taken, affording more and more complete protection to immigrants.

THE IMMIGRANT'S DAY IN COURT

In the immigration stations itself such safeguards are thrown around immigrant passengers that, at the present time, until actual discharge from the custody of the immigration authorities, the immigrant is well protected from economic loss at the hands of swindlers outside of the station.

None but authorized agents of associations working for the welfare of immigrants are allowed access to immigrants before discharge. These agents render such friendly services as the immigrant needs—help him to communicate with friends, give information and advice, and assist in such business transactions as are necessary.

These agents are under the supervision and direction of a "director of social work," an immigration official, who coördinates their activities and assigns workers to meet different needs. This official also affords a valuable connecting link between the employees of the station and the social workers, who in former times were somewhat at odds.

Further protection has been afforded by especial care in granting discharge, and by extension of the supervision of the Immigration Bureau outside the territory of the station itself. Women and girls are not released without a careful examination of the persons who come to claim them, and any immigrant who is booked to an inland destination, with prepaid tickets, is not discharged until he and his baggage are on the train or boat bound for his destination.

Certain immigrant societies represented at the station are permitted to receive immigrants in immigrant homes while they are waiting for friends, or for information of one kind or another, or to secure a job, but

4

these societies are under government supervision, and their homes are under regulation. If they are found engaging in improper practices they are deprived of their privileges at the station.

And for the immigrant who is discharged into the city of New York, protection from the hotel keeper, the runner, the cabman, the baggageman, and the porter, has been secured by special state and municipal legislation which is fairly effective.

So that at this, the largest port of entry, through which perhaps four-fifths of all our immigrants are received, much of the gross exploitation of former years has been done away with.

But those immigrants who have not finished their journey at New York City are exposed to the old practices of swindling as soon as they are discharged from the custody of the Federal government, aboard the boat or train. If their final destination is some large city, they will find waiting for them on arrival the predatory cabman, baggageman, and hotel runner, as in the old days at the port of New York.

A further extension of Federal supervision seems desirable, just as far toward the end of the immigrant's journey as practical considerations will allow. The protection of the port of entry could not be extended to every small village to which the immigrant might be journeying, but at least immigration stations might be established in the larger cities, to which large numbers of our immigrants are destined and in which the business of exploitation is sufficiently profitable to call in a swarm of swindlers.

A general provision in all the immigration laws since 1822—the date of the first Federal statute regulating immigration—authorizing the commissioner "to establish regulations to protect the United States and the immigrant from fraud and loss," might have enabled him to provide such interior stations at any time. And in the law of 1917 it is specifically provided that "the Secretary of Labor shall establish and maintain immigrant stations at such interior places as may be necessary," and may, at his discretion, send immigrant inspectors to accompany the immigrant to these interior stations from the port. But no appropriations have been made for the establishment of such stations, nor are immigrants accompanied by immigrant inspectors on their journey to the interior.

At the smaller ports of entry fewer safeguards are afforded than at New York. At Boston, in 1914, the conditions were described as follows:[1]

In Boston, after the immigrant has passed inspection, he is regarded as needing assistance and direction no more than the cabin passengers. That very much more is necessary for the bewildered immigrant there can be no question. The waiting room in which he finds himself when admitted is a scene of hopeless confusion. Those who are to remain in Boston are not separated from those who are going farther. Certain favored immigrant bankers and agents of transfer companies mingle with the crowd and add to the confusion. There is no uniform method of handling the baggage, and those who bring orders for railroad tickets to their destination, and those who must purchase them here, are not systematically passed along to the different officials with whom they must deal. Some of the immigrants who are going to friends in or near Boston—the very young or those who have suspicious addresses—are detained by the United States officials until their friends have been notified to call for them; but the great majority are released after primary inspection. . . . The employees of transfer companies also solicit patronage in the third-class waiting room, and occasionally obtain

[1] *Report of the Massachusetts Commission on Immigration, 1914,* p. 164.

money from the immigrants on all sorts of false pretenses.
Representatives of some of the immigrant banks are admitted
to the docks and, as the immigrants come out of the inspection
room, take in charge not only those whose prepaid tickets
were purchased at the bank they represent, but others also.
These they take first to the bank, and then to their relatives
or friends. . . . This situation has several ugly aspects.
The privileges given the bankers on the dock may, as in this
case, help to build up the control which is so many times
abused; illegal fares are collected, and, most serious of all, a
person supposed to be entirely ignorant of the language and
the city may be abandoned when friends are not to be found.

The Massachusetts Bureau of Immigration, established in accordance with a recommendation of the
Massachusetts Commission, secured the interest and
coöperation of the immigration commissioner at the
port in plans for remedying these evils, but the outbreak of the European war put a stop to carrying out
these plans, and conditions there are to-day practically
as described in 1914.

The immigrant, then, at the very beginning of his
new life here, may, through the operations of swindlers,
find himself stripped of all the resources he has brought
with him, and his first experiences of a country where
such practices are allowed to prevail are certainly a
poor initial lesson in citizenship.[1]

EMPLOYMENT

Having run the gauntlet of arrival, the next concern
of the immigrant is to find a job. According to the

---

[1] "While the loss of his money, often representing his total capital
in the new country, is a serious matter to the immigrant, the effect
of his loss in determining his attitude toward America, by replacing
his hope with suspicion and frequently placing a desire for revenge in
his heart, is a serious matter to this country."—*Report of the Commission of Immigration of the State of New Jersey, 1914*, p 22.

contract-labor law, he is not allowed to enter if he comes already provided with one. But as a matter of fact he often has as strict an assurance of employment as if he came under contract. The line between a strictly personal and unofficial assurance of some friend, that if he will come to the establishment where his friend is working he will no doubt find a job (in no way a violation of the law), and the use of this same assurance as a step in a regularly organized method of recruiting workers by the managers of the establishment, is hard to draw.

But those who really do come unprovided with work may naturally have recourse to some private or public employment agency. Private employment agencies are licensed and regulated by law in thirty-one states, but, notwithstanding this fact, the Commission on Industrial Relations reported in 1915 that while there were many private employment agents who tried to conduct their business honestly, they were the exception rather than the rule; that "the business as a whole reeks with fraud, extortion, and flagrant abuses of every kind." Another study in the Americanization series[1] discusses in detail the frauds and abuses connected with the private employment agencies and with other methods of filling jobs, so that we need here only to call attention to some of their main features.

The most common evils noted by the Industrial Relations Commission in the operation of the private agencies were the charging of fees out of all proportion to the services rendered; a discrimination in charges to different applicants for the same job; sending men long distances, after paying fees and transportation, only to find that no one at that place had ordered men from

[1] William M. Leiserson, *Adjusting the Immigrant and Industry* (in press).

the employment agent; splitting fees with foremen or superintendents; leading foremen to discharge men frequently in order to have more men hired through the agent and more fees collected; misrepresentation of terms and conditions of employment, so that men were told that they would get more wages than were actually paid, or that the work would last longer than in fact it would or that there was a boarding house when there was really only an unsanitary camp, or that the cost of transportation would be paid when it was to be deducted from their wages.[1]

In placing women, a special abuse of the employment agencies is found in sending them to disorderly houses under the pretext of providing situations as domestic servants—an abuse concerning the immigrant woman particularly, as so great a proportion of the domestic servants are newly arrived immigrants, and as new immigrants are especially liable to be deceived, through their ignorance of the country.[2]

Employment is offered to the immigrant not only by licensed or regularly established employment agencies, but by any number of people engaged in other kinds of business. The saloon used to be a highly popular labor exchange. Jobs are also offered at cafés, poolrooms, coffee clubs, candy stores, grocery stores, lodging and boarding houses, and even on street corners or in parks.

Bankers, steamship ticket agents, and padroni undertake to find jobs in connection with their other businesses, sometimes with, sometimes without, a

[1] *Report of Commission on Industrial Relations, 1915,* vol. i, pp. 110–111.

[2] *Report of the New York Bureau of Industries and Immigration for 1915,* p. 30. *Report of the New Jersey Commission of Immigration, 1914,* p. 63.

license. In Massachusetts, when the Immigration Commission made its investigation, the Italians who did construction work were usually secured not through the licensed employment agent, but through a padrone, who would come to Boston, Worcester, or Springfield to inspect the men whom the immigrant banker had rounded up for him. Sometimes the padrone would canvass the colony himself. Unlicensed agents are in general harder to hold to account than licensed agents, but in Massachusetts, if they carry on their affairs in the public squares or through canvassing from house to house, they are not even liable for a violation of the employment-agency law if caught.[1]

The victim of one of these agencies is not always through with their exactions when he has finally secured a job. Attempts are often made to collect, in addition to the fee, a certain proportion of the wages for a period of time.

One means used by the employment agencies to entice applicants is through fraudulent advertising in the newspapers. Help wanted advertisements are inserted to attract job seekers to their offices, who are then told that these jobs are taken, when as a matter of fact the "jobs" were fictitious. The job seekers are then urged to register as applicants for future jobs, and they frequently do so.

These advertisements are also used as a means of exploitation without any connection with agencies to find jobs or with any jobs at all, playing upon the pressing need of the immigrant for work by which to earn his daily bread. Among those who make use of labor advertisements in this way are white-slavers, fraudulent real estate dealers and stockbrokers, insurance solicitors,

[1] *Report of the Massachusetts Commission on Immigration, 1914*, pp. 44–45.

sellers of inferior or spoiled goods as samples or outfits, agents for theatrical companies, and many others.[1]

Sometimes the immigrant makes application for employment directly at some establishment where he wants to work. Here he may be hired directly by the foreman, who may now be found exploiting the immigrant alone as he did in partnership with the employment agent. Among the tricks of the unscrupulous foremen are, after giving the man a job, for which he has charged a high fee, to require periodical additional payments of the fee, under threat of discharge. He may also charge a fee for securing increases in pay, or for easier and more agreeable work, and he may ask for special contributions and favors besides, such as presents of liquor, fruit, turkeys, and so on. Foremen have been known to borrow small sums of money from an immigrant just after giving him a job, and then to "forget" or refuse point blank to pay it back, threatening the man with the loss of his job if he should report the matter.

From the woman worker the foreman may also claim more than a monetary reward for keeping her in a job. Instances are known in which foremen have taken advantage of their positions to force women into improper relations.

The foreman and his superiors and inferiors sometimes form a regular hierarchy of exploitation in which the ignorant immigrant is the victim.

For instance, a roadmaster on a railway from North Dakota to Montana, had employed a large number of Greeks to work on the various sections under his charge. A Greek subordinate traveled for him over this division, going from place to place, and informing

[1] P. A. Speek, *Report to the Commission on Industrial Relations on the Labor Market in the West.* (MS.)

11

his fellow countrymen that they must pay him $5 each month in order to hold their jobs, or he would have the roadmaster discharge them. He claimed that the roadmaster had bought a farm and must get so much money each month from the laborers to help pay for it, and would see to it that they got this money back in overtime.[1]

We cannot altogether absolve higher officers of companies from complicity in such frauds. In a long-standing case of exploitation recently brought to light, it appeared that the foreman had been protected for many years because he was a relative of the owner of the business.[2] In another case in Massachusetts, in which nineteen Lithuanian workmen had signed affidavits to the effect that they were regularly paying a part of their wages to one of the foremen in order to keep their jobs, within two weeks after the affidavit had been presented to the president of the corporation, the nineteen men were discharged from their employment.[3]

In Ohio a field agent for this study found that a high official of a certain company, on a salary of $8,000 a year, was shown to have been in connivance with several foreign foremen to sell jobs to their countrymen and to levy contributions from time to time thereafter under threat of "firing" them.

In another Ohio city, as reported by the same field agent, when some forty men who had been charged $5 a job by the foreman in the factory where they were employed, and had been threatened with discharge at the end of a couple of weeks if they did not pay another

[1] P. A. Speek, *Report to the Commission on Industrial Relations on Labor Complaints and Claims.* (MS.)
[2] *Records of the Massachusetts Bureau of Industries and Immigration.*
[3] *Report of the Massachusetts Commission on Immigration, 1914,* p. 40.

fee, complained to a social agency, the owner of the factory attempted so strenuously to shield the foreman that some sort of collusion between them was evident.

After the foreign-born worker has secured a job and settled down in it, the next trick to be played on him is the withholding of his wages. This is one of the most common varieties of exploitation. Complaints about wages made up more than one-fourth of all cases brought to seven of the largest legal-aid societies in 1914; even larger proportions are found in the complaints made at the state bureaus of immigration in different years, and state bureaus of labor which undertake the adjustment of wage claims are plentifully supplied with business in this line. The labor department of the state of Washington, after undertaking this task, found the wage-claim business so heavy that they had to give up trying to handle all of it. With regard to the seriousness of the condition in that state the commissioner[1] reports:

It may be said from the experience obtained in handling these claims that the nonpayment of wages causes untold distress among the working people of this state, and exists to a degree that would surprise those unacquainted with it. . . . Here to a great extent we find the fountain head of the I. W. W. movement.

Sometimes wages are withheld on the ground that the worker has left his employment before the expiration of the period—the week or the month—for which he has been engaged, although in general the worker is legally entitled to wages for such portions of time as he has actually worked, regardless of whether a

[1] *Biennial Report, 1913–14*, pp. 194–195.

13

full period has been completed, unless a definite contract has been made for a hiring by periods, and, in some states, even when such a contract has been made.

This particular pretext for refusal is due in some cases as much to irritation on the part of the employer because the worker has suddenly failed him at a busy time and to a desire to punish him for this, as to a desire to make some money out of him.

A side light on some immigrant handicaps is shown in one case of this nature, where a Greek barber worked less than a week, and dropped out without notice on Friday night, leaving the boss barber in the lurch for Saturday, the busy day. His reason for going was that he was the only foreign-born employee in the shop; the rest were Americans and made life unpleasant for him. Before the case was settled he said unkind things about his boss, but as soon as he got his money he wanted to shake hands with the boss, and said he "never wanted to be mad with anyone." The entire amount of the claim was only three dollars— the difference between the amount due at the full rate, and the rate the barber thought proper to pay when men left before the week was up—and certainly not worth litigating from a money point of view. But the vindication of the worker's right, and the establishment of good feeling toward his employer, were certainly worth as much as the money and justified the expense incurred by the legal-aid society that undertook the case.[1]

Sometimes the employer makes a counterclaim against the employee of damage or theft to justify withholding of the wages. This appears to be partic-

[1] Case of Detroit Legal Aid Society.

ularly common in cases of claims by domestic servants, who are often accused either of breaking or of stealing something.

Sometimes it is alleged by the employer that the amount claimed has already been paid. In many cases it is difficult to prove whether the wages claimed have been paid or not, because the small employer seldom requires the signing of a pay roll and often does not take any form of receipt. Consequently, certain employers will go to court with witnesses to contradict flatly the testimony of the complainant, and it is only by careful and painstaking cross-examination that the facts can be elicited, and sometimes not then.

Even when some written evidence of wages due is held by the worker, the claim may be disputed by the employer, who trusts in the ignorance and helplessness of the immigrant to prevent him from having recourse to the law.

One method of withholding of wages is to refuse payment of bonuses or for overtime, as agreed. This often means a considerable saving to the employer, if many workers are employed on these terms.

Unwritten and indefinite contracts are to blame for some of the disputes about wages, and this sort of contract is especially likely to be accepted by the immigrant, owing to his unfamiliarity with business methods. An unwritten contract cannot easily be substantiated, may be honestly forgotten by one or both parties, or may have been indefinite to start with—just a general understanding. And such a contract may be used with deliberate intent to defraud.

Many cases are brought to the legal-aid societies, giving evidence of a deliberate plan on the part of the employer to let wages accumulate in his hands, and finally refuse to pay. This often happens in the case of domestic servants. The Educational Alliance of New York, in a recent report on the legal-aid work, asks, "Have you any idea of the number of immigrant young women employed as servants, who, when their wages become due, are thrown out bodily?"[1]

Certain restaurant keepers evidently have this habit. One, doing a large business in New York, treated all his employees alike—waiters, dishwashers, and kitchen men. Wages would be withheld until the men got tired of it and left.[2] Many times the men treated in this way have no other resources, have no friends able to help them, and are obliged to ask for charitable assistance.

In one case, a young Russian worked in a downtown restaurant in New York for more than a month, and was then "thrown out" in the very literal sense of the term, without any pay. He claimed that he had been promised twelve dollars a month. The employer, on the other hand, insisted that he had taken the Russian in out of charity, to keep him off the streets and away from the temptations and dangers that beset a man who is idle.[3]

In certain trades is found a practice of withholding wages on the ground that the work is unsatisfactory, or that material has been spoiled, or that the worker is being taught the trade, or that work done is merely in the nature of samples to show what the workers can do.

In many instances it is shown that these are ridiculous pretexts to defraud. In one case, for example,[4] a Russian Jewess, engaged as buttonhole maker at $7

[1] The Educational Alliance, *25th Annual Report, 1915*, p. 61.
[2] Case of New York Legal Aid Society.
[3] Case of New York Legal Aid Society.
[4] Case of New York Legal Aid Society.

a week, was informed at the close of the first week that she would have to work four weeks for nothing before she would be entitled to pay. On threat of suit by the Legal Aid Society the employer paid the amount of her claim.

In another case, an Italian woman who had worked nearly two weeks without pay, and had work checks to show for the work done, was refused payment by the employer on the ground that he had taken both the woman and her husband to teach them the trade—"to learn knee pants," as they put it. It was shown that the woman had already learned to do this work and that even a learner could have earned the amount she claimed—$9.98 in two weeks.[1]

In another case,[2] a Russian engaged as a designer at $30 a week, after working two days and a half, and completing a set of designs needed by the employer, was summarily discharged on the ground that his work was merely a test of ability and not to be paid for. When he made a claim for wages, the employer made a counterclaim that the employee had damaged $20 worth of goods in making the designs. It was shown, however, that the full value of the goods made up into designs was less than half of the alleged damage. It was evident that this was just a clever scheme of the employer for obtaining designs without expense, and on threat of suit he paid the amount of the claim.

Another possibility of fraud is found in paying wages by check, as a means of postponing payment, or even evading it altogether. Sometimes the employer may have no funds in the bank when he issues the check. The worker gets his butcher or grocer to cash

[1] Case of Educational Alliance, New York City.
[2] Case of New York Legal Aid Society.

17

it, but in the course of time it will be returned, marked
"no funds." The employer promises to give another
check—a good one—and meantime the man keeps on
working. When he finally gets the check it may be
for the original amount only, payment of the amount
earned after that time being postponed. Sometimes
the employer purposely makes out the check incorrectly,
to profit by the delay in cashing it caused by returning
it for correction. If the employer can induce the
worker to sign a receipt for the corrected or returned
check as "payment to date," he may perhaps free
himself entirely from paying the wages earned between
the date of issue of the original check, and the date
of payment.

Sometimes this trouble arises because the employer
is really short of money. He may be running a specu-
lative business in which he depends upon returns from
the product to pay for its making. Many small employers of all sorts find themselves in this situation.
So do contractors and subcontractors who do not get
their own money until the work is completed, and
sometimes, if they are working for a city or state, not
until long after that.[1] The State Labor Commissioner
of Washington in a late report makes the following
statement:

The Bureau's experience in handling wage collections
demonstrates that the chief offenders are those operators who
engage in the logging business without capital, fully intending to pay all wages if they can, but who expect their workmen
to wait until they can sell their products. Some saw and
shingle mills can also be found in this class of business; once
in a while a contracting firm, and occasionally a manufacturer.
Because of the great number of these cases, the commissioner

[1] P. A. Speek, *Report on Labor Complaints and Claims to the Commission on Industrial Relations.* (MS.)

is convinced that the working people of the state need help
in this respect more than they do in any other, for it appears
they can take better care of themselves when it comes to
finding employment than they can in collecting wages after
they get a job.

INDUSTRIAL ACCIDENTS

While the immigrant is at work on his job, he may
suffer some injury. For several reasons he is more
likely than the native-born worker to suffer injury.
In the first place, he is represented in greater proportion
in the more hazardous occupations. Furthermore, he is
more likely to be ignorant of the processes of industry
and of the machinery. Then, he may not understand
the English language, and in some establishments
instructions and warning notices are posted in the
English language only. He may, in fact, not be able
to read at all, so that he cannot understand written
instructions in any language. In addition, as a peasant,
he has been accustomed to the slow, deliberate, simple
processes of an old-fashioned type of agriculture, and,
being of the unagile type of mind that such a life
develops, lacks the power to make the quick adjustments
called for in the rush of modern industry.

Statistics permitting an accurate general comparison
of the accident rate of native-born and foreign-born
workers, respectively, are not available. Studies made
by the U. S. Department of Labor of accidents in
special industries, however, are at least suggestive. In
the industry of machine building, it was found that
for the years 1910–13 in one large machine plant
employing over 40,000 workers the accident rate for
American-born workers was 60.6 per thousand, for
the foreign born, 101.8 per thousand, and for a group
of Polish workers in that plant taken separately—
the group of foreign-born containing the greatest

19

proportion of non-English speaking persons, and also the greatest proportion engaged in common labor, the accident rate was 115 per thousand.[1]

In a large plant in the iron and steel industry also studied by the Department of Labor, for the years 1906–13, inclusive, the accident rate for each year was higher for the non-English-speaking foreign worker than for the native-born or the English-speaking foreign worker and the rate for the non-English-speaking workers showed little if any improvement from year to year. For the entire eight years, taken together, the non-English-speaking foreign-born workers had an accident rate 2.3 times that of the American born.

Compensation for injuries or disabilities arising in the course of employment was difficult for the worker to secure under the common-law method of procedure which formerly governed this matter. To recover damages court proceedings were necessary, negligence of the employer had to be specifically proved, and the amount of damages appropriate to the injury had to be determined afresh in each case. This meant the expenditure of much time and money on the part of the worker, who could ill afford it, and the possibility that a clever lawyer on the other side could persuade the court to fix low damages or not grant any at all.

At the present time, federal and state legislation dealing with workmen's compensation has greatly reduced the losses to the workers from uncompensated accidents. Only five states—North and South Carolina, Florida, Arkansas, and Mississippi—and the District of Columbia[2] are entirely without statutory provisions

[1] Accidents and Accident Prevention in Machine Building, *Bulletin No. 256, U. S. Bureau of Labor Statistics*, p. 57.
[2] October, 1922.

for workmen's compensation. In 31 states, among them Massachusetts, New Jersey, Pennsylvania, and Rhode Island, important centers of immigrant population, the statutory method is elective on the part of the employer, but if he chooses the common-law procedure, he is obliged to abrogate certain common-law defenses which hampered the worker in establishing his claim. In 12 states the statutory method is compulsory, among them New York, Ohio, Illinois, and California.

In general, the main advantage in these laws is that they establish a definite scale of benefits for specified disabilities which may be collected without proof of negligence on the part of the employer and without a suit at law.

In 37 states the financial responsibility of employers is secured by requiring them to bind themselves by some form of insurance.

EXCEPTED OCCUPATIONS

Statutory provisions have not, however, cleared away all difficulties for the worker. In first place, not all employments are covered by them. Federal statutes apply only to persons in government service and certain occupations outside of state jurisdiction, for example, to persons engaged in interstate commerce. State laws in general do not cover domestic and farm labor, or persons doing work not in the regular course of the employer's business, or workers in establishments employing fewer than a stated number, ranging from two to six.

Of the 43 states having compensation laws, 30 specifically exclude agricultural workers from the benefits of the statute law, and 6 more exclude them as not on a special list of hazardous occupations. Twenty-seven states exclude domestic servants specifically, and 8 more exclude them as not on a list of hazardous occupations. Among the states excluding both classes of workers are Illinois, Indiana, Massachusetts, New York, and Pennsylvania.

Twenty-nine states, among them Illinois, Massachusetts, New Jersey, and Ohio, expressly exclude "casual workers," meaning generally those whose work is not in the usual course of the employers' business.

RAILROAD WORKERS

Certain of the states expressly except persons employed in interstate commerce because of the conflict of jurisdiction with the Federal government. This is an exception of importance to the immigrant worker, because of the large numbers engaged in such occupations and because recovery of damages is more difficult under the Federal law than under the state laws generally. In 1910 nearly 400,000 foreign-born men were employed on steam railroads, of whom nearly 230,000 were laborers. And this is a highly hazardous occupation.

And if the employee has to have recourse to the Federal law, he has to prove negligence of the employer. State courts (New York and New Jersey) have held that the states have jurisdiction in this class of cases when there has been no negligence on the part of the employer, because the Federal law makes no provision for them, but these courts have been reversed by the Federal courts. In summing up various court decisions on this point, the Bureau of Labor in a report on compensation legislation has to say:

Assuming the exclusive authority of the Federal Act in its territory, the question of which Act to seek relief under, whether state or Federal, remains obscure in many cases.

22

MONEY TROUBLES

The rights of recovery are widely different, dependent upon whether the employee is engaged in interstate or intrastate commerce, and the boundaries between these two classes of employment are not only obscure in themselves, but the efforts of the courts in attempting to determine them have been hardly less confusing than clarifying.[1]

If the courts themselves cannot agree as to the appropriate source of remedy in case of accident, how can the ignorant immigrant be expected to know where to go for redress? Many cases are cited in the above-mentioned report in which the beneficiaries have lost their claim to compensation because they had started proceedings under the wrong jurisdiction, and because by the time the question of jurisdiction was decided, the time had elapsed within which the presentation of claims under the right jurisdiction was permissible.

THE LONGSHOREMAN

Another puzzle due to conflict of jurisdiction was found in the case of the longshore worker until very recently. In 1910 nearly 30,000 foreign-born men were employed as longshoremen—nearly six times the number of native born of native parentage in that occupation. Nearly 17,000 of these were employed in New York State. This is also a highly hazardous occupation. The records of the New York State Compensation Bureau show that one-tenth of the accidents reported in this state happen to longshoremen.[2] In this state the longshoremen formerly had the protection of the state statute, and were upheld in this right by the state courts until the early part of 1922. But decisions of the

[1] *Bulletin of the U. S. Bureau of Labor Statistics. No. 272*, p. 167.
[2] T. V. O'Connor, "The Plight of the Longshoremen," in *American Labor Legislation Review*, June, 1921, p. 144.

THE IMMIGRANT'S DAY IN COURT

United States Supreme[1] Court withdrew that protection on the ground that longshoremen, when employed on a vessel, were subject to admiralty law as maritime workers. The New York state court, furthermore, holds that the state compensation law cannot apply to accidents happening to longshoremen on land, but that the state law of torts must be resorted to for a remedy.[2]

Since recovery under the admiralty law and under the state law of torts was difficult, and since it was hard to determine when the worker did or did not come under any one of the three different jurisdictions, as in the course of his daily employment he may pass from one to another a dozen times, it will be seen that the longshoreman had a hard time in trying to secure compensation for injuries. A further complication arose from the fact that should the longshoreman be shifting freight that is moving in interstate commerce, he had no remedy in the state of New York under the compensation law, but was again thrown back upon the common law of torts for his remedy.

A Federal act of June 10, 1922, however, has removed one of these difficulties by amending the Judicial Code to secure for longshoremen exclusive rights and remedies under state compensation laws.

MEDICAL PROOF OF DISABILITY

Another loophole of escape for the employer in the state laws is found in the fact that while they provide a fixed scale of awards for specified injuries or degrees of disability, so that argument and adjudication on

[1] Jensen *vs.* Southern Pacific, 244 U. S. 205, Stewart *vs.* Knickerbocker Ice Co., May 17, 1920.

[2] Status of Longshoremen, Report No. 639. H. R. 67th Congress, 2d Session.

amount of compensation for a given injury are no longer necessary, it is necessary to prove the nature and extent of the disability. In 27 states, including Illinois, Massachusetts, and Pennsylvania, medical examination to determine the injured person's physical condition is made by a medical practitioner provided and paid by the employer. To guard against the possibility that the company doctor will minimize the extent of the injury, in 23 of these states the employee is entitled to have a medical practitioner of his own selection, and paid by him, present at the examination.

But it is readily seen that even with this protection the company has something of an advantage over the workman. The worker may be too poor or too ignorant to make use of the privilege of having a doctor of his own selection present. If he does, the practitioner is likely to be less able and skillful than the one employed by the company. In case of disagreement between these two practitioners, when the employee has a doctor of his own, provision is generally made for submitting the dispute to the industrial commission, if there is one, or to the court, for settlement. In 12 of the 23 states, express provision is made for examination by a third practitioner, designated by the commission, and presumably in the other states where an industrial commission exists this commission must pass in some way on the merits of the dispute. Where no third, neutral physician makes an examination, however, and the dispute has to be settled by presentation of testimony of the representatives of the parties in interest only, the company doctor is again at an advantage, from his usually superior skill in preparing and presenting a case.

In 10 states, among them Ohio and New York, the medical examination is made under the direct jurisdiction of the commission or court, presumably insuring greater impartiality, but the decision so made is not final if some other practitioner disputes it, and as in these states generally the employer is required to furnish medical service to the employee, as part of his compensation, the doctor thus employed may appear as a witness against the injured person when his claim comes up for a hearing before the board. In a recent case reported in New York,[1] a claimant had been examined by 32 physicians, including the medical officers of the Industrial Commission, and in his struggle to obtain compensation he could not rely upon any one of them to act as witness on his side of the case. Commissioner Connor concludes[2] that "the fact that the insurance carriers control the selection of attending physicians has worked to the disadvantage of the injured workman. Aside from this, the medical profession as a whole is greatly dissatisfied with the present system, which has developed into a business undertaking and has destroyed the confidential relationship and the human interest as between physician and patient."

COMPULSORY MEDICAL TREATMENT

One provision found in the compensation laws of 21 states, including Illinois, Indiana, New Jersey, and Pennsylvania, which seems entirely reasonable in itself, is the requirement that the worker shall accept "essential" or "reasonable" medical and surgical treatment, in order to secure compensation for disability, this requirement, however, causes considerable resentment in the mind of the immigrant worker, especially

[1] *Report of Investigation by Jeremiah F. Connor of the Management and Affairs of the State Industrial Commission*, Albany, 1919, p. 22.
[2] *Ibid.*, p. 23.

when it involves hospital treatment of any kind or an operation.

In general he has a great dread and dislike of hospitals and hospital treatment. Some good reasons exist for this dislike. The foreign-born patient in an American hospital, if he cannot speak English, cannot easily make his wants known; he is separated from his family and is lonesome, the food given him is probably different from the kind he is used to, and will be unsatisfactory to him on that account alone, aside from the well-known deficiencies which generally characterize hospital dietaries, and has probably gone to the hospital filled with the gossip that floats through immigrant colonies, about the "black bottle" given to patients to speed them out of this world, and about the use of patients, alive and dead, for medical experimentation. And finally, there is reason to believe that in some hospitals there is a real neglect of poor patients which these workers have heard of. So that it seems to the immigrant workingman an injustice to be forced to encounter these perils.

DIRECT SETTLEMENTS

A fruitful means through which the employer may get the better of the employee in compensation claims is found by inducing the injured person to make a direct settlement for cash with the employer. State compensation laws generally provide that no direct settlement is allowable unless the sum agreed upon comes up to the sum fixed by the law, or unless the settlement has been submitted to the state commission for approval, or both. But in practice the checking-up process of the commission may be imperfect, so that agreements may go through without their knowledge and the commission may also assent perfunctorily to agreements brought before them without sufficient inquiry to determine whether these agreements are or are not in accord with the law and the facts.

To what extent compensation due the worker may be cut down if direct settlement without genuine scrutiny on the part of some state body is permitted, is indicated by the investigation made of 1,000 cases of direct settlement under the New York law before it was amended to prohibit this.[1] In 114 of the 1,000 cases, it was found necessary, after investigation, to make additional awards amounting to $52,279.84, or about four times the original settlement. Had this proportion of underpayment per thousand cases held good throughout the year, the total underpayments for one year alone on the 34,659 cases of that year would have amounted to over $1,750,000. In regard to these cases Commissioner Archer said:

Generally employees are so ignorant of their rights that, left to their own devices, it would be easy to get them to settle for comparatively small sums, totally irrelative to the nature of their injuries or based on the extent of their disabilities.

Employers may further evade their responsibilities to employees by violations of the law which may escape notice for some time. In New York State, the counsel of the state Industrial Commission has recently pointed out that numerous cases occur every year in which the commission's awards cannot be collected from irresponsible employers because they have failed to carry the insurance required by the statute.[2]

Again, although state compensation laws distinctly provide that no part of the expense of compensation is to be borne by the worker, ingenious employers think

[1] *Report of Investigation by Jeremiah F. Connor, of the Management and Affairs of the State Industrial Commission,* Albany, 1919, p. 47.
[2] New York *Times,* May 9, 1921.

up ways to get their money back from the injured men. In a case brought to the New York Legal Aid Society, a firm rated at over a million dollars had paid a claim of $134.55 to a workman for a mutilated finger, after which the workman found his next pay envelope $2 short. On inquiry he was told that this deduction would be made until the amount of the award was made up. He stood this for 9 weeks, and was then discharged. In answer to the legal-aid society presenting the complaint, the firm alleged that as the man was not incapacitated for more than 2 weeks, and as he had received his wages in full each week, they were entitled to the refund. Their excuse for discharging the man was that he had stolen something. That these excuses were baseless is indicated by the fact that the firm paid the claim when pressed by the Legal Aid Society.

A special restriction on the rights of the foreign-born worker under state compensation laws is found in provisions cutting down the benefits for nonresident alien beneficiaries. This ranges from absolute refusal of all benefits to all nonresident alien beneficiaries, to cutting off a greater or less proportion of the full benefit, and granting the benefit to a more or less restricted circle of beneficiaries. Only 10 states, among them Illinois and Ohio, make no distinction between resident and nonresident beneficiaries.

A CASE IN POINT

A case brought to the attention of a social agency in Chicago illustrates some of the troubles and losses incurred through industrial injury, even under a good workmen's compensation law.[1] A Lithuanian woman

[1] Immigrants' Protective League, case running from November, 1915, to January, 1919.

reported to this agency that her husband, after being out of work for two months, and then getting a job with an ice company, on the first night of his employment fell on the ice and dislocated his arm. Apparently, there was no trouble about his compensation except some delay in the payments, but two months after that accident the woman injured her right arm at a fire drill in the packing house where she was employed. (The floor was slippery.) The case shows apparent delay and neglect on the part of the company in providing medical attendance and examination, and at a date a month after the accident they had offered no compensation, but two weeks after the accident they had offered her work. They had given medical treatment only three times, and the woman had gone to a doctor of her own, a man of good reputation who had said that she would not be able to work for three or four months. The company later began to pay her $6 a week for the disability, giving her back pay, covering the time since the accident, and telling her to call for the $6 every week thereafter. She had been earning $6.90 a week. The company discontinued payment after 14 weeks, whereupon the woman went to a lawyer to secure further payments on her claim. Meanwhile she had acquired a profound distrust of the company, its doctors, nurses, and a dispensary to which she was sent, of the last because they had mislaid an X-ray picture which they had taken of her, and she charged them with being in league with the company. Two months later the case finally came before the Industrial Board, which awarded her $126, the doctor appointed by the board to make an examination saying that her arm was in good condition. The expenses falling on the woman for this hearing amounted to $20 for the doctor's bill and the X-ray picture, $9.45 for a stenographic record of the case, and $20 for her attorney's service, all of which, deducted from the company's check for the amount of compensation, left her $76.55. This award was made just one year after the accident. The company, asked to take her back, refused to do so. Two weeks later it was found that the woman was unable to work, her arm was so painful. Her lawyer then took steps to review the case on the ground of recurrence of injury. By this time the company opened negotiations for a new settlement with the woman and offered to take her back, giving her light work. After this the woman was examined by a dispensary doctor, by the company doctor once more, by another dispensary doctor, then by another hospital doctor, who left for army service without giving a certificate of condition, so that it was necessary for still another doctor to make an examination. By this time, the record notes, "she is very much disgusted . . . almost refused to go to see Doctor L., coming Wednesday." She finally took this examination and agreed to pay $10 to still another doctor to appear at a rehearing before the Industrial Board. This doctor proved to be "a very kind man" who would "do his best." Finally, nine months after the first hearing, the second hearing was held by the Industrial Board, at which the company doctor, the woman's last doctor, and a third doctor appointed by the Industrial Board were present, and the woman was again examined. As a result of this examination, the company doctor recommended payment for a 10-per-cent disability, her own doctor, for 40-per-cent disability and more, while the board doctor split the difference and recommended payment of a 20-per-cent disability, which would amount to $240. The company doctor and the woman's doctor agreed to accept the recommendation of the board doctor, and a month later the woman received a check for the amount from the company, at which "she was so glad that she had tears in her eyes."

Eight months after this it is noted that "her arm is very bad." The case record says little about the husband after the first account of his accident. Just before the woman's accident it is noted that the husband "is still working, but he is not well at all. He has some pain in his chest." Then, that he went on strike and was discharged, but soon after that was working again. At that time, just before the woman's accident, he was earning $9 to $10 a week, and out of this and her $6.90 three children were to be supported. The oldest daughter at home finally reached working age, and got employment at $4 a week. The record notes, "It is impossible for Mary to go to school because Mrs. M. cannot work steadily and Mary is compelled to go to work." After the woman's case was settled, the husband reappears in the case. The record states that he was beaten up in the yards where he was employed, and injured so badly he had to stop working for several weeks. The visitor of the agency to which the case was brought writes that she has known him for years and that "he is an exceptionally nice and sober man." The record closes with the statement that the woman's "arm still pains" and that the man is still working, but will have to give up the job because it is too hard, and that he still has bad pains in his head, as a result of the beating.

BANKING

Even while running the gauntlet of the swindlers lying in wait for him at every turn, the immigrant is often able to save considerable amounts of money, through a patient economy. If he is a newly arrived immigrant who has left his family behind in the old country, probably the first thing he wants to do with his money is to send it to his family for their support; the next thing, to purchase a steamship ticket to get them over here.

While the little fund for tickets or remittances is accumulating, however, what is he to do with it? He has the choice of keeping it in his own possession or giving it to some one to take care of. The peasant immigrant, if he were at home and had money saved up, would naturally conceal it in the form of cash somewhere about the premises—in the proverbial "stocking," perhaps. But his places of safekeeping in this country are anything but safe—the belt around his waist, his trousers pocket, his bed, or his trunk in a room which he probably shares with strangers.

If he decides to ask some one to take care of the money for him, he does not naturally turn to the big American bank, for a number of reasons. One is his lack of acquaintance with banks as an institution, and with the operations of a credit system, such as a book account, payment by checks, and so on. The money seems lost to him when he can no longer trace and lay hold of the exact number of material dollars turned in, when he has to go through a series of formalities to get possession of an equivalent value.

And the American banks are not conveniently located for him. They are usually situated at a considerable distance from the neighborhood in which he lives and works, and are open only in his own working hours. So that in order to make use of them he would have to take time off from his work, which he cannot well afford.

If he does make his way to the American bank, he is oppressed by the fine surroundings, the cold white

33

marble, the polished metal, and the no less polished
and cold bank clerks, who do not understand his
wants or his language and are too busy to bother with
him.[1]

And he is a bit suspicious of all this elegance: perhaps
the bank is taking his money to pay for it, he thinks;
furthermore, he is not personally acquainted with any
of these people, consequently is unwilling to trust them.
Banking, to him, is a friendly favor. You trust your
money to the keeping of a friend, not to earn interest
on it, but to have it kept safely, as you would intrust
an important secret, or the care of a wife or child. In
a strange country, if no personal friend is available,
the immigrant will next give his confidence to a countryman—preferably one from his own neighborhood.

The immigrant, then, turns to some one nearer at
hand than the American bank to keep his money for
him, preferably to some one of his own race, often to
some one with whom he is already in business relation—
to the ever-helpful saloon keeper before that functionary was abolished, to the grocer with whom he
deals, to his boarding boss, or to the labor agent
through whom he secures his jobs. Or it may be
to the ticket agency of the steamship line which

[1] "Strange as it may seem its very equipment prevents the
American bank from entering into competition with the immigrant banker. A Slovak immigrant banker, in apologizing somewhat for the appearance of the banking room, stated that it
was necessarily ill kept because the men would come in their working clothes, often covered with mud, frequently intoxicated, which,
together with smoking and spitting, kept the room in a constant
state of disorder. Such a condition would not be tolerated by an
American bank. Moreover, the average immigrant feels a certain
hesitancy in entering in his working clothes a building of the character of some city banks."
The U. S. Immigration Commission: *Report*, vol. xxxvii, Immigrant Banks, p. 216.

brought him to this country. He will be inclined to do this because the line itself is familiar to him, and a link with home, and the agency the place where he expects to spend his money for the tickets to bring his family over.

THE IMMIGRANT BANK

From some such beginnings has developed that characteristic institution known as the immigrant bank. The saloon keeper, the labor agent, the real estate dealer, the ticket agency may find the holding of money, at first undertaken as a casual accommodation, increase to such an extent that it will outweigh the other functions, and the person doing the business will regard himself as a banker primarily, and call his place of business a "bank."

On the other hand, just as the grocer received money from the immigrant as a convenience, the "bank," which has developed from some other business, offers to perform various other services than banking, as a convenience. The immigrant on account of his lack of time to attend to business, and his ignorance of business, needs a general business agent who will attend to all of his affairs at once. So that, whatever the name of the establishment with which the immigrant deals, we may expect to find it carrying on many other functions than those expressed in its name.

The man who calls himself a banker may sell steamship tickets, may meet immigrants at the docks and assist them to secure admission to the country, may find jobs for them, may offer legal advice and notary service, and may render miscellaneous personal services, such as acting as interpreter, writing letters for clients, receiving and forwarding mail, and even finding board and lodging for them, or assisting in the purchase of

clothing and other things that they need, and may
have on sale in the bank itself many little things that
the immigrants want, such as special kinds of food to
which they are accustomed, tobacco, jewelry, musical
instruments, foreign books, and so on.[1] Of 110 immigrant banks investigated by the Immigration Commission, only one had no other business connected with
it, the list of other businesses carried on in connection
with the remaining 109 included collections, insurance,
rentals, real estate, notary public, interpreter, labor
agency, postal substation, books, jewelry, novelties,
saloon, grocery, meat shop, fruit store, general mer-
chandise, wholesale importers, and barber shop.[2]
During the European war certain bankers made an
important feature of offering to secure exemption
from military service.

And these bankers take special pains to be ready to
transact business at hours convenient for their clients—
at night or on Sundays, and to meet the general requirement of the immigrant depositor, that his money is
to be paid at any instant in which he may happen
to want it—even in the middle of the night.

LACK OF SAFEGUARDS

As these banks naturally developed, and as they
were described in the report of the Immigration Commission, they afforded the immigrant banker every
opportunity for exploitation. Few of the immigrant
banks were incorporated; for the most part they were
privately owned and irresponsibly managed. Evidence of deposit was often inadequate, or entirely

[1] The U. S. Immigration Commission: *Report*, vol. xxxvii, Immigrant Banks, pp. 217, 233.
[2] The U. S. Immigration Commission: *Report*, vol. xxxvii, Immigrant Banks, pp. 211–212.

lacking. Many issued no pass books, and the personal receipt of the proprietor was generally accepted as sufficient. It was not uncommon for laborers to lose their receipts and, forgetting how much was due them, take without question whatever balance the banker chose to return. As the deposits were seldom subject to check this form of evidence of withdrawal was also lacking.

The owner of the bank, or the person who received money on deposit in the course of some other business, and the depositor himself, saw no reason for making a distinction between banking funds and the money belonging to the banker personally. It was quite the custom for the banker to keep the money intrusted to him with his own private funds. The grocer or the saloon keeper would meet current bills with these deposits. Another type of banker, while allowing the depositor no interest, would redeposit the funds in an American bank, at interest, in his own personal account. As examples of banking methods, it is noted[1] that a boarding boss would receive money, give no receipt, use the funds as he saw fit. Again, a saloon keeper had only one book in which deposits were entered; and the entries were scratched out when the deposit was withdrawn. In the same book drink bills and board bills were charged against the deposits.

These banks usually had neither capital nor reserves, and often no tangible assets of any kind, so that, should the banker fail, there was no redress for the depositor. Deliberate gathering of funds with the intention of absconding when a sufficient amount had been collected was a common practice, and many of these bankers simply shut up shop and left for unknown regions with all the little wealth of their depositors.

[1] The U. S. Immigration Commission: *Report,* vol. xxxvii, Immigrant Banks, p. 227.

This could be done with ease in states that did not regulate or prohibit private banking, and even in some that did the immigrant bankers seemed to find ways to evade the law.

PROTECTIVE LAWS

The laws themselves have been made more stringent since the time of the Immigration Commission's report. At that time, 1910, only 7 states prohibited private banking; in 1920, 16 states did so. In 1910, 7 states were absolutely without regulation of any kind for private banks; in 1920 only 3 were without regulations.

Of the 22 states in which the Immigration Commission found immigrant banks in operation, 8, among them Illinois where some of the worst abuses existed, now prohibit private banking altogether, 8, among them New York and Pennsylvania, hold private banks under strict state supervision, 3, among them Massachusetts, have enacted legislation especially intended to cover the activity of the immigrant bank, while only 2 of these states have merely minor regulations and only one—no regulations at all—all the last 3 having few immigrant banks and few of the newer immigrants.

At the present time the safekeeping of deposits is fairly well guarded, except for actual evasions of the law, which are especially easy for the immigrant banker, since he can run a small business with little publicity; but possibilities for abuse still exist in the sale of steamship tickets and the transmission of money.

SALE OF STEAMSHIP TICKETS

Swindling in the sale of prepaid steamship tickets is possible, partly because there is such a long chain of intermediaries between the purchaser of the ticket and the person to whom he sends it on the other side. Notwithstanding laws holding the responsible sellers of tickets to account, there seems to be nothing to prevent unauthorized persons from selling orders for tickets, and receiving money, as agents for the authorized agencies, which refuse to be responsible until they have received the money. Even after the passage of stringent laws in New York State regulating the sale of steamship tickets, the Bureau of Industries and Immigration reported (1913) the receipt of 92 complaints against steamship agencies alleging that money was paid for tickets which were never received, refunds on canceled tickets were being withheld, deposits were not returned, although no tickets had been issued and the passengers found that they could not sail, while prepaid tickets which the agent was to have sent abroad to the purchaser's relatives were never mailed. Twenty complaints were made against one notorious licensed agent advertising exclusively in foreign-language newspapers.

MONEY TRANSMISSION

In the transmission of money, also, the immigrant banker, or other person undertaking to perform this service, may take advantage of the transmitter because of the many hands through which the money may pass.

The immigrant banker to whom the immigrant intrusts his money for transmission usually sends it abroad through some larger bank or some express company, which, in turn, sends it on through foreign corresponding banks, to the final destination, which is, perhaps, some remote village with no banking facilities. All that the immigrant gets in the nature of a receipt for his money is the receipt of the immigrant banker or agent, for which the transmitting bank does not make itself responsible, nor does it secure for the transmitter an acknowledgment of receipt on the part of the payee. According to the system in use, the transmitting bank, furthermore, has no means of knowing how long the agent has kept the money before forwarding it for transmission. This gives the agent ample opportunity to use the money for his own purposes.

One means of attracting immigrants to irresponsible agents for the transmission of money, and one means of swindling them, is in juggling with rates of exchange. The large institutions sell orders at rates which are fixed by conventions with the various foreign governments, and are not subject to periodic fluctuations. So that the small agencies attract custom by offering more favorable rates. Some, with intent to defraud, offer impossibly low rates as a bait, and, when a sufficient sum has been collected, run off with the money. This is not at all an uncommon practice.

A particularly mean and heartless form of fraud in this line has flourished vigorously since the outbreak of the European war. In the conditions of distress prevailing in Europe, immigrants have been especially anxious to send money to their families. While the war was stopping communication with certain countries, bankers would receive money to be transmitted to those places at the first opportunity. In such cases the customer would buy, for his dollar, so many rubles or crowns. Finally, the customer, finding that the money could not be sent, would ask for the return of his money. But the banks would allow the return only at the rate of exchange prevailing at that time. As the value of foreign currency dropped steadily after the beginning of the war, and especially after the signing of the armistice, it will be seen that the losses suffered on this score have been tremendous. Even where money could be sent through, these "bankers" have taken advantage of the possibility of holding it without detection, to take advantage for their own profit of a drop in the rate of exchange after the money has been placed in their hands. This sort of exploitation has been especially common in the mining districts of Pennsylvania, but has been reported from all over the country, notwithstanding state laws, as in New York, New Jersey, Massachusetts, and Pennsylvania, providing a time limit (five to seven days) within which money given for transmission must be forwarded. The Massachusetts Bureau of Immigration notes that:[1]

> . . . in some of the cases reported to the bureau the persons sending money to dependents in the home country stated that grave injustice had been done them by the delay in transmission, claiming that money for the imperative need of their families was illegally retained by the banker until war conditions rendered transmission impossible, and that, because of failure to transmit, their wives and families had suffered unnecessary privation, and that, while these persons have redress in civil action, no refund of money could change the privation which the delay caused, nor should the immigrant of little means be forced to expend in such civil suit most if not all the money involved, together with his loss of time.

One case shows in detail the operation of the swindle of holding money for a drop in exchange. On April 16, 1917, a Russian Jew transmitted through a local bank $550 to a government savings bank in Europe, and on June 16, 1917, he sent $40 more. When he called at the local bank in December, 1917, to inquire about the order, he learned that the first order had been sent out on October 9, 1917, and the second on January 18, 1918. The first order, for which he paid $550 in April, should

[1] *Report, 1919*, p. 19.

have cost not more than $320 in October. The man was thus entitled to a refund of $265 and $10.68 interest, under the Massachusetts law that money received for transmission shall be forwarded within seven days of its receipt.[1]

In New York State the legislature of 1920 amended the banking law and the general business law, to place additional safeguards about the transmission of money.[2]

Had the immigrant, however, had recourse to the governmental postal service for transmitting his money abroad at any time during the war, he would have found a gap between the amount he received for his dollars and the actual rate of exchange which hardly any private banker could surpass. Until August, 1920, the rates in effect for outgoing money orders were those which had been in use for many years back. These rates had not been changed by our government during the period of the war, although most of the foreign governments had considered it necessary to change the rates from time to time on money orders issued abroad for payment in the United States. A huge profit accrued to the government by sending such remittances as were intrusted to it during the war period, at losses to purchasers of from 8 to 56 per cent. on the market rate. It is not hard to see why the immigrant turned to the immigrant banker in preference.

There are other reasons, also, why the postal service is not more freely used, even in normal times, for the transmission of money. The official in charge of the registry division in 1909 mentioned the following: First, the illiteracy of immigrants. They are unable to fill out for themselves the necessary blanks, and, as the post office clerks generally do not speak foreign lan-

[1] Case of Massachusetts Bureau of Immigration.
[2] In laws of New York, 1921, ch. 354.

guages, they cannot assume the responsibility of writing the names and addresses as pronounced by immigrants, which might lead to errors, and the consequent liability of the clerk. Again, branches of the post office where money orders may be secured are not scattered widely and close at eight o'clock, so that they are not easy of access. Substations in small places like drug stores, where the proprietor cannot be expected to understand the regulations governing foreign exchange, are not permitted to issue money orders on foreign countries nor are such orders issued in many small-town post offices.[1]

THE NOTARY

The function of notary, which the banker often adds to his business, and which any of the types of business agent may perform, is worthy of mention by itself. The immigrant needs the services of a notary public on many occasions, not only in the ordinary business transactions of everyday life, but in the sometimes difficult and complicated proceedings necessary in attending to affairs in the old country, such as collecting money due, establishing claims to inheritance, transferring property, making affidavits for the purpose of getting a family over from the other side.

Consequently, the banker or steamship agent, or the real estate dealer or any of the business agents who undertake to handle the immigrant's affairs for him, is likely to get himself or some one in his office appointed notary, so that the immigrant will patronize him in that capacity also.

THE NOTARY IN EUROPEAN COUNTRIES

The immigrant is attracted by the title of the notary and ready to intrust his affairs to him, because, so far

[1] *Report of the New York State Commission of Immigration, 1909,* p. 27.

as he has ever heard of the notary in his own country, the name has meant to him a person of education and standing in the community, in whom it is safe to have trust. In European countries generally the duties of the notary are limited to receiving and authenticating documents much as they are in this country. But in European countries a preliminary training in the business of being a notary is generally required, notaries are under strict government control, and the number is limited to a degree which will permit specialization in the notary's function.

In Italy, for example, to become a notary it is not necessary to take the full legal training required for the lawyer's profession, but a two years' university course, based upon the fundamental conceptions of law, is required, and most of the notaries, as a matter of fact, do not confine their preparation within these limits. After the candidate has passed a university examination in these courses, he must have two years of practical experience in the office of a notary already practicing, after which he must pass another examination before the court of appeal. When he is ready to practice he is not permitted to open an office just wherever he likes. Notarial posts, like courts or other government offices, are established by the government, and anyone desiring to practice as a notary must receive government permission to occupy one of those posts. When one is vacant, the applicant considered to be the best equipped as tested by a competitive examination, receives the appointment. Before the successful applicant may practice, he must give security, which will serve, if necessary, to guarantee compensation for damages caused by the notary in the exercise of his functions, or any other pecuniary penalties in which he might be held. Furthermore, he may not carry on

44

other businesses than his own—he may not be a
government official, nor practice as a lawyer, nor be a
merchant or a minister of any religious worship.[1]

These requirements give the Italian notary a high
professional standing and the authority of a public
official.

THE AMERICAN NOTARY

The notary in this country has to meet no such requirements. He must receive authorization from the state
to perform his function, but practically the only requirements for his license to practice in most of the states are
that he shall be at least twenty-one years of age and a
citizen. In some half dozen of the states (Indiana,
Illinois, Michigan, Washington, Wyoming) appointment
is made only on petition of a certain number of citizens
or indorsement by a judge; in three states (Georgia,
Louisiana, and Wyoming) some evidence of "good
moral character" has to be presented. In only two
states (Arizona and Wyoming) has any sort of educational qualification been established. In these, ability
to read and write the English language is required.
Elsewhere a notary may be entirely illiterate and not
even able to speak English. Nor are the numbers limited in any way. In consequence, so many people rush
into the notarial business that it cannot bring in sufficient income to be carried on as a separate business; it
can be only incidental to some other calling.

With so little restriction upon entry into that business, with the opportunity of profiting by the respect
the immigrant has for the official of the same name
but higher qualification in his own country, it is easy to
see how this office will draw to it a class of unscrupu-

[1] Atillio Stanislao Du-Besse, *The Notarial System in Italy*, No. 5,
Comp. Law Bureau of Am. Bar Association, 1912, pp. 32 ff.

lous persons who wish to use it for defrauding the immigrant.

It is easy to see also how little good and how much harm a notary of this type can do in handling the affairs of an immigrant, especially those which involve, as is so often the case, transactions with the other side. For to carry these on successfully, the notary should know something about foreign as well as American procedure, and something about our own immigration law. Even when the notary is perfectly honest and well-meaning, he may be the cause of serious loss to the immigrant by making out papers wrongly and starting proceedings improperly. And we may even call it exploitation because a notary of this type must be aware of his own ignorance of the affairs he is willing to handle.

The deliberate exploiter takes further advantage of the immigrant by undertaking to do various things that he is not legally empowered to perform. The notary's powers and duties are in general limited to administering oaths, taking affidavits, acknowledging instruments, and demanding acceptance of payment and protesting of commercial paper. But the unscrupulous notary is not averse to including in his advertisement offers to undertake legal services, or to do other things for which he is not equipped. He may also show himself willing to violate the law in carrying on the operations he is legally entitled to perform. In instances brought to the notice of social agencies, notaries have falsified dates on papers, have certified to affidavits known by them to be false, and have taken acknowledgments without seeing the persons making them or without knowing who they were. In a case reported from New York, an Italian impersonating a dead brother-in-law induced a notary to certify to his signature for withdrawing a sizable bank account left by the dead man.[1] In an investigation made for the New Jersey Commission on Immigration, it was found that 17 out of 33 notaries written to would agree to execute documents by mail, that in 13 cases witnesses unknown to the grantor were furnished by the notary, in 7 cases the notary did not see the grantors at all: in the case of one document, which was executed by a notary, the grantor saw neither the notary nor the witnesses.[2]

The notary of this type is also found committing plain stealing and swindling through his notarial power of authenticating signatures, or his relation with a client who trusts him with authority to draw money, witness documents, or obtain signatures. Reports of state immigration commissions and commissions of investigation into the exploitation of immigrants afford numerous examples of the losses inflicted upon immigrants in that way. In New York, for instance, a notary secured $110 compensation for accident, in return for a release which he gave the company, without any knowledge on the part of the injured man. In another case a notary drew from a savings bank the money called for by two pass books left with him by a poor Italian woman. It was found that payment was made pursuant to special powers of attorney supposed to be executed by her and her husband before this notary, when as a matter of fact the husband had never seen the notary, and the wife had never signed anything.[3]

A popular method of defrauding employed in case of

---

[1] *Report of the Commission of Immigration, New York, 1909,* p. 215.

[2] *Report of the Commission of Immigration of the State of New Jersey, 1914,* p. 101.

[3] *Report of the Commission of Immigration, New York, 1909,* p. 215.

the sale of a business is for the notary to induce the seller to place in his hands considerable sums of money for satisfying possible claims against the business and then to refuse either to pay the debts or return the money.[1]

BUSINESS VENTURES

When the immigrant has got his family over to this side and settled in a home here, and when as many of the family as are able to do so have gone to work, he begins to save up money again, and now, after a time, is ready to invest his savings in the new country. Sometimes he wants to start up a little business of his own. Here again the swindler is lying in wait for the immigrant. Extensive advertising is put forth to attract him into all sorts of enterprises of a business nature. Sometimes he himself advertises for business opportunities and is picked up by the swindler in that way. Especially attractive to the immigrant is an opportunity for investment involving the employment of the investor, for this will bring in wages to afford livelihood while the business is establishing itself. Often such an opportunity will be offered when no business and no employment exists. In a California case, a young immigrant who had advertised that he had a few hundred dollars to invest, with his services, was offered steady employment at good wages, but was required to deposit $150 as a guaranty of the faithful performance of his duties. The whole scheme turned out to be a fraud. The exploiter's plan was to secure such deposits from each applicant for employment, give them work for a week or two while other victims were gathered in, and then, when a goodly sum had been collected, to disappear with the proceeds. While employed, the men

[1] *Report of the Commission of Immigration, New York, 1909*, p. 48.

were engaged in distributing handbills advertising a fictitious "sale."[1]

Sometimes the immigrant who has been induced to invest in a little business as a partner is frozen out on the pretense that the business does not pay. Sometimes the "business" he invests in does not exist at all. Sometimes it is a "right" in a so-called invention which is not worth anything. Sometimes, and very often, it is a chance to invest in a stock company. Some of the most widespread and notorious frauds carried on in the past have been of this nature, certain foreign-language newspapers acting as agents for the immigrant business of some big promotion scheme intended to catch all classes of people.

A recent example is a scheme worked among Ukrainian immigrants. Certain promoters have been going about among them, selling stock, promising large dividends, and urging, as a special inducement, that the money invested was to be used for the reconstruction of the home country and for the establishment of commercial relations with the United States. After gathering in all the money to be secured within a neighborhood, these promoters close their offices and move to another place for a fresh harvest. There is no "company" and no "investment"; the promoters simply pocket the entire proceeds.

This dealing in business opportunities has given rise to a special class of exploiter, known as the business broker. The report of the New York Bureau of Industries and Immigration of 1913, p. 61, described their activities as follows:

The windows of their offices are covered with large and impressive scarlet seals. Whenever a simple-minded immi-

[1] *Report of the Commission of Immigration and Housing of California, 1916,* p. 115.

grant storekeeper wants to sell his little store, the business broker quickly calls on him, promising to sell it on a commission basis. An advance of $5 or $10 on the commission to cover the expenses, advertising, etc., is asked for. The storekeeper is requested to sign a paper which he cannot read and which states that this payment is not an advance on a commission but a flat payment for advertising expenses. Protected legally by this contract, the business broker spends forty or fifty cents on an advertisement, seemingly sends around a friend or runners to make an impossibly low offer for the store, and makes no further effort to effect a sale. The storekeeper, of course, loses his deposit. . . . When sued, civil judgments have been obtained. But execution can never be levied, as their only assets appear to be their scarlet seals. The contracts signed are so cleverly drawn that prosecution for technical larceny cannot be had.

REAL ESTATE

Immigrants are criticized—especially the newcomers— for a supposed disinclination to take root in our soil, evidenced by the large amounts of money sent to the old country and by an assumed failure to invest in real property in this country. Contact with the actual activities of the immigrant, however, must impress one with the strength and persistency of the immigrant's desire to own land and houses here. In watching actual transactions, one sees this instinct making its way irrepressibly through what would seem to be the most discouraging obstacles, the fraud of others, the immigrant's own ignorance of business dealings, and poverty.

What can happen to an immigrant who responds to the wonderful offers of farm property made to him is told in detail in another volume of this series[1] and need be mentioned here only to make the account complete. Mill or mine workers, anxious to get into agriculture,

[1] Peter A. Speek, *A Stake in the Land*, chap. iv.

are induced by fake land companies to invest in land in some place so far away that they have no chance of inspecting their purchase, only to find later that the property bought is worthless, and their savings lost. Here again, the offer of employment is made to make the sale more attractive. In an instance reported from New Jersey[1] prospective purchasers were told that a factory was to be built on the property, in which men would find employment. To substantiate these promises, the purchasers were shown excavations which, it was claimed, were the beginnings of the supposed factory. In other instances, farm property was offered with extravagant accounts of the crops that could be raised. In still other instances, land was offered as improved and ready to cultivate, when as a matter of fact it was swamp or forest.

A scheme that worked for a while in a Middle Western city was to offer lots in a development in a neighboring state through the medium of lottery tickets drawn at moving-picture theaters. Persons who were notified that they had won lots paid fees for abstracts to title and other papers, to the persons concerned in making the sale, only to find that the lots were worthless.[2] This particular scheme came to an end through the punishment of the exploiters, but similar plans can be concocted and carried on for some time before their contrivers are brought to book.

Equally clever frauds are perpetrated to secure purchasers of suburban or city property. A device very popular for a while, to secure purchasers for either city or country property, was the offering of a lot for the solution of a puzzle given in the advertisement. This "puzzle" was ridiculously simple, but even if a solu-

[1] *Report of the New Jersey Commission of Immigration, 1914,* p. 41.
[2] Case of Chicago Legal Aid Society.

tion sent in was incorrect, the writer would be told that he had won a prize—but that in order to secure the lot offered him free of charge, he would have to purchase another lot. Both lots together would not be worth more than he paid for the one, and frequently much less.

And, of course, an obvious method of defrauding in these real estate deals is to induce the immigrant to sign papers of which he does not understand the purport, which will either give him some property other than he thinks he is buying or introduce, without his knowing it, some stipulation or condition to his disadvantage.

In Chicago many immigrants were taken in by a scheme worked out by a real estate dealer as follows: A prospective purchaser, attracted by extensive advertising, was told that the company would sell him a lot for $300 and put up a house on the lot for him at a very reasonable cost, and for this the purchaser was to pay only $25 down for each lot, and nothing more until the dealer started to build the houses. Then he was to pay at the rate of $7 a month until all was paid for. Purchasers signed contracts to this effect as they supposed, and waited for the building operations to begin. But in vain. The dealer kept putting them off on one pretext or another until the purchasers got tired and demanded their first payments back. It then appeared that the contracts provided simply for the purchase of the lots. Nothing was said in the contracts about the duty of the seller to put up a house. Indeed, the contracts expressly said that the purchase price of the lots did not include houses. This case was prosecuted by the legal aid society of that city on the general ground that the operation was a confidence game, as the contracts seemed to stop any claim on the basis of failure to carry out agreements. This society looked after the claims of 30 people, but these were only a small proportion of the numbers actually fleeced.[1]

INVESTMENT ON SMALL MEANS

Much of the trouble into which the immigrant falls in these real estate transactions, however, is due not so much to deliberate exploitation as to his own ignorance of business methods and the law, and his extreme eagerness to invest, regardless of his inability to carry the financial responsibilities he has assumed. In such cases, however, it is just as important that he should secure his rights as where exploitation takes place.

The narrowness of the margin on which these poor immigrants will buy property is remarkable, as may be seen by the following cases brought to the Chicago Legal Aid Society. A Polish machinist earning $2 a day bought a house worth $4,000, paying $800 down.

A Polish laborer earning $2 a day, but out of work when his case came to attention, was buying a house and two lots for $450 and had paid $150. Another Polish laborer, with an income of $15 a week, owned a two-flat building valued at $1,510, sold it, and bought a lot on which another two-flat house was built. Still another Polish laborer, earning $1.75 a day when working, but out of work a great part of the time, with eight children all below working age, owned a house which he traded for another worth $1,800. A Polish widow who owned a farm in Wisconsin, almost paid for, came to the city and got a job as dishwasher at $10 a week, on which she had to support not only herself, but a thirteen-year-old daughter. After coming to the city she decided to exchange the farm for a piece of

[1] Case of Chicago Legal Aid Society.

city property on which she could pay only half. An Italian laborer earning $15 a week bought two lots worth $649, which he paid for at the rate of $13 a month.

These cases, it will be noted, are nearly all Polish, and the Poles in particular and the Slavs in general are, indeed, the most pertinacious in their endeavors to own property, but this tendency is not confined to them. The Italians also are ready to buy, and it is probably not incorrect to say the same of immigrants generally.

When the immigrant gets the worst of it in these real estate transactions, he will frequently claim that it is because he did not understand the nature of the bargain he was making, and no doubt this is true in many cases.

A Polish purchaser in another case from the Chicago Legal Aid Society, for example, complained that he was rushed through an exchange of property that he did not understand and was made to sign papers without knowing their contents. He had got out of work and fallen behind in his payments, and proceedings were started to foreclose on a second mortgage. The purchaser said he did not understand at all that he had signed any second mortgage—he could neither read nor write.

Sometimes the immigrants are deceived, or do not understand, about taxes due, or assessments for improvements, and suddenly find that their property is seized to meet those obligations.

HARDSHIP UNDER THE LAW

A provision of the common law that works hardship and that is sometimes not understood by the immigrant purchaser is that dealing with installment contracts for purchase of real estate. To protect his own interests, the seller makes a contract for purchase of real estate by payment in installments, according to which the deed is not passed to the purchaser until the payments are made. If the purchaser defaults in his payments, all that he has paid in is lost unless he chooses to take up the matter in an equity proceeding, a process which is so expensive as to make it unprofitable to resort to it in such small transactions as the immigrant is accustomed to.

Often the amounts lost in this way are considerable. For example, in one case[1] an Italian woman, unable to keep up her payments, lost $247 paid on property costing $649 in all. In another a Bohemian widow[2] had paid $500 on four lots to cost $1,300 in all. A man with whom she was negotiating about building paid the remainder, and secured the deed to the property. When the matter was taken to the legal aid society, the attorney tried to explain to the woman that the man had not done anything illegal, but she "could not understand." She said the man had explained the matter to her, but she "didn't know what he was talking about." The comment of the society on the case was that the woman "has simply lost $500 through ignorance." She had fallen behind six or seven months in her payment, and had therefore forfeited all her rights under the contracts.

In another Chicago case[3] a Polish woman bought a lot in exchange for some property and a promise to pay $2,500 additional. Since she did not make the payments as agreed, an action for forcible detainer was brought and the woman was put out of the property. She claimed misrepresentation when the bargain was

[1] Case of Chicago Legal Aid Society.
[2] *Ibid.*
[3] *Ibid.*

made, saying that the seller got her husband drunk, took him at night to the property, and then induced her to sign the contract, making her mark, without having seen what she was buying.

Sometimes the costs attending the settlement of property will wipe out a purchaser's equity, as in the case of V—— P——, another client of the Chicago Legal Aid Society, whose property was sold at foreclosure sale for $1,606, of which $1,000 went to satisfy the mortgage and $606 for taxes and costs of selling the place, leaving him nothing but the $50 he received for giving a quit-claim deed. On the other hand, he had had rent free for several years. This is a frequent situation. The immigrant buys on a narrow margin, cannot keep up his payments, the property is finally taken over by foreclosure proceedings or forcible detainer, leaving him nothing, but meanwhile he has had rent free for a considerable period of time. His feeling about the matter is, however, that he has been deeply injured. This is perhaps partly to be accounted for by the fact that the peasant immigrant has the peasant's peculiar feeling about land. To him it is not simply an object of trade and barter worth so much money, to be changed into something else, but a special good in itself that he cannot bear to be deprived of. This is especially true of the Slavic immigrants, who have in a high degree this attachment to the soil. No matter how clear it is that the value of the property has been enjoyed in rent, and that the payments due have not been made, the immigrant cannot reconcile himself to losing it, gets into a highly emotional state about it, and sometimes goes really insane. Records of the Chicago Legal Aid Society, from which these illustrative cases were taken show such notations as: "Man very excited; appears to be out of his mind." "Could not get from him co-

56

herent account of the difficulty." "Do not think the man is normal." And so on. In one case a man grew more and more unreasonable, refused to accept papers or sign receipts, and finally, after some months of running to the office with complaints and accusations, went and hanged himself.

Insanity is not the only unfortunate result of the attempt to get and hold property on a narrow margin. One poor fellow found himself in jail in consequence of his efforts. This man, Anton B——, a Russian Pole, an ironworker earning $4 a day, with wife and five children, had become a contractor in a small way and bought an old two-story building on a contract. He attempted to raise the building himself, but probably without proper tools, and the ends fell out, damaging the building next door. The owner of the damaged building sued, getting a judgment for over $400, which he was unable to collect through civil process, as Anton had nothing to levy on but his wages, which averaged $18 a week. His wife earned $3 a week by washing, and two children earned $15 and $8 a week, respectively. Anton and his wife insisted that they were not able to pay the judgment, so he was thrown into jail, under the law of Illinois, that a debtor may be jailed for failure to pay judgment in a tort case, when there has been a trial by jury, or a jury trial has been waived by the defendant.

LOANS

One easy way for an immigrant to lose money is to lend it to somebody. He feels about a loan something as he does about a deposit. He will hand his money over to a friend without a definite agreement as to terms of payment, and without a receipt or note or any document to show the nature of the transaction. These loans, like the money placed on deposit with some store-keeper who acts as banker, may get mixed up with other transactions. For instance, they may be regarded as advances on something that will be due later, like rent, as in a Chicago case handled by the Legal Aid Society. In this, one woman claimed to have lent another $300 at different times, but had no note or other security to show for it. The defendant claimed that whatever she borrowed was afterward deducted from the lender's rent, the defendant being the plaintiff's landlady. There was no way of proving this loan except through the indirect evidence of people who had heard conversation about the matter. Sometimes illegal rates of interest are charged, but it is difficult for the immigrant to establish his right in many cases, because of lack of evidence.

The immigrant woman has especial difficulty about loans, as is natural, with her even greater lack of understanding of business methods than that of the immigrant man. A case reported from New York State[1] illustrates such troubles. A Hungarian widow had had no idea what to do with the money coming from the sale of a small business left her by her husband, consequently most of the money was extracted from her by her countrymen. One of them, whom she recognized as coming from her husband's village in the old country, got several hundred dollars from her for the ostensible purpose of starting a grocery business. This business was never started, however, and after a year she became suspicious and applied to the Legal Aid Society. She had no notes or receipts of any kind. When seen about the matter, the man openly stated that he had no reason for not paying except that he in-

[1] Case of Buffalo Legal Aid Bureau.

tended to keep the money; the widow was throwing her money away, and he might as well have it as anyone.

PURCHASES

In the spending as well as in the earning or investing of money, the immigrant may be defrauded. One way is through the grocery book, in which purchases are set down. Sometimes storekeepers make unitemized charges so that there is no way of knowing whether the account is correct or not. A field agent for this study found numerous small merchants doing this in industrial towns visited, where accounts are paid on pay day. It was difficult to prove fraud in any single case, but many families felt sure that the accounts were increased several dollars per week in that way.

It is a pity that the immigrant's reaching toward a higher standard of living in the way of comfortable furnishing, musical instruments, and the like should be made a specially profitable field for exploitation. Through advertisements in the papers, and otherwise, the immigrant's attention is called to articles of clothing, jewelry, household furnishing, phonographs, pianos, and other articles of comfort or luxury to be purchased on the installment plan. Entering into negotiations, he is offered what seem to him very favorable terms, and is induced to sign some paper which he does not understand or the nature of which is misrepresented to him. This paper turns out to be in reality a contract to pay certain amounts periodically, the seller reserving title to the goods until all payments are made by the purchaser. If the purchaser is unable to keep up his payments, he loses the goods and all the money he has paid. Often, he thinks he is signing merely a receipt for the goods. Getting the immigrant to sign what he thinks is a receipt for goods when it really is something else is a common device in all sorts of business transactions.

In one case a woman signed what she thought was a receipt for a small amount of money borrowed on security of goods which she had on storage, but it turned out to be an order on the storage company to deliver the goods. The loan was less than a hundred dollars, whereas the goods were worth several thousand dollars—the woman's entire property—and the man getting the receipt straightway sold the goods and vanished with the proceeds.[1]

INGENIOUS PLANS TO DEFRAUD

A clever and heartless scheme, playing upon the immigrant's homesickness and loneliness, was reported to the New York State Bureau of Industries and Immigration.[2] An offer was made through the foreign press to sell a phonograph "with records of your national songs in your own tongue" on payment of $5 and the balance in small installments. On receiving the initial payment the phonograph company forwarded a machine by express, with instructions to collect on delivery the entire amount of the balance. The immigrant, usually unable to pay so large a sum, had to allow the express company to take the machine back, so that the phonograph company retained both the machine and the original payment. A great deal of money was collected in this way. The fraudulent transactions of one man in this line of business were found to have netted him about $125,000 a year, and it was learned that he kept an emergency deposit of $30,000 to be used for legal services should he be

[1] Case of Detroit Bureau of Information of the Board of Commerce.
[2] *Report, 1915*, p. 19.

arrested. This man when caught and convicted was fined $750.

Another device was the trading-stamp scheme.[1] Agents of companies would persuade persons to purchase stamps at the rate of 10 cents a week, with the understanding that when the total amount of stamps thus purchased equaled $10 or $20, articles of furniture or jewelry could be selected from printed catalogues. When the money was finally paid, the articles secured were such as could have been purchased elsewhere for about half the price at which they were listed. In order to evade the charge that stamps were being sold illegally, the company claimed that the weekly payments were subscriptions to a magazine, and the stamps were for advertising purposes only. As in other installment sales, if payments were not kept up, the entire amount was lost. In one case more than half of the money was paid in and lost, the company holding the purchaser under a contract in the English language which the subscriber signed but did not understand.

Another form of fraud consists in selling by sample and delivering goods of inferior quality. This is a widespread practice. When the goods are delivered, the purchaser may be asked to sign a receipt stating that he has received them according to agreement, and if he does so, and should afterward make a complaint, he is told that his acceptance is binding.

THE CONFIDENCE GAME

The immigrant is peculiarly liable to be victimized by the plain, out-and-out confidence game, with no exchange transactions involved. A bogus express company, for instance, will notify an immigrant that a

[1] *Report of the New York State Bureau of Industries and Immigration, 1913,* p. 24.

package from Europe has arrived for him which he may have on payment of express charges and customs fees. He sends the money as requested, but no package is received. In one case the "express company" consisted of a letter box in a tenement.[1]

The old game of replacing a valuable package with a worthless one is still being played upon immigrants.

In Buffalo not long ago, Joseph K——, a Pole, was met by two plausible strangers who told a tale of making a fortune in Alaska, showing rolls of bills which they said contained thousands of dollars. They were looking for an honest man, they said, to take care of this money for them while they were detained in the city getting their passports for the old country. But he must show that he was thrifty. Joseph thereupon produced a bank book showing a deposit of $1,950. He was told to draw this money, as evidence of good faith, place it in a tin box with the strangers' cash, and keep it until a certain date, when the box would be called for. He did this, but when the time had passed and the strangers did not call, he opened the box and found it stuffed with newspaper. The money represented Joseph's entire savings for nineteen years' work as a laborer in a packing house, and he had intended to buy a house with it.[2]

Still more recently, in a case reported to the Foreign Language Information Service, a Slovak miner, about to take ship from New York with $580 in his pocket, was met by a pleasant stranger with whom he was exchanging confidences, when a third man came running up shouting that he had lost a pocketbook and insisting that one of the other two men had taken it. Both

[1] *Report of the New York Bureau of Industries and Immigration, 1913*, p. 22.
[2] The Buffalo *Express*, August 22, 1919.

presented their pocketbooks for inspection, and both received them back from the excited newcomer with deep apologies. But when our miner opened his purse again to pay for his steamship ticket, he found, instead of his $580, only a one-dollar bill wrapped around a wad of paper.

A plain confidence game is the raffle for which tickets are sold, but the raffle itself never takes place. In one instance the foreman of a mining company issued such tickets to his employees, who had to buy them in order to hold their jobs. No raffle had ever been held, although the practice had been in operation several years.[1]

Sickness and even death are no discouragement to the swindler, for even when under these afflictions the immigrant has to contend with the quack doctor and the undertaker. The devices of the quack doctor are described in detail in another volume of this series.[2] So-called medical practitioners get hold of immigrants through advertisements in the foreign-language newspapers, frighten them by diagnosis of a "dangerous condition," and induce them to spend large amounts of money for needless and even harmful treatments. Certain undertakers are equally rapacious. Playing upon the immigrant's desire for a fine funeral, they will urge the most extravagant expenditures and pile up the charges so as to cover the entire amount of his insurance or savings, if they can find out how much that is.

INSURANCE

To make provision for the expenses of sickness and death the immigrant often joins some fraternal benefit

[1] *Report of the New York State Bureau of Industries and Immigration, 1911*, p. 100.

[2] Michael M. Davis, Jr., *Immigrant Health and the Community*, chap. viii.

society, made up usually of fellow countrymen. Many of these societies are of great service to the immigrant and are conducted honestly. But some of them are not. Sometimes such societies are only accident or life-insurance agencies in disguise, and the paper which the clients sign, thinking it is an application for membership, turns out to be a contract for insurance.

In New Jersey it was found[1] that hundreds of organizations known as fraternal beneficiary societies were flourishing, many of which were run without proper safeguards. In some cases the running expenses of the associations equaled the insurance funds, leaving nothing for the benefit of the insured.

Any insurance company, fraternal or otherwise, may show a disposition to think up excuses for not paying the benefits to which the insured person thinks he is entitled. So that after being offered the most liberal sick and death benefits to secure his membership, the immigrant may find, when he puts in a claim for the benefits promised, that they are hemmed about with limitations he had not suspected.

The tactics of a commercial company's agent with whom the Chicago Legal Aid Society had had dealings are thus described:

This Mr. —— is an old hand at the game. If he sees a possible loophole to avoid paying a policy he will seize upon it. If the deceased drank, he will claim that his death was caused by drinking. If the deceased died of tuberculosis, he will claim that the man had it when he took out his policy, or if the deceased died of an illness of long standing, or chronic, he will try a similar complaint of fraud. He will then make a fairly decent offer "out of charity" to the family, or "to get

[1] *Report of the Commission of Immigration of the State of New Jersey, 1914,* p. 101.

the matter settled," which the immigrant in his ignorance will accept.

BENEVOLENCE

Even the immigrant's sentiments of pity and charity are played upon to defraud him, as in a case reported by the New York Legal Aid Society which we need not regard as entirely unique. A fellow employee of a man who had died busied himself in securing from other employees and friends of the deceased, subscriptions to a fund for the benefit of the widow. Of the $176 collected, only $35 was turned over to the widow, $141 being kept by the collector under various pretenses. Although the widow was in great need, this man hung on to the money for over a year, until the Legal Aid Society forced him to pay up.

Economic exploitation of the immigrant, then, is seen to cover the whole range of his life in this country, from the time of his arrival until his departure through the gates of death, and to come into the experience of so many people that more effective methods of prevention and protection seem to be called for, not only to stop the material but the moral losses involved.

The exploited immigrant may react to his losses in one of two ways, both undesirable in relation to citizenship: he may acquire the idea that exploitation is a custom of the country, which he had better follow himself if he wants to succeed; or he may nurse a growing grievance at the state and the society that permits such practices, and become a dissatisfied and disloyal member of the community.

What is needed to remedy these evils? Good laws and effective enforcement through the courts and other government agencies, of course, but, beyond that, education of the immigrant through intelligent and sympathetic personal dealing to a point where he can take care of himself. The ignorant immigrant will always be a prey for the exploiter. No laws conceivable can protect him at every turn. He must be informed and enlightened, and this is not simply a process of pouring into him facts about the new country, but of learning what is already in his mind, and adapting the instruction to that mental content.

II

FAMILY TROUBLES

ANOTHER broad group of immigrant problems, giving occasion for contacts with the law and the courts, includes those arising from the domestic relations of the newcomers—their troubles with husbands and wives, with children, with parents, with irregular sex alliances. Such troubles are of a more intimate, personal nature than economic troubles, and are less simple to deal with.

But the number of cases of this sort actually brought before the courts is large. In the records of legal-aid societies, which may be taken as some indication of the relative volume of cases, domestic difficulties are nearly as numerous as cases of money troubles, notwithstanding the fact that many of these societies do not welcome domestic cases and do specialize in economic difficulties.

PEASANT BACKGROUND

These family troubles of the immigrant, can be dealt with properly only if they are understood in all their elements, and they can be understood only against the general background of peasant customs and attitudes toward love and marriage.

To the European peasant generally, marriage is a relation entered into primarily not to gratify a personal preference, but to found a family—which is regarded as an economic as well as a social unit. Marriage, to the peasant, is not an individual enterprise, but a group affair, involving the participation not only of the parents of the bride and groom, but of the relatives and sometimes of the whole village.

The bride or the groom is selected as the result of family conferences in which friends may also take part, because of qualities or circumstances that will make him or her a valuable member of the family or the community into which he or she may come. Good looks, personal charm, have little weight. Good character, working capacity, property, habits and customs that fit in with those of the group, are regarded as of great importance. Marriage is brought about only after long discussion of the advantages and disadvantages of the proposed consort, and the matchmaker, a semiprofessional, semifriendly go-between, is a recognized functionary in most mid-European peasant communities.

And marriage is expected of every man and woman. No excuse for avoiding that duty, such as not being "in love" with a proposed bride or groom, or as not being able to marry the person one is "in love" with, is accepted. A full-grown man or woman who is not married is considered a less desirable member of the community than a married person, and is marked with social disapproval.

But the man does not necessarily marry early. He shares in the obligation of supporting the family into which he was born, and may not marry until that obligation is discharged, or until he is economically able to continue to discharge it, with the added responsibility of contributing to the support of the new family he is founding. This means that the man may not be able to marry until a comparatively mature age.

The woman is expected to bring a dowry as her contribution to the family economy, but, since the dowry is contributed in great part by her father or older brothers, her marriage need not be delayed until she can personally accumulate wealth. So that the bride may be younger, and often considerably younger, than the bridegroom.

In marriages arranged in this way, romantic love, as it is known in individualistic societies, has few claims to consideration, although in any human aggregation human nature will manage to have its way at times, and even under a marriage system regulated by the social group, the individuals primarily concerned will often manage to secure partners of their own choosing.

In the peasant family, the husband and father is the recognized head. He holds this position in absolute right among the Latin peoples, handing on the tradition of the old institution of *patria potestas*. Among the Slavic peoples, however, with their tradition of group self-government, which they have outgrown in varying degrees, vestiges are found of the idea that the man is merely the administrative head carrying out the wishes of the group. But for all practical purposes in the peasant groups generally, the man is regarded as the head; he is granted by general opinion powers of control extending on occasion to the physical punishment of wife and children who disobey his orders. There is, however, a noticeable difference in the degree of control exerted by the Latin and Slavic husband, respectively, perhaps due to their differences in traditions. The Latin husband is more implicitly obeyed by wife and children; the Slavic husband, on the other hand, who may be at times as violent and brutal as a man can be, in certain instances, apparently does not maintain the constant control over his family that is exerted by the Latin.

THE IMMIGRANT'S DAY IN COURT

The attitudes of State and Church, respectively, toward marriage in the countries from which immigrants come have also much to do with their ideas about it, and their practices in that relation.

In some European countries, in the past, at any rate, the State surrounded the marriage ceremony with so much expense and so many formalities, that many poor people could not afford to marry, but came together in free unions in which all of the duties and obligations of marriage were met, but to which the legal sanction was lacking.

In countries where Church and State are at variance in their rules about marriage, as in Italy, the peasant is subject to a clashing of influences that will greatly disturb his ideas. If he retains his respect for the Church he will regard the civil marriage as no marriage at all, consequently carrying no responsibilities, and he will not feel bound by it. On the other hand, he may be influenced by the State's disavowal of the religious ceremony to give up all idea of the sanctity of the marriage relation.

Church doctrines about divorce and about the bearing of children have much influence over the conduct of the peasant. The Roman Church, for example, to which so many of our immigrants belong, forbids divorce, and forbids restriction of births by any means except continence in the marriage relation. For the married pair there is no escape—whatever the circumstances of cruelty, unfaithfulness, deficiency—consistent with the fulfillment of religious duty, from living together, and from heaping up the burden of a large family which neither of the pair may want, or be able to provide for, unless they are willing to practice

70

a continence which the peasant does not consider a possibility.

For the peasant is a creature of simple wants, and of simple thoughts about those wants. He has no complicated higher life to occupy him, and to him the sex impulse is one of a few primitive urges in man that, as a matter of course, must be gratified. This idea governs his thought about sex relations generally, as well as about marriage. Marriage is to his mind the normal avenue of gratification of the sex impulse, but if a man has to remain single too long, or loses his wife and cannot replace her, if a woman is widowed, he or she is not blamed overmuch for finding satisfaction outside of marriage in some unobtrusive way.

In the peasant communities of some countries sex relations before marriage between a girl and the man whom she is afterward to marry are not infrequent, and not severely blamed. Such relations are quite usually regarded as an anticipation of marriage, and if the expected marriage does not come off, if the man even had no intention of marrying, the girl is not greatly discredited by the unfortunate experience, and will not find it difficult to make a good match afterward. And often the husband will accept with his bride her child by the man whom she did not marry.

With such a background as this, the stage is set for all sorts of domestic difficulties when the peasant leaves the environment in which these ideas grew up, and which they still fit, to some extent, for an environment in which he suffers a necessary dislocation to begin with, by the mere mechanical fact of the breaking up of all his associations and habits, and in which, in addition, the established ideas and customs of the country are in so many respects, different from those of his own land.

In his own country he was held to the observance

of inherited customs by the force of public opinion in the little village community where everyone knew him, and he was more or less contented with that standard, whatever the personal inconvenience to him, because of the support of public approval.

But village approval does not carry over to the new country, nor is the immigrant brought into a social group which takes the place of the home village as a regulator of his thoughts and conduct. The immigrant colony is not sufficiently stable in itself to fix and enforce standards, and the immigrant is not received into the American social group, so that he becomes acquainted with the American standard largely by way of brief and severe reproof, when he has the misfortune to transgress some of its rules.

In the tide of immigration, the first wave is composed of young adult males, who leave their families at home if they are already provided with families. If they go to work in some labor camp, they are entirely outside of domestic influences, and of social influences as well. Attempts to satisfy the needs of domesticity and sociability will naturally lead them into situations and relations in which they get into serious trouble.

With the peasant idea about the family and the necessity of sex relations, when the married man comes to this country, leaving wife and children at home, he quite instinctively and without deliberate intent to harm anyone, drifts into sex relations with the woman nearest at hand.

If the man finds his way to a city he goes to some lodging house, or becomes a boarder in some family.

THE IMMIGRANT BOARDER

If he has been taken into a family as a boarder, he may take the additional step toward completing the home

relation into which he has entered, by sharing bed as
well as board, entering into sex relations with the
woman of the house. However immoral this practice
may be, the offender accepts more responsibilities
toward the woman and is less sophisticated than the
patron of houses of prostitution. This practice is in
general an attempt on the part of the man to replace the
home left behind, and sometimes involves the essentials
of a true domestic relation. He wants not merely sex
intercourse but the comforts of a home, and will help
to supply them.

In an illustrative case, John M——, a Pole, came to
this country without his wife because she refused to
accompany him.[1] After working here two years and
saving $700 he went back to get his family, and found his
wife living with another man, to whom she had borne
a child. He came back to America and never heard
from her again. On his return to America he went to
board in the family of another Pole who was afterward killed in an industrial accident. John had been
boarding with the family for five years when the accident
occurred, and he was working side by side with the
husband when it happened. He continued to live in
the family of the widow, showed great interest in her
affairs, and was at last suspected of sex relations with
her. This was at first stoutly denied, but it finally
came out that these relations had existed, that the
youngest child was his, and that he would like to
marry the woman if he were not already married in the
old country. At last he did so, taking advantage of a
"presumption of death" of the first wife, through not
having heard from her for more than seven years.
This seems to be a plain case of a marital relation in
substance, although not in legalized form.

[1] Case of Chicago Juvenile Protective Association.

THE IMMIGRANT'S DAY IN COURT

Many cases of this general nature are found. In one[1] a woman, deserted by her husband, bore a child to one of her boarders. He had always wanted to marry her, and did so after the woman had secured a divorce on the ground of desertion. In this case, he in his turn deserted her two months later, and after that he deserted her six times.

Sometimes the boarder takes upon himself so thoroughly the office of husband that he applies marital discipline to the wife, for "immoral" connections with other men, as in a case[2] in which a boarder beat the woman of the house unmercifully, accusing her of immoral relations with some young man for whom she was doing the washing. In another case, when a woman who had run away with a boarder returned to her husband, the boarder was violently angry and swore out a warrant, charging her with stealing $400 from him.[3]

In another case, a woman deserted by her husband was befriended by a decent hard-working man, a teamster, with whom she lived for four years and by whom she had two children. She then decided to apply for a divorce, so that she could marry him. While the divorce proceedings were pending the man was arrested for adultery, on complaint of a woman with whom he had formerly boarded who had tried to persuade him to go away and live with her, and had afterward tried to poison the woman with whom the man was living. The couple were finally safely married.[4]

[1] Case of Chicago Legal Aid Society.
[2] Case of Chicago Juvenile Court.
[3] Case of Buffalo Legal Aid Bureau.
[4] Case of Chicago Legal Aid Society.

FAMILY TROUBLES

In still another case,[1] a Polish woman whose husband abused her fell in love with the boarder and the husband sued for a divorce, but she paid no attention to the divorce summons and did not contest the case. The divorce was granted the husband, but the wife had no idea that she was free and could marry the boarder, so continued contentedly living with him without marriage. Meanwhile, the custody of the child had been awarded to the father, and the wife promptly stole her back again. This procedure brought the matter to the attention of the court. The divorce proctor was so impressed with the good home she made for the children, that through his efforts a petition was filed for the reopening of the divorce case, resulting in an award of the child to the mother. The proctor said that the woman had a very nice home, took unusually good care of the children, and, as the child was too young to understand anything of what the mother had ignored in the way of conventions, he wanted her to have the baby. "The mother is a perfectly good woman in every way," he said. "Her troubles were in her lack of understanding the English language and the American code of morals."

Notwithstanding the elements of palliation to be found in the boarder situation, on the whole it cannot fail to be demoralizing to the family group and to the social group in which it has its setting. How far this will be the case depends to a great extent on the personal character of the people involved. In one instance noted a respectable woman and her whole family were demoralized by an unprincipled boarder, so that three years after her husband's death she was drinking, fighting, and unfit to care for her children.[2]

[1] Case of Divorce Proctor, Detroit.
[2] Case of Chicago Juvenile Court.

75

The children become familiar with a situation which at best is irregular and at worst is positively corrupting. The boarder becomes such a familiar institution that he has the title of "uncle" for the children, and is sometimes known as "pa." The children cannot help knowing about the sleeping arrangements, and will explain as a matter of course that mother and "uncle" occupy the same room. Sometimes the boarder does actual violence to the little girls.

A BAD "BOARDER"

A thoroughly bad boarder is found in the case of Joseph P——, a Pole.[1] Joseph had married in Poland a young woman who brought him as dowry land and property to the amount of $3,500, he contributing to the family equipment only $350. After marrying her, with all her money, it appeared that he did not care to work, and before the fourth child was born he sold the land at a loss and left for America with the proceeds. He went back to Poland after a little over a year's absence, but again got restless, and after about two years at home left his wife and children once more, although the wife begged him to take her with him. In this country it was his habit to form relations with the women with whom he boarded, and he told a friend of his that he would not stay at any place where he could not have intercourse with the housekeeper. In one family where he boarded he enjoyed the wife's society while the husband was away on a milk route; it is uncertain whether the husband knew about this practice or not. In another family, where he lived for two years, he broke up the home, gaining the wife's affections. This was quite aside from attempts he

[1] Case of Chicago Legal Aid Society.

made on other women with whom he was not boarding. He finally met a young married woman, of apparently much the same type as himself, with whom he entered into relations and whom he finally decided to marry, each planning to get a divorce from the former partner. Joseph sent for the oldest three children, who, with the wife, were still in Poland, but the wife claimed that she knew nothing of a divorce, had no papers served or notice given, and after three years started to America to look for him herself. Apparently there was doubt about the woman's divorce, also. Meantime Joseph and his new "wife," were not treating the children well. Some time after the first wife arrived, she brought suit for possession of the children, when some serious charges were preferred against the couple. The children testified that their father and his "wife" had forced the fourteen-year-old daughter to marry a man much older than herself, whom she did not care for, and that they beat and abused the little ones.

Later the children repented of their testimony against the stepmother, and said she treated them well. The oldest daughter said that her own mother had been immoral at home, while Joseph was away, and it appears that a foreman where the first wife was now working was taking a peculiar interest in the case and securing witnesses and paying expenses of testimony. The wife's story about the "immorality" charge against her at home is interesting because it shows the other side of the domestic problem, the possibilities of trouble for the wife who is left behind. She says that a friend of her husband, living next door in the same village in Poland, took advantage of her by force, and told her some time afterward that he did this because Joseph, before emigrating, had debauched his wife while he himself was in America. When Joseph met the neighbor later in America he boasted of what he had done. The neighbor, resolved to get even with him, went home to Poland for that purpose which he evidently carried out. The relation was admitted by the wife, and the fact that the youngest child was the neighbor's. The court was much puzzled by the conflicting testimony in this case, and finally awarded the custody of the children to the father, as they did not look obviously ill treated and as the father was earning good wages and the mother only $7.50 a week.

THE HUSBAND'S ATTITUDE

In studying the domestic troubles of the Poles, one is impressed by instances of the tolerance of the Polish husband, and the independence and self-will, in establishing sex relations for herself, of the Polish wife. Sometimes the husband is so tolerant that he personally will arrange with the boarder for enjoyment of sex relations with the wife, as part of the board, a practice sufficiently frequent to bring into use a special term to describe it—"full board." The Polish husband is not, however, the only one who makes such arrangements. But if an Italian husband does this, it is because he is, and is generally regarded as, a "bad one," while this is not necessarily true of the Pole.

As noticeable as the tolerance shown by the Polish husband to the interloper is the fondness of the latter for the husband's children in many instances. An elopement often means that the man takes not only the wife, but all of her children, and assumes the burden of their support.

But the Polish husband is not invariably tolerant. Sometime he seizes upon the conduct of the wife as an excuse for his own ill-doing, but sometimes he will sue for divorce, or run away, or suffer a general demoraliza-

FAMILY TROUBLES

tion. In a case where a Polish laborer got out of work and a boarder practically supported the family, the wife said her husband refused to work; but her brother said that the husband had always been a steady man until the wife became too intimate with the boarder.[1]

In one case (Lithuanian)[2] a husband objected to the wife's boarders so strenuously that he refused to support her and the children on the ground that the youngest child was not his. In this case the wife's legal right to money came in conflict with the peasant idea about property, and caused trouble. The husband complained that the wife had drawn all of their money from the bank, amounting to $400. It was shown that this money was what was left of $500 which the wife had saved before marriage. This had been deposited in a joint account and some time previously the man had drawn $100. That he complained of her drawing the money to which she was legally entitled and which she had earned herself, and had said nothing about the $100 he had drawn, was evidently due to an idea that the original $500 stood in the place of dowry, which became part of the family fund, to be administered by the man as head of the family. If the husband has deserted or died, it is hard to draw the line between a "boarder" and a new, irregular consort. Whether the man is called a "boarder" or not, the reasons for establishing relations with the woman of the house are much the same and the attitude of mind the same.

Sometimes it is the woman who feels the need of support and companionship in the absence of her husband or after his death, and takes in a boarder who naturally assumes the position of husband. If the husband is dead, there may be a hindrance to marriage

[1] Case of Chicago Juvenile Protective Association.
[2] Case of Chicago Legal Aid Society.

in the fact that the boarder is unwilling to marry or already has a wife. Sometimes the woman actually runs away with the man, frequently taking the children along, and setting up a new home.

In a Lithuanian case,[1] a drunken and cruel husband deserted his wife, who less than two years after that went to live with another man. After living with him for over three years and bearing him two children, the woman applied for a divorce so that she could marry him. She said that she was living with him because she had no money and needed support; the man had quite soberly assumed the obligations of husband. When talked to about the matter, he said he would gladly pay for the divorce and would gladly marry the woman, as he thought she might be better satisfied; but as far as he was concerned he expected to live with her always and marriage or no marriage made no difference to him.

ATTITUDE ABOUT DIVORCE

This tendency to disregard legality in a relation which involves the essentials of marriage is not confined to the man who has taken the place of the husband. It is a constant matter of complaint by social workers that after much pains and trouble have been taken to secure a divorce for some abused woman, she may at any moment forget or ignore the divorce and receive her husband back into her home and resume relations with him without any further marriage ceremony.

This readiness to dispense with a ceremony may be due to regard for the Church doctrine regarding divorce, even in cases where the wife has disregarded it originally and secured one. But it sometimes gives rise to trouble-

[1] Case of Chicago Legal Aid Society.

some complications, as in the case of Mary M——[1]. This woman's husband who was a German and from whom she had got a divorce, had asked her to take him back, but when she consented, told her that they did not need to have a ceremony, as the Catholic Church did not recognize divorces and they were still married. After she went back to live with him he treated her so cruelly that she had to leave him again; but there was no way in which she could claim support for the child that was born to them after her return, except through bastardy proceedings.

Sometimes the husband continues in relation with the wife while the divorce proceedings are going on. If the wife takes a fancy that she would like to have her husband back again, it does not occur to her that she cannot resume the marriage relation at will and at once.

A disregard of divorce is also caused by the peasant's general unfamiliarity with judicial processes. In a case already cited the woman did not know she was divorced. And there are many such cases. In one[2] a Polish woman, whose husband had been abusive and unfaithful, was summoned to court to answer to a divorce suit filed by the husband, on the plea of adultery. The wife was indifferent to this proceeding, paid no attention to the summons, and entered no defense. She denied the charge to the agent of the Legal Aid Society, however. As no defense was made, the husband got his decree and the custody of the children. The wife was greatly distressed at losing the children, although indifferent to the divorce; in fact, two years later she said she did not know whether she was divorced or not. At any rate, she permitted the husband to resume sex relations with her and became pregnant. As he refused

[1] Case of Chicago Legal Aid Society.
[2] Ibid.

to give her money for the support of the child, she took out a bastardy warrant for him and got a judgment. A side light is thrown on the peasant preference for male children by her remark that the man promised to support the child if it was a boy, but not if it was a girl.

CHANGED STANDARDS

It is not necessary in this study to dwell on the elements in domestic troubles that are common to all people— drunkenness, viciousness, cruelty, and the like. We are chiefly interested in those due in part, at least, to the immigrant situation. And yet the immigrant situation may have much to do with strengthening or developing these common elements. Drunkenness may be to some extent caused or at least be incited by the crowded conditions in which immigrants live, and the lack of wholesome recreation available to them; and the boarder evil is certainly made worse through over-crowding.

Directly traceable to immigration, however, is a change in standard that makes a husband dissatisfied with the wife he has left behind in the old country and leads to his deserting her for another woman while she is still in the old country or even after she has joined him.

The wife at home, selected in accordance with a social standard rather than from personal inclination, might not have been loved in the first place and may be devoid of personal attractiveness. The husband remembers her as a plain, hard-working, slow-thinking domestic drudge, and finds an interesting contrast in the more sophisticated, better-dressed, more independent women he encounters in the new country.

Here he finds a greater possibility of following his

own inclinations, where he is not held to account by a social group knowing all about his affairs, and will be found in many instances throwing off the old responsibilities for a new alliance. Any number of cases might be cited.

In one[1] a young Russian with a wife and two children in Russia came to the United States alone and went to live in a German family. Here he fell in love with the young daughter of the house, a girl with modern standards of dress and amusements, who left home and went to live with him. The girl knew he was married, but was determined to have him for a husband.

In the case of Eleanor M——,[2] a couple had migrated together six years before. The man had never been good to the woman, but he was much worse after he came to America. He then began to run around with other women, and four years afterward he deserted his family completely and was not heard of for about two years more, when the wife discovered his whereabouts and moved into the neighborhood where he was living, hoping that he might be induced to return home. Instead, he moved away the very next morning. He was living with a woman who already had two illegitimate children. About two weeks later the wife found him again and had him arrested for desertion. He failed to pay the amounts ordered by the court. The wife then, in desperation, went to the house of the woman, called her out, and threw vitriol at her so effectively that she was disfigured for life.

In another case,[3] a woman who had come over from the old country at the age of sixteen to marry, was treated badly by the husband after she got here. He

[1] Case of Divorce Proctor, Detroit.
[2] Case of Chicago Legal Aid Society.
[3] *Ibid.*

failed to support her, and finally, although she was a good, respectable woman, got a divorce on the ground of immorality, the wife being too ignorant to contest the suit.

The husband's change of attitude toward his family after emigration may influence the wife to take a new partner, as in the case of H——.[1] Here a woman was found living with a man not her husband, with her children by the husband. She explained that her husband had come to this country about ten years previously, and that about two years later she had come, but that her husband had never supported her since her arrival. The oldest four boys were born in Poland and came over with the mother. They did not like the father, but did like the other man and thought he was their stepfather. She said she had not applied for a divorce, but thought she would— but she thought marriage meant very little, any way, as men were better to their wives before their marriage than after. This is a not infrequent attitude on the part of the immigrant woman, to regard marriage as a risk rather than a safeguard, owing to the idea of male domination held by the peasant husband.[2] Her younger children had been properly christened, the priest thinking the woman was married, and she had signed the man's army questionnaire as his wife. She said it was not for the support that she was living with the

[1] Case of Chicago Juvenile Protective Association.

[2] An investigator for this study noted that the Polish women do not care much about the marriage ceremony. They say men are better to women before they are married than after. One woman said: "That began all the trouble, getting married. A man feels sure of you as soon as you marry him. I'll never marry another man if I get free of this one." This woman had been married before and had lived with the last man a year before marrying him, and then "the trouble began," she said.

84

present man, but that he had no home and she took him in.

The man himself said he would not live apart from the woman, because he considered her his wife. They had now lived together six years and had two children. The first husband came around once or twice to see the wife and children, but was not admitted. The wife remarked, "One husband is enough."

In this family apparently all the essentials of a real marriage and home were present, yet in any tabulation of "family conditions" they would no doubt be counted as living in "immoral relations" or words to that effect.

In another case,[1] a woman whose family were prosperous farmers in the old country married, very young, a young man whose parents were also well off. They got along very well in Europe, but after two years of married life they used some money left to her by her father to come to America, where the man deserted her and their two children. He ran away with a young girl and later married her, by public ceremony, in a church. He was finally discovered, was prosecuted, and spent one year and five months in the county jail. Then he was released, for some reason not stated in the case record, and disappeared.

Then the wife, who claimed that she was told by a policeman that she was " the same as divorced" and could marry again, went to live with a man who everyone told her was respectable. She knew that he, too, had been married before, but claimed that he showed her divorce papers. She found later that he had never had a divorce, and left him, but returned when she was shown that the wife had died. The man promised to marry her as soon as she should bear him a child, she

[1] Case of Chicago Legal Aid Society.

said, but the man denied having made any such promise and did not marry her. He was a good, steady workman, but sometimes got drunk, and then abused the woman and her children. This woman impressed the social workers who had dealings with her as a rather high type of woman, and it was certain that she took excellent care of her home and her children.

It is not always the man whose standard has changed after emigration. Sometimes the husband is unchanged and the wife is dissatisfied.[1] In a Polish case, a couple of young immigrants married after they got here and before either of them could speak English. After twelve or fourteen years in the country the woman, who was particularly intelligent, could speak perfect English well and write a good hand, while the husband still had to speak through an interpreter. The wife could make more money than he could and had a higher standard of living and far more ambition to get ahead and educate the children. The result of all this was that the wife filed a bill for a divorce, charging the man with cruelty. Through ignorance he failed to contest the action, but was deeply opposed to divorce and insisted that he would die before he would give up the children.

To match this we have an Italian case,[2] in which the wife, after coming to this country, was desirous of getting ahead and making a good appearance. The husband wanted her to go around with a shawl over her head, as had been the custom in the old country, but this she was unwilling to do. She managed to save up money, which she gave to the landlord to keep for her, and also managed to put some in the bank. When her husband found that she was drawing money from

[1] Case of Divorce Proctor, Detroit.
[2] Case of Chicago Court of Domestic Relations.

the landlord he was sure that she was getting it for an immoral purpose and wanted to take away from her the money she had in the bank. The wife refused to submit tamely, and disputes resulted which brought them before the domestic relations court.

In an Italian case,[1] the woman complained that her husband was abusive to her and the children. She wanted him deported; they had been in the country only eight months. It appeared that the trouble between husband and wife had arisen because the wife had taken over the management of affairs and the man wanted to be recognized as the head of the house.

A case showing various complications of family life connected with emigration of the husband before the wife is that of a Russian family reported from Boston.[2] When first encountered, the woman had made a complaint in court of nonsupport and cruelty, both of which charges the man denied. He claimed in his turn that she was noisy and quarrelsome. On one occasion he said, when he had refused to let his wife go to see her sister who kept a rough house full of drunken boarders, the sister and a boarder assaulted him. After this incident came a long history of quarreling and fighting, and finally the man was sentenced to the House of Correction for three months; but the case was appealed. The next time he was heard of he had been to the State Board of Adult Poor in great distress, to have his "wife" dismissed from the almshouse. Upon inquiry it was found that this was not the woman who had complained against him, but a wife he had left behind in Europe. She had arrived in this country at about the time her husband was convicted of nonsupport of the other woman, and had been in the

[1] Court of Domestic Relations, Boston.
[2] Case of Court of Domestic Relations.

almshouse for two months. After her release the man went to living with her, and the next incident is a request by him to have his wife sent back to Russia, as she was pregnant. She was not sent there, however, for nearly three years later she brought a charge of non-support against him, and for another year we find the man brought up to the court on various charges, when the record ends inconclusively.

FAMILY RESPONSIBILITY

Nonsupport and desertion are troubles of the immigrant involving factors that are more or less common to all poor people, yet are aggravated by the immigrant situation. Sometimes the husband deserts or fails to support simply because the economic burden is too heavy for him. Income may be too small, or the man may have some physical handicap—illness or defect of some sort—that makes it difficult to earn a living. It has been noticed that this sort of trouble is likely to come to a crisis when the wife is about to bear a child; desertion and pregnancy occur together in a great many cases. The economic side of this situation may be regarded as a special immigrant problem because the immigrant enters the lower grades of occupation and is in consequence peculiarly liable to the hazards of unemployment, and to the breakdown in health following industrial accident or as the result of occupational disease. For the same reason, he is found crowded in the tenement districts of cities, or in unsanitary slum quarters of mill or mining towns or villages, to experience all the effects of physical debility coming from those conditions, and the mental irritation occasioned by living in a crowd.

On the social side something in this situation is due to the ideas the foreigh-born brings with him about

88

responsibility for the support and the increase of the family. As far as family responsibility is concerned, the foreign-born peasant is brought up to have as keen a sense of obligation for the support of a family as is the American. It is differently expressed in certain important respects, however. The mid-European peasant considers that family responsibility rests on every member of the family. In marriage the woman as well as the man must bring something to the partnership—a dowry, for example, and potential producing capacity. The Italians and other Latin peoples do not approve of wage earning outside the home for women, but work—contribution to the household of a substantial sort—is expected from the wife. The Slavs do not show so active an opposition to wage earning by the wife, but by them wage earning is not regarded as an individual matter. The earnings of members of the family are regarded as a contribution to a family fund, of which, in general, the man is custodian and manager. In the old country the work is done on the land which is connected with the farm, and the children, as fast as they come and are able to work, are put to work on the soil until the limits of cultivation are reached. The situation is entirely unlike that in the city colony, where the work available is in the form of definite jobs at definite wages. If the woman cannot procure such a wage-earning job, or if her husband objects to her working outside the home, she cannot contribute anything more productive to the family than a limited amount of cooking and cleaning in a little tenement dwelling. And each child is quite definitely an added burden. In the country the child can become a producer of his own food at an early age. In the city the child costs more to rear where all the food has to be bought and paid for, the laws do not permit of his becoming a producer below a certain minimum age, and finally, another definite job has to be found for him when he is ready to work—he does not fall into an inherited task as on the father's farm.

So that the large families that are reared as a matter of course on the farms in the old country, and get along somehow or other, are found to be great burdens, bringing a climax to misfortune in this country.

When this situation becomes too heavy to be borne, to many an immigrant man desertion seems to be the only way out. It does not occur to him to limit the size of his family both because of Church doctrines that artificial restriction is wrong, and his own idea that continence is impossible, and also because of a habit of thinking of children generally as an asset, an idea formed in a state of life in which children could be cultivators and producers.

Consequently, among the immigrant troubles brought to legal-aid societies, we find many cases of nonsupport and desertion where the main difficulty seems to be that the man thinks he cannot support his children. There are also cases where the man thinks himself at liberty to desert or relieve himself of the burden of support because the wife is not doing her part in the family partnership. These claims may be false in individual cases, but the frequency of the claim shows the attitude of mind of the European peasant. To him it is a valid excuse for leaving his family that his wife does not keep the house properly, spends money extravagantly, does not feed the children as she should. This excuse is not in accord with American ideas. In this country the teeming abundance of material riches has made it possible for the man to produce enough to enable the woman to lead a comparatively free life and the American husband in general makes no such claim upon a wife as the European peasant husband. This point of view is embodied even in our laws as they have been developed to regulate domestic relations. The idea at the basis of the older law was that the woman was the property of the man. He was free to direct what she should do; he was responsible for her actions, and was also responsible for her support. But while the law was changed to protect the woman from oppression by the husband and to give her some rights against him, it failed to provide for reciprocal duties on the part of the wife. Under our present laws, the man is bound to provide support, but he cannot make any claim on his wife or enforce the performance of duties on her part in the way of caring for a home.

The immigrant who has come over a single man may get into a situation with a girl which results in a forced marriage. These marriages seldom turn out happily and frequently result in desertion by the husband. If the forced marriage has taken place by a civil ceremony, the husband may feel free to marry again, on the ground that the marriage was not a real marriage, according to religious rules, as happened in a Polish case,[1] in which the husband, after a forced marriage, stayed with his wife until the birth of the child and then went back to his parents in Poland. There he married another girl, thinking himself free to do so, since the priest did not recognize his first civil marriage as valid.

The immigrant husband may also desert because he finds life unpleasant at home, and, in the desertions that take place at the time of the wife's pregnancy, this may be because the husband cannot have sex

[1] Case of Chicago Legal Aid Society.

relations with the wife—she cannot perform what the peasant considers wifely duty or, as they sometimes term it, "family duty." The husband's failure to secure the performance of "family duty" is at the bottom of many cases of "cruelty" reported to the courts. If the husband is refused this "duty," as he considers it, he may relieve his feelings by abusing his wife in some way or other. The real cause of the trouble may not be suspected, as the persons concerned are not inclined to discuss the matter, and even when the wife or the husband does attempt to talk about it, the social worker or the judge dealing with the case may discourage any mention of it.

Another phase of this situation may arise in the foreign family because of the European idea that marriage is a social matter, not intended for the gratification of individual preference. The husband may be much older than the wife and may have been married for his money, not for love. The wife may never have been physically attracted toward her husband, and in the new country sees a possibility of getting out of an unpleasant relation. In the old country both are held to a stricter social accountability by group opinion, and are more contented to abide by their duties. The man thinks he has to be more restrained in his claims, the woman thinks she has to be more obedient. In one case[1] a husband arrested for cruelty and nonsupport claimed that his wife did not fulfill her wifely duties, which she avoided on the plea of ill health. The man in this case appeared to be prosperous, to have no bad habits, and the social worker suspected the trouble to be that the woman did not care for him.

[1] Case of Chicago Legal Aid Society.

FAMILY TROUBLES

In a case of abuse[1] where the man was said to drink heavily, he admitted drinking and beating his wife, but said he did not want a separation. He would give his wife all his wages but a quarter a week, and would try to keep sober, but he complained that she "never spoke kindly to him."

In another[2] case of cruelty the woman herself admitted a lack of affection for the husband. A social worker interested in her case relates that once when they were sitting in a police court together, waiting for the case to be called, the woman began to look at her arms and hands and point out the scars to the worker, saying, "Here is where he burnt me with the poker," and, "Here is where he cut me with a knife," and, "That is where he hit me with a chair." Then in a burst of confidence she turned to the worker and said, "The trouble is I am cold in my heart to him."

The wife in such a situation may use the presence of the children as an excuse for the refusal of intercourse, whereat the husband, exasperated by the turn of affairs, may undertake to have relations in the very presence of the children. This behavior, told baldly, would seem to indicate a low and brutal disposition, and it certainly does show a lack of decency, but it cannot be thoroughly understood unless we know the provocation under which a man not altogether bad and brutal may be exasperated to the point of committing an indecent action, which he would not commit without being wrought up to a high pitch of excitement.

The same thing that often makes the man desert may make the woman refuse sex relations—she does not want any more children, on the ground that the

[1] Case of Chicago Legal Aid Society.
[2] *Ibid.*

pair cannot afford it, or that she is not in sufficiently good physical condition to bear the burden of it.

Or she may object because the man is diseased. This is a situation characteristic of immigrant life. The man who comes to this country before his wife is tempted to form illicit relations with immoral women and to acquire diseases he might be free from in the more normal life of the peasant community.

AN ILLUSTRATIVE CASE

An Italian case[1] illustrates not only the trouble ensuing from disagreement about sex relations, but other aspects of the immigrant's family life. Mrs. I——, a Calabrian, made a complaint to the court against her husband for nonsupport. It appeared that the husband, who worked irregularly, paid for rent and food, but did not give his wife any money. It also appeared that he was accustomed to beat her and the children. The wife's story was that she and her husband constantly quarreled because he wished to have sex relations with her more frequently than she desired, as she did not want to have any more children, since the father was not taking proper care of those he had. She had evidently talked about this phase of the matter quite freely with all the neighbors in the house and even with her own little girl, six years old. The wife said in the course of the conversation that she had been forced to marry her husband by her relatives in Italy, who wanted to get her settled after her father and mother died, and that she had never really cared for him. He was fifteen or twenty years older than she, and she objected to his looks. She kept referring again and again to the fact that he had a badly scarred face.

[1] Case of Court of Domestic Relations, New York City.

FAMILY TROUBLES

She did not bring this fact forward as a reason for leaving him, but simply as a part of the picture of her life. They came to America because conditions in Italy were such that they were always starving. She said her husband had treated her badly ever since they were first married, and she had brought action against him before. Neighbors and friends at first took the woman's part, but some time afterward took the husband's part entirely, partly because they felt strongly that none but a very bad woman would ever leave her husband. A cousin thought the situation was simply that Mrs. I—— was a young woman who objected to her husband because he was older than she and ugly, and he was always afraid she would run away with some younger and handsomer man. Consequently he was afraid to give her very much money, for fear she would save up enough to leave him, and was constantly upbraiding her with his suspicions about any man whom she ever looked at.

The man himself, on the occasion of a visit by an investigator for this study, behaved in a most emotional way over the children, picking them up and kissing them extravagantly, and during the visit continually giving them pennies to buy candy and ice cream. He told the visitor that he had not been giving his wife money for all the expenses of the house, because he did not trust her. He said if he gave her even half of his salary she would probably save up little by little and after a while go off with another man. He wanted to keep her by any means possible, not because he was fond of her, he said, but because he wanted to keep the children together. He resented very much her speaking of him to neighbors as old and ugly, and said she married him of her own free will and that she was tired of him then only because there was some one else in the case. He said all would go well if she would only stay home with him, take care of the children, have his meals ready, and obey him generally. He resented the fact that she would not have sex relations with him and said that if she would not have anything to do with him she certainly had some other man.

INFLUENCE OF RELATIVES

In domestic difficulties generally, the interference of relatives or the presence in the family group of persons who are related, but not in the relation of parent and children, is often found a source of trouble.

In the life of the immigrant this factor becomes important through the crowding into narrow quarters which is a feature of immigrant life. The custom of marrying or taking some sort of companion after the death or desertion of the husband or wife leads to the association under one roof of different sets of children —as the old story has it, "his," and "hers," and "theirs" it may be. Then the father's children may encourage quarrels with the mother, and vice versa.

The European idea of parental authority has its special part to play here also. One of the grievances of the stepfather is that the children will not obey him. This may be either from lack of discipline or because the mother deliberately uses the children as partisans against the husband. The presence of so many sets of children in the family also increases the burden of support which often leads a husband to desert.

The European peasant's respect for parental authority makes more acute the troubles that arise from interference by the parents of husband or wife, or the recourse to father or mother by one of the married pair for backing in their difficulties. If the young wife has to go to the husband's mother's house to live, the old idea that the mother has a position of authority over the group under her roof, and especially over the daughter-in-law, makes the natural difficulties worse. The mother may take it upon herself to keep an oversight of the son, and tell him what he may or may not do.

Sometimes the trouble arises through the doting fondness of the mother for the son, and the feeling of his superior importance, which is also characteristic of the European family in general. The mother and perhaps the father assume rights over the son which no one else is allowed to have, even the wife.

DIFFERENCE IN FAMILY STANDARDS

Difference of standards of families as well as of individuals is also a cause of dissension. In one case[1] a young woman of Neapolitan extraction—her people had come from Naples thirty years before, and she was born in this country—married a young Sicilian, born on the other side, who had, however, come here at a very early age. Her parents did not want her to marry him, because his family had such different ideas from hers. And there had been constant trouble ever since the marriage, because the husband, "like all Sicilians," as the wife's mother expressed it, wanted to be a tyrant in his own home. He not only insisted on obedience from his wife, but he tried to keep her secluded in their home, and, while he wanted friends outside the house, he wished his wife to have nothing to do with them. He told the judge that the reason he had not been supporting his wife since she left him was that he wanted her at home, that he was fond of

[1] Case of Court of Domestic Relations, New York City.

the children, and that he never hit his wife "except when she got very fresh." His wife, in her turn, said that she had put up with his awful temper for years, and finished by saying, "Now I am an American girl and I cannot stand for his treating me like a Dago."

The Sicilian mother-in-law, an intelligent, kindly woman, said she was worried to death over the trouble between her son and daughter-in-law, who was a good woman; but the great trouble came from their different ideas of married life. She said that all Sicilians had much the same ideas as her son, that she herself had always given in to her husband, had never talked back to him, had stayed at home, had taken care of the home and the children while he went out, played cards, and visited his friends, and so she had been respected by him all their married life. She thinks the wife ought not to be jealous of her husband or worried about his behavior, when he is away from home. Almost every evening her son comes to her house and plays the mandolin all the evening. She feels that his wife could not take part in these joyful occasions because it is her duty to stay home and take care of the children.

The husband said he gave his wife $14 a week, on which she ought to be able to run the house and clothe herself and the three children without doing home work, but she had too luxurious tastes.

PARENTS AND CHILDREN

Domestic troubles naturally affect the children of the family, and often provide grist for the juvenile court. Here, too, we see the results of the peculiar circumstances of the immigrant's life in other respects.

The attitude of the parent toward the child as we see it in immigrant families is a strange combination in varying proportions, of strong and impulsive affection toward him and keen calculation of benefits to be derived from him.

In many of the cases, parents who cannot get along together both want the children. The father who is cruel to his wife, and even beats the children, insists with fervor on having an opportunity to see them. This may occur from a desire to torment the wife, as often happens in higher circles, but there is no doubt that many times it is simply from real affection toward the children. In the case of the Italian, for example, ·in spite of his insistence on the power and authority of the father, his impulsive temperament prevents him from exerting a continuous and reasoned discipline, and he is capable of outbursts of the most exaggerated fondness. Italian children are generally undisciplined and unrestrained, especially the sons, who are regarded as potential heads of households and are catered to as such. The girls are kept more strictly after reaching adolescence. From this time on the father is for the most part a tyrant over them. On the economic side, the immigrant parent expects the children to contribute to the family support. He regards the earnings of the children as family property. This causes dissension in the household. The children, brought up in an American community, although in a foreign neighborhood, quickly learn the lesson of freedom and are no longer willing to put up with what would have been taken as a matter of course in the home country, and in consequence conflicts arise about the earning and spending of money, about the use of time and about schooling.

Many of the cases of "ungovernable children" of foreign parents brought before the court show unreasonable parents who want the children to go to work at the earliest possible moment and to turn over all of their earnings to the family coffer.

Environmental influences, on the other hand, do not correct this parental tendency in the right way. In the home is found the rigid idea of parental control; out of the home in the average immigrant neighborhood are found demoralizing temptations to a freedom which is simply viciousness.

CONFLICTS OVER MARRIAGE

The Italian father tries to keep the same authority over the marriage of girls that he had at home. In consequence, instances of a curious reaction on the part of the young people are found. In one case noted,[1] which is probably not unique in this respect, a young Italian, honestly in love with a good girl who was in love with him, was unable to obtain the consent of her father to the marriage because the father wanted the girl to stay at home and look after his younger children, the wife having left his home. After some time had passed the girl was found to be pregnant. The social workers having to do with the case took it as an instance of seduction and wanted to take stern measures with the young man responsible for the situation, who was her suitor, but it appeared that he was perfectly willing to marry her, had been so all along, and had in fact adopted this method to secure the father's consent.

An extreme instance of contest between the father and the suitor was found by an investigator for this study in a Middle Western city, where a number of cases of rape of young Italian girls had occurred. It appeared that these were cases in which men wanting to marry girls whose parents refused consent had

[1] Case of Society for Prevention of Cruelty to Children, New York City.

abducted the girls, in order to secure them as wives, thus rendering themselves technically liable to the charge of rape as the girls were under the age at which they could contract marriage.

These cases referred to by no means exhaust the possibilities of variety in the immigrant's domestic troubles, but they do indicate how far from simple are the elements involved, how much in the situation springs from special attitudes of mind of the immigrant, which need to be understood before the situation can be properly dealt with. These domestic cases are by no means to be understood by cataloguing them under such fixed legal formulæ as "adultery," "desertion," "abandonment," "rape," and so on, or such social formulæ as "vice," "immorality," "cruelty," and so on. Behind each of these terms, in each individual case is a complex of circumstances and motives that not only supplements the bare word of the formula, but may entirely change its meaning, and should guide the treatment to be administered.

III

THE FOREIGN-BORN OFFENDER

Our courts are called upon not only to protect the exploited or abused immigrant, but also to correct and punish the immigrant who is found violating the law. Is this an especially heavy task, and are there peculiar circumstances surrounding the immigrant's offenses that are worth noting?

STATISTICS OF CRIMINALITY

It is generally assumed that the burden of foreign criminality is unduly heavy and attention is called to criminality rates apparently showing that the foreign-born resident of this country is far more prone to offend against the law than is the native born.

In 1910, for example, comparing the white population only, we find that of every one hundred thousand of the native white population 371.3 persons had been committed to prison or jail for some offense; while of the foreign-born population, 746.6 persons out of every one hundred thousand had been committed— or just twice the proportion shown for the native born.[1]

If we take the native-born white of native parentage only, leaving out of account the native-born white of foreign parentage, who may be considered to have some share in the characteristics of the foreign born, the disproportion is even higher. For, of every one hundred

[1] "Prisoners and Juvenile Delinquents in the United States," 1910 Bureau of Census, p. 108.

thousand of native whites of native parentage, only 287.9 were committed to some prison or jail, in comparison with which the foreign rate is 2.6 times as great.

FALLACY OF AGE AND SEX

But statistics may be misleading unless we consider closely just what is being compared. In this instance the fallacy is involved of comparing a group—the natives of native parentage—containing a large proportion of women and children, whose crime rate is always low, with a group containing an abnormally large proportion of young adult males whose crime rate is always high. If we compare the rates for each age and sex group separately—if we compare, for instance, the number of commitments out of one hundred thousand males between twenty-four and thirty-four years of age, of the native of native parentage with the number of commitments out of one hundred thousand foreign-born males of the same age we shall find that the rates show little difference. And this is true of each age and sex group.

COMMITMENTS AN IMPERFECT MEASURE OF CRIMINALITY

But before these statistics could be taken as a measure of criminality, even after this correction, other adjustments would have to be made. They are statistics of commitments only—of persons who were charged with committing some offense, who were apprehended and who were committed to some penal institution. Many persons who commit offenses are not caught, and, on the other hand, some persons who are caught and even convicted are innocent. Again, many guilty persons are punished in some other way than by commitment to prison or jail. If the foreign-born person is more likely to be caught, and more likely to be convicted when caught than the native, if he is more likely to be punished by imprisonment than by fine only, the rate for the foreign born will be higher for those reasons, without regard to the actual commission of offenses. On the other hand, if the foreign-born person is harder to catch and less likely to be convicted, the rate of commitments will be lower for him, irrespective of offenses committed.

It is hard, if not impossible, to measure these possibilities. Some students of the subject think that it is peculiarly difficult to bring the foreign offender to justice because of our ignorance of his language and customs and our failure to adapt our police methods to his peculiarities. On the other hand, if it is true that the poor man finds it more difficult to escape the toils of the law, the immigrant, as a poor man, is particularly involved in this difficulty. We may note here one way in which the poverty of the immigrant can plainly affect the crime rate. A large proportion of the offenses for which persons are convicted are of a minor nature—violations of ordinances, disorderly conduct, and so on, and in many cases the punishment inflicted is alternative—fine or imprisonment. The man with some money can pay his fine and will not be included in the record of commitments; the poor man will go to jail instead, and be counted among the offenders, for the very same act.

DIFFERENCES IN "FOREIGN BORN"

Again, the term "foreign born" includes peoples of many different varieties. The comparison is often made between our older and our newer immigrants, in respect to criminality. If we try to make this comparison we shall be obliged to go all over again through the same process of criticism and modification found necessary in comparing the native born and the foreign born as a whole. The newer immigrants show a higher proportion of young adult males than the older immigrants; the nature of the offenses they are most prone to commit varies among themselves, and from the older immigrants, and the possibilities of detection and punishment may be different.

HOW THE IMMIGRANT MAY BECOME AN OFFENDER

From the statistics at best, with all possible corrections and allowances, we can get only a rough measurement of foreign criminality. Really to understand the immigrant as an offender, we must go back of the statistics to concrete cases, follow the social history of the offender, and note the tangle of circumstances involved.

In many of the cases of foreign criminality, we cannot discover a clear connection between the native qualities or the peculiar circumstances of the immigrant in this country and the fact of commitment for crime. In many others, however, we seem to be able to trace such a connection. Cases are found in which an immigrant who is innocent of the offense charged has been committed to prison for it as a result of his ignorance of our language and customs. In other cases, the changed circumstances of life in the new country, the breaking down of old habits and old restraint, seem to occasion criminal conduct on the part of people who would perhaps have gone straight in their habitual surroundings.

CRIMES OF VIOLENCE

A few instances, gathered here and there, may be cited to illustrate some of these points. First, one or two cases of the most serious type of all, where a human life has been taken.

THE IMMIGRANT'S DAY IN COURT

Nicolo M——, an Italian gardener in charge of club grounds on which trespassing was forbidden, ordered off the grounds some boys who insisted on violating this rule because the path through the club property was the shortest cut to a lake in which they wanted to swim. Turning back to his work, he was stoned by the boys, who refused to leave the property. We may perhaps imagine, without violating the probabilities, that the missiles were accompanied by insulting language. In a rage, Nicolo flung his heavy gardener's shears at the boys, hitting one of them, the point of the shears piercing the heart and causing instant death. The man claimed that he did not throw the shears intentionally, but that a blow from a stone knocked them out of his hand. He was indicted for murder, but the jury failed to agree, and he was reindicted for manslaughter and convicted. After sentence the man committed suicide. In this brief story we see an example of a species of treatment of the foreign born that is going on every day and that is likely to lead to retaliatory conduct. "The foreigner" is fair game to street boys, who will tease and torment him and ridicule him for foreign peculiarities until he may be goaded into some act of violence against his tormentors. The wonder is that not more of such cases occur.

VIOLENCE RESULTING FROM FAMILY TROUBLE

Troubles in domestic relations, which we have seen to arise so naturally and in such variety as the result of the changed circumstances in which the immigrant finds himself are a frequent cause of incitement to violence. The murder of Gianetto C——, an Italian, was apparently the result of his continued interference in the marriage of his daughter. We have noted in

106

our account of the cases of domestic troubles to what devices the suitor has to resort sometimes in order to secure a chosen young woman for a wife, even to "seduction" and rape. In the case of Gianetto, his fifteen-year-old daughter eloped, and for eight years after that it was said that he tried to break up her home. This conduct so troubled the girl that she lost her mind, temporarily, and had to be sent to an asylum. Finally Gianetto was found at his own back door, shot down by an assassin. Before his death, being asked who shot him, he replied, "My son-in-law." For an Italian girl of fifteen to elope, even in this country, is an unusual occurrence, and to the Italian father, accustomed to exercising absolute control over the children, it must have seemed a great blow. Had he resorted to law he might have had the marriage annulled, but he did not do this, whether because he was ignorant of our law or whether because of a distrust of law in general and reliance on self-help for the redress of domestic grievances, which has frequently been noted as an Italian characteristic.

The frequent desertions of wives by husbands and husbands by wives found in immigrant family life, and the intrusion of the boarder, may lead to crime, especially on the part of the husband, if he is the one deserted or wronged. The deserted husband who feels a sense of injury in many instances knows no way of securing redress except through direct action on his part. In some instances it is practically certain that if the right advice could have been given at the right time crime could have been prevented.

In one instance a Pole, deserted by his wife, who had gone to live with another man, made three successive visits to the police station to inquire what he could do in the matter. The police gave him no satisfaction at any visit, and, in despair of getting his wrong redressed in any legal way, he took the matter into his own hands and shot his wife and her lover. In its bare outlines this is a duplicate of another case, which we may give in more detail, as follows:

Jan T——, also a Pole, was sent to prison for life for killing two people. His statement of the circumstances leading to his act bears the marks of truth and well illustrates many characteristic features of the immigrant's domestic life which we have already noticed:

I, Jan T——, came to America and to South Chicago, in 1902; for nine months I have been boarding and lodging at John S——'s on M—— Avenue. During that time I have been working steady in Steel Mills and, thanks to God, I have earned in that short time so much that I was able to send for my wife in the old country, where I had left her, paying $52.50 for the steamship ticket and sending $10 to my wife for her traveling expenses. When my wife came from the old country to America I also had the rooms rented in South Chicago from Frank L—— on O—— Avenue, as well as the furniture I had in my rooms. But there I could not live very long, because of my wife; one day, in the very beginning, on my coming home from my work in the roll mill I caught Frank L—— and my wife in my house in their misdeeds. But I did not lick him for that; I just let Mr. L—— come rolling down the stairs. When his wife Mrs. L—— heard this she came out with the ax and went after him, chasing around the yard and shouting to kill him for that. So I could not live there any longer; I was ashamed of what happened and so I rented the rooms on M—— Avenue. There I lived four years and during these four years I have saved a couple hundred of dollars. I had intention to go back to the old country. But because my wife had objected to our going back to the old country, I said to her I want no more to stay in America and I shall go back to my own country. To this my wife replied: "Now you have money and you better go to the company that builds the houses and buy one and we will have one of our own, because I will not go back to the old country."

And I did as my wife wanted. I went to the company, looked over one of its houses, then went to its agent, told him of my object of visit, and asked him about the price of the house I have looked over. He told me the price and it was $1400. The house was on R——

THE FOREIGN-BORN OFFENDER

Avenue. I went for my money and paid in first payment of $700; after this I have moved into the house with my family and lived there with my wife on very good terms, paying the balance of the sum at the rate of $15 a month and 5 per cent interest a year.

One day when I came home from my work my wife has told me of a visit to our house by a man from our country. I asked his name and she said his name was Joseph B——. I told my wife I don't know him, but the wife said she knows him and was going to take him in as a roomer. I objected to that, but she said she wants to take him in, and I, to avoid a possible quarrel, consented to her taking him in. He came to our house and lived with us one year. During that time there was a harmony in our home, because he had no work and had but little money. But he had the claim against the Steel Company of South Chicago and the company was obliged to pay him a couple hundred of dollars. In two weeks' time after that I noticed my wife's bad behavior and have struck her on the face with my hand. That angered her; she arrested me and I was sent to Bridewell for seventy-eight days before I could chase him out of my house. So he remained in my house while I was taken to Bridewell. In Bridewell I stayed one month, when my wife came to me saying that she wants to go to the old country, that Joseph B—— wants to buy our house, and that I shall sign the papers. I refused to sign the papers and said: if you do not want to keep the house we can sell it after I am out of jail and then we all may go to the old country.

After I regained my freedom my wife took a notion to urge me constantly to sell the house, to put the money away, and to rent the rooms elsewhere until we shall make some more money and then go to the old country. At last I submitted to my wife's will and we sold the house for $1,100. The money we got for the house was kept in the house. Two days later my wife tried to persuade me to get the rooms elsewhere and to move out, but I have told her that there is no need for a hurry and we have plenty of time to do that. At that time the money was kept in the house. I said to her, "I consider you as my wife and you consider me as your husband and therefore I think that you will not give that money to anyone but me."

Two days after when I went to my work she took that money and gave it to the man of her heart, to Joseph B——, who had paid the money for the house; then she took the youngest boy, one year old, and eloped with Joseph B——, leaving the other two children that are now in the Orphans' Asylum of St. Jadwiga at Niles, Illinois. I took these two children to the police station, where I told to the police the whole case and asked it to be so good and find my boy and bring my wife to her children. But there I was told that this matter was none of their business and if I want to find my wife I should look for her myself.

I took these two children and came back to my house. Two days later Joseph B—— came to me and asked me when I was going to move from that house; and he said if I were too slow about it he will throw me out. I said to him thus: "You have stolen my wife and my boy and my money; when you bring my wife and my child and return my money then I will move from this house."

He went to the constable and the constable came to me at my house and said to me that this house does not belong to me any more, that it belongs to the other fellow because he has bought it, and in case I should fail to move out from it in three days' time, he, the constable, shall come and throw me out into the street.

To this I told the constable that it is true that I have sold the house, but I will not move from it until he, the other fellow, shall bring my wife and my child back and until he returns the money he has paid for this house and then stole the wife, the child, and the money.

My wife stayed away from these two children. One morning she came back and gave me the money to pay for the rent and urged me to find and rent the flat. I went out and rented the rooms on the E—— Avenue, after which we have moved there. When we were there I asked her where is our money we got for the house. She said the money is in Chicago and she shall go there to-morrow and get it. And she did so, but when she went away with that little boy, leaving the other two with me, she never came back again. For two months I have stayed alone with these two children, and when I saw that the wife is not coming back to her children, while the children are following me everywhere, crying for their mamma and asking me where she is and making me to tell them that their mamma is gone away and perhaps she is never to come back again. I had no heart to listen to their cries and so I picked up all I had in my house and together with my children I went to Erie, Pa., to my friend Joseph P——, who lived on —— Street. There I got some work soon in a new paper mill on the lake shore, and from this work I managed to pay the board and lodging for myself and these two children for several weeks. The wife learned where I and the two children are and wrote a letter to me asking me to take the children with me and come back. I wrote her back that she shall sell everything she has and shall come to me because I had the work there; in case she was short with the money for her passage I have promised to send her either the money for the passage or the ticket. She answered me, saying that she could not come because she was ashamed of the people, and therefore, she wrote me, I should take the children and come to her.

I quitted the work, took the children with me, and came back to South Chicago, where the wife wrote to me she had the rooms and was living with the other woman, one of them working day work and the other one night work.

But when I came I found it was not true; she had no rooms. Then I said to my wife: "What shall we do now? Which shall we look for first, the rooms or the work?" She told me to go and look for the work and she was to find the rooms. I went and found some work on the railroad track. I thought to myself it was better to have something than nothing, so I accepted the work and worked all day. After the day's work I returned to the place where my wife has stayed with her sponsor, but she was not there. The sponsor said she took the children and said she was going to Chicago and that was all she has said.

I went out to look for my wife and children and have found them at N—— G—— Avenue. That was an old number of the house which is now perhaps changed. That house belonged to the La Buy, whose son at that time was a lawyer and now is a judge in the court on W—— C—— Avenue. There my wife and Joseph B—— had a saloon. I tried to take my wife and my children away from him, but I couldn't do it because he grabbed the revolver and I had to obey him, which I did. But I called the patrol wagon by the telephone from the S—— Avenue station and ordered to arrest him. The patrolman took us all to the police station and there I stated my case. Yet this helped me nothing because my opponent had the money and I had none. Mr. La Buy was his attorney and I was sent to Bridewell for a couple of weeks.

When I got out from the Bridewell I went for my wife and the children again, but I found the place is empty and for rent. But I did not stop there, I went searching and found them rooming on B—— Avenue. There I ordered to arrest him for the second time and the police took him to the N—— Avenue police station. I stated my case again, but the La Buy again was his attorney and the police let him go free again. He went home, but I did not dare to follow him because they were two and I only myself. So I ordered to arrest him for the third time at the C—— Avenue police station and stated my case over again but with the same results.

Then I went to Erie again to Joseph P——, with whom I stayed before with my two children. There I stayed two months. One day

THE IMMIGRANT'S DAY IN COURT

P—— gave me advice, saying that I should better go back to my children. I accepted his advice and went to Chicago to my wife; there I saw my children shabby and barefooted. I took $25 from my pocket and gave them to my wife, asking her to go to the store and buy some clothes and shoes for the children, but she instead kept the money for herself to buy drinks for her lover. Then I told her that I will not let come into the house neither Joseph B—— nor his partner, and will not go to the police station because the police does not care to keep the order.

And I did as I said. I did not let come into the house neither of them for a whole week. But that was too long for Joseph B——, so he persuaded my wife to go with him on Sunday morning to a place on M—— Avenue and there they went and started drinking and paying for the drinks out from those $25 I gave her. When I asked the children where is their mamma they told me she is with Joe and with that other uncle, who stays with us on M—— Avenue. I asked the children what they are doing there, and they told me that mamma and Joe and that other uncle are sitting at the table and playing cards.

I went to the house where my wife was and knocked at the door. They from the inside asked me who is there and I answered, I, the Jan T——, and I want my wife to come home to her children and I want you to let her go. They from the inside answered to my saying that I shall better go to where I came from while I have my head sound (unsmashed).

I went back to the house where my wife was living, and in an hour's time I went back to the house they were in; but the door was locked as before and the men were giving me the same answers. So I went home and went to bed; the children and wife and Joseph B—— have slept there with those other people.

On Monday morning I got up and went to these folks; the door was unlocked this time and I went in. There were three men, Joseph B——, the owner of the house, and the third man unknown to me; I gave them five cents for a beer, and turning to my wife I asked her why does she not go home and wash her children and send them to school, and why she spends the $25 I gave her on cards and beer that is poured down the throats of the other people. To this my wife has said: "Of such men as you are I could get a hundred or three hundred if I wanted.

After she has uttered those words to me some one from behind me has struck me on the head and I fell down; here all rushed to me, but I had enough consciousness left in me to defend myself; I took the revolver from my pocket and fired three shots in self-defense killing one man and my wife, of which I even did not know and learned only the next day when I was laying at the hospital, bleeding through the mouth and nose. Even the guards were saying that I will not live; they may be asked if the truthfulness of my words should be doubted; they were on the fourth floor.

Therefore I do not admit I was guilty; for that was responsible; (1) the police of S—— Avenue station; (2) the police of N—— Avenue police station; (3) the police of W—— C—— Avenue police station; Attorney La Buy; and Joseph B——. If the police at the three stations mentioned above were unable to know the case, their business was to send it to the higher court.

[Signed] Jan T——

VIOLENCE RESULTING FROM IRREGULAR SEX RELATIONS

Sometimes the irregular connections formed by the immigrant who has left his wife in Europe occasion criminal conduct.

Vincenzo G——, an Italian, was indicted for first-, second-, and third-degree assault. He did not actually kill anyone, but came very near to it. Vincenzo was the son of a horse dealer who had been prosperous but had been reduced to poverty, so that Vincenzo could have only two years of schooling. As a child he did odd jobs, until at the age of twelve he established himself as a business man, peddling wooden shoes and old clothes. At twenty he married a girl from a neighboring town, who in course of time bore him ten children. When he had reached middle age his sister sent for him to come to America. Her son gave him a job paying $8 a week and board, and he started in to pay for his passage money in weekly installments. In a job he found for himself later his wages reached $17 a week, out of which he sent $10 a week regularly to his family in Italy. He had intended to stay here three years, earn a thousand dollars, and go back home and set up a little business of his own. But when he got into trouble he had been here five years. People who knew him here spoke of him as a quiet, hard-working man who never showed any disposition to be quarrelsome. He had gone to live in the same house with his nephew, and there he passed the time quietly, spending the evenings playing with his nephew's children. He did not go to church here, as he did in Italy, but on Sunday would buy and drink a bottle of Chianti. The house in which the nephew lived was in a small Italian colony, but the house itself had a mixed tenantry, of Italians and Jews. And it was here that he met Lena P—— the janitress, a Polish Jewess. Lena's husband was in jail, and she so worked upon the sympathies of Vincenzo that he paid her grocery bills, bought shoes for her children, and lent her money besides. And a closer relation sprang up between them, which alarmed and worried the nephew, who tried to break it off. Vincenzo would promise his nephew to have no more to do with Lena, but this was all forgotten when he saw her. After six months of this, Lena gave up her position as janitress and went to live somewhere else, urging him to go with her, so that he might board out her debt to him. The nephew gave him his choice of losing his job and giving up all relations with the nephew's family, or leaving Lena. But Vincenzo found another job for himself, went with Lena, and stayed with her for three and a half years, when she grew tired of him and turned him out. Going back to her house one day nearly a year after that, in the effort to get some of the money he had loaned her, he found another man in the apartment, who, he claimed, assaulted him, so that in self-defense he drew a knife. For this he was convicted and imprisoned. This was his first offense. Whether the act was one of self-defense or not, we have here the picture of a hard-working man of domestic instincts, faithfully bearing the burden of financial support of a large family in Italy, deprived of their companionship, fallen into the hands of a female bird of prey through his loneliness and his kindly feelings for a person in trouble. Had he been with his family, probably none of this would have happened.

A LABOR-CAMP CASE

Andrea S——, another Italian, was not in domestic trouble, but he was living under abnormal social conditions. He also did not kill anyone, but he was charged with firing a pistol and injuring a man, was indicted for assault, and sent to prison. He had been in this country for three and a half years, could not speak English, and could not read or write. He had been married ten years, and his wife and two children were in Italy. He was sending money home regularly, out of his wages of $3 a day in construction work. He had been a poor man at home. His mother owned a three-room house in Italy, and his father one acre of land. No member of his immediate family had ever been to school. From the very start the family was beset with economic difficulties; the father had to incur a debt in order to raise his family, and this debt became a charge upon the children. Andrea was put to work in the fields at twelve years of age, and began to do his part toward paying the debt out of his very small wages as an agricultural laborer. He married at the age of twenty and settled down in his mother's house, but when a younger brother came back from the army he had to move out. Two years later he emigrated to America, on borrowed money. His share in the family debt when he reached his majority amounted to $70, and he expected to clear this away by his earnings in America for three years. When the three years were over he planned to return to Italy. He did pay all of the debt, but was still in America after the three-year period.

When he landed at the port of Boston he secured his first job as a laborer from an immigrant bank, and was shipped to a town in New York State. He then got work with a contracting company, with whom he stayed until the time of his arrest.

After he went to this firm he lived in construction camps. The one in which he was living at the time he got into trouble was an unattractive place. The living quarters consisted of four large shanties containing about twenty-five men each. Near the shanties was the company store. The men worked ten or twelve hours a day, and at night amused themselves by playing games. Sunday was spent doing the week's washing. Around the camp were open fields; there were only two houses within a mile of the place. Men living such a life are shut off from the usual human contacts, and Andrea had the habit of relieving the monotony by going to New York every Saturday night for a concentrated enjoyment that should last him all the week. It was on the ferryboat to New York, on one of these occasions, that the trouble arose which landed him in prison. A crowd of men got to pushing and quarreling, and a shot was fired. Andrea insisted that he did not fire it, but the judge thought he did and he was sent to prison for it.

A LANDLORD MAKES TROUBLE

Sometimes the "boarder" situation leads to conviction for crime even without the incitement of domestic trouble. A young Pole, Jan M——, single, and his sweetheart, Mary K——, to whom he was engaged to be married, boarded with another Pole for about five months, when both left. Mary says that money was stolen from her several times while she was there. Three weeks later Jan returned to the old boarding place, to get his clothes, accompanied by his new landlord, and got into a fight with his former landlord, who, with the help of his wife, fell upon and beat Jan. They had a gun and a poker and would have killed him, but for the interference of the new landlord. During the fight the former landlord's finger was caught and crushed in the door. For this he got out a warrant against Jan, claiming that Jan had bitten the finger. Jan was taken to court, fined $50 and costs, and sent to jail for three months. He and his sweetheart were to have been married the following week, and, as she was already pregnant, she was beside herself with distress at the imprisonment of her fiancé.

The landlord told her afterward that he knew the finger had been caught in the door, but he wanted Jan punished for leaving his house, and he would now secure Jan's release if she would pay $50 to himself.

LARCENY AND BURGLARY

Cases of larceny may be accounted for sometimes by special circumstances of the immigrant situation.

Felix B——, a Czech laborer, was earning $25 a week and doing pretty well, but he had four children, and it was a struggle to provide clothing for them. One day, finding a carload of shoes accessible in the railroad yard, he took some of the shoes, for which he was arrested and charged with larceny. His previous record was good and probation was recommended by the judge.

117

As a result of three months of visiting, the probation officer reports:

B—— is a very satisfactory probationer. He responds to advice. He is a progressive kind of foreigner. Owns his home and has a houseful of children. Has a fifty-foot-lot garden, also 50 ducks and 250 chickens. He took the shoes because he found the car was open and it looked like a good chance to get away with shoes for his family.

This man, of course, really stole property, but he cannot be classed as a criminal type.

An ignorant and helpless immigrant may find himself convicted of burglary without intent of harm on his part.

One Max G—— at the time of his arrest was about twenty years old, had been in the United States about four months, was penniless except for a stray five cents or so in his pocket, and was unable to speak a word of English. He went into a saloon to spend five of his few remaining pennies on a glass of beer, with which he would get a free lunch, and while sitting at a table was accosted in Yiddish, his native tongue, by three young fellows. They learned that Max was without money or work, and offered to take him to a place where he could get a job. Believing that he was going to a place of employment, he followed the men. They took him to a house, which one of the men entered, leaving the other two men and Max standing on the sidewalk. The man who was making his way into the house was discovered, but he and his two friends made their escape, leaving Max standing, open mouthed with astonishment, on the sidewalk, where he was arrested by the police. Brought to court, he was tried and convicted for the crime of attempted burglary and sentenced to twelve years' imprisonment. He served eight years of that term, when a social worker happened

118

upon the case and secured a pardon from the governor. This social worker was confirmed in her original belief in the boy's story and in his innocence of any crime, in subsequent acquaintance with him through a number of years.

The young "burglar" may not always be so plainly innocent of crime, but in many cases in his personal history may be noted a progressive deterioration under the influences of the new country. Many such cases are the result of failure of family discipline conducted upon Old World lines, combined with disintegrating influences outside.

Something of this sort apparently happened to Sam——, whose "burglary" consisted in stealing and selling motor cycles. This boy was eighteen years old, his habits and associations were said to be good previous to this affair, and he had been making $18 or $19 a week for nineteen months after coming to this country, and had been giving satisfaction to his employer. He lived in a comfortably furnished flat with relatives who owned their own property. After a time he began to work irregularly, on Saturdays and Sundays only, for a barber. He worked in this way for about six months and then stopped working altogether. This deterioration seems to have progressed together with his intimacy with another boy whose name, as given in the record, would indicate descent from native stock or from some people of the older immigration. His uncle, finding him staying out late at night, once locked him out, "to teach him a lesson." This resulted in his going with his chum to a hotel and staying away from his uncle's house for over a month. His story is that during this time he committed four or five burglaries, with the other boy acting as lookout, each time taking one or more motor cycles.

119

THE IMMIGRANT'S DAY IN COURT

Even these few cases, picked up here and there, suggest the possibility that a considerable waste of good human material, a considerable conversion of normal humanity into a criminal class, may be going on, simply through failure to understand and deal with the peculiar elements involved. Surely the judge who handles immigrant cases should understand the character, the situation, and the racial peculiarities of the immigrant, in order to adjust the treatment of the case in accordance with true principles of justice. Surely the probation officer should be similarly equipped. Furthermore, something might be done toward preventing the need of court action, if the American community could be brought to regard the immigrant in some other light than as so much industrial man power or as so much social dynamite, and would take the immigrant to itself as a fellow member, with a right to help and sympathy and instruction.

IV

THE APPROACH TO THE COURT

THE immigrant who is charged with committing an offense against the law is brought before some court, whether he knows that there is such an institution or not, whether he knows or does not know by what means he is brought there or what law he is accused of violating; the immigrant who has had some wrong done to him, which the law would take cognizance of, may not find his way to the court at all, unless some one will take him in hand and see that he gets there. He may not know his rights under the law, he may not know where to go to get redress or protection, or what methods he must follow to avail himself of legal remedies. He needs some one to advise him what to do—to inform him of his rights, to explain to him how to secure them.

And when the immigrant does finally stand before the court, either as complainant or defendant, he needs, even more than the native born, some technical advice and aid of the sort given by an attorney. It is of great importance to him, then, that such helpers should be available, and of as great importance not only to himself, but to the community, is the kind of service they render.

For these helpers are the principal media through which the immigrant gets his first impressions of American justice, his first information about our courts and our laws. With every social contact in this country the immigrant is building up a trust or a distrust in our institutions, a respect or disrespect for them, unsuspected by the general public, for the immigrant is as much shut off from its view as it is from his. And some fine day the public is startled by a "spirit of lawlessness" in the "foreigner" which it is utterly at a loss to account for, and considers him depraved and ungrateful, when the attitude noted may be simply the natural result of the only teaching made available to him. Let us see just what may happen to him when he tries to get help in legal matters.

THE IMMIGRANT AS COMPLAINANT

When the immigrant feels that he has been wronged in any way, he is apt to do what we have seen him doing about his business affairs—talk the matter over with his nearest friends and associates, and ask their advice. Some more experienced friend or acquaintance may suggest his calling upon the law for aid, and urge him to engage a lawyer. The friend may perhaps recommend some particular lawyer for the immigrant to patronize. Such advice may be given at one of those street-corner gatherings characteristic of immigrant colonies, or in the saloon, which until lately was a favorite meeting place of immigrants. And we might have seen the saloon keeper adding to his friendly services as banker and employment agent that of giving legal advice or recommending a lawyer. Another near friend often appealed to is the landlord, whom we have also seen acting as banker for his tenants. Sometimes the immigrant in trouble will be advised to go to a bank where the banker will undertake to provide a lawyer. Often the priest or minister is called upon for advice of this kind.

When this species of assistance comes to be asked frequently from the same friendly adviser, he may organize a method of supplying it, and form the habit of recommending certain lawyers, who will pay him in return for the patronage secured through him either by a stated fee or by a share in the proceeds of the case, and thus he will become practically a solicitor of business or "runner" for those lawyers.

Naturally, if the lawyer pays the runner a fee, or splits his own fee with him, he will add this amount or more, to the bill of the client, increasing the burden of expense for legal services, which the immigrant at best is so little able to bear. Naturally also, if the solicitor of custom for a lawyer expects a fee from each client directed to a lawyer, it is to his interest to encourage litigation and stir up trouble rather than work toward a private adjustment of the difficulty. In fact, the possibilities of profitable business along this line lead some of these people not to wait to be called upon for advice about securing a lawyer, but to take the initiative themselves, look for persons who are in trouble, and secure their cases for the lawyers whom they represent. And thus arises the professional "runner," whose activities are familiar.

The employment of runners or solicitors of patronage, by lawyers, or the soliciting of patronage for themselves, is contrary to the ethics of the legal profession, but many lawyers are ready to make use of the runner, and many well-meaning people see no harm in fee splitting and other phases of the runner's activities. A field agent for this study found a Russian Baptist minister specializing in divorce cases, which he regularly turned over to a lawyer friend, getting one-third of the fee. He told the agent that he did not think the immigrant was charged any more because of this division, and thought it was a common practice among priests and ministers in that city to refer cases to lawyers for a share in the fees.

THE IMMIGRANT'S DAY IN COURT

One well-known form of soliciting for lawyers is that carried on by persons popularly entitled "ambulance chasers." In large cities they run a well-organized business. Daily lists of accidents, from the records turned in to the police department or furnished to newspapers, are compiled and sent around to subscribers, who are either runners for lawyers or lawyers themselves.

After the lists are received, the runners descend upon the injured persons or their families in swarms. The homes of the injured are visited, and members of the family, or the injured person himself, is importuned to engage the services of the lawyer whom the runner represents, with the most extravagant promises of what the lawyer can secure in the way of damages. If the injured person has been taken to the hospital, the runners follow him there. In many places it is said that the runners are given special privileges of access at hospitals, when the friends and relatives of the injured person are kept out. In New York City a student in a social agency who had been injured and taken to a hospital could not be reached by a worker in his own office until some personal influence was exerted. By the time the friend had gained access to the injured student the latter had already signed a contract with an attorney.

In a case reported from Buffalo by a field agent for this study, a young Pole, who had lost a leg and had been taken to a hospital, was not allowed to see his friends until one of them, a lawyer, succeeded in getting access for them through the influence of an interne. The young man said he was glad to see them, for he was worn out with the solicitations of the insurance people and the ambulance chasers, fifteen of whom had

124

besieged him. The insurance people were trying to make him accept a sum of money and sign a release to the company, thrusting bills to the amount of two thousand dollars into his hands and assuring him that if he did not take their offer then he would get nothing. The runners, on the other hand, insisted that they could do much better for him than the insurance people.

The ambulance chaser may be in the employ of some one attorney for whom he solicits patronage, or he may be in business for himself, inducing the victims to sign contracts in blank for legal services. After the runner has secured signatures to a batch of these blanks he will trade them off to the attorney making the highest offer. A man of this class brought into a Chicago court was found to have been making four thousand dollars a year on such contracts. He was a Russian Jew, an entirely ignorant man, who could scarcely read or write English, but he was able to make this considerable income from such work.

It is not strange, then, that the injured person, or some member of his family already distracted by the misfortune of the accident, confused, excited by extravagant hopes, pressed to the limit by the solicitor, ignorant of business methods, should sign something or other that the solicitor puts before him, not realizing to what or to whom he is binding himself. In a Polish case,[1] the wife of an injured man was found to have cards of two attorneys, while still a third, whom both husband and wife claim never to have seen or heard of, appeared to be handling the case. The man had been in the hospital five weeks, and perhaps a runner got his signature to one of the blank contracts described

[1] Case of Chicago Legal Aid Society.

above, turning the case over to a lawyer whom the man had never seen.

In another Polish case[1] a man was struck by a train just five hours after he had taken a job as railroad laborer, losing an arm, part of the other hand, and breaking his leg. While he was in the hospital he and his wife were importuned by runners, so that later he found himself in the position of having assigned a half interest in his claim to one lawyer, another half to a second, and still another half to a third. The runners were not even daunted by the fact that the man had no hands with which to make a signature. One of them, foreseeing a hindrance to the deal in this circumstance, asked him how he could sign a contract, with no hands to write with. "I will show you," said the victim, with a cheerful smile, and, taking a pencil between his teeth, made a cross mark on the paper. This was taken as binding him to a contract, and so he was secured. In this instance the services of a lawyer were unnecessary, as the railroad had given every indication of willingness to fullfil its obligation. The injured man was grateful for what the company had already done for him, and said he had not intended to sign up with any lawyer until he was out of the hospital; but the ambulance chasers made him believe that he would not be treated fairly in a settlement and that the only chance he had of getting justice was through the employment of a lawyer. When he found what a complication he had got into he would have been glad to get rid of his band of lawyers, but in order to do that he would have to sign some more papers, and by this time he was afraid to sign anything, and refused to do so.

The ambulance chaser may stage an elaborate scene to capture the patronage of the immigrant. One trick

[1] Case of Chicago Legal Aid Society.

is to have the injured person visited by some one in league with the runner, purporting to be the insurance agent, who will make an offer of compensation so low that the patient will refuse it. This visit will then be followed by one from the runner, who makes a better offer. If the true insurance agent makes his appearance at any stage of the proceedings the immigrant is so bewildered that he does not know who is who or who is to be trusted.

The claim of the ambulance chaser that he is performing a real service to the injured person, has, as a matter of fact, some basis in the practice of the insurance agents and claim agents, whose activities have been described, of pushing for direct settlements for small sums, through the same arts of forcible persuasion used by the solicitors. And as long as these practices continue, the ambulance chaser will be provided with this justification for his work and will be just so much the more difficult to dislodge.

In cases of industrial accidents the workmen's compensation laws providing for the submission of direct settlements to an industrial commission or to a court, and regulating the fees of attorneys acting in accident cases, go far toward remedying these evils; but even under such regulations, the runner and the attorney for whom he acts still find it possible to swindle the immigrant by deceit and evasion of the laws.

The runner and unscrupulous lawyer are clever in knowing how to take advantage of the law of contract in different states. In Illinois, for example, a contract, once signed with a lawyer, holds against future contracts, so that if an immigrant falls into the hands of a bad lawyer at first, he cannot replace him. In one case, for example,[1] an Italian widow, whose husband

[1] Case of Italian Consulate Legal Aid, Chicago.

127

had been killed in a coal mine, had been awarded over $6,000 in the courts, with the aid of attorneys provided by the Italian consulate. After the suit was won an attorney produced a contract which the woman had signed soon after the death of her husband, which gave him 25 per cent of any sum which she might get from the coal company. He sued on the contract, and, although he had done none of the work, the contract was considered valid and he collected the sum of $1,580 from the judgment. After defending this litigation the woman had only $2,294 of the original award of $6,000 left to her credit.

On the other hand, in states where, as in Ohio, for example, a contract with a lawyer may be revoked at will, the runners have an opportunity to pursue their victims indefinitely, giving them no rest from solicitations to make a change of attorneys. To effect their purpose they will make the most extravagant promises on behalf of the lawyer for whom they are working, and the most damaging misrepresentations of the lawyer already in charge of the case. Under these circumstances, the reputable lawyer who is conducting a case honestly is continually at the mercy of the runners and the unworthy attorneys whom they represent, and the foreign client is not only losing the benefit of honest legal service, but is acquiring false ideas about justice and his rights under the law.

THE IMMIGRANT AS DEFENDANT

When the immigrant is brought before the court as defendant and needs some one to look after his rights, the runner is again on hand. Runners are found swarming about the criminal courts, as near to the court room as court regulations will permit. They infest the corridors of court buildings, get access to jails, and may be found operating in the court room itself, in the absence of strict rules to the contrary, or in evasion of them.

An investigation made in 1918 by the Massachusetts Bureau of Immigration, covering about two hundred cases of runners, showed that over twenty individuals were found daily in the corridor adjoining the First and Second Sessions of the Municipal Criminal Court of Boston, soliciting business for attorneys and furnishing bail for persons arrested.

These runners dealt mainly with the foreign born, ignorant of our customs, our language, and our legal procedure. Pretending to have great influence with the courts, the police, and the district attorney, they were ready to guarantee the discharge of accused persons, whether innocent or guilty, on payment of a fee to them or to the attorney whom they represented. On the other hand, they threatened with severe penalties,— long prison terms or heavy fines,—persons accused of even minor offenses, for which in any case the penalty would be light, should they fail to engage the attorneys recommended by the runners.

Notorious among these runners were a certain Joseph W—— and his partner, Wladislas K——. These men found a particularly profitable opportunity for gain in connection with the enforcement of the liquor laws. Joseph W—— acted as spy and informer for the police, reporting persons to them for the illegal sale of liquor. When an arrest had been made in consequence of a report by him, his partner, Wladislas K——, would approach the accused person, offering to furnish an attorney who could "fix" the police, the district attorney, and the judge.

In one of their cases a woman who had been reported

THE IMMIGRANT'S DAY IN COURT

by Joseph W—— to the police for the illegal sale of liquor and had been arrested, had already engaged a lawyer and was waiting for him in the corridor of the court, when she was approached by K—— who told her that her lawyer was ill and that he would furnish her a lawyer. He threatened that unless she did engage this lawyer, who was a friend of the judge, she would be fined $50 and sentenced to a long term in prison. She did engage the lawyer recommended, and in her case the decision was a suspended sentence. As the runner had told her that without the lawyer's services the penalty would be heavy, she would naturally think that the mild decision secured was due to the efforts of the attorney.

This illustrates a delightfully simple and effective method—in common use because of its effectiveness—by which the runner or other person boasting of "pull" or "influence" can make good with the ignorant immigrant and retain his hold over him. He promises, as the result of influence, something which he knows is going to happen in any case, and when it does happen the immigrant thinks that the runner or his lawyer brought it about.

Among the cases brought to light by the bureau were some in which innocent persons had been arrested and sums ranging from $50 to $150 extracted from them by these two runners. This happened not only in liquor cases. In one, the runner K—— induced a Polish woman to secure a warrant for the arrest of an innocent man on the charge of larceny. After the man's arrest, K—— went to him and, posing as his friend, offered to secure a lawyer for him, getting from him $190 for bail and attorney's fees. The lawyer who was introduced to the man by K——, as his attorney, proved to be, however, the attorney of the woman,

130

and made use of the information and evidence turned over to him by the would-be client to the latter's own disadvantage.

Joseph W—— had a long criminal record. He had been convicted on three different occasions of being an idle and disorderly person, for keeping a disorderly house, and for deriving support from the earnings of prostitutes. He had, however, never served a prison term, and even during a period of probation was soliciting for attorneys in the courthouse corridor under the eyes of the court officials. Many of the professional runners are of similar low character.

Among the runners shown up by this investigation we find a banker, adding to the numerous functions of a "banker" as already described that of runner. This banker, well known in the immigrant colony, was in the habit of advertising in foreign-language papers as follows: "Are you arrested? Do you need a defender or one who will bail you out? Apply to ——." This man advertised himself variously as a Russian, a Pole, a Lithuanian, or a Jew, according to the paper in which he was advertising. As a banker he was able to make something over and above the usual exactions of the runners, through opportunities to exchange fees offered in foreign currency for American money, in which he could falsify the rate of exchange, and by getting hold of the funds of the accused person to deposit in his bank, after which it was easy to withhold the entire amount as an attorney's fee, or under some other pretext.

Sometimes the court interpreter may be found acting as runner. This is a natural avenue of approach to the foreign-born client. While the accused person is telling his troubles to the interpreter, the latter may quite honestly give advice about the securing of a lawyer, and indeed the prisoner may appeal to him to find some one. It is difficult to know just when the activities of the interpreter in this direction cease to be helpful and become harmful, but that the interpreters in some courts are actually carrying on a regular business as runners seems to be quite generally known. They are tempted into this business in part, no doubt, by the extremely small salary or the scanty fees accruing from their purely official duties.

Persons in other branches of the public service are sometimes found to be acting as runners. In the spring of 1919 a judge in the Court of Domestic Relations in Chicago censured in open court an employee in the Bureau of Social Service for urging applicants at the Bureau to engage the services of a lawyer when legal services were not necessary.

THE PROFESSIONAL BONDSMAN

The immigrant accused of an offense and held for trial may need some one to make arrangements for letting him out on bail. The runner will undertake this job also, for a fee, which is supposed to be used in securing the service of a professional bondsman.

Many of the bondsmen are themselves runners and carry on the bad practices of the runner. One of these professional bondsmen, in a Lithuanian case reported,[1] came to the house of a woman whose husband had been arrested for the loss of two barrels of wine from a truckload that he was moving, took all the money ($55) she had, and said he would get her husband released and charge her only $5. The man was released on Sunday, and when the case came up on Monday he was fined $18 and costs, $22 in all. The

[1] Case of the Immigrants' Protective League, Chicago.

bondsman paid the fine and kept the rest of the money, saying that he had paid a bribe to the judge and the police to release the man on Sunday.

In the Massachusetts investigation of 1918[1] a form of partnership was found between attorneys, bondsmen, runners, and certain bail commissioners, officers who are empowered to accept bonds for prisoners. One combination of this sort did a flourishing business in certain police stations. Like an ambulance chaser following accidents, the bail commissioner would frequent the police stations at night, and as soon as a person was arrested approach him in his cell, offering to release him on bail. He would suggest a bondsman, also an attorney, and use his position of authority as a means to force the prisoner to make the arrangements he proposed.

THE IMMIGRANT LAWYER

If the attorney to whom the runner leads the immigrant would really do something for him, we might perhaps excuse the irregular practices of the runner. But as a matter of fact the lawyers who depend for their business upon runners are only too frequently found engaged in practices of exploitation that could not be surpassed by any of the varieties already mentioned in this study. They may charge excessive fees for small services or for no services at all, and, even worse, like the runners, may stand in with the other side.

Many complaints against attorneys are brought to the legal-aid societies by immigrant clients. A common complaint is that money has been paid an attorney to start a suit and nothing has been done. Sometimes the attorney is not really at fault; the delay is neces-

---

[1] Investigation of the Municipal Criminal Courts by the Massachusetts Bureau of Immigration.

sary and the client does not understand the situation. But in many cases the delay is a simple fraud.

EXTORTIONATE CHARGES

Excessive charges are common, often measured quite literally by the amount of money or property possessed by the client.

In a Chicago case[1] a man paid a lawyer $90 to get a divorce for him, when the necessary work could probably have been done for $40 or $50. His wife also engaged a lawyer, who charged her a fee of $30. As noted in the report of the case: "This she had, and this she paid. She had nothing left." She did not even know the lawyer's name.

In a case reported by a field agent for this study in a small Ohio city, a man and a woman who purported to be his wife were arrested on a trifling charge. The man had $215 in cash, a gold watch, and a few trinkets; the woman, $275 in cash, a ring, and a necklace. Three lawyers appeared to defend them, only one of whom had been regularly retained by them for a stipulated fee of $50. At the conclusion of the case, one of the two self-appointed lawyers, a Hungarian Jew and a countryman of the accused, got out a writ of attachment against all the remaining valuables of the couple in return for alleged legal services, although he had not touched the case in any professional way. This writ covered not only the valuables just enumerated, but the gold eyeglasses of the woman. Since the couple could not speak English, it was several days before the facts became known, when the judge of the Common Pleas Court ordered the money and valuables to be returned, and threatened the offending lawyer with disbarment if a repetition of the offense occurred.

[1] Case of Juvenile Protective Association.

In another instance the same lawyer was asked by another lawyer to interpret for a client who had just secured a refund of $5.43 in a petty case. It was only necessary to speak two or three sentences, but when the client emerged from the office he had only the forty-three cents.

In the same city a case was found in which a lawyer had acted for both sides. This lawyer, being consulted by a woman who wished a divorce from her husband, took advantage of the couple's ignorance of legal procedure and of American methods and succeeded in representing himself as attorney for both of them, and in extracting a fee of several hundred dollars from husband and wife for alleged services rendered. The wife was granted by the court a lump sum of $2,000, but within a few weeks the husband had recovered practically all this with the assistance of the lawyer by a virtual system of blackmail.

PROMISES OF ILLEGAL PRIVILEGES

The lawyer as well as the runner is found promising to secure special privileges not allowed by law, in return for a substantial fee, or to insure a favorable court decision through bribery.

These practices flourished with special luxuriance in the war period. Lawyers could be found everywhere who would promise to secure exemptions or other privileges in connection with military service. Cases reported to the Massachusetts Bureau of Immigration illustrate the nature of this particular form of swindling.

In one, a Pole paid an attorney $10 for exemption from military service. In another a Pole who was drafted was promised exemption by a lawyer on the payment of $25 down and $100 when discharged. This man had a valid claim for exemption on account of

135

family obligations and was discharged on his own affidavits. The attorney then threatened to put the man back in the army if he did not pay him the $100.

In another case, the father of an Italian boy under eighteen who had enlisted in the army wanted to get him out on the legitimate ground that the boy was under age. He was referred to a lawyer and placed $100 in escrow with a relative of the lawyer. The boy was discharged from the army without even the knowledge of the lawyer, to say nothing of his doing anything to bring about this result. When the attorney learned of the discharge, without the authorization of the father he took the money which had been placed in escrow with his relative and wrote that he had collected it for his services.

A BAD CASE

What lawyers and runners together can do to some poor immigrant accused of a minor offense is indicated in another case reported from Boston.[1] As stated in the affidavit of the woman in question, the facts were as follows: the woman, an Italian, was arrested for striking a man with a bunch of keys, an act which she claimed she committed to defend herself from assault by him. When she was arraigned in the court, after a night in jail, the interpreter told her that she ought to have a lawyer, although she said she did not need one, as she was not guilty and the offense was not serious in any event. She told him that if she did need a lawyer, the court ought to furnish one free of charge, as she was a poor woman. Next day an attorney appeared at the prison, saying that he was sent to take her case, and that his fee would be $25. She told him that she had

[1] Case of Massachusetts Bureau of Immigration.

no money and he left. After him came an Italian woman offering to supply bail and secure an attorney for $22 and received the same reply. After her came an Italian man making the same offer for $15, and again the same reply was made. The woman had never seen any of these people before.

When she was brought before the court, six days later, the lawyer again made his appearance, saying that the interpreter had sent him because she needed a lawyer badly. She finally admitted that she had $25 in the bank and she would pay it to him if he would secure her release. This he agreed to do. She was then released on bail, and the lawyer, in order to secure the $25, asked for her bank book, which showed a deposit of $100. Taking her to the bank, he had her make a mark on a piece of paper and, presenting this at the window, received $90. When she saw this amount of money she objected, but was informed that his fee was $125 and he was only taking $90 of it at the present time. The affidavit goes on:

I said to the attorney that he had agreed to secure my release on bail and defend me for only $25, whereupon he said that unless I pay this money I must go back to jail. I again objected and cried, whereupon they gave me back $15. They kept for themselves the sum of $75. I am a poor wash-woman, depending on the few cents I would earn by going out and doing a day's work occasionally for my support, and the $75 taken from me by this attorney constitutes a good deal to me.

Later another Italian appeared at her house, asking at first $50, then $25, and then $12 for continuing the defense of the case, saying that the case could not be defended if she did not pay some more money. The attorney also notified her that she must pay him $50 more, and when she reminded him that she had paid

him $75 already, when he had agreed to take the case
for $25, he replied that at the time he took the case
she told him she had only $25, when as a matter of fact
she had a hundred dollars. Upon her protest that she
was a poor woman and could not pay so much he told
her that she did not understand anything about court
procedure, or the expenses he would have—there were
twelve jurors, and each had to have $4 a day and
meals, and $125 was very cheap in comparison with
the expenses and the amount of work involved. As a
kindness to her, however, he would only ask her for
the remaining $25 in the bank, but if he did not appear
for her she might have to spend six months in jail.

As a matter of fact, the grand jury had failed to
indict the woman, and the attorney had not told the
truth when he said that the case would be tried and
that the money was necessary for expenses.

A NOTORIOUS LAWYER

The California Commission on Immigration and
Housing has recently had before it the case of an
Italian lawyer whose practice illustrates a great variety
of the methods of swindling by attorneys to which the
immigrant is liable. The Commission had nine cases
against this man in one city, and he had a bad record
in other cities. He is the type of lawyer who advertises
as a "specialist in criminal cases and the friend of the
Italian people." The way in which he is a "friend"
to them is shown by the cases handled by the Commission. In one, an Italian immigrant was arrested for
wounding one of four thugs who attacked him in front
of his own house, and was quickly acquitted by the
judge on the ground of self-defense when the case came
to trial. But meanwhile the man had borrowed $300

for his release on bail, and when the case was dismissed the lawyer succeeded in getting hold of this amount by inducing the man to sign what he supposed was only a receipt for a bank book returned by the lawyer. The paper, however, contained a stipulation that $300 was to be used for the expenses of the defense. The man claimed that he was expecting to pay only about $25 for the lawyer's services, which consisted in securing the man's release on bail, and then saying about three words to the judge at the trial. The lawyer was finally forced to return $125, but in the end kept over $100 that he should not have had, an amount which it took the client months to repay to his friends out of the money he was earning as night janitor in a business building.

In another case, this lawyer charged an Italian $200 for assisting him to evade the draft. He wanted $500 more, but, as the Italian said $100 was all he had in the world, he decided that that would do. The lawyer did not succeed in securing exemption by the local board, but the man was discharged from the camp to which he was assigned, for physical disability. In other cases he served false summonses with the object of frightening the victims out of substantial sums of money.

In another instance he promised an Italian woman to obtain the release of her husband from a hospital for a stated fee, and in addition tried to extract another $200 on the pretext that the hospital authorities demanded it as a bond, or a bribe to the doctor in charge of releases.

Perhaps the worst case of all was one in which he appropriated for himself and an accomplice $750 out of $3,250 due to a little Mexican girl who had been crippled in a railroad accident. He secured this without rendering any legal services whatever, and by means of a succession of frauds, not only upon the child, but upon her guardian, an ignorant Mexican, and upon the court and the surety company acting as bondsman for the guardian.

NATIONALITY OF LAWYERS AND RUNNERS

From what class of the population are these unworthy lawyers and runners drawn? Many of them are of foreign birth or descent, of the same nationality as the immigrants whom they cheat. This does not mean that no one else would be bad enough to cheat them, but that the person knowing the language and habits of thought of the immigrant, and trusted by him as a fellow countryman, as we have seen in the case of the bankers, has the best opportunity to take advantage of him. And in fact, not all of the runners and swindling attorneys are of the same nationality as their clients or even of foreign birth.

The runner is more likely than the lawyer to be foreign born, of the same nationality as the victim, because he makes the first connection with the immigrant, and this is easier when the one who makes the approach is a fellow countryman and knows the language, so that he can understand and be understood. This is not so necessary for the lawyer, who, on the other hand, should know more about the courts and legal methods than the runner needs to know, and would naturally, for that reason, be some one of longer residence in the country and more experienced than the runner. So that we find many of these unworthy lawyers to be of the older immigration or native Americans, who depend upon the foreign runner to make the contacts with the non-English-speaking peoples and secure the trade. The nationality combinations between runners and lawyers are various. Sometimes the runner deliberately chooses to work for a lawyer of another nationality, so that he may take advantage of the lack of mutual understanding between lawyer and client, to make additional money as interpreter and general go-between.

Reputable firms headed by native Americans are found connected with this species of business. Sometimes such a firm will have a foreign specialist in the office to handle the foreign cases, and personally to take the blame for bad practices if trouble arises; the firm disavowing all knowledge of the matter.

EQUIPMENT OF THE IMMIGRANT LAWYER

What is the professional equipment of these lawyers? Some of them are not lawyers at all, but are practicing law without a license. State laws prohibiting unlicensed practitioners are enforced with varying degrees of severity, so that it seems to be quite possible in many cities where the foreign born are found in great numbers for persons without a license to be carrying on legal practice, and in many states the requirements for admission to the Bar are so low that even a license to practice does not guarantee a high level of intelligence or acquirement. Some of these unlicensed practitioners have law offices to which they give an aspect of regularity by employing some one who has been admitted to the Bar. In several cases women were found by investigators for this study to be carrying on this kind of business. In Buffalo a Russian woman was discovered who had tried repeatedly to be admitted to the Bar, but had always failed because of her reputation, and was then posing as an attorney. She had been especially active during the war in draft proceedings. She claimed that she could get men exempted from military service and had collected large sums, in separate fees ranging from $1 up to $300 a case, according to the resources of the victim. She took pains to impress her clients with the weight of her influence with the authorities and would advise them that she would interview the President himself, if need be, so that they would not be called to military service.

Another woman in the same city, well known under the title of the "Polish Queen" has passed as a lawyer and has been doing business for twenty-five years. She has a decrepit attorney attached to her office, and does much advertising.

In Pittsburgh another woman, known as "Polish Rosy," was found wielding great influence in a large Polish colony and handling any sort of legal affair for her countrymen for a generous consideration. She was able to bring practically all the lawsuits before a certain alderman with whom she divided profits, and social workers were convinced that she falsified interpretations upon occasions, but so far they have been unable to gather evidence in sufficient quantities to put a stop to her activities.

The bankers or other business agents who advertise to render legal services to immigrants are usually acting only as runners for lawyers, but sometimes they pretend to be lawyers themselves and to be competent to undertake any legal affair turned over to them, using the notary's commission with which they so often provide themselves, as their authorization in the eyes of the immigrant, who has so high a respect for the office of the notary.

EFFECT ON THE IMMIGRANT

As a result of such practices as are described in this chapter we might expect that the immigrant client, after being swindled once, would learn a lesson and break off with the exploiting lawyer and runner. Sometimes he does, but in many cases he persists in going to people of this sort; in many cases he gets into such a state of bewilderment that he does not know whom to trust, and oscillates between unreasoning confidence in anybody and everybody and equally unreasoning and indiscriminate disbelief.

An immigrant will often suddenly begin to suspect that a lawyer whom he has employed is not doing the right thing by him and will run to another, and then another, without notifying any of their predecessors. Or he will be found willing to sign anything and everything given him, without knowing the contents of the documents, and then will suddenly refuse to sign anything whatever.

The immigrant may distrust his lawyer not because he is swindled, but because of his own inability to understand a legal situation, even when the lawyer is doing everything in his power. The foreign client, in his ignorance of the nature of legal transactions, is often insistent on having everything explained to him, and is then unable to understand when the explanation is made, and demands an explanation over and over again. This habit makes him a trying client, and it is not surprising that a frequent form of complaint by the immigrant against the lawyer is that the lawyer is not keeping his client informed as to the progress of the case.

In a Polish case[1] where a woman had brought her husband before the court it is noted that "the proceedings were too intricate for her to know what happened," and her Polish attorney told her "he didn't care to talk

---

[1] Case of Chicago Legal Aid Society.

to her," but would write anything he had to say. This woman could not speak a word of English, and was confused and unintelligible even in her own language, and one can well imagine the numerous visits to the lawyer's office, and the numerous demands for explanations which did not explain.

Different peoples seem to differ in their attitude toward lawyers. The Italian immigrant is apparently more suspicious than the Slavic immigrant, and less willing to seek legal advice. The Slavs are generally ready to trust a lawyer, and the Poles in particular seem to have a genuine enjoyment of litigation, which leads them into connections with lawyers that a less litigious people would avoid.

The attitude of the immigrant toward the law and the courts, in so far as it is determined by the teaching of the lawyers and runners, will naturally be one of distrust and disrespect. Because, from what has been shown of the practices of the lawyers and the runners it is plain that the immigrant is being taught erroneously about American courts and American justice. He is taught that bribery and influence are the regular methods of securing favorable decisions, that the extortionate fees he is called upon to pay are necessary to provide the expected bribes, that the immigrant has no chance before the American court without the aid of a lawyer skilled in a special kind of trickery.

V

THE COURT

WHEN the immigrant is finally brought into relation with the American court, civil or criminal, as plaintiff or defendant, what does he find there? How far does it meet the needs of exact justice in his case, and inspire him with the respect for law, the confidence in our institutions of justice that he should have as a loyal member of the community?

What should he find in the courts in addition to the strict and impartial justice which it is their function to administer? The immigrant who has been defrauded of his money in some of the numerous ways shown in a preceding chapter, in so far as he is a poor man, and he usually is, should find the operations of justice sufficiently cheap and rapid for him to be able to avail himself of their protection in his particular case. The foreign-born workingman who has a claim for wages amounting to $10, for example, cannot afford to spend anywhere from $2 to $10 for court costs, and as much more as a lawyer can screw out of him for counsel fees, in order to collect the small amount due him through legal proceedings. And yet the loss of such a small amount as this means a serious deprivation to him, especially if it is repeated over and over again, as may easily happen.

Nor can the foreign-born workingman afford to wait weeks and months for a decision in such a case. He cannot even be sure of being in one place long enough to see the end of a case dragging along, through protracted court proceedings, as he is so frequently a migratory worker of one sort or another.

If he is accused of some offense, delay is equally hard on him, for, until his case is decided, he must either be at a considerable expense for bail or he must spend the time between arrest and the verdict in confinement—practically a prison sentence upon one who has not been declared guilty and may eventually be declared innocent.

More than this, as he is a newcomer, unfamiliar with our institutions and customs, who is building up an opinion about the country to which he has come bit by bit out of his daily experiences, it is important not only that justice should be done in his case, but that he should feel that it is done. For if he does not understand what the court is doing, or if he thinks it is dealing with him unjustly, he is to this extent hindered in developing respect for the institutions of the community.

THE IMMIGRANT'S ATTITUDE TOWARD THE COURT

The immigrant's feeling about courts in this country is partly determined by his impressions of courts and legal procedure gained through his home experiences and traditions.

It must not be supposed that the average immigrant has any clearly worked out philosophy of law and of court functioning. As a peasant at home he has had little experience with either courts or laws. He knows the policeman and the tax gatherer and the officer in charge of enlistments for the army, but only once in a long while does he get into court. But even from his limited experience he may have acquired a certain general attitude toward courts and the law which will influence him here, and he may notice differences in the way such legal matters as he has had experience with are treated here, that may puzzle him or make him dissatisfied.

Some of our immigrants bring with them a distrust of courts in general. This may arise because the immigrant comes from a community of primitive type, which has never recognized the authority of the state, through its courts or otherwise, to interfere in certain personal matters.

In the Polish peasant community of the old type, for example, in which the family was the social unit, an appreciation of individual rights within the family was little developed. It was expected that the family group would look after the interests of its members, and an individual who should undertake legal proceedings against a member of the family group would be under severe disapproval in his community.

Among many of the immigrant peoples questions of family honor and family discipline are considered to be outside the jurisdiction of courts. According to their ideas, justice in these cases is to be administered and punishment inflicted by members of the family, or personal friends who may have undertaken the family obligation.

Private vengeance may be undertaken in other kinds of cases, and organized into a system of private justice, outside of the courts, in localities where the courts of the country are found notoriously inadequate to render justice. Some such system of private justice was the Sicilian Mafia in its original form.

The immigrant from a community where any such ideas prevail may, then, bring with him to this country a general indifference to the court as a source of justice, and may refrain from bringing his wrongs to it for that reason. And he may be actually afraid to come before the court in any capacity, for fear of the harm that may be done him by fellow members of his own group who have also been accustomed to the idea of private vengeance as a means of adjusting wrongs.

When we find our immigrants afraid to prosecute, afraid to appear before the court as witnesses, we are inclined to blame them severely for their lack of confidence in the institutions of law, for their unwillingness to further the ends of justice. But we should remember that such a state of mind is by no means unknown in our own country districts, among our own people. Many a native-born farmer has refused to complain to the court of small thefts, or to press a small claim, for fear the person complained against, or his friends, might burn the complainant's barn or kill his cattle.

Again, the immigrant may bring with him a distrust of courts because in his own country he has known them as the agency of what was to him practically a foreign power—a dominant nationality ruling over a subject nationality. The Pole would expect to find in the Russian court, the Armenian in the Turkish court, an instrument of political oppression. And furthermore he has found such courts susceptible to bribery. In fact, he has often found his only opportunity of securing justice through bribing the officials of justice—a practical paradox working havoc with the building up in his mind of any ordered conception of the functions of the courts.

As a large proportion of our newer immigrants have come from just such subject nationalities, it is easy to see that very many of them may be affected by a general distrust of courts, so that when they are told, by the unscrupulous lawyers described in a previous

THE COURT

chapter, that the courts here are unjust and corruptible, they are ready to believe it.

The immigrant may also distrust our courts, or misunderstand their operations, because he sees them proceeding differently from the way he was accustomed to at home, so far as he has had any experience with courts. Or if he himself knew nothing about courts, his attorney if of foreign birth, might contrast our courts unfavorably with those at home. For the attorney trained to practice in a foreign court is frequently inclined to prefer the system he is accustomed to, and even when he is quite honest and upright may give the client an unfavorable impression of the American court because he really thinks it inferior. If he is one of the unscrupulous type described in the preceding chapter, he will find in abuse of our courts and our methods an effective means of emphasizing his own importance and the necessity for securing his help in getting justice for the immigrant.

When he comes before the court, certain immediate contrasts may strike the immigrant who has had experience with courts at home. The Italian, for example, remembers a court surrounded by a visible pomp of authority, filled with officials resplendent in robes and uniforms. In such a court, however, notwithstanding the glitter of the surroundings, the Italian feels at home and as free to behave without a constraining solemnity of demeanor as he does in the beautiful churches of his country, in which he strolls about, chats and laughs, with full reverence for the saints, the Madonna, and Almighty God Himself.

For the Italian trial judge is not a stern keeper of

149

order in his court. Futhermore, in the conduct of a
case he does not hold the persons before him to certain
fixed rules of evidence or strict canons of relevance,
in the bringing of testimony, or the presentation of the
case in other ways. Nor in jury cases does he control
in any way the verdict of the jury. The attorneys,
then, may make long and impassioned and oratorical
appeals to a jury which may disregard both law and
the fact freely, and in obedience to their emotions
render a verdict which cannot be reversed by the judge.

In this country, the outward trappings of the court
are not impressive. But the judge is a powerful being
in his own court room. He holds every one present to
a strict order and decorum, and in the higher courts,
in the presentation of a case he requires adherence to
certain forms of procedure, to certain fixed rules of
evidence, and he controls the jury to such an extent
that he may set aside their verdict under certain
circumstances.

It may, then, be a surprise to the Italian who finds
himself in the apparently informal and workaday
American court to be brusquely called to order by a
court official, or even punished, for some incautious
word, some sudden motion, that would seem to him
perfectly compatible with respect for the court and
law.

And as he views the proceedings, the Italian coming
before the court may find it rendering justice on the
basis of what seem to him dead and complicated
technical rules which have no meaning for him; he
may find the court unaccountably severe toward
accused persons in adjudging them strictly by rule,
in cases calling out his natural sympathy; and on the
other hand, if acquittal results, from the lack of technical evidence in cases where there seems to be every

moral certainty of guilt, he may get the notion that
courts are too easy.

In the immigrant's attitude toward our law and
courts, then, we have to reckon with preconceived
ideas which, as far as they are mistaken, should be
altered, perhaps by definite instruction directed to
that end, or, more slowly, perhaps, but even more
effectively, through experiencing exact and even-handed
justice from the court itself, on each occasion in which
the immigrant appears before it.

SUBSTANTIAL VS. TECHNICAL JUSTICE

For beneath and behind all his feelings based on
special acquaintance with a legal system, on habits
and likes and dislikes and prejudices and preferences,
what the normal, noncriminal immigrant really wants
is justice—substantial as distinguished from technical
justice—that is, the right solution for the particular
case, even though it may run contrary to the rule
contrived to meet cases of that kind in general.

This desire for substantial justice is not peculiar to
him. The distinction is one of a kind that any social
group will naturally make as rapidly as it finds the
legal institutions and processes established to meet a
given need failing to do so in all particulars.

If we prefer our legal system to that developed on
the continent of Europe, it is because we think that it
affords a greater amount of substantial justice. If the
Italian prefers his own court methods, it is because he
fails to discover the working out of substantial justice
through the mazes of our unfamiliar technical procedure. When the lawyer in Italy is appealing to a
jury to disregard the code law and acquit an accused
person, it is in the name of a higher law, a law of

justice and of conscience. When the Polish peasant community, dissatisfied with the operations of the Russian court, took the law into its own hand, it was with the same excuse.

What "substantial justice" may mean to the peasant seems to have been well expressed through the peculiar institution of the "peasants' court" as it existed in Russia. This "peasants' court" was a court having jurisdiction in a small district over minor civil and criminal cases, in which one of the parties at least was a peasant of the district. It consisted of ten judges, all peasants and members of a village commune, who in trials held before them rendered their verdicts according to the customary laws and traditions of the local peasantry, unrestrained by official codes.

The theory guiding such a court, the feeling it expresses, are described as follows:

The mir in the management of its affairs recognizes no permanent laws restricting or guiding its decisions. It is the personification of the living law, speaking through the collective voice of the commune. Every case brought before the mir is judged on its own merits, according to the endless variety of its peculiar circumstances. In foreign lands, too, the laws tacitly acknowledge the necessity for making a considerable allowance for the voice of pure conscience in the more delicate questions of society as to the culpability or innocence of its members. But by the side of the jury sits the judge, the representative of the written law, one of whose duties it is to control and keep them within their strictly defined limits—*i.e.*, to the mere verdict as to the facts of the case. With a Russian mir the law is nowhere, the "conscience" everywhere. Not merely the fact of the criminal offense, but every disputed point is settled according to the individual justice of the case, no regard being paid t the category of crime to which it may chance to belong.

These villagers have to deal with living men whom they

know and love, and it is deeply repugnant to them to over-shoot the mark by so much as a hair's breadth for the sake of a dead abstraction—the law.[1]

The English and American mind has greater satis-faction in the rule of an abstract, uniform, and definite law.

To a truly independent man [says Stepniak], even a hard law, because abstract and dispassionate and known to him beforehand, is a better thing than the most benignant des-potism. That which is the most abhorrent to him is the sense that he is dependent on the good pleasure of another—be it the benevolent despotism of one master or even the still more benevolent despotism of a friendly crowd.[2]

The same conception is expressed as follows in a little different way by one of our American legal authorities, discussing the distinction between law and justice:

Law protects us against the incompetence, whimsicality, corruption, and variability of the human judge, among thousands of whom there will be few who are wise and sound enough always to do justice.[3]

Perhaps, then, there may be some lack of adjustment between the immigrant and the American Court be-cause of this contrast.

THE MINOR COURTS

Let us now turn to the courts themselves and see how far this substantial justice, needed and desired by the immigrant, is dealt out to him. In this survey we will confine our attention to the minor courts, for one reason because most of the troubles of the immigrant

[1] Stepniak, *The Russian Peasantry*, p. 139, ff.
[2] *Ibid.*, p. 141.
[3] Wigmore, *American Judicature Society Bulletin VIII*, p. 19.

requiring the intervention of the law—such as the money difficulties, and the domestic situations described in previous chapters—are under the jurisdiction of the minor court. For another reason, because the immigrant who appears before the minor court is rather more likely to be the average individual, than the serious criminal who is among those brought before the higher criminal courts or the well-to-do and experienced business man involved in large civil cases. The immigrant goes to the minor court from the neighborhood to have his trouble adjusted, and soon goes back to the neighborhood to take with him his impressions of American justice and impart them to his friends. If he has secured his claim against some swindler, he is further grounded in a good opinion of our institutions. If he has been accused of some small offense and the case has been handled with intelligence and justice, he may, after paying his penalty, go back to his neighborhood a wiser man and a better member of the community. If he has not received the proper treatment, he may go from bad to worse and land before the higher courts as a serious criminal.

The importance of the minor courts in their treatment of the immigrant population, both for securing justice and for developing the right feeling about our institutions of justice, has been emphasized over and over again by those who have studied their workings.

The Committee on Inferior Courts of Suffolk County (Massachusetts) said in its report:

These inferior courts represent in large measure the vital point of contact of the law with the common people. As they serve or fail to serve the purpose of their creation respect for law increases or diminishes. More especially is this true since they deal with that portion of the community, often the poor and ignorant but lately come to the country,

THE COURT

whose conceptions of American justice must depend very
largely upon their knowledge and experience of the inferior
courts, whose judgments are for them in large measure final.[1]

In an address before the New York Bar Association,
Charles E. Hughes said:

I never speak of this work of our higher courts without the
reflection that after all it is courts of minor jurisdiction which
count the most so far as respect for the institutions of justice
are concerned. And I wish to make especial application of the
point at this time. We are fond of speaking of Americanization. If our Bar Association could create a sentiment which
would demand that in all our cities the police courts and minor
civil courts should fairly represent the Republic as the
embodiment of the spirit of justice, our problem of Americanization would be more than half solved. A petty tyrant in a
police court, refusals of a fair hearing in minor civil courts,
the impatient disregard of an immigrant's ignorance of our
ways and language, will daily breed Bolshevists who are
beyond the reach of your appeals. Here is work for lawyers.
The Supreme Court of the United States and the Court of
Appeals will take care of themselves. Look after the courts
of the poor, who stand most in need of justice. The security
of the Republic will be found in the treatment of the poor
and the ignorant; in indifference to their misery and helplessness lies disaster.[2]

THE JUSTICE COURT IN THEORY

In this country the lowest member of the court hierarchy
is the court held by the justice of the peace and known
generally as the "justice court." This is the minor
court of the rural districts, and it might be thought that
it concerns the immigrant very little, as he is found so
largely in the more thickly populated localities. But

[1] Report of Committee on Inferior Courts of Suffolk County (Massachusetts), 1912, p. 7.

[2] *New York Law Journal*, January 24, 1919. Address before New
York Bar Association, annual meeting, 1918.

the justice court is by no means confined to the agricultural regions. It is found exercising its functions in cities and having concurrent jurisdiction in counties in which cities are located, so that city cases may appear before it. And in many of the small towns in which the justice court more properly belongs may be found an immigrant population drawn there by some special form of industry.

The justice court, which has summary jurisdiction in small cases within defined limits, as well as powers of examination for the higher courts, is characteristic of the English system from which our courts derive their origin. Such courts, with power to hold for trial or dismiss at discretion, are not known in continental countries. But although borrowed from England, the American justice court has developed along lines of its own. The American justice has jurisdiction in civil as well as criminal cases; the English justice has jurisdiction in criminal cases only.

In this country in its early years it was necessary to provide for the administration of justice to a comparatively small and poor population scattered over a wide area. To meet the need, courts had to be numerous and they had to be cheap; and the number of persons trained in the law was too few to permit of a general requirement of legal training for all judges. Consequently, this requirement was not made for the American justice. It was also not a requirement for a justice of the peace in the English system. The English justice, however, had to be a man of property, was, presumptively, a man of education, and held his post by a commission from the government, on an indeterminate tenure. His office involved no special advantage to himself, other than the consciousness of performing a social duty and the standing in the community that performing this duty would bring. These qualifications tended to secure intelligence in the performance of duties, and a certain disinterestedness in rendering decisions.

The American justice, on the other hand, was elected by the little group of neighbors whom he served, was likely to be a poor man, like them, and he might have had very little general education. He could not afford to serve for nothing. And the small community he served could not afford to pay him a salary adequate to compensate him for giving his whole time to the work. Indeed, the volume of business in such a community was not sufficient to warrant it. So that payment for his services was made in the form of a fee for each occasion.

In the American justice court, we may perhaps presume because of the lack of technical legal knowledge and training on the part of the justices, many of the formalities of procedure characteristic of the English court generally are dispensed with, and the justice exercises a considerable amount of discretion in applying the law to a given case—discretion, not to depart from the treatment prescribed by law for one who falls within a stated category, but, unchecked by rules of procedure, or by a jury, to decide freely whether a case does or does not come under the provisions of the law.

This court, then, would seem especially fitted to meet the needs of the immigrant in certain respects. It was organized to afford justice cheaply and rapidly, and the legitimate expenses attached to proceedings in this court are not high. And through the powers of discretion vested in the judge a "substantial justice," resulting from taking into account circumstances outside of those which would be admitted under strict rules of procedure, may be administered.

The justice court as thus organized is seen to resemble

the peasant court of Russia in some of its characteristic features: it is a court drawn from the neighborhood and free to deal out justice in accordance with community standards, within the limits of discretion allowed the presiding officer, and on the basis of that intimate knowledge of the persons and circumstances of the cases before the court which comes of common life in a neighborhood. The judge of such a court may also follow up as a neighbor the treatment he administers in the court as a judge. He may instruct, or help in other ways, the person in difficulties who has come before the court. For we are coming to see that the appearance before the court is only one event in a long social history, and that if the function of the court is to aid in social adjustment as far as it can do so, as well as to secure the observance of a rule in a given case, certainly the opportunity to render these services is a power for good in the justice court.

Judge Brown, of the Philadelphia Municipal Court, looks to the justice court, in its possibilities, as a model for the activities of the modern, socialized court, in a big city. He says:

It is my wish, and that of my collegues, to give the people the personal service that was once rendered by the judge of a less busy age, when those who came to court to be tried, or to bring trial, to bring suit or to be sued, were the judge's neighbors, his acquaintances, his friends.

The judge of that day knew those who needed help, those who were in want of correction, and those to whom should be extended compassion. In the smaller communities the judges are still the advisors and counselors of the people. It is only in the crowded complex centers of city life that the people fear the courts and the judges, because here the personal touch has disappeared.[1]

[1] *Report of the Municipal Court of Philadelphia, 1916,* p. 3.

THE COURT

Unfortunately, the justice court as it has developed has by no means lived up to its best possibilities, and especially in its relations with immigrants. The lack of an educational qualification for the office of justice has permitted the entry into it of large numbers of persons who are not only untrained in the law, but deeply ignorant generally. The uncertain remuneration of that office, derived from fees, makes it impossible, in most localities, for a man of ability who wants to conduct the affairs of the office honestly, to make it his main business and give full time and attention to it. He can only carry on the duties of justice incidentally to some other occupation. The dishonest and ignorant man, on the other hand, sees in the office an opportunity for making money through unworthy devices to swell the number of cases before the court, and will push them to the limit. Such justices will be found constantly stirring up legal trouble, in opposition to the proper function of the law officer, of composing differences. They will be found actually creating cases out of nothing, or, in cases brought before them in the regular way, selling their decisions to the highest bidder.

The fact that the justice is elected by a small local constituency for a short term tends to place him under obligation to the constituency and subjects him to the local influence of small politicians. The lack of any central supervision permits the dishonest justice to go on unchecked in his bad practices, and the ignorant justice to continue in his bad methods, or at the best allows a variation in principles of procedure that is not to the interest of the clients of the courts. And these evils will be emphasized where the population is split

159

into classes of the rich and the poor, the educated and the ignorant, and, most important for our purpose, the native and the foreign-born. The "neighborhood court" no longer works as such where the neighborhood itself is no longer an organically united group, and where the court represents one class, the clients another.

How the foreign born may be treated in these justice courts may be indicated by some examples from states where immigrants are found in great numbers. In New York, for instance, the Bureau of Immigration has been much concerned with the manner in which immigrant unskilled laborers have been maltreated by justices of the peace in industrial communities of the state. A general practice, with a striking instance of abuse is described as follows:

Unfamiliar with our legal procedure, they (the immigrants) are thrown into jail or fined heavily on the slightest pretext, even though no crime has been committed. . . . The ignorance of many of these justices, and the opportunity for collusion with superintendents and foremen of industrial corporations largely controlling the political destinies of such communities, have resulted in fixing criminal records upon aliens without due process of law. . . . Four immigrant workmen in a recent case signed a contract at a New York City employment agency to work for a corporation in Saratoga County. Under one of the clauses of the contract they agreed to pay the corporation for advancing their traveling expenses to the scene of work. On arrival there, hungry and tired, they were not given and were unable to obtain any food, and accordingly became dissatisfied. They left the following morning and started to walk to the nearest town. The superintendent and a deputy sheriff pursued them in an automobile and brought them before a local justice of the peace without having first obtained a warrant of arrest. The justice then accepted a charge of petit larceny against them, and all four were sentenced to remain thirty days in jail.

THE COURT

. . . At the worst they were liable only for civil breach of contract, as they had never committed any criminal offense.[1]

The Bureau of Immigration was not mistaken in this view, for in a habeas corpus proceeding brought before a higher court by the Bureau, the four men were immediately released.

In Illinois, serious abuses in the operations of the justice courts in both civil and criminal cases were described as follows, with special reference to those having jurisdiction in Cook County, in which the city of Chicago is located.

The justices having jurisdiction throughout the county . . . and the county being large . . . many lawyers began suits against citizens of the city in remote courts, far from their homes, from thirty to forty miles. Many suits were begun out in the country and they were set occasionally at ten minutes before the early-morning train arrived. If the train arrived at nine o'clock, the case was heard at eight forty-five, so that the defendant was obliged to go there the night before with his witnesses if he wanted to be on hand. There were no hotel accommodations and generally the defendants did not go, but appealed the case to the Circuit Court. . . .

Other abuses were common and general throughout the city, one complaint being, and the principal one, that judgments were rendered for the plaintiff in many cases, notwithstanding the evidence. . . . Some of the justices in the Loop District or the center of the city, were honorable men and tried their cases fairly. It was the acts mostly of a few of the justices that brought the whole system into contempt. The constables were men of no particular character. Many of them were "plug uglies." Some of them were common criminals. Citizens were shot during the making of levies. Money was extorted from people. False returns were made. In many cases the defendant never knew that he had been

[1] *Report of the New York Bureau of Industries and Immigration, 1913*, p. 60–61.

161

THE IMMIGRANT'S DAY IN COURT

sued at all until the constable arrived with an execution to make a levy. The latter had made a false return that he had served the defendant when he had not, and abuses of that kind were quite common among the constables. One in particular became so notorious that public attention was focused upon the whole constabulary and the justice-of-the-peace system.

I think the action of the justices and constables in civil suits was the one first to attract public attention, but I think their action in criminal cases was more serious than their action in civil suits. The justices were often selected by the mayor at the instigation of the alderman of a particular district where the large police force was located. The bailiff of the court was selected in the same manner and usually through the influence of the alderman of a particular ward. So was the Clerk of the Court. The machinery therefore for the administration of criminal justice in the court of first instance was an adjunct of the political machine that happened to control the administration of the city. The jurors in the justice courts were picked up from the body of the county. The bailiff had the duty and the right to go and pick any citizen he saw fit. The result was that in these cases plaintiffs frequently engaged the counsel or the bailiff to select a particular class of jurymen to sit in the court. He might take those any place he pleased. Abuses of various sorts were engaged in by the bailiff of these courts: Among others, they acted as agents for the alderman and his chief henchman in seeing to it that bail was furnished defendants. They became very active agents in notifying the chief bailor as to what defendants were arrested the night before and what sureties they had and what the prospects were as to what they could pay for bonds in these cases. The clerk was a part of the system occasionally also in some of these courts. . . .

In short, the whole system for the administration of justice in the minor cases had become such as to have lost the confidence of the bar and public in many of the men charged with its administration.[1]

[1] Testimony of Judge Harry Olson, chief justice of the Chicago Municipal Court, before the Page Commission; *State of New York*

THE COURT

While in this description no special mention is made of immigrant cases, in fact a large proportion of the business before these courts concerned the foreign born.

In Ohio also the justice courts became notorious for bad practices, especially in their relations with the immigrant. As described by Judge Manuel Levine, of the Common Pleas Court of Cleveland:

Most of the officials of the justice court, including the justice of the peace himself, were unscrupulous and dishonest. . . . So far as Cleveland and other large cities are concerned, we have come to regard the country justice of the peace and his fellow workers as nothing less than a public menace which had to be resisted with grim determination.

At least fifty per cent of the cases handled by our justices of the peace should never have reached the stage of litigation. If the justices had been men of peace, honest and just arbitrators, more than half of the number of cases could have been settled through their friendly intervention. But peace among the litigants meant no fee to the justice of the peace and the vampires surrounding him. Strife, contention, and litigation were productive of lucrative income for all the servants of justice.[1]

Due to this competition for business, nearly forty thousand cases were annually brought into the justice courts of the county in which Cleveland is situated, and of these at least three quarters were cases of immigrants or children of immigrants.

The justices were not only unscrupulous, but in many cases totally ignorant of the law and lacking in general education. At one time, according to Judge

Proceedings of the Commission to Inquire into the Courts of Inferior Criminal Jurisdiction in Cities of the First Class, vol. iii, pp. 2871–2872. Albany, New York, 1909.
[1] *American Judicature Society Bulletin VIII*, p. 5.

Levine, only five of the fifteen justices having jurisdiction in the city of Cleveland had made a pretense of studying law. Yet the justices of the state were not all on this low level, and it is only fair to say that among them might have been found quite a number who carried on the duties of their office with intelligence and integrity.

SOME TYPICAL JUSTICES OF THE PEACE

While the justice of the peace has been displaced from Chicago and Cleveland by improved court systems, he still flourishes in many parts of the country. In Ohio and Pennsylvania the justice courts are of especial importance in dealing with the immigrant because so many immigrants are to be found in the many small industrial towns in which justice courts have jurisdiction, and a special survey was made for this study of the justice courts in some of these towns with special reference to their treatment of the immigrant. In this survey a great variety of personalities was found among the justices.

In one place, of the three justices, one is an elderly lawyer, fair and able, and sympathetic toward the immigrant—his only drawback is his age. The second man is mercenary, illiterate, has little legal training, has no sympathy with his clients, and insists upon his fees even in cases where payment would mean a great hardship. The third justice is not so venal as the second, but intends to make his office a paying business. He is openly and loudly prejudiced against the foreign born in this country and considers them all Bolshevists and Anarchists of a dangerous kind. From his views, and the excitement of his manner even when discussing the question, it is a fair assumption that the average immi-

grant appearing before him receives slight consideration and a far from sympathetic hearing.

In another place one justice is obviously carrying on
his work for the money there is in it; the other is an
elderly man with little legal training or ability, but he
is regarded as perfectly honest and he is inclined to be
sympathetic in immigrant cases. A justice who had
recently died, however, was notoriously corrupt, and
had made the exploitation of the foreign born one of his
business specialties.

In another place, of the three justices, one is very old
and has practically turned over his business to one of
the other two justices. This second justice is an intelligent man who is apparently quite fair and just
toward the foreign born. But he quite frankly admits
the existence of exploitation of the foreign born in connection with his own court, at the hands of runners and
lawyers.

The third justice is a less educated and less able
man than the second justice, and is on the whole
inclined to be somewhat less fair in his dealings with
the foreign born.

In another town were found justices, one of whom
was practically a nonentity, because the "justice
shop"—significant and commonly used phrase—interfered with his regular business; another was a qualified
lawyer who did a fair and legitimate business; another
was a young man with an interest in the immigrant;
a fourth was an old, uncouth, unlettered person who is
in the business for the money, speaks no foreign language, and makes no provision for interpreters in his
court.

In still another town two of the three justices are
paid a salary, so that they are not dependent on fees,
and are unanimously reported to be perfectly straight

in their dealings. One of them has made a special study
of court methods and is genuinely interested in trying
to bring about improvements in the justice court.
Since these justices are paid a salary they can afford to
discourage litigation, and it is found that they are
making a conscious effort to keep out of court as many
cases as possible by advising settlements through
mutual agreement. But the third justice, operating
under the fee system, carries on most of the bad
practices associated with that system.

In another place one of the justices is a notorious
grafter, but two others, one a young attorney, are
much interested in Americanization work and teach
English in night schools.

In a certain small city the four justices are men of
average integrity and intelligence, as justices go, and
perform their duties with fair ability and little tendency
to take advantage of the foreign born who come before
them.

In a near-by town, one of the two justices is felt to
be making a fairly respectable attempt at maintaining
decency and a semblance of honesty and fairness in his
court, but the other justice is unqualifiedly and undoubtedly bad.

THE CONSTABLE IN THE JUSTICE COURTS OF OHIO AND PENNSYLVANIA

As in Illinois, a leading feature of the operations of the
bad justices in Ohio and Pennsylvania was found to
be the employment of the court constables to drum up
trade. Such justices were found to have from two to
five of these officials, whose practice it was to go out
and make arrests, with or without cause, for the sake
of the resulting court fees, These were shared with
them by the justice. Under this plan ignorant immi-

grants were arrested and fined upon every conceivable minor charge, and the fees ran into tremendous figures.

One of the constables working with a corrupt justice in an Ohio town, who is kept manifestly to drum up trade among the immigrants with whom he comes in contact, is foreign born himself. In numerous instances he has been known to stir up little differences among his countrymen, or to encourage little misunderstandings already existing, in order to have them brought before the court. In other cases he has persuaded some one to file petty charges, often purely imaginary or exaggerated, against an immigrant, for the sake of the fee involved.

Fines also are a source of revenue, for, although fines are supposed to be turned into the town or county treasury and not to go into the pockets of any court official, the unscrupulous justice seems to find a way to get hold of them.

In one case reported for this survey from a Pennsylvania town, two immigrants were fined $50 and costs, amounting to $8.50, for fighting. The justice entered the full amount on the record in pencil, but when he thought he was unobserved erased it and wrote down the $8.50 only, in ink. Tossing over to the constable his share of the $50, he pocketed the remainder, and the incident was closed.

The larger the fine imposed, the greater, naturally, will be the revenue, so the unscrupulous justice who has planned to take over the fine himself will put it up as high as he thinks the defendant can pay. In a certain case in a Pennsylvania town, an immigrant who was going home from a restaurant was arrested for "loitering." In court the justice found out how much money he had, and inflicted a fine amounting to a little above that sum. He then remitted the few odd cents of the fine above the amount of the culprit's possessions, and told him he ought to be grateful for the favor.

In another case, two men of foreign birth were charged with loitering, one of whom, it appeared, had some money; the other did not. Evidently the constable knew of this and it had been arranged between him and the justice to fine the man who had money. At any rate, the justice dismissed one and fined the other, while the constable was out of the room. But before the two men had left the court the constable, returning, found that the justice had fined the moneyless man and released the other, whereupon the justice, hastily informed of this by the constable, called the two men back and reversed his decision, this time fining the man with money and letting the other man go.

THE JUSTICE AS COLLECTION AGENT

Some of these justices carry on a special line of business, in which they practically make themselves collection agents for credit houses or firms selling on the installment plan. This plan is most often carried out through garnishment proceedings. One company, reported by a field agent as a most active patron of the justices, sold sewing machines on the installment plan. Upon delivering the machine at an immigrant's home, the delivery man would persuade the immigrant to sign a paper which he supposed to be simply a receipt for the goods, but which really acknowledged the machine as a necessity, and thereby gave the company the right to garnishee wages upon it under the laws of Ohio. On the least pretext of default in payment the case would be taken to the justice and the garnisheeing process begun. It is commonly supposed that the justice is

compensated by such firms. At any rate, it is presumed
that firms which throw a large part of their business of
collection, garnisheeing, and eviction to any particular
justice are favored in the decision.

The case of a young Polish girl at an industrial plant
in an Ohio town, found during this survey, illustrated
the troubles an immigrant may get into through the
workings of this system. During the winter she bought
clothing on the installment plan amounting to about
$70, and kept up the payments regularly out of her
small earnings, until only about $20 was left unpaid.
Then she fell ill and for two weeks was unable to make
any payments. Although the situation was explained
to the collector, garnishment proceedings were filed
and she was notified to appear before a justice court in
an outlying township, several miles from the plant.
She was unable to pay the remaining sum on the installment, to which had to be added the fees for court
proceedings and the doctor's bill, so that she was
loaded down with an accumulation of debt from which
she could not free herself. Several weeks later she was
arrested in a coffee house on a charge of immoral
conduct, which a social worker interested in the case
thought could be traced more or less directly to the
distress to which she was reduced through the garnishment proceedings.

An allied method of exploitation is found in the unscrupulous justice's activities in the attachment of
property for the collection of a debt. Certain collection agencies have formed the habit of turning over
to the justice of the peace for collection bills against
railroad men or others whose business takes them out
of town. These would be presented to the wife or some
other relative when the man was known to be away
and when it was thought improbable that payment

would be made. Upon failure to meet the bill the man's property was attached to the amount of ten per cent of the bill, which was all that could be taken under the law, and this would be turned over to the collection agency. To this an eight per cent fee could be added, and in another week or two the process would be repeated. In this way the debtor would be made to pay nearly twice as much as the original debt, the additional amount going into the coffers of the justice.

In one place in Ohio visited by a field agent for this study the justice courts would allow attachment proceedings and garnishment for saloon bills, although a saloon bill is not incurred for necessaries and is not allowed as such under the Ohio law.

In another Ohio town a curious abuse in which the constable is involved is based on an old state law which provides that a person upon removing to another county of the state cannot take with him any property purchased in the county from which he is removing, that has not been completely paid for. Frequently an immigrant will purchase a suit of clothes and move out of the county, explaining the situation to the firm from which he has bought the articles, and making definite arrangements for payments before leaving. Often in such instances a constable is sent after him to bring back the balance of the payments for the installment house and substantial fees for himself, usually far in excess of the amounts legally allowed. This is a favorite practice of the constables, as they can claim traveling expenses from the immigrant besides the ordinary fees.

OTHER ABUSES IN JUSTICE COURTS OF OHIO AND PENNSYLVANIA

In Ohio, as discovered through this survey, as well as in Illinois, a standard swindle of the justices consisted in summoning clients and witnesses for hearings in some remote quarter of the justice's jurisdiction and at an impossible hour, so that the persons summoned could not arrive in time and judgment could be rendered against them by default.

Besides these standard methods of exploitation, individual tricks of the trade were found developed by different justices. Many of the justices charge large fees for simple services, and during the war period they had special opportunity for such practices in connection with military service and taxation. Some were known to charge $3, $4 or $5 for filling out a questionnaire and $5 for going out of the office to take an affidavit. Fifteen or twenty dollars was often charged simply for giving advice in regard to the filling out of naturalization papers.

In a Pennsylvania town where large numbers of immigrants are employed in a great basic industry, the field agent found the justices inclined to take advantage of the foreign born and anyone else where possible. One in particular resorted to all the common methods of extortion, and would even issue separation papers for $50 each, and other papers which he had no legal right to issue for correspondingly large amounts.

In Pennsylvania townships either party to a trial can demand a jury if desired, under certain conditions, and many of the justices were found practically maintaining a professional jury by encouraging a certain clique of hangers-on to keep within easy reach. As their jury fees depended upon the degree to which they pleased the justice, he was able in practically all cases to obtain the kind of decision wanted.

In a series of cases reported by the field agent, justices had combined with certain railroad detectives to arrest immigrant women for stealing coal from the railroad tracks. The value of the coal stolen in most cases was not more than ten or fifteen cents, but the women, who were brought before the judge in large numbers for trial, had to pay from $20 to $25 for fines and costs. As the women were seldom able to pay this in one amount, it was made payable in weekly installments of $1 to $2, and for a long time it was a common sight to see a line of twenty or twenty-five women standing outside these justice courts, waiting to pay the weekly installments of their fines.

In some of these justice courts the practice has arisen of identifying foreign workmen with difficult names by their check numbers in the establishment where they work. In accordance with the practice, if papers are to be served on immigrants, the constables have formed the habit of leaving them at the plant where the men work, with the timekeeper, or pinning them to the time-clock card instead of serving them personally as the law requires. This results often in holding one man responsible for the sins of another. In one case found in an Ohio town a newly arrived Italian found pinned to his first pay envelope an attachment to cover a bill from a saloon which he had not even had time to visit. It was found that the bill had been contracted by another employee who had left and whose number had been assigned to the newcomer. The justice, however, on being informed of the mistake, refused to rectify it until much pressure had been brought to bear, and until, in addition, he had been assured that the fees in the case would be paid. This justice was the one mentioned on a preceding page as considering all foreign born dangerous Anarchists and Bolshevists.

Space is lacking to report all of the ingenious tricks found by the field agent in use to exploit the immigrant in these courts. In one town the justice had a scheme of making his cases pay his poker bills of the night before. If his losses had been large the fines next day were correspondingly heavy, so that he was never permanently out of pocket by his card games.

In one Pennsylvania town a case was reported, in which it was claimed that a quack doctor had come to an agreement with a squire interested in the insurance business that patients under treatment by the doctor should take out insurance through the squire, and then, on some pretext or other, be induced to sign over their rights in the insurance to the squire and doctor. The doctor on his part was to see to it that the patients did not recover. The number of deaths among the clients of these two aroused suspicion and the doctor and squire were brought to trial for murder. The doctor pleaded guilty to murder in the second degree, but the squire, standing trial, was acquitted. In the community he is, however, generally credited with having a direct part in the events which led to the doctor's confession. Aside from this suspected crime, the whole tendency of his term of office has been toward exploitation and practicing all the worst evils associated with the justice courts. One of his practices when business was slack was to toss pieces of money to any chance immigrants who happened to be around and tell them to go out and get a drink at a certain saloon. He would then send one of his constables to arrest the men on a charge of drunkenness or disturbing the peace, and assess as heavy a fine and costs as he thought the arrested men were able to pay.

RUNNERS AND LAWYERS IN THE JUSTICE COURTS

In these justice courts the runner and unscrupulous lawyer have unusually good chances for their activities. In one small city an attorney was found who speaks seven different languages and is consequently able to obtain and hold the bulk of the foreign-born clients and command exorbitant fees for his services. He maintains a number of runners. Two or three other attorneys of foreign descent are suspected of engaging in similar practices. Such instances of wrongdoing as charging $125 for defending a client on a simple charge of intoxication to which he pleaded guilty, allowing a man to remain in jail without making any effort to have his case brought to trial, while bleeding his family for successive fees of $25 and $50 each, were found and are illustrative of this type of procedure.

Advantage is usually taken of the immigrant's ignorance to frighten him unduly in connection with minor offenses. In an Ohio town the offices of a negro attorney and a white foreign-born attorney who employ runners with whom they split fees are located just across the hall from the office of the justice. These runners stand about the entrance of the building, in the heart of the business district, and when they see an immigrant one of the runners approaches him and addresses him in his own tongue. If he finds the man is in a legal tangle of some kind it is a simple matter to lead him to one of these attorneys, assuring him that his trouble is a very serious affair and that he needs an attorney and an interpreter at once.

These practices are carried on the more easily because the justice courts do not make provision for interpreters, and the runners and lawyers themselves may undertake that function, which gives them another opportunity to deceive the client.

THE ALDERMANIC COURT

In Pennsylvania cities is found a form of court which has the same function as the justice court, but is presided over by the alderman of the ward and known as the aldermanic court. These courts have long been notorious for bad practices and have been vividly described as they existed in the city of Pittsburgh a few years ago in the *Pittsburgh Survey*.[1] One improvement effected in the Pittsburgh district since the date of that survey has been the extension of the jurisdiction of the county court, to cover the minor cases formerly heard in the alderman's court only, thus affording a means of escape from the abuses of that court. In the alderman's court itself, however, there has been little change since that time. These courts are perhaps a little more affected by the power of public opinion, a little less glaring in their abuses.

The alderman's court has jurisdiction anywhere within the county, which makes possible all the abuses of concurrent jurisdiction. The aldermen, like the justices, are paid by fees, and their incomes are out of all proportion to the services they perform. In Pittsburgh quite recently it was estimated that one alderman received $10,000 a year in fees, another over $20,000. In no case does an alderman take in less than $5,000 a year. The aldermen, for the most part, are men of mediocre abilities and attainments, without legal training, and in their courts are found the usual evils of the justice court. In one small Pennsylvania town visited by a field agent for this study, of twelve aldermen, only one had had any legal training, and all were persons with little general education and no social outlook. One was a barber, two were mill hands, several were low-grade politicians, and one was an immigrant leader who is growing rich at a suspiciously rapid rate. In general, wherever they are found,

[1] Baxter and Kerr, "Aldermen and Their Courts," *Pittsburgh Survey*, vol. V, pp. 139–155.

the aldermen presiding over the aldermanic court, like the justices, employ constables to go out and bring in cases when business grows slack.

In Pittsburgh the field agent found certain of the aldermen employing foreign-born runners, who make it a business to know and encourage the little jealousies and quarrels amongst their own people and urge them upon the slightest pretext to take the matter to a certain alderman's court. If the nature of the case permits, it is a common practice of the alderman to multiply the charges, which multiplies the fees. Thus, if several immigrants are found fighting they may be charged with "assault and battery," also with "carrying concealed weapons," also with "disturbing the peace," also with "assault with intent to kill," and any other additional charge which the ingenuity of the alderman or the ignorance of the litigants might render plausible. Even if the case is dismissed the fees are payable by the county, so that whether an accused person is held or discharged the alderman gets his fee. It is easily seen that this circumstance encourages the bringing of charges without the least regard to the likelihood of their being well founded. The various aldermen of the county have in the past been amassing an annual bill of many thousands of dollars in this way which has been paid by the county. In some years as much as $30,000 or $40,000 has been paid by the county for cases brought into the aldermanic courts without a sufficient justification of fact to render possible anything but a dismissal even in these courts.

In one of the small Pennsylvania cities a fertile field of exploitation for the alderman and his constables has been found in certain provisions of the state game laws, whereby an alien is not allowed to have in his possession either firearms or a dog of any kind. The law provides a fine of $25 for these offenses, half of which is to go to the informant, and costs, which average $6 or $7. In many cases the alien was fined because his children had some small pet dog, obviously not used as a game dog. And as to firearms, a story is told that in one case a constable was known to have arrested several foreign-born residents under this law because their children had been playing with toy pistols.

Could any piece of petty graft be more likely to cause a sense of irritation and injury among decent immigrants?

From these examples it is plain that the justice court, at least as it is found operating in the more crowded communities where immigrants are settled in large numbers, cannot be trusted to give the immigrant a square deal, and all the arguments brought forward against this type of court generally are of especial weight in relation to the needs of the immigrant. He is less able to protect himself than the native-born person, and he will suffer more harmful consequences of a failure of justice.

VI

DEVELOPMENTS IN THE MINOR COURTS

In the larger communities, where the volume of court business warrants, we find minor courts known under various names, such as police court, magistrate's court, district court, or the like, which are a step in advance of the justice courts as we have seen them in operation, in that the judge and other court officials are paid for full-time services by a fixed salary instead of by a fee for each case, and that the judge must have had legal training. In such courts the judge is no longer under temptation to stimulate court business for the sake of a money return to himself, and he may be expected to render more intelligent decisions because of his knowledge of the law.

THE OFFICIAL INTERPRETER

This larger court may add to its staff a court interpreter, who, although comparatively low in rank in the court hierarchy, is of especial importance to the immigrant. We have already noted examples of the harm coming to the non-English-speaking client, not only in his material interests, but in his thoughts about matters of justice, from unofficial interpreters—his friends, or his lawyer or the runner who secured the lawyer for him, through their false representations.

If the non-English-speaking client finds an official interpreter in the court, he is no longer entirely at the mercy of his foreign-speaking lawyer, or of some

178

volunteer interpreter he has brought with him, for his understanding of what is going on at the court hearing, for the court's understanding of him.

The court interpreter may also render a great service to the immigrant, beyond his stated duty of giving accurate literal translations, by making such explanations of the meaning of what is said on both sides, as will help to bridge the gap between the native-born judge and the foreign-born client, with their different habits of thought, their different understanding, perhaps, of the very same words, and let each see what is really in the mind of the other.

He often has the opportunity also to act as friendly adviser to the foreign-born client, to enlighten him as to his rights, and to tell him something of the meaning and methods of courts and the law in this country.

But the court interpreter also has it in his power, just because of his position of advantage as a court official, to mislead and cheat the immigrant, either on his own account or in partnership with other swindlers like the runners and lawyers already described.

The official interpreter who is not employed for his full time, but is called in only when needed and paid a fee for each service, is especially under temptation to engage in these unworthy partnerships to supplement an inadequate income.

The court interpreter who is honest but ignorant can also do much harm. The court interpreter must know something of both the foreign language and our own, and should know both languages sufficiently well to make a translation which shall carry over the real meaning from one language to another. Many times a barely literal translation fails to do this. An idiomatic expression in one language may mean nothing when

179

literally translated into the other, and the person using it may be entirely misunderstood. The interpreter should also know enough of the rules of court procedure to make proper explanations to the client of the meaning and bearing of questions and answers, and to give the right phrasing to his translations of both, so that the client shall not put himself at a disadvantage.

Where one court has to deal with a great variety of nationalities, and not a large number of some of the kinds, it is usually not possible for the court to provide a separate official interpreter for each language. But serious misunderstandings may arise when this is not done. In such a court an official interpreter understanding one language may claim to know one or more in addition with which he really has only a superficial acquaintance, and the judge may accept his services as interpreter for the languages unprovided for, because he needs some one, and he himself has no way of measuring the interpreter's proficiency.

The best service of interpretation, then, is likely to be rendered in courts that maintain a staff of full-time interpreters, who are paid a living wage, and who are able to translate well all of the foreign tongues heard in the court.

SIMPLIFICATION OF PROCEDURE

The most significant feature in the development of the minor court, and the one of greatest moment, perhaps, to the foreign-born client, may be found in the growing use of discretion in the treatment of individual cases. This line of development away from the original tendency of the American to stick to the letter of the law, as did his English ancestors, has been entered into because in one class of cases after another it was discovered that strictly technical methods were failing to afford substantial justice. We have already seen that the justice of the peace had the power to exercise discretion of a certain sort, consisting in his power to hold or dismiss cases at will, and to dispense with technical rules of procedure. So that in handling the civil cases arising out of the many money troubles of the immigrant, the justice had it in his power to render the process of law inexpensive and rapid, as is needed to make the remedies of justice available to the poor man. We have also seen that in great measure the justice failed to do this.

Minor courts of higher rank were more strictly bound by rules of procedure, involving much delay in getting a case settled, and much expense. For where legal technicalities have to be strictly observed, court costs must be levied for the handling of the legal papers required, and a legal expert must be paid because he will be needed to see the client safely through the maze of the proper presentation of his case.

In this newer development, in order to reduce the delay and expense involved in the ordinary civil trial in a court of higher rank than that of the justice of the peace, special courts for the hearing of cases of small claims have been established[1] in which court procedure has been much simplified and court costs either reduced or done away with. Such courts exist in some half dozen cities, and in them, in general, the services of a lawyer are not needed. In some of them, in fact, a lawyer is not allowed to appear. The judge takes upon himself the function of counsel, and sees to it that both parties have the opportunity to make a fair showing of the merits of their cases.

[1] For a description of these courts, see Reginald Heber Smith, *Justice and the Poor*, chap. viii, "The Small Claims Court."

DISCRETION IN TREATMENT

The characteristically modern uses of discretion in the courts, however, are based upon a general conception that the character and circumstances of persons before the court should be taken into consideration in rendering judgment, as well as the acts defined by the law. Under this conception the purpose of the action taken is not merely to secure the performance of certain acts by the client—to pay a claim, or to go to prison, or to pay a fine, but to try to bring about a state of mind—to bring the client into right relations with his fellow beings; if he is an offender, to keep him from future offense, if he has been wronged, to secure a permanent and genuine righting of the wrong.

According to this conception the attitude of mind of the client is of the greatest importance. What is desired is not only to secure a physical compliance with the terms of the law, but a mental state which will favor a wholesome social adjustment. So that to the extent discretion of this sort is exercised in the court, the court officials will find it their task not only to enforce but to persuade, to conciliate, to educate.

This is a considerable broadening of the functions of court officials and it involves a broadening of the qualifications for service in the courts. The officials in such courts should know people as well as the law, should know how to persuade as well as how to command, and should have in mind all the time the possibilities of doing some educational work with the clients before them.

Courts embodying this general idea of discretion have been established especially for juvenile cases and questions of domestic relations, and these are the courts with which the immigrant is especially concerned in settling the domestic difficulties which we have seen to be so large a part of his troubles. In these courts there is especial need for the education of the foreign-born client. Immigrants from Central and Southern Europe, in particular, have quite different ideas of the legal as well as the moral rights of husbands in relation to wives, of parents in relation to children. The laws of Central and Southern European countries generally give the husband more power unchecked by law within his own family, more legal remedies against members of his family, and hold him to less responsibility than do the laws of this country. The average immigrant is astonished at what the law requires of him here in relation to his family. His wife is bewildered at possibilities of legal action against him which she does not fully understand and does not know how to use, or may use improperly. Painstaking work is needed to make the immigrant families realize the meaning of our laws about family relations.

THE PROBATION OFFICER

In nonspecialized courts dealing with minor offenses we also find the use of discretionary methods of treatment, in the choice between different forms of punishment prescribed by the law or of suspension of any form of punishment, with or without the supervision of future conduct by a court officer. This latter possibility introduces us to a new court functionary, also of great importance to the immigrant—the probation officer. He is found not only in the minor criminal courts, but in the juvenile courts and the courts of domestic relations. In all of them it is his function primarily to see that the orders of the judge are complied with; these orders may involve only certain acts, like the payment of money, but they may also involve the attainment of a certain character, or attitude of mind, by the client, to show that he is fit to take up his social obligations, free from further responsibility to the court. The probation officer also may assist the judge before decision is rendered by collecting the information about the client which the judge needs in order to know what treatment is appropriate.

EQUIPMENT OF THE JUDGE

In courts of this wider discretion what would be a desirable equipment for the judge who is to deal with the foreign-born, beside a knowledge of the law? To begin with the negative side, "a weak, or incapable, or narrow-minded judge," says Reginald Heber Smith,[1] "can do more harm in a court of wide discretion, such as a small claims, a juvenile, or a domestic-relations court, than anywhere else." On the positive side, he ought to know the types of people who come before him. The same considerations that have led to the regarding of the juvenile client as a special type, needing special treatment, should lead to the recognition of the newly arrived immigrant as a special type. The immigrant, like the child, is not fully aware of the consequences of his acts, he is not fully able to carry out the responsibilities laid on him in the way that the grown-up native-born person may be expected to do. To understand them and to help them then, the judge dealing with the foreign born might well try to learn something about the peoples they represent—their history, their customs, their ideals and aspirations.

[1] Reginald Heber Smith, *Justice and the Poor,* p. 47.

DEVELOPMENTS IN THE MINOR COURTS

In our study of the troubles that bring the immigrant before the court we have seen, even in the money difficulties, certain complications due to the experiences of the immigrant which a judge should understand in order to settle the case justly. These special experiences are of even more moment in cases appearing before the criminal courts. But the domestic troubles above all are interwoven with such a network of ideas and habits regarding the family relation, peculiar to the community from which the immigrant came, that it would seem hopeless to try to deal with these situations through the method of persuasion and conciliation adopted by the modern court without a thorough knowledge of these peculiarities, and an unprejudiced view of them as elements in the situation, which cannot be disposed of simply by disapproval.

The fact that the court officer possesses this equipment, aside from any special use made of it, has a favorable effect on the foreign-born client. For just as we are inclined to think an immigrant stupid when he does not understand something quite familiar to us, in the same way the foreign-born person may think us stupid when we are ignorant of something he knows very well. Even such apparently small matters as using the foreign names correctly, spelling them and pronouncing them with some approach to accuracy, and using the last name instead of the first in speaking to foreign-born clients, will give them a greater respect for the officials addressing them.

For, although we may use the same consideration for the immigrant and take the same interest in him, that we would in a child, we must remember not to push that analogy too far. The foreign-born adult before the courts has in general the adult appreciation of his

185

personal dignity, which may be wounded if he is addressed familiarly as "Tony" or "Mike."

Sympathy usually comes with knowledge about any people, and if the judge can feel a genuine sympathy and interest in the foreign-born client before him, as the representative of a national type, he will be so much the more able to secure the good will of the client for the court and the court's orders.

The judge would be greatly aided by understanding the language of his non-English-speaking clients. This would enable him to make a direct approach to the client and to see through any attempts to deceive on the part of interpreters, official or unofficial. In practice we cannot, of course, ask a busy judge to learn ten or a dozen languages; we can only say that as many as he can muster will be useful.

If the judge is of foreign birth or descent himself, he naturally will understand his own people in a way that the average native-born American does not. He will in most cases be able to address them in their own language, and may be expected to know something of their habits of thought and their customs.

EQUIPMENT OF THE PROBATION OFFICER

Something of the same qualifications might be expected in the probation officer, who is the extension of the judge's mind in relation to the case. On him rests the responsibility of securing for the judge information about the true circumstances of cases. He has a far wider opportunity than the judge for educating the client, and for persuading him to right courses of action. It would seem even more necessary for the probation officer than for the judge to know the languages of the peoples with whom he has to deal, and to know the history, habits, and characteristics of the people, and the social and economic class they come from. And the probation officer of foreign birth would seem to be the best able to understand his fellow countrymen.

Let us look at some of these minor courts, of higher rank than the justice court, and see what the various types of courts actually are doing for and with the foreign-born client, how the court officials regard their work in relation to the foreign born, and how the foreign born feel about them.

First let us turn to a police court in which the judge has a high appreciation of the opportunities before such a court of establishing respect for American institutions in the minds of the foreign born. He says, about his methods:

Above all things, impress the foreigner who has reason to have business with your court that your court is a court of justice and that you are firm for that which is right. Go out of your way, if it is necessary, to listen to his complaint, although you may not at the outset think that it has any standing or place in court. Never let him leave you with the impression that he is not being justly and fairly dealt with. There are so many small things that happen and come to the notice of a magistrate in his everyday life that really are not part of his court work in which he can play a part. . . . Yesterday morning before I left home, a group of foreigners, eight or ten, came into court. It seems that they had been sent from New York or Albany up to the woods to work. Their transportation was paid. They worked so many days and they were given transportation to Albany, and there they were without means and there was money owed them by the man they worked for. They were to receive so much pay. They were Polish and Lithuanians, a mixed group. The spokesman came to me—some one suggested he go to the police court. The police court magistrate, not only in Albany,

187

but every other city, is the public adviser. In the few minutes that I had to talk with these men through their spokesman, it came to me that a wrong had been done. Finally I found that one of the men interested in the concern was in Albany and I sent for that man. . . . I asked if what they said was true, and he replied, "Yes, it is true, but there has been a difference of opinion between the men in this concern and the money is tied up." I said to him: "You are doing this group of people an injustice, and let me tell you that this is one of the reasons why the foreigners at times say they are not being justly treated here, and what wonder the ignorant become radicals. If anything happens you are responsible; it is up to you; it is your duty to see to it that these men are compensated to-day. Fight your own battle out with the men you had your difference with." Now, those poor men eventually might have come in as vagrants, and that is just one of the many things that one will meet with.[1]

A police court conducted according to such principles must be an influence for good with its clients. There they may get advice and instruction as well as a decision, and in this instance we may note an attempt to settle a trouble by conciliation.

Police courts of this character are not, however, found everywhere. In the Ohio and Pennsylvania towns and cities surveyed for this study, it appeared that, although the police courts generally were somewhat better than the justice courts, they were not of the highest type. The police judges in the towns visited, paid by a fixed yearly salary, were not found promoting litigation in the manner of the justices. But in their respective communities they had the reputation of being subject to local political influences.

[1] Judge John J. Brady, of the police court of Albany, New York; Remarks at the Annual Meeting of the New York State Magistrates' Association, *Twelfth Annual Report of the New York State Probation Commission, 1918*, p. 467.

DEVELOPMENTS IN THE MINOR COURTS

In some of the courts visited, foreign-born clients were seen to be treated with scant consideration and in a rough and brutal manner; in others the technical rights of the immigrant, involved in the particular case before the court, apparently received as much attention as if the client had been of native birth. But in general in these courts was to be noted a more or less marked lack of sympathy with the immigrant, a more or less thinly veiled feeling of contempt for him, and a tendency toward impatience with his ignorance and illiteracy.

In these courts the dishonest attorney, the runner, and the professional bondsman seemed to have excellent opportunities of plying their trade. They were found in the jails, in the corridors of the courts, and even in the court room itself. And in some of these courts the official interpreters were found in league with the runners and the lawyers who employ them. Many of these interpreters were not only dishonest, but ignorant, pretending to speak languages of which they knew little or nothing.

MINOR COURTS IN MASSACHUSETTS

In Massachusetts the justice of the peace has no trial jurisdiction, and the lowest minor court is the district court, the police court, or the municipal court, presided over by a salaried judge. Each of these courts is an independent unit, even in the city of Boston, where separate courts still represent the old town governments later united in the greater city.

In these courts we find provision for probationary treatment. Every court in Massachusetts in which criminal cases are tried, or juvenile cases heard, is required by law to be provided with at least one probation officer. Boston maintains two specialized courts, one for dealing with juvenile cases and one with domestic relations, both of which are equipped with probation officers.

In the Boston Court of Domestic Relations which as a city court in a city with a large foreign-born population might be expected to have special knowledge of different foreign peoples, the probation officers are none of them of foreign birth, nor do they speak any foreign language. Occasionally the court interpreter makes an investigation in a home where English is not understood. More often the workers depend upon a chance interpreter among the neighbors and relatives. Each officer has more cases than he can handle effectively, consequently some of the work has to be neglected. Evidently, personal instruction and character building cannot be carried on effectively under such circumstances. Apparently little personal discrimination is made between cases; a standard period of probation is set in each case, and during this time little attention is paid to the probationers. The probation officers seldom take the responsibility of prosecuting for actual violation of probation, to say nothing of carrying on the educational side of the probation officer's work. Individual probation officers with a special interest in the matter are trying to carry out the principles of probation, but they are so overburdened with work that it is impossible for them to be really efficient. Complaints are sometimes handled in such a way for the foreign-born woman who asks protection as to make her feel that the court does not help her because she is foreign born, so that she loses respect for the court and is unwilling to have anything to do with it again.

The minor courts of Massachusetts generally do not employ full-time interpreters on a salaried basis, although large foreign-born populations of many nationalities are to be found in the industrial towns and cities of the state. Interpreters are called in as they are needed, in some courts from lists of names approved by the judge, and are paid by a fee for each service. In these courts, then, we might expect to find the same troubles with interpreters that are noted in other places where the fee system prevails. In the Boston courts the interpreters were found, as a matter of fact, to be so ignorant, and so dishonest, that after great effort salaried interpreters were secured for the criminal session of the Central Court of Boston.[1]

One feature of the procedure in these minor courts is of great help to the immigrant. The judge, when imposing a fine, need not demand the payment of the entire amount at once, but may permit it to be paid in installments to a probation officer. Many an immigrant, who may be too poverty-stricken to pay the whole amount of a fine at once, can pay it in installments, and in this way be relieved from the stigma of a jail sentence in default of payment of his fine.

METHODS AND IDEALS OF THE JUDGES

To gain some idea of how the judges in the Massachusetts minor courts themselves felt about the foreign-born client, and about the conditions in their own courts, some fifty of them were asked for information on these points, for the purposes of this study. Of these only eleven responded, a small number on which to generalize, but as these were presumably the judges with the most interest in the question, their views are of value.

All of them had considered the problem of the

[1] *Report of the Massachusetts Commission on Immigration*, 1914, p. 295.

foreign-born sufficiently to note differences in the kinds of offense persons of different nationalities were most likely to commit, and seven of them recognized special circumstances in the experience of the immigrant in his own country or here which would to some extent account for a tendency to commit offenses. One thought that inability to understand the law, and what obedience to law means in relation to community life, and too close segregation were accountable. One special misunderstanding mentioned by him should be noted as applying in many communities—that is, the misunderstanding of the license to marry. Many immigrants, unfamiliar with the formalities of civil marriage in this country, think that procuring a license to marry is the ceremony itself, and that the license is their marriage certificate. More than one case of illegal cohabitation may be explained in that way. Another judge thought that lack of education, especially in standards of living, and poverty lead to violation of law by the foreign born, and that in so far as the immigrant gets education and the means for a proper living, he is no more of a "problem" than the native born.

Another judge attributes the immigrant's trouble in court to ignorance. Another says the average immigrant, having had experience with corruption in his home country, comes here with the belief that justice is not to be expected from court officials, and is inclined to take the law into his own hands. Another thinks that, in addition to ignorance, a feeling that he was persecuted at home influences his attitude toward obedience to the law in this country unfavorably. Another judge thinks that the trouble with the immigrant is that he comes to this country with the idea that liberty means license; then he acquires the American idolatry of the dollar, and becomes "like the rest of the inhabitants—he heartily approves and supports all law not affecting him." Another gives the immigrant's reluctance to change observances and ceremonies attended by the excessive use of liquors as a cause of many of his troubles. Only one of the judges would say that he considered the foreign born a serious problem in law enforcement.

Eight of the judges state that they make use of their opportunity to instruct the foreign-born clients in the meaning and purpose of laws and ordinances, and four of these note that much of the work is done by the probation officers attached to their courts. Two more, who do not undertake the instruction of the foreign clients themselves, tell of work done in this line by the probation officer and in one of the two courts by the interpreter in coöperation with the probation officer. The judge of the Juvenile Court in Boston, who was one of the eleven replying, says:

In every case that comes before me, which a foreigner is interested in and concerned with, I explain the meaning and purpose of the laws and ordinances; and in addition the probation officer having charge of the case makes the explanation.

Another judge says:

In every case coming before me I try to impress our foreign element that this is the best country in the world for them if they will only obey our laws and become good citizens.

Another says that he instructs foreign clients when they have been accused of violating some town by-law or have committed some minor offense which they would not consider an offense. Two of the judges give instruction "now and then" and "a little, but not sufficient," evidently thinking this a desirable thing to do, but lacking time for it, while one, who does give such instruction as would naturally be called for in the ordinary course of the court, says that he finds the foreign-born client fairly well instructed already, knowing not only the procedure of the criminal court, but the tendencies of the different judges.

In most of these instances the purpose of the judge in his instruction seems to be to explain the laws in question in the particular case before him; in one, however, the judge seemed to have in mind rather the inculcation of general civic duty.

In exercising discretion as to the kind of penalty inflicted in cases of minor offenders, few of the judges noted making any differences with different nationalities. One remarked that it is well known that some of the races appreciate the value of money more than others, so that a fine as a form of punishment makes a special impression on them, and some feel imprisonment more keenly, but he did not state any rules of practice based on these differences. One thought that no distinction should be made in method of treatment between different kinds of immigrants or between the native born and the foreign born, and another said that he made no such distinction. These last opinions emphasize the equality before the law which is an essential element of justice, but fail to reach the idea that equal treatment of unequals leads to inequality, which is the reason for establishing discretionary methods. If a choice is made between fine, imprisonment, or suspension of sentence on the basis of differences in character due to age, or the repetition of offenses, surely the same principle is valid with respect to differences in character shown as a result of different historical experiences and social traditions.

Another judge thought that suspension of sentence under probation was not understood or appreciated by the immigrant who has an imperfect knowledge of English, and that in their cases fine or imprisonment is more effective, moderated in terms to suit the condition and circumstances of the defendant, as well as the character of the offense. He is persuaded of this by the interpreters of the court, whom he considers to be men of high character, understanding their fellow countrymen thoroughly.

One of the judges has no hard and fast rule for dealing with foreign-born clients, but he does note that the Polish people particularly dislike any restraint on their liberty. We may note that at least this little group of the Massachusetts judges, has taken into account the foreign-born client as an element of interest in the operations of their courts, and is showing a disposition to study the problem.

What suggestions have they to make as to the improvement of court methods or the conditions surrounding the operations of the courts? All but one of them seemed to consider the interpreters, called in as they are wanted, on payment of a fee for each service, adequate for the purpose. One judge, in a small industrial city, however, thought that in the system of court interpretation as carried on in these courts there was room for improvement. Interpreters, he says, vary greatly in ability—few know their business. He thinks volunteer interpreters are not satisfactory. Courts in large cities should have regular interpreters present every day, and the position should be made a responsible one. In his court the parties in interest often bring their own interpreters, and he fears that they frequently act as law brokers. Three other judges express disapproval of the volunteer interpreter. One of the three says that in his court attempts to secure volunteer interpreters always end in failure.

The volunteer is apt to be a partisan. Another says that he would not have a volunteer interpreter in his court, and that good interpreters are rare and should have some court training.

Eight of the eleven judges say that the runner evil does not exist in their courts; one knows of a "very few;" one says that his court is free from runners except in so far as the professional bondsman is a runner; and one has already been noted as saying that he suspects the volunteer interpreters coming to his court to be acting as law brokers—much the same thing as runners, except that they do no business at the police station or at the courthouse.

Only one of the judges whose opinions have been given represented a Boston court, so we may add here a view of the lower criminal court of the Central Court of Boston, as seen by an investigator for this study, to give one more example of theories and methods of treatment in the Massachusetts minor courts. A large number of the persons appearing before this court are foreign born. Many of the cases involve quarrels and disagreements which are more effectively treated by arbitration than by legal decision. Notable about the procedure of this court is the dignity and privacy with which it is conducted. The persons concerned and their lawyers stand at one side of the judge's desk, and the case is discussed quietly. The desk is so far removed from the benches given over to the use of the public that the discussion is heard only by the persons in interest. The trouble bringing the clients to court is presented informally and talked over frankly. Only occasionally is it necessary to take formal testimony.

DEVELOPMENTS IN THE MINOR COURT

The attitude of the justice is that of an arbitrator rather than that of a deciding official.

In this court most of the persons appearing are represented by counsel, but because of the care taken by the judge himself to secure a fair presentation of the cases, services of counsel are practically unnecessary. Most of the cases brought by the foreign born are trivial. Many are cases of quarrels, and at times a complainant will be found bringing some one before the court only to gratify a personal spite. On such occasions it is the policy of the judge to dismiss the cases with a rebuke, and he often takes a little time to point out to clients the unwisdom of certain courses of action and to instruct them in the right way of handling their affairs.

In the daily operations of the court there is no indication of prejudice against the foreign born, unless evidences of a rather general feeling that they are inferior persons may be counted as such.

BIRTH AND DESCENT OF THE JUDGES

The judges in the minor courts of Boston, and throughout the state as well, are largely of American or Irish birth or descent, which might occasion a lack of understanding of the newer immigrant races, and possibly some prejudice in dealing with them.

In Boston the Italians are numerous and would like to see their people represented on the Bench. Reasons that may be urged for this sort of national representation were well expressed in a leading Italian-American newspaper of Boston.[1]

A person familiar with the customs, habits, and language of a certain race, other things being equal, ought to make a

[1] *The Italian Voice*, March 15, 1919.

better arbitrator in matters affecting that race than one not so familiar. In civil and criminal matters involving members of this race he can grasp the spirit behind it all. He can determine what sense of honor the litigants possess and he can determine how much of the serious there is in the cause. To be able to speak the language of the litigants must of necessity be a great advantage to the presiding officer and a benefit to the machinery of the law. Incompetent and interested interpreters would find it impossible to continue that vocation; their day will draw to its end. . . .

To-day, in the vicinity of Boston there are about one hundred thousand people of Italian descent, thoroughly American, well represented in the electorate, who are ambitiously striving to see some of their number attain responsible positions. They have seen their ambition realized in all the walks of life excepting one. Among them there are bankers, business men, and doctors, who have made their mark and who have gained more than local reputation for their ability. In Boston, of their number, only one has received an appointment as judge and that has been a rather insignificant appointment, what one might call a minor office.

On the list of names of judges of our courts we cannot fail to notice names that are Irish, French, and Jewish in their origin. These men were appointed in the first instance to give representation to their race. They deserved it and should have it; there is no ground to complain on that score. In such appointments we see the desirability of gaining the confidence of the race and making it feel as though it were part and parcel of the great American nation. Of course, they were sufficiently strong in numbers to be considered as entitled to representation. Why not extend the same courtesy to the Italian race who are sufficiently strong in numbers and who in the great war gave life freely and willingly that the dictates and ideals of America might govern the civilized world?

It would be a brave man who would declare that an Italian American would not be qualified to be a judge. The country which gave to the world its law of partnership, insurance, bills and notes, must surely have amongst its inhabitants to-day men of legal mind. The laws of heredity still apply and the "mind to law" of the forefathers must as a result of the law of heredity pass down to the descendants. Let us not overlook the code law, which is also of Italian origin. The Italians have always shown great executive and judicial ability.

WHAT LEADERS OF THE FOREIGN BORN THINK OF THE BOSTON COURTS

Opinions of certain leaders of the foreign born in Boston gathered by a field agent for this study may give an idea as to how the immigrant himself feels about the courts with which he has to deal.

An Armenian lawyer, a man of fine personality and socially minded, thinks a great prejudice exists in the courts against all foreign born. He thinks that most of the judges and district attorneys are unsocial in their viewpoint, and that the socialization of the courts is one of the most necessary reforms. In his opinion it is impossible for one not in touch with the political forces, and therefore nearly always impossible for the foreign born, to get a fair chance in court. In his experience with cases he has found that the court will not give as much weight to the testimony of the immigrant as to that of the American. He has found that in cases which he has had in the courts the testimony of one American would be taken in preference to that of two Armenians. In the eyes of the judges all the foreign born are liars, a judgment which he resents and feels is especially unjust in the case of the Armenians, who regard truth very highly. He cited two cases which he considered illustrative of injustice to the foreign born in the courts. In one, about twenty Armenians were arrested in a coffee house, charged with gambling. The whole group were taken to the

199

police station, where they were told by the police that they might as well plead guilty, for the result would be the same in any case. There was no attempt to ascertain which ones, if any, of the group were guilty of gambling. Each man was summarily fined $25.

In the other case, in which an Armenian was killed by an Irish boy scarcely eighteen years of age, the district attorney failed to hold the offender for trial, with the understanding that he should be kept under observation for three years. The Armenian lawyer was satisfied with the result from a humanitarian standpoint, but felt that the leniency was due to political interference and the fact that the man killed was an immigrant.

As to the general feeling of the Armenians toward the courts, this lawyer said they had little respect for the American institution of justice, not only because of actual injustice they had met with in the courts, but because the runners and lawyers into whose hands they fell taught them that everything depended on favoritism and bribery. They naturally believed these men because they remembered the Turkish court, in which, if a man gets justice he must buy it, and consequently does not think it strange that a court in another country should be of that sort also.

An Italian social worker and leader among his people says that Irish domination in the courts operates against other European groups. Another Italian leader, a lawyer, has found that there is little respect among the foreign born for the American courts, and attributes this in part to the fact that in America the courts and the judges are open to political influence. The Italian, he says, has a profound respect for the courts and judges in his own country, because the judiciary is a profession entered into for life, and because, under a central supervision, judges may be sent from district to district, and cannot, therefore, build up a system of graft.

Another Italian, a lawyer who has had much experience in handling cases for Italians in court and has been prominent in Boston politics, says that, although he has had experience with the court in which individual judges have shown antagonism to foreign-born people, and lack of respect for them, this is not representative or general. There are a few of "the old Yankees" who dislike the foreign born. One judge dismissed a case brought by a Portuguese woman because she fainted in the court and the judge thought this behavior might prejudice the jury. When the case came up for another hearing, he alluded to the incident and said he hoped the lesson had been sufficient, as if the fainting had been an attempt on her part to influence the jury. The same judge upon another occasion was so rude to Italian witnesses that counsel asked for an apology and got it.

In another case a judge ordered an Italian witness to stop using his hands to gesticulate while giving his testimony. The witness politely acquiesced, but in a moment his hands were going as hard as ever. The judge became impatient and shouted at him to stop, which he tried to do, but when counsel suggested that the man, being an Italian, could not help this method of expression, the judge was angry.

An Italian editor thinks that the attitude of the courts is lenient rather than severe toward the immigrant, and that this paternalistic attitude is dangerous. He also thinks the American courts are controlled by politics, so that it is difficult for anyone to secure justice, and that the Italians have little respect for the American court, "because they soon learn that justice can be bought and sold." They have greater respect for the courts of Italy, because of the greater ceremony connected with them, and their freedom from control by local politics.

A Hungarian lawyer had not found in his experience that the immigrant was mistreated in the courts. The judges are rather likely to excuse him because they think he does not understand the law. Cases of injustice he thinks are no more frequent among immigrants than among the Americans, and are due to dishonest and unprincipled justices and police officers. A Lithuanian editor agrees with this view.

A Lithuanian lawyer thinks that on the whole the courts are fair and considerate. He notes that Lithuanians take it for granted that the fee paid a runner or lawyer or interpreter or other agent will be divided with the judge, because the Russian courts to which they are accustomed are so corrupt. The procedure in the Russian minor court, however, is more simple; difficulties are settled by the judge without the aid of lawyers. But when the Lithuanian tries to handle his own case in an American court the practices of the court are so involved that he makes out very poorly. Another Lithuanian lawyer has found the judges usually friendly.

An Italian woman social worker says that for the most part the Italians have little respect for the American courts, because they lack the dignity and ceremony which characterize the courts in Italy. A Belgian social worker had observed that the foreign born generally think the courts are corrupt, that everyone connected with the court was ready to take advantage of them, and that bribes were necessary. A Russian Jewish social worker says that failure to secure justice in an American court is not a surprise to the foreign born from Russia, because in Russia there is no justice for anyone. It is taken for granted that the courts are corrupt.

An American social worker says that the courts and the district attorney's office are not trusted by the people, on account of the political influence that exists, but the injustices suffered by the foreign born are no greater or less than those experienced by everyone in the courts of Boston.

A Syrian editor says that in the courts the Syrians feel that they are looked down upon by the officials. He hears few complaints of unjust sentences, but many of the attitude of the court toward the foreign born. In the event of more immigration he thinks that the Federal government should take greater care to protect the immigrants and explain American life to them. The Syrians come from a country which has long been dominated by Turkey and in which dishonesty and bribery are openly practiced by public officials. They come to this country expecting to find justice. When they are exploited they become convinced that conditions are no different in this country from what they are in Turkey.

A Greek lawyer thinks that on the whole the judges and the court are considerate and friendly. There are individual cases where judges are prejudiced against the foreign born and these are the source of much hard feeling.

It will be noted that a considerable proportion of these leaders think the minor courts of Boston and their judges are fair and unprejudiced. Of those who criticize the courts in their treatment of the foreign born the greater number ascribe the trouble to improper political influence rather than to a direct prejudice against a certain nationality.

There is more general agreement among them, however, that the immigrant client himself has a general distrust of the courts, due partly to actual injustice or lack of consideration experienced there, partly to what the runners tell them, partly to their experiences of corrupt courts at home which they expect to be repeated here, partly to admiration of home courts, which they think superior to ours. Evidently, in Boston, the avenues of communication between the court and the foreign-born client are not yet completely clear and open.

OPINIONS ABOUT THE INTERPRETERS

About the interpreters the foreign leaders had much to say. Those of them who themselves had had the longest experience in this country, the greatest familiarity with the American courts, thought the court interpreters fairly satisfactory. One criticism made by those who complained of the interpreters was that men were accepted by the courts because of their familiarity with one foreign language, as adequate interpreters of other related languages. For example, familiarity with one Slavic language would be taken as evidence of ability to interpret for any or all of the others. Another complaint is that for the smaller national groups interpreters are not provided at all. It is said, for example, that there is seldom a Portuguese interpreter in court—the parties concerned must bring their own.

An Armenian leader thinks that the interpreters are a menace, as they fail to interpret correctly, either through ignorance or intent. He has frequently found it necessary to stop a case in the middle and request a change of interpreters. This is not always possible to accomplish, as the judge has no way of knowing whether the interpreter is adequate or not. Another Armenian, a former interpreter himself, said that the situation was better than it had been for some time, but that there would be no permanent improvement until the courts employed salaried interpreters, appointed through examination for fitness.

An Italian leader thinks that one of the greatest difficulties with the interpreters is their lack of special knowledge of court procedure, so that they are not qualified to interpret accurately. Most of the interpreters, he says, have no knowledge of legal terminology or of the difference between a leading question and a direct question. When a lawyer puts a direct question it is likely to be interpreted as a leading question and the testimony brought out may be unfair to one side or the other. This is a pitfall the foreign-born interpreter is likely to fall into, if he has had any experience with European courts, in which so much more freedom in the introduction of testimony is allowed, but it is especially to be guarded against in the American court, in which so much emphasis is placed upon procedure. Time and again he had seen witnesses for the defense play into the hands of the other side because of clumsy interpretation.

He complains, also, that the interpreters are not intimately acquainted with the languages they use, and are not skillful in giving idiomatic translation where direct translations would give an entirely wrong idea of the real meaning. He thinks that the interpreters should be required to pass examinations, which should cover knowledge of the common legal terms and of idiomatic expressions. They should also know something of the rules of direct examination and cross-examination so that they may coöperate with lawyers.

THE IMMIGRANT'S DAY IN COURT

Some of the foreign-born leaders think that there is still some dishonesty among the interpreters. One woman active among the Italians felt that the interpreters had no sympathy with the clients and did not assume a helpful attitude toward them. Frequently they grossly misinterpret. In a case observed by her in which two Italians were on trial for quarreling, the judge dismissed the case with a few words of admonition, telling the accused persons to go home and not quarrel with each other any more, that quarreling was not the American way. The interpreter, however, translated this into an order to go home and not try to kill each other, for if they did they would get into trouble. A number of Italians in the court room took the matter to one of the Italian newspapers, but nothing was done about it.

According to these leaders the Boston courts are still infested with runners, notwithstanding the fact that a special law was passed in 1916 regulating the solicitation of cases for lawyers, and that under it the State Bureau of Immigration in 1918 made special efforts to prosecute offenders and drive them out of the courts.

One of these leaders says that in three years after the passage of the law there were only three convictions, and that most of the old offenders are now back on their jobs, infesting the corridors of the court, lying in wait for the unwary immigrant.

COÖRDINATED COURTS

Another step in the improvement of the minor courts is made by uniting them under the supervision of a presiding justice. This is an especially valuable improvement under a discretionary system because it affords to the individual justice, who can no longer rely on a cut-and-dried rule of law as a basis for his decisions, something to take its place as a standard— the results of the experiences of a group of judges, co- ordinated under a presiding judge, so that each member of the group gets the benefit of the wisdom of all, and no member, due to this system of conference and supervision, can make "discretion" a cloak for purely arbitrary action on his part.

In many localities where more than one minor court is needed we find such courts united into coöperating groups.

MUNICIPAL COURT IN CHICAGO

In Chicago is found a court of this modern type with various branches coördinated under a presiding judge. This court, called the Municipal Court, has jurisdiction in both civil and criminal cases, provides special courts for special classes of cases, among them a Small-Claims court, a Court of Domestic Relations, a Boys' Court, and a Morals Court, and makes use of a psychiatric clinic.

This court succeeded in its first year of operation (1907) in reducing litigation from the enormous number of over 92,000 cases in the last year (1906) of the justice courts in the city of Chicago, to approximately 57,500 cases.

The court claims for itself to be not only a judicial force, but a constructive social agency. In this court are to be found a number of judges of foreign birth or parentage, of high character, who show a special appreciation of the problems of the foreign born.

Chief Judge Harry Olson, of this court, who has done so much toward establishing this modern method of court organization, not only feels the seriousness of the problem of the foreign born, but the desirability

THE IMMIGRANT'S DAY IN COURT

of considering their standards and experiences in trying to solve it. As an example of his general attitude may be cited some remarks of his before the Page Commission about voluntary probation officers. He says:

Quite often many of those who volunteer to act as probation officers have notions of their own as to how other people should live and act. A young lady whose antecedents are from Vermont or New England might think the Russian Jews do some things they ought not to do, and that the Poles do some things that they ought not to do, and that the Scandinavians do some things that they are accustomed to doing that they ought not to do, and. . . many of them may seek to impose their ideas of behavior on these citizens of foreign extraction and foreign customs, their own ways of thinking and living. That causes some trouble.[1]

The Social Service Department of the Court of Domestic Relations affords an especially good opportunity for coming into relations of confidence with the foreign born and giving them instruction and advice in domestic troubles. As described in a report of the Municipal Court[2] the first purpose of the Court of Domestic Relations is to keep families intact. Consequently, every resource at its command is used to reunite husbands and wives whose quarrels and misunderstandings threaten to destroy their homes and leave their children without parental guardianship. When a complaint is made, on some matter under the jurisdiction of the Court of Domestic Relations, the person complained against is asked to come to the Social Service Department for a "friendly talk" either with a representative of the department or with the presiding judge. The official who was head of this de-

[1] *Proceedings to Inquire into Courts of Inferior Criminal Jurisdiction in Cities of the First Class*, vol. iii, p. 2963. Albany, New York, 1909.
[2] *Report of the Municipal Court of Chicago, 1916–17*, p. 108.

partment at the time of the report shows a clear appreciation of the value of understanding the language and customs of foreign-born clients, in what she says of a social worker in that division, whose transfer to another branch she regrets.

Miss S—— [she says] speaks several languages, and, what is much more important in the business of home mending, she understands the customs and traditions of the foreign women who submit their home worries to the court. Custom has much to do with conduct, and though our foreign-born citizens are rapidly absorbing American ideals and learning "American ways," their conduct must still be judged to a large extent in the light of their national customs. No matter how sympathetic a social adviser may be, she finds it difficult to counsel the woman whose language she does not understand and whose views on home management and the upbringing of children are strange to her.[1]

In contrast to the attitude of this worker toward domestic problems is that of a former judge of the Domestic Relations Court in the same city, whose prescription for the alien husbands guilty of cruelty, desertion, and nonsupport was deportation—the mechanical instead of the psychological method.

The Chicago Municipal Court is well supplied with foreign-born probation officers, the staff including officers of Italian, Polish, Bohemian, Lithuanian, and German nativity or extraction. The chief probation officer of this court thinks that they are likely to be more effective than native Americans in dealing with their own people. The chief probation officer of the Juvenile Court (not a part of the Municipal Court), however, who has the same population to deal with thinks that it is difficult to secure foreign-speaking

[1] *Report of the Municipal Court of Chicago, 1916–17*, p. 114.

probation officers who come up to the standard set by native American probation officers.

Strangely enough, this highly developed modern court has no official salaried interpreters, but has to depend on those called in for special services. The salaried official interpreter, however, is badly needed in a city with so large and so litigious a foreign population.

The judges have attempted to clear out the runners and lawyers and get rid of the exploiting bondsmen, but with not altogether complete success, because here, as elsewhere, their jurisdiction does not reach beyond the precincts of the court itself. Judge Olson says that the runners and lawyers in the Chicago Municipal Court are still a genuine menace.

MUNICIPAL COURTS IN OHIO

The evils of the justice court in Ohio led to the establishment of municipal courts on the general plan of the Chicago court. The court in Cleveland in its civil branch has undoubtedly brought about great improvements as far as the foreign born are concerned. The various foreign-language publications speak of it with approval, and it is well-known to and much used by the immigrant colonies. The fees are comparatively low and there is a much more sympathetic attitude shown toward the foreign born than previously. A real effort seems to be made to understand the foreign-born client and assist him in his problems. This is especially true of the court of small claims called the Court of Conciliation. It is estimated that during its first year some ten thousand people were directly or indirectly saved from arrest through the operation of this court, a large percentage of whom were foreign born.

An interesting feature of the small-claims court is

the work done by a special clerk of the court in preparing cases for trial and in effecting settlements without trial. Perhaps one reason for the success of this work is the fact that a year before a special branch court for the handling of small claims was established, a rule of the newly organized municipal court provided that a court clerk should be designated to assist persons in small cases in drawing and filing the necessary papers required by the Municipal Court procedure, and that this clerk should also endeavor to adjust claims between parties where opportunity offers. The fact that the clerk assigned to these duties, William F. Burke, performed them so well led directly to the organization of the small-claims branch of the court, and his services in fulfilling these particular duties were continued in that court. Through this office thoroughly social and preventive work is accomplished.

This court is exceptional among civil courts in making provision for the services of an interpreter, without cost to the client. But in practice an interpreter is not always on hand.

In the criminal branch of the court, however, there is still much to be desired in the relation of the court to foreign-born clients.

An investigation recently made[1] showed that the criminal branch of the Municipal Court was hardly above the level of the old time police court.

The dignity and decorum desirable in the conduct of the court's business, in order to inspire respect in the immigrant offenders who receive in this court their first impression of the majesty of the law, are conspicuously lacking. Criminal cases are conducted in the old police-court rooms, which, during proceedings,

[1] *Cleveland Foundation Survey of Criminal Justice in Cleveland, 1921.*

are crowded with lawyers, defendants, witnesses, police, hangers-on, and sightseers, many chewing gum and tobacco even when addressing the court. Loud talking in the court room is general, and in order to make themselves heard in this court room lawyers and others have to lean over the bench to address the judge. This produces the impression of a confidential communication, which, although false, lends color to the belief that certain lawyers have "pull with the judge."[1] But observers for the survey saw no attempt to man-handle or intimidate the foreign born who thronged the court. The treatment accorded them was courteous on the whole.[2]

A practice of shifting cases from one judge to another when the calendar gets crowded exposes the clerks in charge of the changes to pressure of solicitation to transfer cases from a "hard" judge to an "easy" judge. And the crowding of cases also prevents proper attention on the part of the judge to individual cases. If a case is of public importance, or has news value, or has interested influential people, it has a chance of securing attention, but the poor or ignorant petty offender gets short shrift. In 1919 the average number of civil cases disposed of, per judge, in the Municipal Court was 2,422. During the same year the number of criminal cases per judge was 11,888—over four times as many.[3]

The judges of this court are characterized in this survey as "inferior in quality and ineffectual in character," but they are generally believed not to be influenced

---

[1] *Cleveland Foundation Survey of Criminal Justice in Cleveland, 1921.* Reginald Heber Smith and Herbert B. Ehrmann, "The Criminal Courts," pp. 51–52, 134.

[2] *Ibid.*, Alfred Bettman, "Prosecution," p. 15.

[3] *Ibid.*, "The Criminal Courts," p. 54.

DEVELOPMENTS IN THE MINOR COURTS

by money considerations; political considerations, however, are openly of weight.[1] The judges are chosen by election, and to serve during election year in the "police court," as the Municipal Court is still popularly termed, is regarded as a political asset. In fact, the schedule of the judges is so arranged that judges facing reëlection are given the opportunity of serving on the criminal side during the preceding nine months.[2]

To secure reëlection or election to some higher judicial position, judges are tempted to use their judicial duties as a means of publicity. In the winter of 1920, it is noted in the report of this survey, a Municipal Court judge made a specialty of fining liquor-law violators—for the most part foreign born making home brew—unprecedented sums.[3]

In this court it was found that certain lawyers of the unscrupulous type described in a previous chapter were handling a large proportion of the cases in the court. Men of ability or fine sensibilities do not care to practice there. And trailing after these lawyers were found the runner and the professional bondsman, with all of their rascalities.[4]

In Cincinnati is found a municipal court organized according to the same general plan and showing a decided improvement over the old justice court which it supplanted. But it has not become sufficiently well known to the immigrant. It is still too expensive to be fully available for his needs, although cheaper than the old justice court as operated in that city, and the procedure has not been sufficiently simplified. Before

[1] *Cleveland Foundation Survey of Criminal Justice in Cleveland, 1921.* "The Criminal Courts," p. 25.
[2] *Ibid.,* p. 43.
[3] *Ibid.,* p. 42.
[4] *Ibid.,* pp. 58–61.

certain of the judges the immigrant secures justice and a fair amount of sympathetic understanding. But in general the judges and other court officials seem to lack a knowledge of the history and customs of the immigrant and an interest in the psychological problems involved, which would give them a sympathetic and understanding attitude toward the foreign born. On the whole the judges have no particular interest in the problems of Americanization, and in fact are often prejudiced to a slight degree against anyone of foreign birth who has had time to become a citizen and has not done so.

And in this court generally is found a certain prejudice against an immigrant if he cannot speak English, and a tendency to regard all non-English-speaking persons as Bolshevists and dangerous radicals against whom it is proper to assume a tyrannical and unsympathetic attitude.

In the criminal branch the assistant city solicitor who prosecutes practically all the immigrant cases is interested in "Americanization," so called, but apparently has a narrowly limited idea of the meaning of the word, and little imagination as to the possibilities of his position for dealing with the immigrants. He does not even profess to have sympathy with them, and feels strongly that the fact that a client has not become naturalized or does not know the English language or understand American customs makes a strong case against him, regardless of the merits of the particular charge that has brought him to the court. In his attitude in the court room he is overbearing and tyrannical, apparently regarding the foreign-born clients as a necessary evil upon whom any great expenditure of time and energy would be a waste.

The number of cases in which an interpreter is

required does not exceed one a day, accordingly no provision has been made for the regular employment of salaried interpreters. Volunteer interpreter assistants are called in when needed, from a list of court attaches and foreign-born merchants in the vicinity. Sometimes they are given a witness fee in payment for their trouble. On the whole this system seems to work with a fair degree of satisfaction in this court. There are still runners, unscrupulous lawyers, professional bondsmen, and unreliable interpreters hanging around, sufficient in number to constitute a real problem, but they are not nearly so great an evil as in the old justice courts.

The Municipal Court and the Juvenile and Domestic Relations court in another Ohio city are in charge of judges who have a sincere and sympathetic desire that the foreign born shall get a square deal at their hands, but both admit that there is a large amount of exploitation by lawyers and runners that they are not able to stop because practically all of it is done outside the court, especially before the case comes to a hearing, when the judge has no cognizance of it. Both courts have salaried interpreters. But in many cases the parties bring their own interpreters, who, in the opinion of the judges, are often found misinterpreting. One of the official interpreters is a woman, a former saloon keeper, who speaks ten different languages; but social workers suspect that she can be and has been bought off on occasion. They have little positive evidence of this nature, but in one case at least a social worker found her giving an intentional misinterpretation which served to favor materially the interests of one of the litigants.

In still another city in Ohio the Municipal Court is found to show a great improvement over the old justice courts. The judges, however, are not all imbued with the most modern social ideals. One of them, a man of considerable ability, seems to have a social point of view in the conduct of his office; another is a literalist in the application of the law, and imposes merciless sentences in many instances. His personal honesty is unquestioned, but he has no idea of preventive justice. The third has no striking characteristics, but the fourth, a former police judge, is commonly supposed to be too lenient with offenders of the underworld. In his own expressions of opinion as to the methods of carrying on the duty of a magistrate, however, he shows sympathy with the idea of justice as preventive and not entirely punitive. The impression prevails that various members of the court are influenced by political considerations.

This court has no official court interpreter, and non-English-speaking clients have to depend upon the various attaches of the court, and upon volunteer interpreters whom the parties in interest may bring.

It is the common impression that the average foreign-born client in this municipal court gets as fair a hearing as the American, and this seems to be corroborated by the general attitude of the judges themselves as expressed in interviews with them. None of them expressed any prejudice against the foreign born as such. In fact, many persons familiar with the court thought that the immigrant had a better chance in court than the American because of the foreign vote, which is solidly organized in this place, in various foreign-born groups under strong leaders.

Complaint of political influence in the Municipal Court is made in another Ohio city, where the presiding judge is considered a clever politician. But he is admitted to be clever and able, and his decisions are based on what seem to him the merits of the case and not on technicalities, so that the social workers in the city are on the whole agreed that he shows an appreciation of the social viewpoint.

In New York City the minor criminal courts of first instance are organized as a coördinated court, known as the Magistrates' Court, under the supervison of a chief magistrate, while the civil courts of first instance are still uncoördinated. In the civil court, however, are found some of the improved methods adopted in the modern small-claims court—provision for conciliation and arbitration, and for trying cases without cost to those who cannot afford to pay. In 1919 about twenty per cent of the cases were tried without cost to the clients.

The law of New York State makes provision for relieving the civil courts by authorizing arbitration outside of the courts. Tribunals composed of one or more persons may be established which may make decisions as binding as those of the court of law, if clients go before them under agreement to accept their decisions. Under these laws an interesting agency has come into being in New York City, which is directly intended to meet certain peculiar needs of one of the religious groups in the city's population. This is the agency called the "Jewish Court of Arbitration."[1] It is an unofficial body, made up of rabbis, and of justices from the city's courts, lawyers, and business men of the Jewish faith. This body is drawn upon to furnish three judges—one justice, one rabbi, and one business man or lawyer—for each session of the court.

[1] Executive offices, Room 416, 38 Park Row, New York City; Louis Richman, Executive Secretary.

THE IMMIGRANT'S DAY IN COURT

An executive secretary receives clients wishing to submit their cases to this court, decides whether the cases are of a nature to appear before the court, and arranges for the hearings. Cases appropriate for consideration by the court are such as involve disputes between two religious congregations or between a congregation and one of its members. This court will also take up domestic troubles, in which it has no legal authority, but acts as conciliator, endeavoring through persuasion and instruction to adjust difficulties between married people so that recourse to a court will be unnecessary.

This court can deal more rapidly and understandingly with such cases as come before it than the ordinary court, because members of it understand the customs and habits of the people, their beliefs, their psychology, and their language. For, although this court is open to all Jewish cases of the kind described, without restriction to any particular country of birth, as a matter of fact the people coming before it are mainly of foreign birth and have been reared in social and religious traditions unfamiliar to the average American magistrate. And the variety of experience represented in this court adds to its effectiveness, The rabbi contributes a specialized knowledge of religious questions, the business man a knowledge of concrete business situations, the members of the legal profession, the knowledge of legal rules and procedure needed to bring the decisions of the court in line with accepted legal practice.

Like other courts of arbitration, this court may also save time by dispensing with many of the formalities of ordinary court procedure, and it has this great advantage for the poor client, that its services are rendered absolutely without cost.

Its sessions are held in a neighborhood accessible to its foreign clients and at hours when they can attend without interruption of their work.

Here, then, is a court that works rapidly, cheaply, and understandingly, for one group of foreign-born clients, and to their satisfaction. It is a type of agency which might well serve as a model for other communities, but up to the present time the court in New York is the only one of this nature found in any of our cities. This court was established only recently, however (February, 1920), and we may hope that eventually the example may be followed in other places.

The reorganized criminal courts are generally admitted to be rendering far better service than the courts they displaced. The magistrates generally are of distinctly higher type than their predecessors. Some of them are of foreign birth or parentage, but more generally of the older immigration than the new.

The magistrates are chosen by appointment of the mayor, and each is assigned by the chief magistrate to the court or the district in which he is to serve. In the district courts the magistrates serve in rotation, any one magistrate remaining in one court only two weeks. These features of the system greatly reduce the chances for establishing local ties and obligations of a political nature that might interfere with the impartiality of the magistrate's decisions.

On the other hand, the chief magistrate assigns certain magistrates to long-time service of a specialized nature, such as dealing with domestic relations or with traffic cases, so that such cases can have the benefit of the special experience or fitness of a given magistrate for dealing with them.

These courts employ salaried interpreters, and the

uniformed police formerly serving as court attendants, who aroused much hard feeling by their rough manner of dealing with persons in the court room, have been replaced by civilian attendants who are generally found to be courteous and considerate, while upholding the dignity of the court.

The magistrates have wide powers of discretion as to the treatment of cases, in which they are assisted by a staff of probation officers.

Under such broad discretionary power, the methods of carrying on the work of a court, the success in administering justice, will depend to a great extent on the personality and social philosophy of the magistrate, and in the New York magistrates' courts we find a wide variety in these respects.

In their decisions, for example, the proportion of cases discharged by different magistrates is found to differ greatly, also the relative proportion of discharges for different offenses. Some magistrates are to be classified as "hard" judges, some as "easy" judges; some are particularly severe in cases of intoxication, but easy on some other offense. Others are easy on intoxication, but come down hard on disorderly conduct; some are severe against both of these forms of offense, but are relatively easy on vagrancy—and so on through the list of offenses.

They differ greatly also in their choice of penalty in cases where the accused person is found to have committed the offense. Some make much use of imprisonment, and little of the suspended sentence or of probation. Some use the suspended sentence freely, and give very few jail sentences. An interesting measurement of these differences, helping to depict the differences in personality of the magistrates, is to be found in the statistical reports of the magistrate's court, showing the decisions of individual magistrates in the various classes of cases.

Consequently the treatment the immigrant receives in the magistrate's court, will depend to some extent on the personality of the particular magistrate before whom he appears. Let us try to picture some of these personalities, in action, one by one, as we see them at work in their courts, or as they have expressed themselves to investigators for this study on the problem of dealing with the foreign born.

Magistrate A may be classed as a "hard" judge, and he is apparently hard on everything alike—intoxication, disorderly conduct, vagrancy, peddling without a license, violation of corporation ordinances. He makes very little use of the suspended sentence and of probation. This magistrate, however, theoretically recognizes the suspended sentence and probation as useful means of treatment, and makes it his practice to consider each case separately, taking all the circumstances into account in determining which penalty shall be employed. He appreciates differences in the kinds of offenses committed by peoples of different nationality, but he thinks there are no marked peculiarities in the way the offenses are committed, or in the circumstances which lead to the commission of the offenses. In his official capacity he tries to instruct the immigrant to the extent of briefly informing him of the requirements of the law and the ordinance which he is charged with having broken. He does not think any changes in the court are needed to help in dealing with the foreign born, but believes that it would be of great practical use to the immigrant and a help to the court to have him taught the English language, respect for and obedience to the laws and ordinances; to have him impressed with the fact that law is supreme in this country, that he should be careful to comply with the requirements of the laws and ordinances, to respect the authority of the police, and not take the law into his own hands, but seek the proper legal tribunal for his remedy.

A snapshot of him as he officiates in his court shows us an elderly gentleman with a strict expression and the general air of a court official that reminds a Russian of the officials he remembered at home under the old régime. It is a hot day and cases are disposed of rapidly. A crippled candy peddler—Jewish—is fined five dollars, but begins to wail loudly about something in Yiddish, which no one understands. Notwithstanding the official provision for interpreters in the New York magistrates' courts, there is none on hand in this court at this time, and a visitor has to act as interpreter. The Jew explains that he cannot pay the fine—he would rather go to the workhouse for two days, as he does not make so much money in that time. The magistrate agrees, but a kind visitor pays the fine and the peddler goes free.

In another case, two Italians have had a fight and one has scratched the other with a knife. The defendant is trying to explain how it happened, with great gesticulation and in the Italian language. Again no one understands. There is no interpreter, but the officer at the door understands Italian, so he is called in. The defendant pleads guilty—he had too much to drink, and in the quarrel used a knife, but no great harm was done. The judge tries to reconcile the two, through the interpreter, but the complainant wants the defendant punished. The case is put over until the next day. Next comes a West Indian who does not know a word of English. With great difficulty he is made to understand that he is to bring his own interpreter if he wants his case heard.

Magistrate B is another "hard" judge in all classes of cases, as far as the proportion of discharges tell the story, but he makes more use of the suspended sentence and less of the workhouse, which mitigates his severity. On a visit to his court an Italian girl, convicted of stealing a waist from her mistress, is seen weeping bitterly. She claims she only borrowed the waist to wear to a party and meant to put it back. The magistrate suspends sentence, gives her some fatherly advice, but tells her he will put her in jail if the offense is repeated.

In the next case an Italian woman complains that the defendant, another Italian, had done something to her little girl—no one can find out what. The chief clerk happens to know a little Italian, translates a few words, and gives up. It turns out that she is speaking the Sicilian dialect. No one in the court knows that language; the chief clerk tries again, and in a few seconds the case is discharged. The mother leaves the court boiling with rage; all signs indicate that she will be in court again before long, for taking the law into her own hands. Then come ten or twelve immigrants, holding money in their hands for a fine which they know is about to be imposed. One dollar each is collected from them, and they walk off satisfied. These are cases of peddling without license.

Magistrate C discharges a greater proportion of his cases than do Magistrates A and B, but still he may be counted among the fairly strict judges. He uses suspended sentence very little. He does not think that the foreign born present any separate problem in the magistrate's court, other than that of securing adequate interpretation, and has noticed no significant differences in the kinds of offenses committed by people of different nationalities, or in the way the offenses are committed, or the circumstances leading to the offense. He is not able to instruct the foreign born in any way during court proceedings except as to the particular law or ordinance which has been violated, and he would not base his own choice of fining, imprisonment, or suspension of sentence on any difference noted in the manner in which different racial varieties would react to those methods of treatment. He thinks that discretion in this regard has no special application to the foreign born.

Magistrate D is even less severe than Magistrate C in holding cases, but he is not what would be called an "easy" judge. Fining and suspended sentence are the forms of decision he makes most usually.

He thinks that the foreign born as such present no different problem from the native born except that they are more apt to infringe minor laws through ignorance, and hence their court experience ought to be viewed as a part of their education. The more serious offenses he thinks are more often committed by the American-born or American-bred children of foreign born. It has been his practice to consider each case separately and to explain briefly the meaning and purpose of the particular statute or ordinance which has been violated. No other person connected with his court has made any systematic effort to do this, but he has frequently noticed that the interpreters emphasize, amplify, or simplify what he has been undertaking to explain. He could follow what they were doing because he understands half a dozen languages himself, although he is not foreign born.

Magistrate E discharges only a small percentage of his cases. But he is not what would be called a hard judge, for he makes great use of the suspended sentence, for all classes of cases.

DEVELOPMENTS IN THE MINOR COURTS

In his court room he is seen to be rather young, kind, and understanding thoroughly the sheep he is shepherding. On the occasion of one visit, a case is brought up of a peddler who has been caught selling in forbidden territory. His excuse is listened to, the judge suspends sentence, but with a little lecture, asking for the man's word of honor not to repeat the offense. Cases which followed were treated in the same general way. Only repeaters were fined, but all were reasoned with.

Magistrate F also discharges a comparatively small proportion of his cases. This magistrate makes great use of the suspended sentence, even more than Magistrate E. In fact, he is one of the magistrates who use it the most frequently. He thinks that difference in nationality rarely has any significance in deciding which form of treatment to use; this is best determined according to the nature of the act and the individual history of the defendant.

In general, he thinks that the problem of the foreign born in the court is the problem of ignorance and poverty, but that certain peculiarities are shown by different nationalities, arising out of the national history and psychology. He finds many differences in the offenses committed by different people. This magistrate has interested himself especially in the development of the probation system, and has worked personally for the reforms embodied in the improved magistrate's court, which he would like to see carried on still further.

Magistrate G discharges a large proportion of his cases and also employs the suspended sentence with frequency. In his court he gives the impression of not being very attentive to his task. He chews tobacco, disposes of the results in full view of the court, sits with half-closed eyes, is constantly yawning, and seems very little interested. As cases are brought before him he seems to make no attempt to grasp any differences involved. In certain cases of peddling without license, the same questions are asked by him of Jew, Pole, or Russian. The interpreter knows so well what is coming that he hardly waits for the judge to ask the question —he repeats it in the foreign language without delay, and all there is left for the magistrate to do is to say "three dollars fine" and the case is over.

A case is brought up involving a quarrel between two Russian Jewish families, resulting in a black eye for the old grandfather of one of them. While the case was going on the magistrate paid little attention, but as the evidence showed that the old man had been hit, his assailant was found guilty by the magistrate. One may suspect that more understanding of the psychology of the people dealt with would have resulted in a different decision. For the Jewish people of this neighborhood are in the habit of fighting over their respective children and their rights, but make up as easily as they fight. In the present instance, when the victim himself, the old man, was told by a bystander that the assailant was locked up and would probably get from three to six months in the workhouse, his face fell, and, when he was asked if he did not want the man punished, he replied, "Oh! Oh! I did not want him to go to prison; I just wanted to scare him. Oh, young man, take my advice and run whenever you see a fight. Let them fight it out between themselves, and make up by themselves."

Magistrate H also discharges a large proportion of his cases and makes great use of both the suspended sentence and probation. His expressed policy is to use probation and suspended sentence wherever possible, then fines, and finally, in extreme cases only, jail sentences.

He thinks the immigrant is a problem in the courts largely because of a mistaken idea given him by unscrupulous politicians that if he gets into trouble the politicians will get him out; partly because he has not been educated in American ideals. This magistrate notes differences in the kinds of offenses committed by different people among the foreign born. In the court he always takes great pains to explain our laws and customs to the foreign born, and endeavors to make a better citizen out of the immigrant client before he leaves the court than he was when he came in. He is always careful to see that the immigrant understands his rights before the court, and takes pains to look after his interests when he is not represented by counsel.

Magistrate I is foreign born himself, and shows in his court an appreciation of the difficulties of the foreign born. In one case the defendant, a man of the same nationality as the judge, was brought into court on the charge that he had entered an apartment with the purpose of stealing something. His explanation was that he had made a mistake in the number and got into the wrong house. The magistrate accepted this excuse and let the man go, probably with more assurance that he was right in his judgment than a magistrate who was unfamiliar with the characteristics of that nationality could have been.

Magistrate J is scholarly and somewhat severe, with a high appreciation of the responsibilities and dignities of his office. He notes that the larger proportion of minor offenses are committed by the foreign born, but thinks that these offenses do not necessarily involve any malice toward society or its members. They are largely due to ignorance. The immigrant is a problem in the courts because of his tendency to colonize in little isolated groups, in which only the foreign-language newspapers are read and only the foreign language is spoken. He would remedy these conditions by teaching English to the foreign born, compulsorily if necessary, and would break up the foreign districts.

So far as the courts are concerned, the most that can be done he thinks is to use every opportunity to impress on the people as they come before the judge the meaning of the American law and bring to their attention the fact that they are expected to learn the English language and become American citizens.

When foreign-born clients appear before him he always asks them how long they have been in this country and whether they are citizens, and can speak English or not. He does this as a species of Americanization propaganda. He thinks that much of this is wasted on the person to whom it is addressed, but that it has a wholesome effect on persons in the court room. In his opinion foreign-born clients often pretend an ignorance of English when they understand it well enough, so that they will have the extra time to frame their answers which is afforded when an interpreter is used. Notwithstanding this feeling of distrust, however, he always postpones a non-English-speaking case until a day when the interpreter of the required nationality will be in court. Occasionally a court attendant or an attorney well-known to the judge is allowed to act as interpreter.

He does not try to instruct any of these foreign-born offenders in the meaning of the laws from the bench, for he does not consider this a judicial function. In the use of the different forms of penalty, he says that in his court "the foreign born receive the same measure of justice as the native born," this meaning, presumably, that his relative use of fine, suspended sentence, imprisonment, and probation is not determined in any way by the nationality of the offender. And he says that he sees no reason why justice should be more tender with the foreign born than with others.

Summing up the general impression made by these individual magistrates, it cannot be said that in the handling of the ordinary cases of small offenses any special prejudice against the foreign born or any marked discrimination is shown. A number of the magistrates have considered the foreign client as a distinct variety worthy of study, and some of them try to give him the instruction he needs to enlighten him as to his rights and duties. Too many of them, however, are not aware of any special need for studying the nature of the foreign-born client, and are not giving him, as a distinct social type, the benefit of that intelligent discrimination on the basis of knowledge which is the essence of discretionary treatment.

In some of these courts the field agents found that interpreters were not available. The service, however, is perhaps as good as it is practically possible to supply. The interpreters, who are engaged for their full time and paid a salary, are selected from lists prepared as a result of civil-service examinations. The requirements for court interpreter are that he shall know at least three languages besides English, that he shall speak English well, and that he shall be of good reputation and of good moral character. The examinations are strict, and are both oral and written. Each court is supposed to be equipped with at least one permanent interpreter who knows three or four languages. These are usually a related group, such as Yiddish, Russian and Polish, or Italian and French, or Greek and

Turkish—related, that is, not necessarily as members of the same linguistic family, but as those which a person living in a given country might have occasion to use. But by no means all of the languages for which interpretation is necessary in some one court may be in the group spoken by the official interpreter. To one district court, for example, in which the one official interpreter speaks Yiddish, Russian, and Polish, many Italian cases are brought, and many involving persons from other Mediterranean countries.

No provision is made in the magistrates' courts for the interpretation of any dialect, which perhaps might seem an unreasonable requirement. But in a large city there may be a sufficiently large colony of Sicilians, for example, who do not speak the literary Italian, to make it as necessary to have an interpreter who speaks the Sicilian dialect as to have one who speaks Greek. There is frequent need in New York, also, for the interpretation of the Ukrainian dialect.

To interpret languages not provided for in the staff of interpreters, the court must use volunteers. One of the court attachés may be called upon, or a client may bring in a friend to interpret. Some of the magistrates consider the volunteer interpreters untrustworthy. One has refused to allow them in his court because he has found them collecting fees from parties to proceedings, and one magistrate says that the employment of volunteer interpreters is of questionable legality.

New York State, like Massachusetts, makes provision in the law against the improper solicitation of trade for lawyers, under which proceedings may be taken to check the runner evil. But apparently little or nothing has been done under this act. The magistrates themselves have taken measures to keep their courts clear of runners and to a great extent have succeeded, but the evil is not entirely ended. One of the magistrates, when asked for his opinion as to the extent of the trouble, said that the runner and the shyster lawyer had been disposed of quite thoroughly, except in one or two of the courts in which it had been found very difficult to clear them out. Another says that they work so much under cover that it is hard to get at them; another considers the progress made very great, but believes that only drastic remedies will eliminate the evil altogether, which under present conditions seems to defy all assaults upon it. Another magistrate says that personally he has been very successful in waging war on the runner, lawyer, and professional bondsman because he has made them fear a jail sentence at his hands, but he thinks that this class of exploiters is still a menace.

The probation officers of the New York magistrates' courts are appointed after a thorough civil-service examination, conducted by experts in probation and social-service work. This assures not only general intelligence, but some knowledge of scientific principles of dealing with persons. But special knowledge of habits and customs of foreign people are not among the requirements, and on the list of probation officers we find only a few persons of foreign nationality—mostly of Irish or Jewish extraction.

The chief probation officer, however, has a clear conception of the foreign offender as a type, and of the importance of educating him.

Many offenders are found to be foreign born [he says], and often they have broken the law because of ignorance and misunderstanding. Some of these who have not understood why they have been arrested and have been bitter and sullen at what they considered injustice, now through the practical helpfulness of the probation officers have come to understand the reason for the laws they have broken. Probation officers of their own nationality have been able to bring them the great message of democracy and have inspired them with the desire to become not only citizens, but public-spirited and valuable ones.[1]

And in cases of delinquent girls, he notes that the probation officer must educate the foreign mother, who is continuing in this country customs and habits suitable at home, which do not fit the new conditions.

NEW YORK COURT OF DOMESTIC RELATIONS

Attached to the New York magistrate's court is a specialized court of Domestic Relations. This court has a staff of interpreters and probation officers, and makes use of volunteer social workers who assist the judge by making preliminary investigations. The probation officers are not especially equipped with a knowledge of the languages and customs of foreign peoples and the volunteer workers represent religious rather than racial or national differences. On the staff is to be found one colored worker, who would have special knowledge of the customs and habits of thought of her own racial group, and during the progress of this study a volunteer worker with a knowledge of the Italian language and of Italian customs was detailed to the court to look after Italian cases. Cases in which her services were needed were so numerous that she was not able in the half-time service she was able to give, to make sufficiently detailed investigation or do sufficient follow-up work for them. Of the clients under her care somewhat over a third could not speak English, somewhat over a fifth could not speak it well, less than half could use the

[1] "The Progress of Probation," *Magistrates' Courts*, New York, 1920, p. 17.

language adequately. To meet the need of the foreign cases coming before the court, at least two workers who know the languages and customs of the Eastern Jews could be kept busy, also, one similarly equipped for the Italians, and one, who should know several Slavic languages, for the Slavic cases.

In the treatment of cases in the Court of Domestic Relations notwithstanding the fact that the law recognizes the right of the wife to leave the husband and get separate support, the officials of the court hold to the same leading idea found in the work of the Chicago court—that it is their business to keep as many families together as possible, and, if husband and wife are living apart, to induce them to come together again, on account of their children.

The officials of the New York court believe that social workers should not encourage a woman in feeling that she may be right in separating from her husband, because if she thought that she would be upheld in such a step she would be much less likely to attempt to put up with him. They consider that even in case a man and wife are hopelessly uncongenial they are better off together, financially, because one man's earnings can better support one household than two, and socially, because without a home the man will drift about and become even more demoralized.

The usual procedure at the hearing in cases where a couple is separated and there is no moral obliquity on either side is to ask first the woman and then the man whether he or she wishes to go back to the other. If one wishes to go back, the other is urged strongly to do the same, with little or no consideration of more intimate facts of the family history or the characteristics of both parties, or whether they have or have not made previous attempts at a reconciliation. As a matter of fact, in most of the cases the family does not have recourse to the court until after genuine efforts have already been made to effect an adjustment. This slowness to bring a situation to court until it is almost hopeless is probably accentuated among the Italians on account of a general distrust of our courts and legal methods, but it is found in cases involving other nationalities as well.

THE MUNICIPAL COURT OF PHILADELPHIA

The Municipal Court of Philadelphia is a minor court which is distinctly recognizing a duty toward the foreign born. The policy of the court, as outlined by President Judge Charles L. Brown, is based on principles of especial value for the treatment of the immigrant. He not only emphasizes the modern doctrine of adjusting treatment to the individual according to his nature and needs, but brings strongly into view an aspect of the relation between court and client that is often overlooked, the client's reaction to the action of the court and his right to be considered not simply as a passive recipient of a ready-made "justice" handed down to him, but as an active coöperator in the result.

Justice in the modern social court [he says] should lay aside her sword and cast off the bandage from her eyes. She should investigate through her probation system before trial, and not only after judgment, and she should weigh her evidence in the suppliant's presence and should let her suppliant see what she is about.[1]

Of the Municipal Court, he says:

We are studying impulses—conduct as expressed in personality—inclination. . . . The modern emphasis is on per-

[1] *Report of National Probation Association, Thirteenth Conference, 1919*, p. 79.

sonality, on its value and sacredness; the new insistence is on the right of independent judgment.[1]

And he distinctly recognizes the foreign born as a special human variety to be studied and understood. He says on this point:

Very often when a Polish couple or an Italian couple or a Jewish couple come before me in court, I find it very difficult to understand what the cause of their trouble may be, because in the first place they speak a different language, and, in the second place, their manners, their customs, their standards and ways of living are totally different from ours.

The interpreter, whether he is Italian, Polish, Lithuanian, Russian, Czech, or Jewish, clarifies the whole situation for me, which enables me to dig into the roots of the matter and to see and to understand, so that justice administered by the court may be dispensed more equitably. It is a process of drawing out the good that is in the individuals by sympathy and understanding.[2]

Making clear the necessity for coöperation of the client in the process of rendering of justice, he says we must not consider the family or the man or the woman as a court's problem of the court that we are solving.

We must think of ourselves as if we were on the other side of the bar of justice; we must ask, "What does this man or this woman or this child think of his or her own problem?" . . . We must keep in mind the thought, "What does this man or this woman expect from justice?" . . . We must admit the man or woman who is before the court into a place where he or she may have a share in shaping the legal decision. The legal decision is the man's future. No man's future in America can be denied him.[3]

[1] *Report of the National Probation Association, Thirteenth Conference, 1919*, p. 80.

[2] The Philadelphia *Record*, February 29, 1920.

[3] *Report of the National Probation Association, Thirteenth Conference, 1919*, p. 79.

THE IMMIGRANT'S DAY IN COURT

He sees also the court's possibilities for the task of Americanization in its best meaning, and in this aspect also he insists on the right and necessity of self-determination on the part of the immigrant himself, to bring about the desired results.

He says:

> To me the process of Americanization is one of interpretation—interpretation in its broadest and finest sense. . . . We must not only interpret America to the immigrants, but, the immigrants to America. . . . You cannot club Americanization into immigrants. They had too much use of force in their native countries. . . . It is right to say to the immigrant, "You must learn English." That is good and fine, but it should, however, be tactfully done. We must not forget that even when the immigrant knows English we still do not know him. He may know English and not know us of America. We need a link, and that link I find to be the foreign-language workers. . . . We have in our courts thousands of immigrant cases every year who often come into clash with the law because they do not know our ways. I do not know what I would do if we had no interpreters to send into the homes to adjust these cases.[1]

With this attitude about the learning of English compare the attitude of certain other judges as shown in decisions from the bench. In a court in the Middle West, a Lithuanian who had been in the country for nine years and was suing for damages in an accident case asked, through his attorney, for an interpreter.

> This man doesn't need an interpreter [the judge said]. He needs a school teacher, and I am going to give him a chance to get one. This case will be continued until July 1st to allow him to learn English. If he makes enough progress by that time the case will be heard, otherwise it will be continued again and again until he is able to speak our language.

[1] The Philadelphia *Record*, February 29, 1920.

236

DEVELOPMENTS IN THE MINOR COURTS

This man has applied for his first papers, but has never taken out his final papers. He wants all the benefits accorded a citizen, yet he doesn't bother to learn the language or to take enough interest in the country and its institutions to understand them. He has been sending his money back to his wife and child, who are still in Lithuania. I have no patience with a man of his type.

In a New York City court not long ago a client was similarly "sentenced," and in another city in New York State a judge refused an interpreter in a desertion case to a woman who could not speak English intelligently, although she was born in the city where the trial was taking place, and he stopped the trial, telling the woman that she must learn English before he would hear her case. He considered that it was her own fault that she could not speak English, and urged her to go to night school at once, overlooking the fact that the woman was not illiterate and that she had been educated as the law permitted, in a parochial school where English was not taught.

In the Philadelphia court the probation officers are sufficient in number to attend to their work carefully and well. They are not, for the most part, equipped with a knowledge of foreign languages and customs, but where they fail in entering into relation with the foreign client for this reason, the services of the interpreter are made use of. Provision is also made for foreign-language workers to make preliminary investigations in the social branches of the court.

An especially interesting feature of the work of this court is the use made of the interpreters as social workers. The interpreters themselves are of unusually high character. On the staff are editors, teachers, men of high culture and standards, representing the principal nationalities dealt with. When the probation officer has a case on hand in which he fails to make himself understood, or himself to understand the attitude of the persons involved, he calls to his aid one of the interpreters.

In a domestic case, for example, the interpreter will pay a visit to the home, and, as expressed by one of them, "through his understanding of what is in the minds of man and wife can explain to them in their own language the changed conditions under which they are living and thus gain their confidence, where a social worker ignorant of their language and customs would only arouse their suspicion and resentment. . . ." In cases turned over to them, he said, further, the Municipal Court interpreters rarely fail to adjust the family differences in the home without further recourse to court proceedings. In from 90 to 95 per cent of such cases the parties are reconciled and the husband becomes law abiding.

And this is not all that is attempted and accomplished by the interpreter in his function of social worker. At the very start he finds out whether the man is a citizen or not, and, if he is not, urges him to become such and aids him by instruction in our laws and in the procedure necessary for naturalization. But no official pressure is brought to bear on him to make him acquire citizenship. The man's confidence and consent are gained through persuasion, and he undertakes the duties of citizenship as a matter of choice, not of necessity. Nor is this all. As explained by one of the interpreters:

After the immigrant has agreed to take out his first papers, the interpreter has little, if any, difficulty in the process of assimilation, and not only has his subject become a good family man, but the whole family rapidly become Americanized. If the man is out of work, the interpreter gets him employment. He sees that the children are sent to school, or, if old enough, that they get suitable work.

238

DEVELOPMENTS IN THE MINOR COURTS

The relations of the members of the family to one another become different, he says, further; the head of the house shows more consideration for the women and children, the wife begins to dress and act like American women, the family larder is kept in good condition, the father begins to patronize the savings bank and is well on the way toward being a good American citizen. Perhaps this picture is a little too highly colored to cover all of the cases, perhaps some of these things would have happened without the aid of the interpreter, but at any rate the principle of operation is sound.

But even in this highly socialized court, carried on according to the principles laid down by the president judge for individualized treatment, the visitor to the Court of Domestic Relations will note a rather general tendency on the part of the judge to disregard objections raised by the wife against returning to her husband, or, on the other hand, by the husband against returning to the wife, and urge the coming together of separated couples as a general policy, without full regard for the special situation in each case.

THE MINOR COURTS SUMMARIZED

From this rapid survey of the minor courts dealing with the foreign born in the ordinary civil and criminal cases, it appears that in the lowest court, that of the justice of the peace or the court of similar functions under a different name, there is much actual abuse and defrauding of the immigrant, in both civil and criminal cases.

In courts of the next higher grade, in which no opportunities are presented to the judges for direct money-making out of the immigrant because they are paid by a salary and have no share in the returns for court costs, we do not find open swindling of the immigrant by the higher officials of the court. We do find, however, the court of this type frequently charged with conducting its operations in obedience to political influences. But this frequently results to the advantage of the foreign-born client in a material sense, if his national group is sufficiently important to count as a political factor. This is especially likely to happen where judges are elected in their own small local districts to serve in the district. It is not, however, to the advantage of the immigrant in a moral sense. It does not set before him a high ideal of American justice. In such courts he learns that the important matter in a case is not the right of the client, but his influence with some one in power. And he should not be blamed for his low standards if he has acquired them in the court itself.

Some of the minor courts, found to be carefully guarding the strictly legal rights of the foreign-born client, show a lack of consideration in personal dealings with him during the progress of his case, and a certain amount of contempt for his ignorance and his strange ways, that cannot but hinder the growth in him of a feeling of friendly confidence in the court.

Improvements in the minor courts intended for the general good of all classes of clients have been of benefit to the foreign born. The small-claims court, wherever it is found, is of great service to the immigrant client. But these courts are as yet too few in number to come anywhere near to filling the need for rapid and cheap adjudication of civil cases.

The enlargement of powers of discretion in the courts has opened up a greater possibility of adjusting treatment to the actual needs of the immigrant. But in practice, for all classes of cases, the detailed understanding of the problems involved, the equipment of information and technique needed as a basis for discretionary action, are not as yet as widely extended among our court officials as are their powers of discretion.

Many of the judges have apparently not arrived at any general principles for governing the exercise of discretion. Many of them have not acquired the appreciation of human varieties that is needed to apply the right remedy in the particular case. They seem to be especially lacking in knowledge of the foreign-born client as a special variety, worthy of study. We also find a lack of that feeling of sympathy with the type, which goes so far toward making the modern method of treatment successful. The judge who deals with juvenile cases looks at the child as an object of interest, a human value to be saved from depreciation and destruction; there is no such general feeling about the immigrant client, who is just as strictly the product of his heredity and experiences as the child, who is in many instances just as ignorant and irresponsible, and, in many instances, also, is just as susceptible to treatment. It is too much the practice on the part of judges to hold the foreign-born client to the same standard of knowledge and responsibility to which it is fair to hold the native-born American; to assume that our standards of right and duty, our principles of conduct, are intuitive possessions of all "good" human beings, and that if they are rejected the person who does so is deliberately "bad."

Few of the judges are familiar with the languages or the habits and customs of foreign-born clients. Only in the largest cities do we find a few judges of foreign birth or descent who do understand the language of their fellow countrymen and something of their customs.

Probably hardly any of the native-born judges have this equipment.

And only in the largest cities do we find probation officers having knowledge of the language and customs of the foreign-born clients. And where these are found they, too, are mostly of foreign birth or descent.

With neither the judge nor the probation officer understanding the foreign-born client, recourse must be had to the interpreter. But even he, so indispensable a link between the non-English-speaking client and most of the courts in the country, is not always available. In the smallest places and the lowest courts, no official interpreter is employed. The non-English-speaking client has no direct and official means of communication with the court. Of the minor courts employing official interpreters, a large proportion pay them by fees, opening the way to the abuses we have seen connected with the fee system. Even in the larger cities the smaller national groups may be unrepresented by an interpreter.

The difficulties in the way of making provision for these deficiencies cannot be altogether removed. We cannot, in practice, insist that a judge, a probation officer, or even an interpreter of his own nationality be provided for every variety of foreign client who comes before every court.

As a matter of fact it would not be altogether desirable to do so. It would not be desirable in court treatment of the foreign born to segregate them into groups to be dealt with only by representatives of their own nationality. This would tend to perpetuate the very isolation and lack of assimilation that we are trying to put an end to.

The foreign-born judge or probation officer who understands the foreign side of the relation into which the foreign-born client is to be brought may not know the American side as well as the native American; furthermore, he may bring to his task social or class prejudices which are as bad perhaps for the client as race prejudices. A tendency of the foreign-born resident of this country, who has succeeded in raising himself above the level of the newly arrived immigrant, to lord it over his poorer and more ignorant fellow countrymen and to impress upon them and upon his American associates his own superiority, has been frequently noticed, and may conceivably show itself in the relation of judge to client and of probation officer to client.

But if we cannot require foreign birth, or knowledge of the foreign languages, on the part of the judge and the probation officer, we can at least ask that the judge have added to his legal knowledge a certain broad sociological and psychological equipment, and at least some knowledge of the racial varieties with which he deals. And we can certainly ask that the probation officer who is to deal with the foreign born be definitely tested in knowledge of foreign-born peoples, since he has to come into long and intimate contact with his clients and carry on with them a distinctly educative process. It would be desirable, but we probably could not require, in all cases, that he should understand the language of his probationers.

Especial effort should be made, however, to increase the supply of competent interpreters, and to include in their equipment so much of the qualifications of the social worker as would enable the interpreter to supplement the work of the probation officer who is unfamiliar with foreign languages, but does understand the principles of probation and the institutions of this country.

243

VII

THE IMMIGRANT WORKINGMAN BEFORE THE COURT

So far we have seen the immigrant before the court in the ordinary cases arising in the activities of everyday life—cases of civil claims for some money loss, cases of the sort of minor offenses which appear on court calendars year in and year out.

There is another, special class of cases, occurring not so frequently or regularly, in which the immigrant, however, is as vitally concerned, and in which impartial treatment by the courts is of as great importance as in the types of cases already considered.

These are the cases in which a workingman comes before the court because of something he has done in connection with the operations of a labor union, when occupied in the attempt to adjust the relations between employers and employed.

It is natural that the handling of such cases in the courts should be of especial interest to the immigrant, for a large proportion of the working people are immigrants, and nearly all of the immigrants are working people.

First of the immigrant's needs is to make a living, and unfair treatment that thwarts him in this necessary activity will be as deeply resented by him as any species of injustice—perhaps more deeply than any other.

PICKETING

The labor cases in which the rank and file of the immigrant workers are most closely involved personally are those arising in connection with picketing during a strike.

In considering how these cases are treated, the first question to ask is: How does the law itself regard picketing? What is picketing, in the definition of the law? Is picketing in itself legally permissible or not permissible?

Legal questions arising from the operations of labor unions show in this field also the strain put upon the old framework of technical law when new conditions arise which were not contemplated when the law was laid down, so that modifications and adjustments of the law are necessary in order to prevent a failure of substantial justice in the administration of the law according to established technical rules.

The labor union is a comparatively new institution, a growing organism, which the old formulæ of the law as yet fail to cover completely and satisfactorily. The courts, in the attempt to adjust old law to the new situation, have to fall back upon special reinterpretations of old principles, and in the process of tucking a new meaning inside of an old word, of drawing a new situation under the cover of an old definition, there is much room for choice and much room for disagreement. And the choices made, the new meanings added, the cases included under the old headings, will necessarily depend somewhat upon the general point of view of the person making the new interpretation.

In court decisions on labor cases there might, then, naturally be found all degrees of stretching of an analogy, and all degrees of variation in judgment on a given situation on the part of the interpreting judges, which it would not be unfair to ascribe in part to their general views on social and economic problems.

THE IMMIGRANT'S DAY IN COURT

DECISIONS ON THE NATURE AND LEGALITY OF PICKETING

A survey of judicial decision in the courts of this country, in cases relating to picketing, reveal wide differences of opinion, both as to what picketing is and as to whether picketing in and of itself is lawful, the latter question, in fact, somewhat involving the former.

Certain judges regard picketing as an activity which necessarily involves intimidation or violence. One says:

> To picket complainant's premises in order to intercept their teamsters or persons going there to trade is unlawful. It itself is an act of intimidation. . . . It will not do to say that these pickets are thrown out for the purpose of peaceable argument and persuasion. They are intended to intimidate and coerce.[1]

Other judges accept a definition of picketing which does not include intimidation or violence as part of its essential nature. According to this view, if picketing does not involve violence and intimidation, it may be lawful. The courts of Ohio, Minnesota, Montana, New York, Oklahoma, and New Hampshire recognize peaceful picketing as legal.[2]

The courts of California, Illinois, and Michigan in general follow the doctrine that all picketing is illegal.[3]

But even in the states where picketing is generally recognized as legal individual judges may in effect declare all picketing illegal. In the New York Supreme Court, Justice Erlanger ruled that, although the New York courts had held that they will countenance a certain kind of picketing as legal, the purpose of picketing

---

[1] Justice Grant, Peck *vs.* Railway Teamsters' Union, Michigan, 1898, 77 N. W. 13.

[2] Truax *et al. vs.* Corrigan *et al.*, Supreme Court of the United States, 1921, 257 U. S. 42 Sup. Ct. 124.

[3] Francis Bowes Sayre, *A Selection of Cases on Labor Law*, p. 213.

made it necessary to carry it on in such a manner that it was likely to become unlawful. He says:

> Picketing unaccompanied by threats and intimidation is a useless weapon. Its effectiveness and its very essence is in the terror that it excites. If done peaceably it would be futile.[1]

Justice Van Siclen also of the New York Supreme Court made substantially the same ruling a few days earlier. He said:[2]

> To my mind there can be no lawful picketing, because if it is lawful picketing it can be of no use to the union. The purpose of picketing is interference one way or another. The only reason human beings do it is to try to injure some one.

Judges may even declare picketing illegal when they admit the possibility of peaceful picketing and agree that in the case in question there has been no violence. Judge Mitchell says:[3]

> It is further urged that the strikers, through their committees, only exercised . . . their right to talk to the new men to persuade them not to go to work. There was no such right. These men were there presumably under contract with the plaintiff, and certainly in search of work, if not yet actually under pay. They were not at leisure and their time, whether their own or their employer's, could not lawfully be taken up, and their progress interfered with, by these or any other outsiders, on any pretense or under any claim of right to argue or persuade them to break their contracts. Even, therefore, if the arguments and persuasion had been confined to lawful means, they were exerted at an improper time, and were an interference with the plaintiff's rights which made the perpetrators liable for any damages the plaintiff suffered in consequence.

[1] Pre Catalan *vs.* International Federation of Workers, etc., N. Y. *Law Journal*, March 23, 1921, p. 2126.
[2] New York *Times*, March 15, 1921.
[3] O'Neil *vs.* Behanna, Pennsylvania, 1897, 37 Atl. 843.

THE IMMIGRANT'S DAY IN COURT

And in the interpretation of what constitutes intimidation, another ground for difference of judicial opinion is found. One judge says:

There is and can be no such thing as peaceful picketing any more than there can be chaste vulgarity or peaceful mobbing or lawful lynching. When men want to converse or persuade, they do not organize a picket line. . . . The argument seems to be that anything short of physical violence is lawful. One man can be intimidated only when knocked down. But the peaceful, law-abiding man can be and is intimidated by gesticulations, by menaces, by being called harsh names, and by being followed or compelled to pass by men known to be unfriendly.[1]

Another judge admitted that in the case before him there had been

. . . no public disturbance, no physical injury, no direct threats of personal violence or of actual attack on or destruction of tangible property, as a means of intimidation or coercion. But I do not understand that intimidation . . . necessarily presupposes personal injury or the threat thereof. The clear weight of authority undoubtedly is that a man may be intimidated into doing or refraining from doing by fear of loss of business, property, or reputation.[2]

Two recent decisions of the United States Supreme Court are of interest.

One[3] involved the interpretation of Section 20 of the Clayton Act. This section is an attempt to establish a definite rule of law governing the issue of restrain-

[1] District Judge McPherson, Atchison, Topeka, and Santa Fe Railway Company *vs*. Gee, U. S. Circuit Court, 1905, 139 Fed. 582.

[2] Vice Chancellor Green, of New Jersey, Barr *vs*. Essex Trades Council, New Jersey, 1894, 30 Atl. 881.

[3] American Steel Foundries *vs*. Tri-City Central Trades Council *et al.*, Supreme Court of the United States, 1921, 257 U. S. Decided December 5, 1921, 42 Sup. Ct. 72.

ing orders in cases between employers and employees which involve disputes concerning terms or conditions of employment. That portion of the section especially applying to picketing provides that:

. . . no such restraining order or injunction shall prohibit any person or persons, whether singly or in concert, from terminating any relation of employment, or from ceasing to perform any work or labor, or from recommending, advising, or persuading others by peaceful means to do so; or from attending at any place where any such person or persons may lawfully be, for the purpose of peacefully obtaining information, or from peacefully persuading any person to work or abstain from working.

The decision of the court in this case turns on the definition of "peaceful" and "lawful" in the section. The decision says:

How far may men go in persuasion and communication and still not violate the right of those whom they would influence?

We are a social people, and the accosting by one of another in an inoffensive way and an offer by one to communicate and discuss information with a view to influencing the other's action are not regarded as aggression or a violation of that other's rights. If, however, the offer is declined, as it may rightfully be, then persistence, importunity, following, and dogging become unjustifiable annoyance and obstruction which is likely to savor of intimidation. From all of this the person sought to be influenced has a right to be free and his employer has a right to have him free.

The nearer this importunate intercepting of employees or would-be employees is to the place of business, the greater the obstruction and interference with the business and especially with the property right of access of the employer. Attempted discussion and argument of this kind in such proximity is certain to attract attention and congregation of the curious, or, it may be, interested bystanders, and thus to increase the obstruction as well as the aspect of intimidation which the situation quickly assumes. In the present case the three or four groups of picketers were made up of from four to twelve in a group. They constituted the picket line. . . . It is idle to talk of peaceful communication in such a place and under such conditions. The numbers of the pickets in the groups constituted intimidation. *The name "picket" indicated a militant purpose, inconsistent with peaceful persuasion.* The crowds they drew made the passage of the employees to and from the place of work one of running the gauntlet. Persuasion or communication attempted in such a presence and under such conditions was anything but peaceful and lawful. . . . Our conclusion is that picketing thus instituted is unlawful and cannot be peaceable and may be properly enjoined by the specific term because its meaning is clearly understood in the sphere of the controversy by those who are parties to it. We are supported in that view by many well-reasoned authorities, although there has been contrariety of view.[1]

In consequence, the court refused to accept a modification of the injunction ordered by the Circuit Court of Appeals, which added the words "in a threatening or intimidating manner" to the act of picketing enjoined.

This qualification [says the decision] seems to us inadequate. In actual result it leaves compliance largely to the discretion of pickets. It ignores the necessary element of intimidation in the presence of groups as pickets. . . . The phrase really recognizes as legal that which bears the sinister name of "picketing" which it is to be observed Congress carefully refrained from using in Section 20.

That there can be no doubt of the intention of this decision, a reference to it in the opinion of the court in the second case referred to says:

[1] American Steel Foundries *vs.* Tri-City Central Trades Council, Supreme Court of the United States, 257 U. S. Opinion of the court delivered by Mr. Chief Justice Taft, December 5, 1921, 42 Sup.Ct. 72.

IMMIGRANT WORKINGMAN BEFORE COURT

We have but recently considered the clauses of Section 20 of the Clayton Act. (American Steel Foundries *vs.* Tri-City Trades Council.) We held that under these clauses picketing was unlawful, and that it might be enjoined as such, and that *peaceful picketing was a contradiction in terms* which the statute sedulously avoided.[1]

The effect of this decision is in the first place to restrict the activities that may be lawfully carried on for purposes of observation and persuasion to such an extent that anything which may be called "picketing," as generally understood, whether "peaceful" or not, is deprived of the protection of the Clayton Act, and turned over to the discretion of individual courts as before the passage of the Act.

Furthermore, the declaration that there is no such thing as peaceful picketing will tend to influence future judicial decisions toward the same conclusion.

In the second case referred to,[2] a section of the State Code of Arizona, embodying substantially the same provisions as Section 20 of the Clayton Act, was declared unconstitutional. This decision has the effect not only of removing the protection of this section in this state, but of discouraging other states from establishing similar rules of law.

In a still more recent case[3] a temporary injunction was issued restraining the defendants not only from overt acts of hindrance and obstruction, but from peaceful persuasion of employees or would-be employees, and

[1]William Truax *et al. vs.* Michael Corrigan *et al.*, Supreme Court of the United States, 257 U. S. Decided December 19, 1921, 42 Sup. Ct. 124.

[2] *Ibid.*

[3]U. S. *vs.* Railway Employes' Department of the American Federation of Labor *et al.*, U. S. District Court, Northern District of Illinois, September 25, 1922.

251

even from being "unnecessarily" in the vicinity of the places of employment concerned in the strike.

From these recent, important instances it might appear that the present tendency of the courts is toward greater and greater restriction of picketing.

Some ten years ago it appeared that in general the law regarded peaceful picketing as legal. [1]

That this is also true of the present time is the view of United States Supreme Court Justice Brandeis, who said in 1921:

By no great majority the prevailing judicial opinion in America inclines toward the legality of peaceful picketing.[2]

"One cannot read the opinions," says Groat,[3] however, "without feeling that many judges admit the legality with reluctance," and that where they do admit it, it is most frequently in cases where violence and intimidation have been most flagrant, so that an unfavorable decision can be rendered on that ground, and "where the acts are less flagrant, and the picket has been conducted in a more orderly and peaceful manner, these general statements of the lawfulness of the picket in itself give way to finer spun definitions

[1] Judge Stimson in his handbook concluded that at the time of writing the law had . . . "pretty well settled down to the view that picketing, for the purpose of mere persuasion of workmen not to take employment, and not attended with any disorder or physical and moral intimidation, is now held legal; at least when conducted in a reasonable manner and with not too great a crowd."

Stimson, *Handbook to the Labor Law of the United States*, p. 290.

[2] Dissenting opinion in Truax *et al.* vs. Corrigan *et al.*, Supreme Court of the United States, 257 U. S. Decided December 19, 1921, 22 Sup. Ct. 124.   See also Francis Bowes Sayre, *A Selection of Cases on Labor Law*, 1922, p. 211.   "According to this weight of authority mere peaceful picketing, if it involves no intimidation, is not illegal."

[3] Groat, *Attitude of American Courts in Labor Cases*, pp. 128-9.

of intimidation, to the drawing of the line so that the boundaries of lawful picketing are considerably narrowed." "The conclusion suggested by the opinions is that judges do not look with favor upon the picket, but that they are led to admit its legality within very narrow limits by the force of logical inference flowing from well-known and generally accepted legal principles."[1]

Whatever may be the general trend of opinion it is clear that decisions in individual cases vary, and the principles expressed vary from one judge to another, even under the prevailing judicial practice of considering previously decided cases of weight in establishing a principle. Furthermore, judges may not only disagree with one another in the doctrines on which different decisions are based, but may disagree as to the meaning of the same decision. In the case of American Steel Foundries, the majority of the court thought they were establishing the principle that picketing in itself was unlawful because it could not be peaceful. Justice Brandeis, on the other hand, in a dissenting opinion in the case of Truax v. Corrigan, says, "This court has recently held (American Steel Foundries) that peaceful picketing is not unlawful."

Passing along down the line from the highest court of the United States through the court hierarchy, noting the varying decisions, until we come finally to

[1] This attitude is well expressed in the description of a parallel situation in England: "The practice of picketing has, therefore, received explicit legislative sanction. . . . This, however, the average magistrate seldom understands. He habitually assumes that strikes, though not criminal, are morally reprehensible; and he chooses, in defiance of the intention of Parliament, to consider the moral suasion of the most peaceful picketing as an unwarranted interference with personal liberty."—Sidney and Beatrice Webb, *Industrial Democracy*, p. 855.

the immigrant worker who is the picketer, we wonder how he can ever know whether, in picketing, he is engaged in a lawful or an unlawful activity. It must be very confusing to him. And so far as he is acquainted with the latest decisions of our highest court, he must feel that they are unfriendly to the picketer.

PROOFS OF ILLEGAL ACTS ON THE PICKET LINE

The next difficulty is to prove the actual commission of unlawful acts. What is likely to happen on a picket line is something as follows: Before an establishment on strike, or near it, will be found a group of pickets, a stream of ingoing and outcoming workers actually on the job, and a detail of police, sent there to preserve order. The pickets exchange remarks with the strike breakers, and with the police, perhaps. The talk grows loud. Then some scuffling is seen. The police make a dash, seize upon some one who, they claim, is interfering with some one else, and march him or her or them, off to the station house, to be brought before a minor court on such technical charges as "assault" or "disorderly conduct" or perhaps "resisting an officer."

Unfortunately, activities on the picket line are not under general observation at every moment. In fact, the greatest activity goes on at the time when the fewest impartial witnesses are likely to be around, in the very early morning, when work is just beginning. So that when cases come up in court, frequently the only testimony offered is "he did" on the part of the complainant, who is often the officer charged with the duty of arrest, and "I didn't" on the part of the defendant, both *ex parte* witnesses. Between these two the judge has to decide the question of fact, and if he invariably sustains the complainant, and if the person seized in case of disorder is always the striker, never the strike breaker, the union workingman is sure to feel that the police and the judge are unfair and that the judge is siding with the boss against the workers.

ATTITUDE OF JUDGES IN PICKETING CASES

Are judges, as a matter of fact, found to have a bias in favor of the employer, so that we see in this class of cases a distinct differentiation of court and defendants into opposing groups, and the court thus abandoning its proper position of disinterested umpire? Some careful students of their decisions think that they are.[1]

Judges are, in general, drawn from the more successful and prosperous part of the community, whose interests are more or less closely knit with those of the employing class. It is perhaps natural that, on the whole, their sympathies should be with this class. At any rate, the working people are rather inclined to think that they are. A prominent immigrant leader in Boston, when asked about the attitude of his people toward the courts, said that there was a general feeling among all the foreign-born groups in that city that there was no justice for them in the courts, not because they were foreigners, but because they belonged to the labor class.

PICKETING CASES IN THE MAGISTRATES' COURTS OF NEW YORK CITY

Let us see how such cases are actually handled in some of the courts already observed in their dealings with ordinary cases and by the police who make the arrests for these courts. Let us look first at the magistrates' courts of New York City, which we

[1] H. R. Seager, *Report of Commission on Industrial Relations*, **xi**, p. 10558.

THE IMMIGRANT'S DAY IN COURT

have seen to be showing such great improvement in method and spirit over the old police court which it supplanted.

The New York magistrates' courts hold peaceful picketing to be lawful and an order of the New York Police Department, issued November, 1918, and still in force, with some changes in the order of paragraphs, defines peaceful picketing and prescribes the manner in which strikes are to be handled as follows:

POLICE DEPARTMENT
NEW YORK CITY
OFFICE OF THE POLICE COMMISSIONER

NEW YORK, *November 1, 1918.*

GENERAL ORDERS No. 100
STRIKES

a. Circular 19, Series 1916, is revoked.

b. The manner in which strikes are to be handled is largely at the discretion of the commanding officer.

c. The best police work is that of prevention. At the outset of a strike, the commanding officer will advise employer and striker of the meaning and intent of this general order by which the Police Force will be governed.

d. The employment of professional bullies and thugs by either side to a strike will be discouraged, and unlawful conditions and acts that might ultimately lead to disorder and violence will be prevented.

e. There is no compulsion upon an employer to keep in his employ any individual or individuals against what the employer believes to be his best interests; nor, on the other hand, need an employe or employees continue to work under conditions that are unsatisfactory to them, be those conditions what they may.

f. Peaceable picketing has been held by the courts to be lawful. Striking employees may picket in the vicinity or in front of their former place of employment with a view to persuading those still employed to strike; or to persuade those they have reason to think are considering taking their former places not to do so; or to advise prospective customers of the establishment where they were formerly employed of the existence of the strike and the character of their grievances. In all such cases, members of the Force will require that the manner of address and the language used are of a sort not to create disorder or violence, nor to offend public decency; and they will prevent violence or even physical contact between opposing factions.

g. Strikers will not be permitted to have pickets so numerous as to interfere with the free passage of pedestrians nor of vehicular traffic; nor will intimidation be permitted by the presence of an unreasonable number of pickets nor by the acts or demeanor of the pickets. The number of pickets that may be employed in any specific instance will be left to the discretion of the commanding officer, due regard being had to the width of the street and sidewalk; the number of persons still at work; the size of the building involved, the number of its exits and their size; the number of neutrals using the sidewalk; etc., but they will not be permitted in such numbers as to obstruct the free entry into and exit from the employer's place; nor to allow the assembly of crowds which might intimidate or obstruct the passage of persons to or from such place.

h. It is to be assumed, unless advice to the contrary is had from the courts or other competent authority, that the purposes of a peaceful, orderly strike are legal. It is imperative, therefore, that the law be enforced with strict and even-handed impartiality; favors being shown none, and justice being done all.

i. The general duties of the Police Department in connection with strikes and industrial unrest are the same as under unusual conditions of more common occurrence—*i.e.*, to protect life and property and to maintain order.

j. Effective 12.01 A.M., November 2, 1918.

RICHARD E. ENRIGHT
Police Commissioner.

The unions also stand for the principle of picketing by peaceful means. It is the policy of the modern, well-organized labor union in New York City, and elsewhere, to forbid its members to use violence.

In the shirtmakers' strike, in July, 1919, of the Amalgamated Clothing Workers, largely composed of foreign born, pickets were given cards with instructions for their duties as follows:

When on picket duty, don't walk in crowds. Walk two by two.

THE IMMIGRANT'S DAY IN COURT

Don't put your hands on anybody.

Don't stop walking back and forth in front of the shop.

When a police officer tells you to move, don't stop to argue with him. Keep on walking.

When asking anyone to join the strike, ask in a kindly spirit.

If a police officer interferes with you, report to the union.

If gangsters attempt to intimidate you, notify the nearest policeman.

If a picket is arrested, telephone details to the union.

If you are arrested, telephone from the police station to the union.

In court ask for the union lawyer, who will always be in court.

Notwithstanding the pacific principles laid down by the police and the unions, there is usually much complaint of violence during strikes by both sides concerned. Looking back only to the strikes of the past year or two, in the shirt workers' strike just referred to, the general strike committee gathered evidence for presentation to the police commissioner to show that guards employed by the employers were terrorizing the girl pickets, and that the police were permitting assaults on the pickets by the guards, without interference. Many complaints were made in various strikes during the same summer of violence committed by the police themselves; on the other hand, the newspapers reported daily arrests of strikers for disorderly conduct or assault while picketing.

An official of the Ladies' Waist and Dressmakers' Union, another union of heavy foreign-born membership, in an interview with an investigator for this study, bitterly criticized the methods of the police and court officials toward the strikers and the union generally in their strike in the spring of 1919, and said

258

that he had noticed little, if any, improvement within recent years. He claimed that the police interfere with the strikers while picketing, and handle them roughly; and that the judges consistently take the word of the manufacturer's representative—for example, the detective employed by the manufacturer to protect strike breakers—rather than that of the striker; that they require unduly heavy bail, and impose unduly severe penalties of imprisonment or fine. In the strike which had just ended and which had lasted eleven weeks, over 400 arrests had been made, in no case was the bail less than $500, and the fines ranged from $3 to $25, averaging $8 per person fined. Many strikers, he said, bore for a long time the marks of the rough handling they were subjected to by the police officer when he made the arrest.

Five hundred dollars bail seemed to him a disproportionate amount for a minor offense such as "disorderly conduct" or blocking the sidewalk. The fines also seemed to him disproportionate to the offenses committed, and he had noted that for the same offense the fine imposed on a striker would be from $10 to $15 while that imposed on the ordinary offender, not connected with a labor trouble, would be only three or five dollars.

As the bail money and the fines are supplied by the union, this heavy imposition is a form of repression of union activities, for the demands soon drain the treasury, and the union is obliged to borrow at a high rate of interest.

This attitude of the police and court officials he considered a great hindrance to the Americanization of the worker, who is in almost every case an immigrant. Knowing nothing of our tongue and form of government, and experiencing the unjust treatment of our minor city officials, he becomes indifferent to citizenship.

ATTITUDE OF THE NEW YORK MAGISTRATES

It seems to be, however, the policeman rather than the judge who is considered the most unfair and is most objected to.

As to the judges in the minor courts, the investigator, on visiting the courts and talking with the workers, finds that in labor cases, as in the ordinary cases previously considered, they decide them in a variety of ways, apparently according to personal predispositions.

Some judges are regarded as "hard"; others as "easy"; and workers are pleased if brought before the latter type. One unfortunate result of variations of decision in the court and experiences of rough treatment from the police seems to be a blunting in the immigrant worker's mind of the sense of respect for law and the court as an institution, and that quick sense of revolt against injustice which is the safeguard of law and order in a free community. If the foreign-born striker learns to accept the court calmly as a machine grinding out arbitrary decisions, which do not mean anything one way or another except in so far as the individual before it is lucky or unlucky in escaping a penalty, he is getting a poor preparation for taking part in the task of keeping the institutions of justice on their proper level, or for becoming an intelligent, law-abiding citizen himself.

Following up the handling of strike cases by some of the individual magistrates we have already watched in the treatment of ordinary cases, we may see some of the varieties of decision and how the different magistrates feel about the problem.

IMMIGRANT WORKINGMAN BEFORE COURT

Magistrate E who was found to be so careful and kindly in ordinary cases, seems to be pretty sharp after picketers. In the waist and dressmakers' strike in March, 1919, out of one day's haul of eighteen girl picketers he sentenced one girl to the workhouse for ten days, on a charge of "assault," another on the same charge for two days, while upon the remainder he inflicted small fines or suspended sentence. To throw a workingwoman into the surroundings and the companionships of the workhouse might well be termed a "cruel and unusual punishment" for such offenses as are committed on the picket line—getting into a fuss with another girl, talking back to an officer—and may result in lasting harm to the woman or girl who experiences the treatment. In the same session he imposed a fine of $5 on a man alleged to be a gangster in the employ of the bosses, charged with assault by girl strikers. In another strike case, of bakers, where the testimony consisted only of a complaint and a denial, this magistrate said he hoped "something can be done to end this nuisance. . . . These men are out fighting for what they claim are their rights. But it appears to me that if drastic punishment is meted out to any person under these circumstances the moral effect will be tremendous."

In another baker's case before this magistrate two pickets were charged with attacking a strike breaker, while they claimed, in opposition, that the strike breaker had attacked them. One of the pickets was a Czech who had been in the country six years and had taken out first papers for citizenship; the other, a German, had been in the country five years and held no papers. Although this case occurred in the spring of 1919, after the ending of active hostilities in the World War, and although one of the men was a Czech, the complainant's attorney urged upon the magistrate that the defendants "were not even citizens, and Germans at that." The magistrate explained that he believed in collective bargaining, but that "foreigners who were allowed in this country must be thankful, obey the law, and keep their mouths shut." He justified the strike breaker in his refusal to answer the questions of the picket on the ground that the strike-breaker was formerly in the United States army and was therefore right in not answering the questions of a mere "foreigner." In conclusion he said, "Every picket brought before me for an offense of this kind will be severely punished. Many things have been happening lately. They [the Germans] especially must keep their mouths shut." The defendants were sentenced to three days' imprisonment.

The onlooker at this trial could not but feel that the presumptions were in favor of the pickets. The strike breaker stumbled badly in his testimony. His physical strength was much superior to that of his alleged assailants, and, as he was a tall fellow, he would have had to bend over decidedly in order to be hit in the eye by the two short strikers. Furthermore, he showed no evidence of injury. And the only testimony to the assault was offered by a detective who claimed not to have been in the employ of the baker but just happening to pass. He was, however, on terms of acquaintance with the strike breaker and with the plaintiff's attorney.

Magistrate A the strict, formal judge of ordinary cases, in an expressmen's strike gave workhouse sentences of ten days each to pickets.

In a recent strike of clothing workers, however, this magistrate was considered quite fair by the leaders of the strike. He imposed small fines where the cases warranted fining, and was so interested in seeing that exact justice was done that he visited the picket line himself early one morning, subsequently instructing the police officers to be more careful in making arrests. He was ready to coöperate with the union, and the union with him. On one occasion the union turned over to him ten pickets who in the opinion of the union leaders had been guilty of violence and disorder, and, with the concurrence of the union, all were fined by the magistrate.

Magistrate K, who in the handling of the ordinary cases that come up in a magistrate's court, was seen to be a sympathetic man who patiently analyzed cases of the foreign born and was considerate in imposing fines according to the circumstances of the case and the defendant's ability to pay, took occasion in one labor case to lecture some girl picketers, saying that the right to labor was as sacred as the right to picket, and no striker had the privilege of interfering with the sacred right of any other person to labor. Eleven of the picketers were fined by him, all, except in three cases, on the charge of girls still at work.

Magistrate J the scholarly magistrate who thinks instruction to immigrants from the bench is not part of the judicial function, is considered by the unions as an archenemy of the working man and of all liberal movements. A visitor to his court, seen by one of the labor representatives present, during a strike case, to be reading the *Dial*, was cautioned by him, "If the judge sees you with that paper he will have you arrested as a Bolshevik!" This remark is typical of the attitude of the workingman toward this court.

In one case before this judge the officers could not prove that the men arrested had committed any violence—they merely charged that they had seen the men with their hands raised as if to strike. The men denied that they had committed any violence. None of them could speak English. Upon learning this the judge asked how long they had been in this country and whether they were citizens. It appeared that they had been in the country about five years and were not citizens. Thereupon the judge gave them a lecture on the wrong they were committing in enjoying the blessings of the United States and not assuming any of the responsibilities of citizenship. "I will tell you something that will make you wake up to a knowledge of the English language in a hurry. How would you like two years for your misbehavior?" In the end, however, the cases were dismissed.

Another labor case illustrating the attitude of this judge was that of a young Russian Jew who had been arrested on the charge of having struck a man. He claimed that he pushed into the crowd to question the right of the foreman to carry a pistol. A policeman took them all to court to look into the matter, whereupon the young man was arrested and put in jail. It was found that the foreman had no permit to carry a pistol and it was not proved that the boy had struck anyone. The testimony presented seemed to exonerate him, but the judge placed him on six months' probation, which was a great humiliation to the boy. He felt that he might as well have gone to jail. The strikers suspected that the judge took this means of curtailing the boy's activity in the strike because he was a leader.

A gruff and forbidding attitude in the court room gives the impression that this judge is antagonistic to the foreign-born worker, and unsympathetic with him. But a visitor to the court, in the course of a personal interview, found him deeply interested in the problems which come before him for settlement and honestly desirous of getting at the root of the various troubles, as a basis for a fair decision. He expressed particular interest in the foreign born and the problem of Americanization, and blamed the American people for their neglect of the immigrant. In discussing the strike cases he did not take the part entirely of either the employer or the worker; he thought that there was occasion for criticism on both sides. In handling strike cases he said his policy was to try to impress the workers with the necessity of preserving order and obeying the law, usually by scaring them with a severe talk. Sometimes he imposes a small fine. But in general he feels that the matters involved are private affairs, to be settled out of court.

Sometimes a magistrate rebukes the police for overstepping the bounds of lawful activity.

The police commissioner's orders previously quoted expressly give the commanding officer power to determine the number of pickets who may be lawfully employed in any specific instance, with due regard to various circumstances noted, and under this order precinct captains individually undertook to establish a lawful number. But in one case in the summer of 1919 a magistrate discharged nineteen pickets who had been arrested for refusal to limit their numbers to two or four pickets in front of each shop, and denounced the policeman for making the arrests. "Strikers may have twenty-five pickets in front of a shop," said he, "if they behave properly in accordance with the law regarding peaceful picketing."

But in the strike of the Amalgamated Clothing Workers in the winter of 1920–21, another magistrate ruled that the number of pickets could be limited by individual captains for their respective precincts, and levied fines on pickets above the number allowed.

Another magistrate was found by a visitor to the court, while strike cases were going on, to be inflicting fines of $25 for apparently slight offenses, substantiated only by the testimony of the policeman who made the arrests.

Still another magistrate, who had expressed himself decidedly in affirmation of the right to picket, in one case observed, dismissed a complaint made by a picket against some one who attacked him, against what would seem to have been fully as clear evidence as that which is usually accepted against strikers accused of violence, and said, in the bargain, that if the pickets did not carry on their operations in an ordinary legal manner he was going to send some of them to jail. This in a case where the nonpicketer was defendant and the picketer complainant seems a little inappropriate.

In cases brought up in connection with the strike of white-goods workers in the spring of 1919, in one of the courts, the magistrate impressed a visitor to the court as being open minded and honestly trying to decide the cases which came to him on their merits. The strikers much preferred him to magistrate G who will be recalled as the rough, tobacco-chewing magistrate of a former chapter. There seemed to be a general disposition to accept the decision of the judge without very much complaint, although in one or two instances where the judge refused to hear the case the girls expressed their despair at trying to get any consideration.

In this court the attitude of the judge and of the lesser officials, on the whole, was courteous and kind in a bluff way. The proceedings were informal and due consideration was given to the unfamiliarity of the clients with the ways of the law.

The disorder while on picket duty, with which the defendants were charged, consisted sometimes of trouble with nonunion workers, sometimes of interference with the police. The judge dismissed almost every case which involved trouble with the nonunion workers, evidently taking the attitude that the matter was one for industrial settlement, not for judicial decision.

In one of the instances of complaint by the police of interference by a group of girls, the judge imposed the very small fine of one dollar each.

From these glimpses of the magistrates in action it would appear that in New York City the foreign-born workingman finds it difficult to know beforehand what sort of behavior during a strike is or is not lawful, since the decisions of the magistrates vary so widely in individual cases, as well as their theories of what constitutes lawful behavior.

It would also appear that the magistrates, while not universally satisfactory to the workers in their decisions, are, not as a whole, unmistakably ranged on the side of the employer, as is perhaps natural in a city too large and embracing too great a variety of elements to be dominated exclusively by any one class.

ATTITUDE TOWARD THE NEWER UNIONISM

Organizations of men united to improve their economic conditions often meet with difficulties in securing legal recognition of their activities because of the feeling of those in power that these activities are directed not simply toward the adjustment of individual cases to an existing order of things, but toward a change in that order.

The old type of craft union did, as a matter of fact, accept in general the economic and political principles on which present-day society is founded, and their activities, by crafts, were concentrated only on those special points were a particular craft was concerned. And seldom could the craft union apply enough pressure to disturb seriously an entire community, even had it desired to be revolutionary. So that in recent years we were becoming sufficiently accustomed to the principles of the craft unions to regard them as part of the prevailing system, and accept a labor disturbance as an indication of dissatisfaction in a particular bargain, rather than a movement to upset the principles on which such bargains are made.

Meanwhile another form of unionism was in the course of development, the industrial union, as opposed to the craft union, organized by establishments instead of by crafts. And whereas the craft unions covered only certain skilled or semi-skilled employments, the industrial union took in the great body of the unskilled, a class of growing proportions in the man power of industry.

So that where the industrial union was well organized, in case of a strike all classes of workers could be called out at a given plant, making it possible to apply a more effective pressure on the employers.

Then came our entry into the European War, and with it the fear that the worker from a foreign country might use his industrial position to the advantage of an enemy power, by slackening production, or by sabotage of other kinds, or through the strike. And when, in addition, the workers in European countries were seen to be gaining broader economic rights through political revolution, the fear was aroused that workers might attempt the same methods here, so that a real terror of the foreign-born worker was awakened in this country which introduced new complications into labor cases.

IMMIGRANT WORKINGMAN BEFORE COURT

But in fact, during the war, before the armistice, strikes were few in number; after the armistice without assuming any revolutionary stimulus there was abundant economic basis for strikes in the rising cost of living, which was rapidly outstripping increases in wages. But after April, 1917, any sign of a labor disturbance was likely to be interpreted as a symptom of revolutionary activity, and measures were likely to be taken to treat it as such.

In this new development the courts and police did not limit their activities in labor cases to the checking of actual violence, but, through the restriction of the freedom of speech and public meeting, attempted to reach back to the incitement of violence or disturbance and in the handling of cases of disorder the courts emphasized considerations of state.

Let us look at a few recent examples, in which foreign-born workmen were especially concerned.

STRIKE OF CLOTHING WORKERS IN CINCINNATI

In Cincinnati, in the strike of the clothing workers, called by the Amalgamated Clothing Workers in the spring of 1919, many persons were arrested and brought before the Municipal Court. This court has already been noted as one which, although improving upon the justice court it replaced, was found in ordinary cases to be somewhat unsympathetic with the foreign born and somewhat lacking in adjustment to their needs. This characteristic was apparently exaggerated in the treatment of strike cases. A large percentage of the strikers were unnaturalized immigrants and those coming before the court were severely dealt with.

According to the attorneys for the strikers, in no case were they given a fair trial, and the fact that they were foreign born practically convicted them before their cases came up in court. We might disregard this as an *ex parte* statement but for the circumstance that the attorney for the employers quite frankly admitted that decisions in strike cases were influenced by the prejudice of the court against the defendants as "foreigners and Bolshevists." Some such feeling as this is plainly indicated in the remarks made by Judge Fox, of this court, in sentencing a striker charged with assault to six months in the workhouse and a fine of $200, an unusually severe punishment for an assault which had inflicted little injury on the person attacked. Among other things he said:

The punishment to be imposed on you in this case is to be determined not so much by the injury inflicted upon your victim, as by the injury done to society. The forces of anarchy and destruction at this hour are in full control of Russia and to a lesser degree in Germany. . . . The tactics employed by you are the same as those used by the Bolsheviki of Europe. . . . All things respected and cherished by us in this country you seek to overthrow, that you may get some personal advantage for yourself. You are an alien, a citizen of Russia. You were permitted into this land because of the generous spirit of the country. Here but a short period, here by toleration only, you defy the laws of the land that gave you refuge, you seek to supplant law by anarchy. Such as you have no appreciation of the blessings you enjoy in this land, you have no respect for our laws, our institutions are not dear to you, our traditions are not sacred or a source of pride, and our civil and religious liberty are but obstacles to the furtherance of your plans. All these considerations which would deter a citizen of the United States can in no wise restrain you. Fear of punishment is the only thing that will stay you and your associates.

The court will therefore impose the severest punishment

the law permits. . . . Further, the court will bring this case to the attention of the United States authorities with the confident hope that at the expiration of the sentence it will now impose upon you, they will deport you and free this land forever from your evil influence.[1]

It is perhaps permissible to wonder how far civil liberties are being protected when a person arrested on a charge of minor disorder, of a kind common enough ever since the beginning of a labor movement in this country, is practically convicted of "anarchy," of which there was no evidence but the assault, and is recommended for deportation, a remedy which cannot be administered for minor misdemeanors of this nature.

Later in the strike Judge Bell of the same court ruled that there was no clothing strike in Cincinnati, giving as his reason that it had been called by the Amalgamated Clothing Workers, an industrial union, and had not been authorized by the American Federation of Labor. He therefore fined seven strikers for carrying banners with the announcement that a strike was on. There was no charge that the banner carriers had disturbed the peace or in any way violated the law.

TEXTILE STRIKE AT LAWRENCE, MASSACHUSETTS

In Lawrence, Massachusetts, a strike of the textile industries was declared in February, 1919. This is a city in which over four-fifths of the population are either of foreign birth or of foreign parentage, and somewhat over two-thirds of the foreign born are from non-English-speaking countries. In 1910, over

---

[1] *Advance*, April 11, 1919. Judge Fox has been kind enough to verify this report of his remarks. In a letter to the writer he said that according to his recollection the above quotation is correct.

half of the foreign-born men were aliens. The town can show representatives of over thirty different nationalities, and in the carrying on of the strike the workers were organized in fifteen different national groups, each with a meeting place of its own.

This strike was no product of union agitation; no union, conservative or radical, was responsible for it. It came into being as a spontaneous expression of the working force of the mills, without incitement from outside of any description. The Industrial Workers of the World, hearing of the trouble, sent representatives to assist in organizing the strike, but these representatives were sent away by the strikers.

When the strike was declared, on February 3d, the city authorities took measures to establish a strict and repressive discipline. Not satisfied with the home force of police as a means of keeping order, the city government brought in mounted police from other cities and made ready to suppress the first signs of unrest.

From the beginning permits for parades of any description were refused, on the ground that under the circumstances parades would "encourage Bolshevism," notwithstanding the fact that the demands made by the workers were purely economic.

From what could be learned of the activities of the police from day to day, it would appear that the handling of the police situation was calculated rather to provoke disorder than to quell it, and that the police began demonstrations before there was any trouble from the strikers. The leaders of the strike, two or three of whom were Christian ministers, and opposed to the use of violence as a matter of principle, on their part exerted all the influence they possessed to keep the strikers from resorting to force and intimidation.

IMMIGRANT WORKINGMAN BEFORE COURT

As the strike went on complaints of interference on the part of strikers with persons wanting to work and of general disorder in the city caused by strikers became more and more frequent.

The most open instances of violence, however, were furnished by the police. Early in the strike a troop of mounted men "dispersed" a band of twenty respectable citizens who had come to Lawrence to study conditions, riding after them, blocking them from certain streets, using insulting language to the women, and beating some of the men over the head with their clubs.

Soon after that, strikers who had been attending an outdoor meeting, held on private property before such meetings had been prohibited by the police, on dispersing, were treated as an unauthorized "parade" and ridden into from two directions by the mounted police. Mrs. W. Z. Ripley, of Boston, who was present during these occurrences, stated, in an affidavit under oath, that perfect order had prevailed during the two hours of the meeting, that when the strikers began to come from the meeting mounted police rode into the midst of them, beating heads on every side; that from a window she watched groups of police beating men already lying on the ground; that she saw one old man with a deep cut in the back of his head still bleeding, who was lying on the sidewalk and offering no resistance, beaten by four policemen with their long sticks, and at no time did she see any one interfering with the police in making arrests.

A few days later two of the preacher leaders, after a day on the picket line, were driven along the street by the mounted police, were beaten as they ran, without offering resistance, and were finally taken to court on charges of inciting to riot, of loitering, and of assault. When their cases came to trial both were acquitted. In later cases in which the evidence of violence on the part of the strikers was no more strongly substantiated than in this case, but the person complained of was a foreign-born workman with an imperfect knowledge of English, the defendants were not let off so lightly.

In the hearing of the cases of the preachers, it developed that the police sergeant did not know that there was a Massachusetts law protecting "peaceful picketing"[1] and the judge himself said that there was no such thing as peaceful picketing.

A week or two later a "strikers' guard" of ex-service men was charged by the mounted police, and a young Italian, with an honorable record of fighting in France as a volunteer, was clubbed, arrested, and later fined $20 by the court for "making a disturbance." A circumstantial story was told that he was severely beaten in his cell after arrest. A police-court attendant expressed doubt about this. "They don't beat them in here," he explained, "they do it in the street."[2]

The Commissioner of Public Safety denied that the police had been brutal at any time, but said that hitting people on the head was the way to disperse a crowd.[3] A visitor to Lawrence was told that the mounted men had a special technique of clubbing, the art of striking a glancing blow that drew much blood but did not inflict deep injury. However that may be, the results of police activities were seen in dozens of bandaged heads and surgeons' patches during the active days of the strike.

On another morning a crowd of strikers on the

[1] Jerome Davis, *The World To-morrow*, May, 1919, p. 138.

[2] John A. Fitch, *The Survey*, April 5, 1919.

[3] *Ibid.*

street was regarded by the police as an unauthorized parade, and dispersed with much clubbing. Twenty-two persons, all foreign born, were arrested. From this time on, day by day, the police gathered in one and another striker, on various charges. By the time of an inquiry undertaken by the State Board of Arbitration, about the middle of April, 224 arrests had been made, according to the city marshal.

In the drives of the mounted police upon the crowds, apparently some innocent bystanders were involved, to their injury. According to affidavits made by the victims, one old man going out to buy cigarettes was caught in the crowd, could not get away fast enough, and was beaten over the head; another, a young fellow, hurrying to get medicine for a sick child, was treated in similar fashion; another man going to the grocery to buy sugar, not a striker at all, had his head laid open by a mounted man. The foot police, of the city itself, were generally regarded in the town as comparatively mild in their methods, one reason given being that the mounted men from out of town felt less responsibility for the way they behaved, since they would go away home again, after the trouble, while the foot police would stay, would be in contact with the workers later, and would be in danger of reprisals for any injuries inflicted.

The court before which the strikers were brought for trial was a district court of the type described in a previous chapter as the minor court of Massachusetts towns. Three judges took turns in hearing the cases, and all three expressed sentiments unfavorable to the strike and the strikers. One of the judges, as has been noted, expressed the opinion that there was no such thing as peaceful picketing. Another of the judges, in discussing the strike before the State Board of Arbitration, attributed the strike troubles to attempted revolution, arraigned the "outside agitators," and contrasted the peaceful picketing of the telephone strikers, mostly native-born girls, in a strike then going on, with the violence of the foreign-born strikers. The third judge, during the hearing of cases before him, took occasion to complain of agitators from out of town and to deplore the "spirit of unrest" that had arisen.

A visitor to the court on a day when several of the strikers were tried did not see any rough browbeating of strikers and their witnesses by the judge, and noted that the interpreter was intelligent and sympathetic and apparently competent; but after all the evidence was in the decision was invariably against the striker. Among the cases heard on this particular day were two in which the accused men were bandaged and patched to an extent that showed some terrible punishment by the police. From all outward signs, it would have seemed that the men were the objects of assault, rather than the assailants, for the policemen, whom they charged with attacking, were free from injury of any kind. In behalf of one of these bandaged men a bystander testified that she had seen him beaten as he lay on his back, helpless, on the ground, by a mounted policeman until the blood ran in streams. The only evidence against him was that of the policeman. The striker was fined $20. The Superior Court evidently agreed with the witness for the defendant, however, for on appeal this case was not pressed by the district attorney. The other man, all bandaged and plastered, was charged with disturbance and given thirty days in the House of Correction. On appeal this sentence was reversed and the case placed "on file," a method of procedure saving the accused person from the stigma of a criminal record, on payment of a fine of $25.

It was interesting to note that on this same day a man charged with choking his mother-in-law in the course of a chronic domestic dispute, an offense which he practically admitted, was tenderly turned over to the care of the probation officer for two weeks, in order that all the circumstances might be ascertained.

In the strike cases this judge habitually inflicted heavy penalties—jail sentences and large fines—and imposed heavy bail. Of the 22 persons arrested in connection with the so-called "unauthorized parade," 4 were given jail sentences of 30 days, and 8 fined $25 each. This judge gave warning, as the strike went on, that the penalties would grow heavier; in well-defined assault cases, he said, jail sentences would be imposed as fines did not seem to be effective. And he reproved counsel for suggesting appeals in the hope that the decisions of the lower court would be reversed, because, he said, past experience had shown that it would be sustained.

As a matter of fact, the judge's expectation was not justified. Of 108 cases arising in connection with this strike and taken on appeal to the Superior Court from the Lawrence district court, by November, 1919, 29 had been dropped by the district attorney, 26 had been placed "on file" without record standing against the defendant, and in 37 other cases the sentence of the lower court had been very much reduced. The remaining 17 cases were still pending.

In these cases the justice administered by the higher court was practically the opposite of that administered in the lower court, a rather bad lesson to the immigrant if he is to be impressed with the exactness and impartiality of the administration of law.

In the present instance it looks as if the lower court showed signs of that partisanship from which a court should be free, while the higher court, removed from local influences and prejudices, was free to give its decisions in accordance with the real evidence in the cases. A glance at the political and social organization of the little city of Lawrence shows how this can happen and is typical of other places, dependent upon one dominant industry.

In this city the directing forces in the dominant industry are largely persons of native birth and descent. They exert a strong influence also in all the affairs of the place, through their control of its general prosperity and through the money they supply for community purposes, public and private, to say nothing of an influence, suspected, if not proved, in the election of public officials.

An element distinct from the mill officials and their group, and yet capable of making an alliance with them against a common enemy, is the city government, made up in the main of a stock of the older immigration—the Irish, many of them graduates from the working force of the mills. As former workers they are inclined to criticize and even oppose the employers, but, on the other hand, having risen to prosperity out of the ranks, and seeing a new kind of people now making up the bulk of the working force, and seeing them organized in a union disputing the control of the old craft unions, they are not altogether sympathetic with the lower-grade mill workers.

The strikers, on the other hand, represented for the most part the newer immigration and the unskilled worker, with whom the other two elements feel very little sympathy and regard with the fear that comes from imperfect understanding, and sometimes from unfair treatment—the fear of the exploited felt by the exploiter.

In such a place it is not surprising that the police, as part of the city government, should further the interests of the element they represent, and that the courts, linked closely with both the city government and the employers, should show some bias against the foreign-born workers.

Whatever the technical rights involved in these court and police cases, there can be no doubt of the effect on the minds of the workers. They felt that they were being dealt with unjustly and that this country, which promised so much of justice and freedom was as oppressive as the autocratic countries they had come from.

In several of the national groups among the strikers action was taken looking to arrangements for their return to their own country, where they thought conditions would be better. The Italian group asked that the ports be opened so that they could go home, and the Russians, Lithuanians, and Poles expressed a similar desire. Outside visitors to the daily meetings of the strike committee could not fail to note the growing excitement, the growing resentment of the workers against the rough treatment they received at the hands of the police, against the severe sentences of the court. Any wild proposal for reprisals on the part of excited members, however, was instantly combated by the strike leaders, who were incessant and unwearied in their exhortations to the strikers to keep the peace, under any provocation, and deprive the authorities of any excuse whatever for proceeding against them.

During all this trouble a "citizens' committee" in the town was carrying on a campaign of "Americanization," according to a plan devised by an outside

expert. This plan included activities along the lines
of education, housing, citizenship, industrial welfare,
arbitration, employment, thrift and savings, health,
recreation, and the holding of open forums. Posters
urging the necessity of "getting together—all dwellers
in Lawrence—for a common civic purpose," and
presenting the plans of the committee were printed
in the newspapers and circulated among the population.
But the foreign-born resident reading them must have
felt the contrast between the beautiful principles set
forth in them and the actual happenings of every day
in the town. And he would not unnaturally have
taken offense at some of the adjurations to "obey the
law," because "the true American stands for justice,
the square deal, fairness. He will work with all his
strength to get justice for those who are unjustly
treated," and "the American obeys the law of the
land," and, furthermore, he might perhaps wonder if
the circular was quite right in saying, about "our
foreign-born friends" that "we want them to see
clearly that they can get what they want by service
in obedience to American laws, and that if they will
make their requests in obedience to the law, not in
defiance of it, all they earn will be given to them
gladly."

Apparently little was done in the working out of
the plan beyond the holding of open forum meetings
in various parts of the city. The meetings most
widely advertised were hardly of a character to attract
the immigrant worker. The proceedings were carried
on in the English language, the speakers and topics
and the treatment of the topics were of a kind that
would appeal to the prosperous native, nurtured in
American traditions. Foreign-speaking forums were
held, with some success, but from the programs one

would infer that the topics were a bit remote from what the foreign workers felt were the live issues of his part of the community life. There is no indication that the rank and file of strikers were reached by any of these meetings. The foreign-born people reached were of the more prosperous classes, and it appears that more interest was shown in this plan by them than by the native-born, for the chairman of the Citizens' Committee, reporting on their activities in April, said that up to that time the least vigorous response to their appeals had come from the native-born citizens of the city.

After some weeks had passed, wages in the woolen mills were raised, the strikers went back to work, and nothing revolutionary had happened.

TEXTILE STRIKE IN PASSAIC

During the same spring of 1919 strikes of the textile workers were called in Passaic and Paterson, New Jersey, and branches of the Amalgamated Textile Workers, an industrial union, were organized in these places.

In Passaic, as in Lawrence, the strikers were almost all foreign born of the newer immigration, and little sympathy was felt for them by the people of the towns generally.

A Committee of Public Safety charged with maintaining order and protecting life and property was active during the strike, and the ranks of the police were augmented by ex-soldiers. According to local social workers, the police were unreasonable and brutal and by their conduct antagonized and irritated the strikers. One social worker said that the slightest act on the part of a striker was noticed and punished;

if a girl so much as put her hand on the arm of another girl who was a nonstriker, she was harshly reprimanded and not infrequently arrested by the police, and their whole conduct was such that the strikers could not look on them as other than enemies.

The court record shows that in strike cases the judge was at first inclined to be lenient; the first persons arrested were dismissed with a reprimand. The Committee of Public Safety, however, felt that such procedure was too easy and insisted that the judge be more severe, and the later dispositions of cases show that in every instance the heaviest penalties were inflicted. In Passaic also the strike was interpreted as a symptom of revolution, and the trouble laid to "outside agitators."

Whereas in Lawrence the authorities had been content to allow strike meetings to be held indoors, in halls placed at the disposal of the strikers by private owners, in Passaic, as the strike progressed, meetings even under such circumstances could not be held without a permit. A police rule, prohibiting the holding of meetings without a permit from the Commissioner of Public Safety was supplemented by a city ordinance to the same effect. The provision that the permit was to be issued only after the commissioner was "satisfied that said meeting shall not be detrimental to the public welfare" made possible a use of the power to refuse a permit such as to stop discussion of any nature. To the Amalgamated Textile Workers this rule seemed a violation of the right of free public meeting and free speech guaranteed in the constitution of the state, and they consequently held a meeting without permit for the purpose of making a test case. The police, however, instead of making arrests so that the principle could be tested in the court, cleared out the audience by force, turned out the lights, but permitted the speakers to proceed with the reading of the constitution of the State of New Jersey without an audience, by the glimmer of two candles.

TEXTILE STRIKE IN PATERSON

In Paterson, at the very beginning of the strike the chief of police had issued an order that no out-of-town agitator should be allowed to speak at local meetings. Two delegates from the Amalgamated Textile Workers who came to Paterson to a meeting of the local I. W. W. were, in consequence of this ruling, pounced upon and sent out of town, with a warning to stay out of Paterson for the future.

Later the Amalgamated Textile Workers opened an office in Paterson and were forthwith visited by the chief of police, whose purpose was, as he said, to find out what connection the union had with the "Russian Bolsheviki," as he had learned that the union at its first convention had passed a resolution of greeting to the Russian Soviets. As soon as the Amalgamated local began its work and attempted to hold meetings, the chief of police refused to issue permits for meetings, and was supported by the mayor in his action, for reasons stated in a letter to the executive secretary, as follows:

I have considered your letter and your representations made to me at your recent interview, and I have concluded that Chief Tracey is right. At your interview with me you stated to me that, while members of your organization considered themselves radicals, yet they did not believe in, or undertake to gain their objectives by force, but there are times that actions speak louder than words. The Soviets of Russia, to whom you extended your fraternal greetings, did believe in, and actually exercised force to the extent of killing owners of factories and other businesses, of which they took control, and their published regulations relative to the women of Russia were beyond the pales [*sic*] of civilization.

I cannot conceive of an organization which does not believe in these things sending a fraternal greeting to those who not only believed in them, but practiced them, without in the greetings uttering some words of condemnation of such conduct.

With these facts before me, I can but approve of the action of the chief in withholding permits for public meetings.

It is of interest to note that this very chief of police, backed so heartily by this pure-minded mayor who was so shocked at the "nationalization of women" of Russia—that picturesque legend which gained such wide currency—was later found expressing absolute ignorance of a particularly foul nest of prostitution, so well known that a stranger could be directed to it by a policeman stationed before the City Hall, and so bad that the grand jury brought indictments against several proprietors of houses. We cannot say that the chief was "protecting" these places, in the technical sense, for the grand jury exonerated him of this offense. But a leading newspaper of the place,[1] while approving the action of the grand jury, says it is inconsistent to say that the police have exercised "care, caution, and diligence. . . . This is slopping the whitewash over, just a bit, for the *News* ventures the opinion that there is not a member of the local force, from the chief down, who did not know that these houses were operating in —— Street. It was a matter of public property."

In answer to the mayor's letter, approving the action

[1] Paterson *Evening News*, February 26, 1921.

of the chief in refusing to issue permits for meetings, the secretary of the local pointed out that the resolution in question was in no way a statement of their program or intentions, and that nowhere could it be proved that the activities of the organization were other than lawful. But the mayor and the chief, uninfluenced by these considerations, persisted in their policy of suppressing the Amalgamated. Even membership meetings on the premises of the association were forbidden. The executive secretary was informed that before any meeting could be held the authorities would have to be satisfied that the men conducting the affair were American citizens and not in sympathy with the Bolshevist movement. Later, two organizers for the Amalgamated were fined $50 each by the recorder, in the police court for distributing circulars—"in order to teach them a lesson," as he said, although the fine imposed was the extreme penalty, and this was their first offense against this ordinance.

Still later a regular monthly membership meeting of the local, which had been held in spite of a warning that it would not be permitted, in order to test the constitutionality of the police procedure, was raided by the police, two officials of the union were arrested, and the papers of the union were seized—without a warrant, it was claimed by the officers of the union. Next day, these two men and two more were arrested when they went to ask the return of books and papers seized in the raid, and were committed to jail by the acting recorder in default of $1,000 bail, charged with advocating the overthrow of the government by force. The charge in detail recounted that they "wilfully and unlawfully did in public attempt by speech inciting and printing to incite, promote, and encourage hostility and opposition to the government of the United States and the State of

285

New Jersey by circulating literature and by speech advocating the Soviet form of government instead of the government now existing in the United States and the State of New Jersey." When this matter was brought before the higher court on writ of *habeas corpus*, attorneys for the city asked that the case be dismissed. This was done, and after a conference with the chief of police a permit was granted to the union to hold public meetings in the city, "upon the express promise of the officers . . . that said meetings will be held in an orderly manner."

But the chief of police could not reconcile himself to picketing. In the following month, during a lockout, he issued orders that strikers stationed in front of mills or stopping other workers who are not on strike should be charged with "picketing"; if they were found standing on the sidewalks conversing with one another, they should be arrested for loitering or unlawful assemblage or disorderly conduct.[1] This amounted to a prohibition of picketing as such by the city authorities, although, as claimed by the attorney for the strikers, the Supreme Court of New Jersey clearly allows strikers to picket.

The recorder warned the strikers that the picketing laws would be strictly enforced by the court, and as a result the union had to pay fines amounting to about $150 for different complaints made against their members during this strike, notwithstanding the fact that the chief of police had taken occasion, through the newspapers, to "compliment the strikers both in the silk industry and the machine shops of the city for the orderly manner in which they are conducting their fight for changed conditions."[2]

[1] Paterson *Evening News*, August 3, 1919.
[2] Paterson *Morning Call*, August 7, 1919.

IMMIGRANT WORKINGMAN BEFORE COURT

The great steel strike of the autumn of 1919 is a notable instance of a labor trouble in which large numbers of foreign-born workers are concerned, and from the handling of which by the governmental authorities they would gain a vivid impression of the way law is administered in this country.

In the region involved in the strike, at least two-thirds of the total number of persons employed in the industry are of foreign birth.

Of the 365,600 men who walked out on September 22, 1919, when the strike was called, a much larger proportion were foreign born, for they left behind in the mills office workers and supervisors of various degrees not concerned in the strike, who were almost entirely native Americans, and they also left behind many of the native-born skilled workers, who were enjoying more favorable conditions than the mass of the strikers.

The foreign born are found in great variety in the industry. In one industrial unit, the 14,687 employees were split up into 54 nationalities.[1] The 6,075 employees of the Duquesne Works in August, 1919, represented 29 different nationalities. Of these, the white Americans made up a little over a third, colored Americans, 5.5 per cent. Another 8 per cent were of the northern and western European nationalities. The remainder, over half, were from southern and eastern Europe, with a scattering few from Asia Minor. In this southeastern European group the most numerously represented peoples were the Slovaks, constituting over 15 per cent of the total number of employees, and

[1] Investigation of the Strike in the Steel Industries, Hearings before the Committee of Education and Labor, U. S. Senate, Sixty-sixth Congress, First Session, p. 480.

the Magyars, over 12 per cent. Slavic peoples of other nationality groups than the Slovaks made up the bulk of the remainder—Russians, Poles, Serbs, and Croatians—together with some Lithuanians.

This strike was widely heralded as a revolutionary movement, partly because of the general temper of the time, partly because its chief organizer was known as a "radical," partly because so many foreign born were concerned in it, and partly, we may suspect, because the employers wanted to enlist public sympathy against it, by alleging other than economic grounds for its origin, although, as a matter of fact, the demands made were entirely economic, the strike was organized under the auspices of the staid and conservative American Federation of Labor, and carried on according to regularly established union methods, and no revolutionary action was ever taken or even proposed.

In the Pennsylvania district severely repressive measures were taken from the beginning of the attempt to organize the steel workers. Meetings were prohibited, and after the strike was called the strikers found themselves under a harsh rule. From all accounts of the happenings during the strike, it seems that the strikers were unusually orderly. The mayor of Pittsburgh, speaking for his district, congratulated the men on the good order maintained by them.

Concerned in the making and carrying out of orders relating to picketing, public meeting, and other manifestations of strike activities were forces coöperating in a way which would naturally lead the foreign-born worker to believe that his industrial boss was his civil governor, and his government indistinguishable from his industrial boss.

In general charge, in the steel towns or cities, was a

mayor or burgess, who could make regulations, was in control of the police force charged with enforcement of the regulations, and who, finally, as we have seen in a previous chapter, sat as magistrate in the courts to decide upon cases of violation of his own regulations.

This same mayor or burgess was frequently either an official or higher-grade employee in a steel plant, or had close personal relation with some one who was. Even without this connection, he and his fellow officials were likely to be openly and obviously under the influence and direction of the companies.[1]

One notable and picturesque instance was found in Duquesne. The mayor of that town was himself president of the First National Bank, his brother was president of the Port Vue Tin Plate Company, and his own official duties included those of city commissioner, president of the city council, director of public safety, and magistrate. He was especially severe in refusing permits for meetings, and on the occasion of one refusal made a frequently quoted remark that "Jesus Christ himself could not hold a labor meeting in Duquesne."

And it was in his town, earlier in the year, that a meeting gathered to hear a Russian speaker deliver a lecture on Lincoln, was raided by the police, most of the Russians present were taken to jail for an examination, and the lecturer himself was arrested and held in jail for thirty-six hours. A certain humor in this proceeding lay in the fact that the speaker was sent out as the representative of an agency of the Federal government in a campaign of "Americanization."

[1] "'Free elections' were customarily impossible in steel towns in western Pennsylvania, due to clearly understood manipulations by steel-company officials or by steel-company officials who were also public officials." *Interchurch World Movement Report on the Steel Strike of 1919*, p. 239.

The forces actually on guard over the strikers included, in one place or another, the state constabulary, the city or borough police, the private industrial police of employers, known as "coal and iron police" or as "company police" or otherwise, city or borough detectives, company detectives, specially sworn in deputy sheriffs to any number and drawn from any class of the population the powers in authority desired to call upon, and, it was freely charged, gangs of out-and-out thugs and criminals. And the personal connection between the city police and the industrial police and the city and company detective staffs was often close. Men passed rapidly and freely from one force to the other.

In Pittsburgh it was made known that city policemen detailed to the strike zone had received pay for their services, in addition to their city salaries, from a steel company.

These forces all worked together as one body and were systematically upheld by the courts and others in authority, in all of their acts.

In Gary, Indiana, the regular army of the United States was added to the forces assembled to guard against the strikers, and brought the Federal government directly into the chain of influences the strikers had seen stretching from the industrial plant to the court.

As described by the Commission of Inquiry of the Interchurch World Movement, the Federal soldiers were equipped with bayonets and steel helmets, and the force included many trucks, mounting machine guns and bringing field artillery. Rules for picketing established by the commanding general were so interpreted and carried out as to break up the picket line. Delays and difficulties attended the release from jail or the bull pen of picketers who had been arrested. Army officers sent soldiers to arrest union officers in other trades than the steel industry for such offenses as threatening to call a strike on a local building operation. As a result of all this procedure workers throughout the city believed that the Federal government opposed them.[1]

Accounts of this strike give instance after instance, in many cases supported by affidavits, of violence committed by these mixed forces in working-class neighborhoods against the foreign born, who might or might not be strikers. Groups of people, men, women, and even children standing quietly in the street were ridden down and scattered by mounted men, or arrested and taken to court as "disorderly" or "suspicious persons"; individuals were sought even in their homes, and haled to court on similar charges. Instances in plenty, with the supporting evidence, will be found in the hearings before the Senate committee and the reports of other investigations.[2]

The state constabulary in particular apparently translated its nickname of "Cossack" into grim reality for the foreign-born workers, who, experiencing from them the same sort of rough handling with which they were familiar from the Cossacks at home, would naturally infer the same sort of cruel and arbitrary government behind them as they knew in the old country.

When cases were finally brought before the court,

[1] *The Interchurch World Movement, Report on the Steel Strike of 1919*, pp. 241–242.

[2] Investigation of the Strike in the Steel Industries, Hearings before the Committee on Education and Labor, U. S. Senate, Sixty-sixth Congress, First Session, Senate Resolutions 188 and 102: "Closed Towns," S. Adele Shaw, *The Survey*, November 8, 1919; *The Interchurch World Movement Report on the Steel Strike of 1919*.

there was much complaint of injustice. Attorneys claimed that they could not get access to clients or to their records, that they could not secure the release of clients on bail, that in the hearing of the cases they were not allowed opportunity to cross-examine or even to hear what was going on. In the decisions the industrial status of the man, as well as, or perhaps rather than, the specific charge for which he was brought before the court seemed to have weight.

One attorney testified before the Senate committee that in the court before which his cases were brought the magistrate would ask the man before him, "Are you a citizen?" and then, "Are you working?" If his answer to the latter question was, "No," the magistrate would impose a fine or jail sentence; if the answer was, "Yes," the man would be discharged.

It was charged that the same discrimination was made by the arresting officers. In one place, it was stated before the Senate committee, it was the custom for officers to round up the strikers standing before the mills, set free those who would agree to go to work, and send the rest to jail. Testimony was also given that men were terrorized after arrest, while in the jail, by threats that they would be "hanged in the morning" if they still refused to go back to work. Other instances may be found in the reports of investigations already referred to.

The report made by the Senate committee was not regarded by the labor element as especially favorable to them—in fact, quite the reverse—so we may accept the conclusion of this committee on the activities of courts and police as at least a moderate and conservative statement of the case, and this report substantially sustains most of the charges made by the strikers and their attorneys.

IMMIGRANT WORKINGMAN BEFORE COURT

These conclusions were as follows:

Since the strike there has been complaint that the strikers have been denied the right of free speech and that the treatment by the officers has been brutal and that their treatment in the courts does not accord with the high ideals of American democracy. In some places all meetings have been denied. In others, street meetings have been denied and indoor meetings permitted. The orders of the mayors and burgesses that no outdoor public meetings, or, in some places, no public meetings, should be held, was most distasteful to them. While apparently they were trying to obey this order, they regarded it as aimed wholly at them. They are to be commended for their observance of law and order.

It may be open to question whether permits to hold meetings should have been denied to the workers, and, while generally the orders denying permits were obeyed, yet in most instances where clashes occurred or arrests made it was because of attempts to hold meetings after the request for a permit had been denied.

Freedom of speech is one of the bulwarks of American liberty. Freedom of speech does not, however, mean unbridled license. It does not mean the right of men to advocate the overthrow of this government, but it seems to us that where a strike is carried on in a peaceful way the least possible amount of restraint and the largest freedom of speech where meetings are conducted in an orderly way are certainly to be desired in the American Republic. The suppression of frank discussion only serves to accentuate a bad situation.

Officials should not hesitate to prevent meetings called together for the purpose of advocating the overthrow of the government. On the other hand, they ought not to be permitted to prevent men meeting and talking over their grievances and presenting to the men their arguments in favor of joining the union or refraining from joining the union.

Incidents have been presented in the committee of unnecessary force by police officers. Probably there will always be abuses in times of excitement, but apparently there have been cases of unoffending men and women arrested without reason by the officers, put into jail, and in some cases fined by magistrates without warrant or justification. It is not necessary to refer to special cases as disclosed by the evidence. The action in many instances was such as to lead one side of this controversy to the belief that the officers of the law were acting on the side of the steel company. Such a situation is unfortunate and tends to breed discontent. As long as officers are human beings they will make mistakes. They should be very careful that in maintaining the majesty and dignity of the law they do nothing to bring it into disrespect.

As to the complaint of the action of the courts, we are inclined to believe that there is some ground for complaint and that the magisterial courts in the taking of bonds and the forfeiting of bonds, in the arresting of people merely as suspicious characters and sending them to jail therefor, have not in every instance been justifiable. The courts should be very careful that they are not subject to just criticism for curtailing the rights of defendants.

The foreigners whom the needs of our industries bring among us cannot be dragooned into love for America and loyalty to its institutions. Public officials should always be ready to receive sympathetic suggestions for the relief of just complaints or violations of or interference with the legal or humane rights of labor, as well as the insistence upon a protection of the property rights of capital and the preservation of law and order.[1]

That the repressive policy followed in Pennsylvania was necessary in order to prevent disorder seems to be disproved by the happenings in the neighboring state of Ohio, where a different plan was followed. In Ohio strikers were allowed to picket, both indoor and outdoor meetings were freely permitted, no speakers were arrested, no meetings dispersed. Public officials entered

[1] Senate Report No. 289, Sixty-sixth Congress, First Session, *Investigating Strike in Steel Industries,* p. 24.

into relations of coöperation with labor officials as well as with the mill authorities, and the general maintenance of order was noteworthy.[1]

Were the foreign-born workers in the strike really revolutionists, and was the thought of revolutionary agitation at the bottom of their minds in striking? The Commission of Inquiry of the Interchurch World Movement, as the result of a first-hand investigation, concludes that neither their purposes nor their methods were revolutionary. Their report states that while hundreds of strikers were rounded up in the "radical" raids going on during the strike, none were tried and convicted in state courts of anarchistic belief or practice. A mere handful were held for deportation, and these, not because of radical agitation during the strike, but for general radical propaganda or membership in organizations considered dangerously radical.

Perhaps Andrew Pido will do as well as anyone to typify the average steel striker and illustrate some of his experiences and reactions. He appeared before the Senate committee and testified that he had been arrested for making a "remark" to the son of a borough officer. He was put in jail, the officer came around with his son, unlocked the cell, and looked on while the son gave Andrew a good beating up. Andrew was punched so badly that he could not open his mouth for three days. The officer was not in charge of the jail, but he opened the cell just the same. This Andrew was a Slovak, twenty-three years of age. He had taken out his first citizenship papers and wanted to get the second papers. He had purchased Liberty Bonds. He had been in the war, and had tried to enlist in the army that year (1919), but had been rejected on account of an oper-

[1] *The Survey*, November 8, 1919, p. 89.

ation he had undergone. He was a striker because he wanted eight hours a day and better conditions. He thinks a man ought to work eight hours, have eight hours sleep, "and eight hours he can go to school and learn something," and he thinks "that an education is better than much money." He himself had gone to night school about twenty nights—this is all the schooling he had ever had. He says the men would like to go to school, but they work too long hours.

Asked about his relations with the boss, he says: "Well, I do not have much kick, but I was not very satisfied with them, either. The first thing that was wrong, they would call me a Hunky."[1]

This is by no means a complete account of the labor troubles of the past few years in which foreign-born workers have been concerned. But the instances given here may be regarded as indicative of what is happening generally.

Judging from these, we may conclude that in our municipal governments and minor courts we find in normal times and in large places not given over to the dominance of one strong interest a more or less grudging recognition of the foreign-born worker's rights in labor troubles, ready, however, to be transformed, in certain places, or in times of stress and excitement, into a concealed or open hostility which tends to make the worker feel that the government and the court are nothing of his, nothing in which he has a part, but an alien, perhaps an "alien enemy" power.

[1] Hearings before the Committee on Education and Labor, U. S. Senate, Sixty-Sixth Congress, First Session, Senate Resolutions 188 and 102, p. 599.

VIII

SPECIAL PROVISIONS OF LAW RELATING TO THE ALIEN

THUS far we have been considering the experiences of the immigrant under laws that applied to the native-born citizen equally with himself; the text of the law for both was the same, the penalty prescribed was the same, court procedure was the same. If any discrimination was made against the foreign born, it was at least not authorized by any law, or any rule of procedure. There are in our statute books, however, laws making different provisions for aliens from those for citizens, and laws applying to aliens only. Let us look at some of these and see whether there is anything in them that would tend to make the foreign born feel that he was unjustly treated.

DISCRIMINATION IN THE FEDERAL CONSTITUTION

It is commonly supposed that the Constitution of the United States itself embodies discriminatory legislation; that its guaranties of rights apply to citizens only. Many persons will be surprised to find, if they turn to the text of the Constitution itself, that the word "citizen" is used only in establishing qualifications for Representative, Senator, and President, in defining the jurisdiction of United States Courts, in defining citizenship, and in prohibiting discrimination by states against citizens of the United States. All other provisions and guaranties of rights relate to "persons" or "people," are not defined in their application, and necessarily affect everybody.

FEDERAL AND STATE LAW

The general body of state law, and of Federal law, aside from the laws regulating the admission of aliens to the country, contains few provisions relating specifically to the alien. Such provisions as there are relate mainly to the right to acquire land, to the right to enter into some specified occupation, to the right to vote, and to taxation. The alien also may have special rights under a treaty with the foreign country from which he comes.

RIGHTS TO REAL PROPERTY

As to landholding, acquirement of land from the public domain of the United States (under the Homestead law) is permitted to aliens who have declared their intention of becoming citizens, but is not permitted to nondeclarants.

Under state laws, some fourteen or fifteen of the states restrict in some way the right of the alien to acquire and hold real property. Nonresident aliens only are restricted in the greater number of these states. They are not allowed to acquire land by purchase, but various provisions are made permitting them to take land through inheritance, or in satisfaction of a claim, but under the condition that they dispose of the property within a stated time. A smaller number of states make the same general restriction against aliens, whether resident or nonresident, who have not declared their intention of becoming citizens, or restrict the amount of land the nondeclarant may hold. A very few of the states forbid ownership by any class of aliens.

In 1907, Oklahoma set up a barrier against the ownership of real property by all classes of aliens, and provided that any alien who thereafter acquired real estate must dispose of it within five years.

Arizona forbids all classes of aliens to acquire land other than mining land, by purchase, but allows them to take title and hold land coming to them by inheritance for five years. If at the end of that time they have not disposed of it or become citizens, the land becomes the property of the state. Pennsylvania restricts the amount of land to be held by purchase, by any class of alien. Illinois and Kentucky permit any alien to acquire land, by purchase or otherwise, but make provision that it must be disposed of within a period of years. In Illinois the term is six years; in Kentucky it is eight years, but it is further provided that a resident alien may hold land for his own residence or place of business for a period of twenty-one years. California has a land law especially directed against the ownership or acquirement of land by the Japanese.

The rights of aliens to own land are further extended in practice by the fact that the legal procedure prescribed for carrying the restrictions into effect is frequently not invoked. In Illinois, for example, which has a strict law against alien ownership, aliens are seldom disturbed in their possession, since a special form of action is necessary to oust them, and this is seldom resorted to.

On the whole, it would seem that the land laws are not greatly restrictive. Under them the immigrant who is a resident alien is interfered with hardly anywhere or hardly at all in any ordinary uses he may desire to make of real property.

THE IMMIGRANT'S DAY IN COURT

Restrictions on the alien's right to carry on an occupation are found mainly in relation to positions under Federal, state, or municipal government. In a few states, all positions in the civil service, whether classified and subject to examination or unclassified, are closed to aliens. In some of the states statutes have been framed to prevent the employment of aliens in any capacity on public works, but in many instances the constitutionality of the legislation has been disputed, and denied by the courts.

Restrictions on entering into private occupations are few, and when such exist it is usually on the ground that the occupations are affected by a public interest. For instance, the practice of law is forbidden to aliens in most of the states. Some of these restrictions also have been disputed as unconstitutional and found void by the courts.

TAXATION

Discrimination in taxation has affected the immigrant mainly through the provisions of the Revenue Act of 1918 of the Federal government, relating to the income tax. Taxation in general bears only indirectly on the poor man; but with the income tax for the first time came the audible rap of the tax collector at the door of rich and poor alike, and it was a particularly hard and disturbing rap at the door of the immigrant workingman.

The Revenue Act of 1918 provided that the non-resident alien individual should pay a tax of 12 per cent on his income for the year 1918, of 8 per cent for 1919, rates exactly double those imposed upon resident aliens and citizens. And unless the country of which the nonresident alien was a citizen or a subject allowed similar credits to citizens of the United States non-resident in that country, the nonresident alien in this country was allowed no exemptions for income below a certain limit, or for dependents.

As the nonresident aliens among the immigrants are for the most part the poorer people on the lower levels of industry, and as they customarily have dependents in the home country, a high rate of taxation with no exemptions was a great hardship to them, and was felt as such. The fact, furthermore, that provision was made for the collection of part of the tax by employers gave rise to much misunderstanding and suspicion. Workingmen suspect all deductions from the pay envelope, in the light of past unfortunate experiences with foremen and others.

It was exceedingly difficult, also, for the immigrant workingman to understand the procedure of collecting the income tax, to know what his status was, in the first place, as resident or nonresident, then to know when he had fulfilled the requirements of the law and whether he had secured his full rights under it. Under this cloud of uncertainty the immigrant could imagine all sorts of unfair treatment, and very often got it, owing to misunderstanding on his part and lack of explanation on the part of officials.

It was not, indeed, altogether easy to determine whether an alien was a resident or a nonresident. The law does not define the term. In the earliest proceedings taken under the act, persons charged with collecting the tax were disagreed as to a definition. Employers collecting the tax were likely to consider any alien a nonresident. Regulations of the Treasury Department,[1] issued to explain the meaning of the law and

[1] Regulations 45 Relating to the Income Tax, under the Revenue Act of 1918, Washington, 1919.

clear up doubtful points, define the nonresident alien negatively by saying that any alien who is not a "mere transient" is a resident of the United States for purposes of the income tax. As explained in the regulations whether he is a "transient" or not is to be determined by his intentions with regard to his stay. The best evidence of such intentions is afforded by the conduct, acts, and declarations of the alien. A mere floating intention, indefinite as to time, to return to another country is not sufficient to constitute him a transient. But if he genuinely intends his stay to be transient, he will remain a transient although he continues to live in the United States for a considerable time. The fact that an alien's family is abroad does not necessarily indicate that he is a transient. But an alien who enters this country intending to make his home in a foreign country as soon as he has accumulated a sum of money sufficient to provide for his journey abroad is to be considered a transient, provided his expectations may reasonably, considering the rate of his savings, be fulfilled within a comparatively short time. Thus the regulations explained "nonresident" and "resident."

Although these regulations did somewhat clear up the matter, even under them to determine "nonresidence," it is necessary to determine that hidden and changing thing, an "intention," to know whether it is "floating" or "genuine," and to check up this determination by certain imperfectly defined surrounding circumstances.

Furthermore, since, according to the regulations, aliens employed in the United States are *prima facie* regarded as nonresidents, so that the burden of proof is placed on them to show that they actually are residents—if such is the case, every alien workingman has to puzzle out these distinctions for himself, and if he fails to show clearly that he is a resident, he remains among the nonresidents, subject to the higher tax rate. The distinction is not entirely clear at best, and the immigrant will naturally be confused by it. And even the officials charged with administering the law did not find it any too plain, so that their explanations to the alien were not always enlightening. In some cases one official would tell the alien one thing, another another.

As a result of this confusion, a considerable number of aliens registered themselves as nonresident who had a resident status. In many cases they did this because of an idea that if they registered as residents they would not be allowed to go back to see their families, or ever be able to see their country again. And after the armistice many of them were in the greatest anxiety to go to Europe to search for their families, whom they had lost track of during the war and who might be in distress of some kind.

Owing to these general misunderstandings, also, they saw persons in the same situations taxed differently, which, of course, would seem to them an unfair discrimination. The files of the Foreign Language Information Service, to which aliens in need of advice were invited to appeal, are crammed with pathetic letters relating hardships and misunderstandings in great number.

One man, a steel worker, wrote that in 1918 he had earned $920, and that the company was withholding the tax from the wages. He had already paid $18.40, and now they were making him pay 10 per cent for 1918, 8 per cent for 1919, "and do not give any receipts. . . . I cannot understand how it is. There is nobody here who could explain it to me, for I do not speak English. I believe what anybody tells me, and I pay.

Of course I am willing to pay according to the law, because I know that the government needs the tax, but I am afraid of being misled too often. I am a poor man, married, and have five children in Europe. So please let me know whether I have paid right. Answer soon."

Perhaps this man did "pay right," but a deduction of $110.40 from a $920 salary seems a rather heavy burden on a man with a wife and five children to support.

Another unfortunate who had to pay 12 per cent on $1,000 earnings, writes, "They want me to pay, and by living God I do not know what to do. The mine does not work but twice a week." Another man made $1,122.46 in 1918, in a smelting and refining company, spent $100 for a Liberty bond and $100 for War Savings Stamps, and paid $134.64 income tax, although he stated that he had no definite intention of leaving America.

These are but three chance instances out of thousands, some of which, more picturesque and dramatic, have already seen the light in print.

IX

THE IMMIGRATION LAW

THE most distinctive and important set of laws, referring especially to the alien, are, so far as the immigrant himself is concerned, the Federal laws governing the admission to this country of aliens, their exclusion and expulsion from it.

These laws, unlike the general body of law, are enforced against the immigrant not through the courts, except as the last resort, and in a limited degree, but by an administrative body, the Department of Labor. Because this is so, and because it is asserted that no questions of criminality or of civil rights are involved, it is frequently urged that any test of the law and the methods of its enforcement in accordance with principles of justice worked out in the laws enforceable through the courts and in court procedure is not to the point. Perhaps not, if we regard only legal technicality. But if we have in mind the substantial justice, that every human being feels aggrieved at not receiving, as distinguished from technical justice, there is certainly ground for comparison. Wherever a law of any sort exists, surely a corresponding right to substantial justice under it exists.

The immigration law, like other laws, is a rule laid down to be followed in particular cases; it may be considered just or unjust, in so far as it does or does not show the characteristics we recognize as fundamentally desirable in the laws enforced through the courts.

The process of administering justice under the law

in the courts consists in deciding whether or not a specific case falls under the general rule laid down in the law and prescribing the appropriate action to be taken in that case. This is essentially what happens in the enforcement of the immigration law by the administrative department in charge of it.

There would seem to be good reasons, then, for scrutinizing the immigration law and the procedure under it in the light of principles laid down for laws and legal procedure in general to see how far substantial justice is rendered.

In the immigration laws the provisions of special importance to the immigrant are those defining what classes of persons shall be kept from entering the country, or sent out after they have entered.

EXCLUSION PROVISIONS

In the provisions for exclusion as the law has developed, two distinct purposes are shown, somewhat in conflict with each other—one, to restrict the competition of foreign labor with the labor force already in this country, by prohibiting the entry of persons who had previously contracted to do work here; the other, and this covers the greater part of the provisions for exclusion, to establish a selective process by which persons below a certain moral, mental, physical, and economic standard shall be kept from entering the country.

The first Federal law establishing excluded classes, that of 1875, shut out prostitutes and criminals other than political offenders. A law of 1882 excluded any convict, lunatic, idiot, or any person liable to become a public charge. In 1882, also, a beginning was made of Chinese exclusion legislation.

THE IMMIGRATION LAW

Successive enactments have added to the excluded classes, both by establishing new kinds of disability and by adding to the specific disabilities belonging in some general class already established that was found not to be sufficiently defined.

To the mentally defective have been added epileptics, imbeciles, feeble-minded, persons who have been insane at some former time, whether "lunatics" at time of admission or not, and persons of a "constitutional psychopathic inferiority." To secure a certain amount of educational acquirement as well as normality of intellect, by the law of 1917 illiterates were excluded.

In 1891 a standard of physical condition was set in the provision for excluding those afflicted with a "loathsome or contagious disease," and to this has been specifically added, tuberculosis, in any form.

The economic standard, set to prevent dependency, and beginning in the provision excluding persons liable to become a public charge, has been expanded, in successive laws, to include paupers, immigrants whose passage has been paid by some society or government agency (assisted immigrants), professional beggars, and vagrants.

As both defective and dependent, under the law of 1907, persons who had a mental or physical deficiency which might affect their ability to earn a living were to be excluded, and as dependent, with a possibility of moral harm, children under sixteen, unaccompanied by a parent, were to be excluded at the discretion of the administrative head of the service.

As not measuring up to the moral standard have been added persons admitting the commission of crime, polygamists, persons who believe in the practice of polygamy, persons connected in a number of defined

307

ways with the business of prostitution, anarchists, and persons variously defined who are grouped with them in the law.

EXCLUSION OF ANARCHISTS

The first provision for the exclusion of anarchists or persons of that type appeared in the law of 1903, after the assassination of President McKinley. As the provision is worded it provides for the exclusion of "anarchists, or persons who believe in or advocate the overthrow by force or violence of the government of the United States, or of all government, or of all forms of law, or the assassination of public officials." In 1917 the "anarchy clause" was expanded and changed in phrasing to read as follows:

. . . anarchists, or persons who believe in or advocate the overthrow by force or violence of the government of the United States, or of all forms of law, or who disbelieve in or are opposed to organized government, or who advocate the assassination of public officials, or who advocate or teach the unlawful destruction of property; persons who are members of or affiliated with any organization entertaining and teaching disbelief in or opposition to organized government, or who advocate or teach the duty, necessity, or propriety of the unlawful assaulting or killing of any officer or officers, either of specific individuals or of officers generally, of the government of the United States or of any other organized government, because of his or their official character, or who advocate or teach the unlawful destruction of property.

In both these laws, the phrases following the word "anarchy" may be interpreted as definitions of that term—the comma and the word "or" after "anarchy" marking the beginning of a restrictive or descriptive passage.

THE IMMIGRATION LAW

A law passed October 16, 1918, however, separated the descriptive phrases from the term "anarchy" by replacing the comma with a semicolon and eliminating the word "or." This left the term "anarchists" entirely without definition. Other changes bring the offenses of the alien personally and of the organization, membership in which is to cause his exclusion, into agreement. There had been some small discrepancies between the two in the law of 1917, as will be noted in the text given above.

A law passed in 1920 adds the preparation and distribution of literature, or membership in an organization that prepares and distributes literature, advocating or teaching the various forms of opposition to government named in previous clauses, as causes for exclusion, expands "organization" by adding "association, society or group," and provides that the supplying of money for the teaching of the forbidden doctrines shall be regarded as the teaching of the doctrines, and that contributing money to an organization shall constitute affiliation with it.

EXCLUSION ON RACIAL GROUNDS

The Chinese exclusion acts provided for the debarring of immigrants because of their race. But in other cases, Congress has carefully refrained from making a racial or a national distinction a ground for exclusion, notwithstanding a public sentiment in this country which has favored certain peoples and has been opposed to others. Japanese laborers are kept out without the enactment of a law against the Japanese by agreement with the Japanese government.

In the law of 1917, however, we find a provision that, without expressly making a racial distinction, practically has this effect. This is the provision excluding, "unless otherwise provided for by existing treaties," persons born within specified geographical boundaries, who are not members of specified occupational classes. These boundaries include a large part of the Asiatic continent, and of the islands of the southern Pacific, and through this provision Hindu and other Asiatic laborers are shut out without being named as such.

An act passed in 1921, as a temporary measure, establishes a group qualification for admission by restricting the number of aliens of any nationality who may be admitted to the United States in any year to three per cent of the number of foreign-born persons of that nationality resident in the United States according to the Census of 1910.[1]

This law, although not openly discriminating against any racial or national group, does, in effect, do so against the peoples of eastern and southern Europe and of Asia Minor, because immigration of these peoples, being comparatively new, had accumulated only small populations in the United States by 1910. So that, on the basis of population, immigration from northern and western Europe is practically without restriction, while immigration from southern and eastern countries is held within narrow limits.

THE SPIRIT OF OUR LAW

Are the exclusion provisions in accord with the principles regarded as fundamental in the general system of law handed down by our ancestors? One of these principles is that the thing permitted or not permitted shall be clearly defined, so that one may know beforehand exactly what to do or to refrain from doing, in

[1] *Report of the Commissioner General of Immigration, 1921*, p. 16.

order to comply with the law; may know what the enforcing officer will or will not punish him for doing or not doing.

VAGUE DEFINITION OF EXCLUDED CLASSES

The more ill defined and vague the terms of the law, the greater is the power of the enforcing officer practically to establish *ex post facto* legislation, by declaring that a given situation after it has arisen, falls within the definition of the law, and the greater is the injustice to the defendant, the less opportunity he has had of knowing beforehand what was right or wrong for him to do.

Many of the provisions for exclusion are of this vague nature. "Liability to become a public charge" is nowhere defined. It is left to the discretion of the examining inspector to decide how much money in the immigrant's possession, what personal circumstances will determine this in each particular case. The immigrant cannot find out before he starts just what will insure his compliance with this provision, and it is a hardship to him to be turned back after he has made the voyage. Similarly vague is the term "constitutional pyschopathic inferiority," or "physical defect of a nature which may affect the ability to earn a living."

Again, what is an "anarchist"? As we have seen, in the latest enactment this word is absolutely undefined. The head of one of the immigration stations being asked by the writer how he determined whether a man was an anarchist or not, at first failed to understand the question, and then, after some explanation, said that an "anarchist" was one who "was established to be such to the satisfaction of the commissioner under rulings from Washington." Asked what these rulings were, he said he could not divulge them, as it was against public policy.

How, then, could an immigrant know whether he would or would not be classed as an "anarchist" in the meaning of the law if no information is given out as to what constitutes an anarchist? He may assume that it means only one who has a definite theory of government which he is ready to carry out in practice; it has been interpreted in certain decisions of government officials to include anyone who believes that under certain circumstances government will become unnecessary and will disappear of itself. And the word has even wider meanings in popular usage, as when "anarchism in art" and so forth is referred to.

PENALIZING OF BELIEF

Again, it is a general principle of the law, as developed by our English ancestors, not to concern itself with beliefs, or even with intentions, unless these are shown through some overt act. This principle, which has been worked out to secure religious toleration, is, however, now being disregarded in state legislation against political heresy; and in the immigration law we find beliefs penalized in the provisions against "anarchists" as just noted, and against those who "believe in" as well as practice polygamy.

ESTABLISHMENT OF GROUP RESPONSIBILITY

Furthermore, according to the spirit of our law, responsibility is personal; that is to say, one is chargeable only for his own acts, and not for those of other people. Instances are few in which the law holds an individual responsible for the acts of a group to which he belongs.

It is held unjust to make an individual responsible

for what he cannot control, and if a group is at all considerable in size the individual certainly cannot control its action, and sometimes may not even know what action is being taken. If the member of a group is to be held to full responsibility for the actions or beliefs of the group, the group may get him into trouble faster than he can get away from the group. An illustration of the working out of this principle is seen in the laws limiting the liability of individuals holding stock in a corporation. Under the older forms of partnership, the group was so small it could be presumed that each member knew what was being done by the others and could exert influence upon the actions of the others. But with the corporation came so extended a partnership that the individual no longer knew or could control the action of the group and the law recognized this changed state of affairs by limiting the liability of the individuals accordingly.

In the immigration laws, however, we find an increasing number of provisions establishing group responsibility, as in the provisions for excluding because of membership in an organization, or because of belonging to a certain race, or because of birth in a certain locality, or because of the number in the country of a group to which an individual belongs.

DIFFICULTY OF PROVING VIOLATIONS

Even where the class is clearly defined by law, if it cannot be determined what individuals fall within it, this also is a hindrance to the effective rendering of justice. Under these circumstances the law will either be unenforced, or enforced against the wrong persons in many instances. If the law is evaded with impunity, this causes disrespect for all law; and if it is enforced against the innocent, this arouses a feeling of injustice.

313

THE IMMIGRANT'S DAY IN COURT

Just this difficulty arises in connection with a number of the exclusion provisions of the immigration law, especially those that deal with belief and membership. What is to prove the belief of the incoming immigrant, except his own statement? If he thinks a true statement of his belief will shut him out, he probably will not make it. What is to show membership in an organization? What is to show the fact of previous insanity? Some of these difficulties can be met by establishing investigating stations in the countries from which the immigrants come. They certainly are not met in the examinations on this side.

How little practical effect the exclusion provisions regarding belief have had may be seen, for example, from the fact that up to June 30, 1921, eighteen years after the passage of the first provision against the admission of "anarchists," only 38 persons had been debarred for that reason. If the 38 excluded are the only persons of anarchistic belief who applied for admission to the country, what is the basis for the complaint against the immigrant as the importer of anarchy? If they are not, the law is shown to be ineffective. This latter was the view taken by the Commissioner General of Immigration in 1912, who says:

It is even more difficult to detect anarchists. . . . During the past year only two anarchists were rejected and only four arrested and deported. Yet it is a matter of common knowledge that there are many alien anarchists in the United States. Persons of this belief usually are found fully acquainted with the provisions of the immigration law, and therefore appreciate the importance to themselves of concealing their status in this regard at the time of entry.[1]

[1] *Report of the Commissioner General of Immigration, for the year ending June 30, 1912*, p. 6.

THE IMMIGRATION LAW

Our immigration laws make provision for sending aliens out of the country after their arrival, as well as for excluding them. Leaving out of account the Alien bill of 1798, an Act passed for a two-year period only, to meet a special political emergency, which gave the President the power to deport any aliens whom he regarded as dangerous to the country, the provisions for deportation in the immigration law began as a logical extension and supplement to the provisions for exclusion, intended to remedy evasions of those provisions, and make them fully effective.

As the disqualifications for entrance are necessarily such as the immigrant brings with him, such as have arisen in the country from which he comes, in the same way the earlier deportation provisions cover only disqualifications existing at the time of entry, and the period after landing within which deportation could be effected was restricted to the period within which a violation of the requirements for admission might reasonably be discovered.

In succeeding immigration laws, however, the period within which deportation might be effected was lengthened more and more until all time limits were removed for certain classes of disqualifications, and disqualifications arising after landing were recognized as grounds for deportation.

Under the law of 1917, an alien who had become a public charge in this country within five years after landing, might be deported unless he could bring positive proof that the cause of dependence arose after landing. An alien might be deported at any time after entry who was found connected with commercialized vice in any one of a number of defined ways, or if he

315

had been a major or habitual offender before or after arrival, or if at any time after entry he should be found advocating or teaching the unlawful destruction of property or advocating or teaching anarchy, or the overthrow by force or violence of the government of the United States or of all forms of law or the assassination of public officials.

In the provisions of this law for the deportation of persons of the anarchist classes only those actually found advocating and teaching anarchy and violence of various kinds were deportable at any time after entry. Other persons coming under the definition of the provisions for exclusion, persons shut out for beliefs, or for membership in organizations, could be deported only within five years after entry and if it could be shown that the disqualifications were present at the time of entry.

The deportation provisions, then, in the law of 1917 held more strictly to the principle of individual responsibility, for the concrete act, than do the provisions for exclusion.

The law of 1918, however, which deals only with members of the anarchistic and similar classes, after defining those who are to be excluded from admission, in a second section provides that "any alien who at any time after entering the United States is found to have been at time of entry, or to have become thereafter, a member of any one of the classes of aliens enumerated in section one of this Act," shall be deported, thus adding belief and membership as causes of deportation, regardless of their origin, and of the time the alien has lived in the country, and the same section retained in the law of 1920 adds the stricter provisions for exclusion of that law to the provisions for deportation.

The recognition, then, hitherto embodied in the im-

migration law of the obligation of each country to undertake the responsibility of caring for its own waste
products, has now been withdrawn in the case of serious
criminals and persons belonging to the anarchist classes,
without adequate reason, it would seem. Under the
present law, an immigrant brought here as an infant,
who has grown up in the surroundings of our cities
and towns and farms, who has been educated in our
schools, and who has learned all that he knows in our
communities, if he is found under the circumstances
just mentioned, may—if he or his parents have failed
to become citizens—be deported to a country which
is not responsible for him in any way for disabilities
plainly arising in this country.

And much more personal hardship to the individual
is involved in deportation than exclusion, so that the
penalty for the same disability is made greater after
the immigrant has once been admitted than at the time
of entry and it becomes greater the longer the immigrant is here.

If the alien has lived here so long that this country
has become his home, his situation when deported is
something like that of the English criminal who was
sent to the colonies, with perhaps less opportunity of
establishing a normal life once more. In a case brought
before a Federal court, in which an alien who had been
in this country since childhood was ordered deported
on the ground that since her arrival she had become
immoral, the court said:

It seems to me that no greater hardship could be occasioned than by deporting an alien who had come here at a
tender age and lived here until after majority. Deportation
in such case is tantamount to exile.[1]

[1] Redfern *vs.* Halpert, 186 Fed. 150.

317

THE IMMIGRANT'S DAY IN COURT

Every moment of the immigrant's life here forms an additional link with the country in which he is investing his personal energies and his money, in which he is forming personal and business relations, in which he is weaving himself more and more into the network of social life, and which is making its influences felt more and more, in making him what he is, whether for good or for bad. Residence in this country is in fact a sort of vested interest, growing with lapse of time, notwithstanding a technical state of alienage for those who have not become naturalized. And this is to some extent recognized in the immigration law itself, when it makes special provisions for the admission of "aliens returning after a temporary absence to an unrelinquished United States domicile of seven consecutive years."[1]

REVOCATION OF CITIZENSHIP

As the immigration law now stands, it holds control over the alien through some of its provisions most at variance with the spirit of our law, as long as his life in this country lasts, if he fails to become naturalized, and even after naturalization, under certain circumstances. The citizenship granted to the alien is, in fact, something different from the citizenship enjoyed by the native born. In the first place more conditions are hedged about entering into citizenship. The alien, in order to become a citizen, must show that he is not a disbeliever in or opposed to organized government, or a member of or affiliated with any organization which entertains or teaches disbelief or opposition to organized government, or one who advocates the killing of officers of government, or a polygamist. He must be of good moral character, at the time of application for citizen-

[1] Act of February 5, 1917, Section 3.

ship, and must also be shown to have been such for five years preceding the application. None of these qualifications are required of citizens by birth.

And the native-born citizen loses his citizenship only for conviction of serious crime; the naturalized alien may lose his[1] through court proceedings to set aside and cancel the certificate of citizenship on the ground of fraud, or that the certificate was illegally procured. That is, among the causes of canceling the certificate would be that at the time of granting the certificate the alien belonged to any of the classes mentioned above, and also if at the time of naturalization he had not in fact renounced allegiance to his former country or government, or was not "attached to the principles of the Constitution of the United States and well disposed to the good order and happiness of the same." None of the above circumstances would cause the withdrawal of citizenship from a person born in this country unless he had first been convicted under some state law making any of these circumstances a serious crime. After a certificate of naturalization has been canceled, the person again becoming an alien is liable to deportation according to the provisions of the immigration law.

CASES OF "DENATURALIZATION"

Certain cases brought up in Federal courts illustrate the wide range of reasons for cancellation of naturalization and of inference in proving illegality.

In 1912, one Raverat was deprived of citizenship on the ground that he was not of good moral character when admitted to citizenship.[2] In the same year, one Leonard Olsson[3] lost his citizenship in the state of

[1] Section 15, Naturalization Laws, Act of June 29, 1906.
[2] U. S. *vs*. Raverat, 222 Fed. 1018.
[3] U. S. *vs*. Olsson, 196 Fed. 563 foll.

Washington, apparently because he was a Socialist, or rather, because of his affiliation with the Socialist party. The decision states that at the hearing in denaturalization proceedings the man denied that he was an anarchist, but omitted to make any declaration affirming loyalty, and on cross-examination his answers respecting attachment to the Constitution were evasive. He admitted that he was a Socialist, and a "frequenter of assemblages of Socialists in which he participates as a speaker advocating a propaganda for radical changes in the institutions of the country." He claimed to have a clear understanding of the Constitution and knew that deprivation of "life, liberty, and property" without due process of law was forbidden, "and yet the evidence introduced in his behalf proved that the party with which he is affiliated and whose principles he advocates, has for its main object the complete elimination of property rights in this country. He expressed himself as being willing for people to retain their money, but insisted that all the land, buildings, and industrial institutions should become the common property of all the people, which object is to be obtained, according to his belief, by use of the power of the ballot, and when that object shall have been attained the political government of the country will be entirely abrogated because there will be no use for it."

The judge interpreted all this as hostile to the Constitution. "He has no reverence for the Constitution of the United States, nor intention to support and defend it against its enemies, and he is not well disposed toward the peace and tranquillity of the people. His propaganda is to create turmoil and to end in chaos." Had the judge based his decision to cancel on the general ground of lack of attachment to the Constitution as shown in the evasive answers of the naturalized person, we could better understand it; but when he introduced the man's connection with the Socialist party, and the usual Socialistic beliefs as an important factor in the decision, we cannot understand it, since this party has legal standing, which at that time was not even questioned. Perhaps "anarchy" is implied in the idea that when the means of production are owned by the people, government will be unnecessary. But this is a commonplace of current political discussion.

In 1918, one Carl Swelgin was deprived of his citizenship in Oregon[1] on the charge that at the time of naturalization and during the five year period previous to that time, he was not attached to the principles of the Constitution of the United States, is not well disposed to the good order and happiness of the same, is not of good moral character, and that since two years before his admission to citizenship he was, and at the present time is, a member of the Industrial Workers of the World and an organizer in it, and that this organization has advocated and does advocate resistance to the existing governmental authority of the United States, and the complete control and ownership of all property in the United States through the abolition of all other classes of society, and that such purposes are to be accomplished without regard for right or wrong, but by the use of such unlawful means and methods known as sabotage and direct action.

The entire body of proof brought forward in the decision is connected with the principles of the I. W. W. and contains no evidence showing lack of "good moral character" or attachment to the Constitution other than connection with this organization.

[1] U. S. *vs*. Swelgin, 254 Fed. 884.

THE IMMIGRANT'S DAY IN COURT

In 1919, one Stupiello[1] was deprived of his citizenship in New York State on the ground that he was an anarchist at the time he was given his certificate. He had been arrested by the Bureau of Immigration on warrant of deportation for anarchy, but was released from custody as a citizen. Thereupon action to cancel his certificate was undertaken. This man admitted that he was a "philosophical" anarchist; he believed in "evolution by education, in order to reach a state of education of mind that it won't be necessary to have a government." But he said he thought it necessary to have a government as long as society is organized as at present.

During the World War, a number of naturalized citizens of German birth were "denaturalized" on the ground that they did not, in fact, renounce allegiance to the country of birth at the time of receiving citizenship. In one of these cases the man had been in the country for thirty-two years.[2]

In these proceedings also we may note the difficulty of establishing belief, and the unfairness involved in holding the individual to responsibility for membership in a group.

METHODS OF ENFORCING THE IMMIGRATION LAW

Turning again to consideration of the immigration law, we find that the method of carrying it into effect departs materially from the general principles of court procedure worked out in our legal system. Congress makes the law—the general rule: an administrative department, the Department of Labor, performs the police function in searching for and making arrest of sup-

[1] U. S. *vs.* Stupiello, 260 Fed. 483.
[2] U. S. *vs.* Wusterbarth, 249 Fed. 908.

posed violators of the rule, acts as prosecutor in presenting them for judgment before itself as judge, acts as jailer in holding in forcible custody doubtful cases for admission and persons under charges for deportation, and finally as executioner, in shipping deportees and the debarred from the country. It also invades the legislative domain in laying down rules of operation which under its discretionary power have the effect of law.

In this process the check afforded by the separation of judicial, executive, and legislative functions, which is considered one of the characteristic safeguards of our legal system, is wanting.

And other checks are wanting, resulting in opportunity for unfair treatment of the immigrant. This unfairness may consist in inflicting some hardship that the immigrant feels is unfair, or it may consist in granting special privileges, which the immigrant considers a favor, but which really is a detriment to him, in giving him the idea that the law may be evaded through personal influence or bribery.

Let us see where some of these possibilities are to be found in the procedure at entry.

The medical examination which the immigrant first undergoes is necessarily hurried and superficial, because of the inadequate force assigned to this duty, and many immigrants defective in one way and another must slip through without detection. But there is apparently no defect in the system. The medical officers are well equipped for their task, have a high standard of professional honor, and would be glad to carry out their work more completely.

The examining inspectors of the Immigration Bureau before whom the immigrant next appears have full authority to admit such immigrants as are not clearly admissible under the law. They may also detain immigrants temporarily, to await the arrival of funds or friends. But they have no power of exclusion. They cannot, therefore, inflict the final hardship of sending a man back after the long journey, but through the discretionary power they hold of interpreting the general provisions of the immigration law they can be lax in admitting special cases. A civic organization making an investigation at one of our ports learned that an officer in charge of the examining inspectors was in the habit of looking over the lists of immigrants and checking certain names with the remark that he was "interested" in those cases. It would be quite easy for the examining inspector to give such cases the benefit of any doubt and let them through.

The law provides that all aliens who may not appear to the examining immigrant inspector to be clearly and beyond a doubt entitled to land, shall be turned over to a board of special inquiry for further examination.[1]

The civic organization already referred to found an occasion for graft on the part of the lower officials of the immigrant station in arranging for the early appearance of cases before this board, to avoid long waits in the detention rooms, and concluded, as the result of their investigation, that bribery by relatives and friends of aliens was common. Within recent months over a dozen employees at that port have been discharged for dishonesty.

A board of special inquiry consists of three members, chosen from the immigration officials, who act as judges. These boards are equipped with interpreters and official stenographers. A large station may have a number of such boards. These boards have authority

[1] U. S. Department of Labor: *Immigration Laws*, third edition, p. 18, Law of 1917, section 17.

to order the exclusion of the immigrant, as well as to admit him over the doubts of the examining inspector. As exclusion is a matter of such serious concern to the immigrant, and unfair treatment here will involve such real injustice, the proceedings of this board should be surrounded by special safeguards. To some extent this is the case. The decision is reached by a majority vote of three persons, not by the arbitrary pronouncement of one man. The story of the alien is heard, interpreters are present to make sure that he is understood, and a record is kept of the proceedings. Furthermore, the alien has the right of appeal from an excluding decision of the board to the Secretary of Labor except in cases of mental defect and contagious diseases. On the other hand, the hearings are deprived of the safeguard of publicity. The immigration law provides that the hearings must be held "separate and apart from the public."[1] And while the immigrant may have "one friend or relative present" at the hearing, it is provided that this shall be allowed only after the preliminary part of the hearing is completed, that the friend or relative shall not be employed as counsel or attorney, that, if he is a witness, he shall have already completed the giving of his testimony, and that he shall not be a representative of an immigrant aid society.[2] This means in practice that the alien brought before the board may not understand the situation in which he finds himself, and may be unable to present his case to proper advantage.

Former Attorney General Palmer, in discussing the procedure in deportation cases, gave it as his opinion that "if there is any time in the immigration proceedings when an alien needs counsel more it is when

[1] U. S. Department of Labor: *Immigration Law of 1917*, section 17.
[2] *Ibid.*: *Immigration Rules of 1917*, rule 15, subd. 2.

he arrives at Ellis Island without knowledge of our laws and without any knowledge whatsoever of the procedure.[1]

It may be doubted also, whether the members of the boards of special inquiry have the juridical qualifications necessary for a task of this kind. The matter at stake, the success or failure of an enterprise that has involved the breaking up of a home, the expenditure of perhaps all of one's little capital, a long and hard journey, is certainly of as much consequence as the liability to pay a ten-dollar fine in a police court for some minor offense. And the application of the law to the specific case involves an even greater exercise of judgment. It does not seem unreasonable to ask that the judges of such a court should be as well equipped for their task as the police magistrate is for his.

The member of the board is usually a member of the regular inspection force, chosen from their ranks by a superior officer for fitness for the task, so that the most intelligent of these are probably secured. But the standards for selection of examining inspectors are not very high, and the salaries are so low that men of ability are unwilling to remain in these positions. At the port of New York, the most important station in the country, the maximum salary for an inspector, including the members of boards, is $2,220, and only 4 of the force of 112 get this amount. Only 20 of them are paid $2,000 and over. Seventeen of them are paid $1,380.

The right of appeal is freely resorted to. In the year ending June 30, 1921,[2] in which for the first time immigration rose to pre-war proportions, and 805,228

[1] *Hearings before the Committee on Rules,* Sixty-sixth Congress, Second Session, p. 56.

[2] *Report of the Commissioner General of Immigration, 1921,* p. 124.

immigrant aliens were admitted to the country, appeals against excluding decisions were taken in 7,442 cases, or in 42 per cent of the cases ordered excluded.[1] In cases of appeal, 3,541, or 48 per cent, were actually debarred after appeal, and 52 per cent were admitted to the country, 1,710 of them without bond or any other security. That is, in somewhat more than one case out of five the decision of the board of special inquiry was reversed. And the proportion at the port of New York taken by itself was even greater. This port in 1921 received about 70 per cent of all alien immigrants admitted to the country. Of these 6,941 were ordered excluded; in 4,459 cases, or 64 per cent, appeals were taken, and in 3,122 of the appeal cases, or about 70 per cent, the aliens were admitted. This means a reversal of the decision of the board in nearly half (45 per cent) of the cases in which exclusion was ordered.

This large proportion of reversals must have a bad effect on the morale of the board, and make a bad impression on the immigrant, especially in view of the way so many of these appeals are carried through. It is a common practice, not concealed in any way, and not considered worthy of special reprobation, for the appeal in behalf of some doubtful immigrant to go to Washington accompanied by letters from the Congressman of the district in which his friends live, or from other officials. Among such officials have been found the Commissioner of Immigration at the port in which the board has taken action. However proper the reasons urged in the letters, the practice gives occasion for the use of political pressure and for general belief that such pressure is exerted.

[1] If we may conclude that the number of excluding decisions is learned by adding the number of those debarred, and those ordered debarred but not debarred after appeal.

This is certainly a bad lesson for the immigrant. A better lesson for him would be a system in which the tribunal invested with the power of exclusion and admission should carry on its work with such safeguards that its decisions would be trusted and reversals on appeal infrequent, because the original decisions had been so fairly and so intelligently made.

Deportation procedure, since it works more of a hardship to the individual than exclusion, should be even more carefully safeguarded than procedure for admission. And in general this is done. The beginning of that process is a complaint by some one to an immigration officer that a certain alien comes within the deportable classes, in consequence of which the officer may make application for a warrant of arrest to the Secretary of Labor. Rules of the department provide that officers shall make thorough investigation of all cases where they are credibly informed or have reason to believe that a specified alien is subject to arrest and deportation, and the application for a warrant "must state facts showing *prima facie* that the alien comes within one or more of the classes subject to deportation after entry, and, except in cases in which the burden of proof is on the alien (Chinese) involved, should be accompanied by some substantial supporting evidence."[1]

If the facts stated are within the personal knowledge of the inspector reporting the case, they need not be in affidavit form. But if based upon statements of persons not sworn officers of the government, or not

[1] U. S. Department of Labor: *Immigration Laws and Rules of May 1, 1917,* third edition, March, 1919, rule 22, subd. 3, p. 67.

THE IMMIGRATION LAW

officials of institutions where persons deportable as public charges are confined, the affidavit of the person giving the information, or a transcript of a sworn statement taken from that person by an inspector, must accompany the application. Warrants may be requested and given by telegraph in case of necessity, or "when some substantial interest of the government would be subserved thereby." The alien for whom the warrant is issued is then arrested and taken before an official of the Bureau of Immigration, where he is granted a hearing "to enable him to show cause, if any there be, why he should not be deported."[1]

One departure from regular legal procedure is seen in the fact that practically all of the steps to be taken in the process of deportation are prescribed in rules of the department, which may be changed at will, without notice, and are not laid down in a general law, recorded in a statute book.

The actual process of complaint, investigation, and arrest under those rules is, however, fairly parallel with the regular procedure in criminal cases. One variation is seen in the departmental rule providing for the immigrant to show cause why he should not be deported, as that places the burden of proof on the person under charges, in opposition to the established legal principle of placing the burden of proof on the complainant. This is an addition to the law through an administrative rule, for the law itself says nothing about the "burden of proof" being on the deportee except in the case of a person who has entered "in violation of any other law thereof which imposes on such person the burden of proving his right to enter or remain," meaning the Chinese, under the Chinese exclusion acts.

[1] U. S. Department of Labor: *Immigration Laws and Rules of May 1, 1917*, third edition, March, 1919, rule 22, subd. 5, section a, p. 68.

THE IMMIGRANT'S DAY IN COURT

Pending determination of the case at a hearing, the alien may be taken into custody, at the discretion of the immigration officer in charge, or allowed to remain in a place considered by that officer to be "secure and proper."

At the hearing the alien is allowed the right to know the charges against him, and to employ counsel, but until lately both of these rights might be withheld until the hearing had proceeded sufficiently to guard the government's interests.[1] At present, both of these rights are granted at the beginning of the hearing, and counsel may offer evidence and subpœna witnesses.

If the alien cannot speak or understand English it is provided that an interpreter shall be employed "where practicable."

A full record of the examination must be made and forwarded to the Bureau of Immigration, together with any written argument submitted by counsel, and the recommendations of the examining officer and the officer in charge as to whether a warrant of deportation should or should not be issued. The record, however, need not and usually does not embody the original evidence on which the warrant of arrest was based. The hearing is conducted in other respects at the discretion of the examining inspector. He is bound by no rules of evidence and may allow or induce the alien to testify against himself. He is not required to conduct the hearings as secret proceedings, either by the law or by the rules of the department, but as a matter of practice the hearings are secret. No member of the family, no friend, no representative of the press or public is admitted, to afford the check of publicity if something wrong is going on.

[1] U. S. Department of Labor: *Immigration Laws and Rules of May 1, 1917*, second edition, November, 1917, p. 65.

THE IMMIGRATION LAW

The examining inspector may even be his own interpreter, or there may be no interpreter present if it is not "practicable"; and the inspector may be his own clerk and stenographer, and make up the record himself. Except for the presence of counsel, he may have the entire proceeding in his hands. And the counsel can do little to check irregularities in the procedure, in the absence of witnesses to substantiate his complaint, nor can he fully check the correctness of the record sent to Washington as a basis for issuing the warrant of deportation.

The Secretary of Labor, or his authorized representative, is the only person entitled to decide whether a warrant of deportation shall be issued and to issue it. But in practice, the examining inspector really decides the matter in the majority of the cases. The Secretary of Labor has to base his decision on the record as prepared and sent to him by the examining inspector, which he has no opportunity to check by a personal knowledge of the proceedings. He has not seen or heard the person under charges, or his witnesses or the witnesses against him. He has no way of knowing whether the record is correct and complete or not. It is quite possible for the examining inspector to omit facts from the record, or state them in such a way that a false impression is produced, without detection. And the inspector is under the constant temptation to which a prosecuting officer is always subject, of making out a case against the person under charges. And then, if the volume of deportation cases is large, the Secretary will find it difficult even to examine thoroughly such records as are sent him, and he may satisfy himself with the recommendation of the examining inspector or of the Commissioner of Immigration, who also indorses the cases with a recommendation for action, he, too, without first-hand contact with the cases.

According to departmental rules, pending determination of the alien's case, he may be released on bond, which is set at $500 "unless different instructions are given by the department," but aliens who are unable to give bail "shall be held in jail only in case no other secure place of detention can be found."

If the alien or his counsel thinks injustice has been done him, he may apply to the Secretary of Labor to grant a rehearing, and the Secretary may order a rehearing in cases where he desires to have new evidence against the deportee presented. This may be either before or after the warrant of deportation has been issued.

In deportation proceedings appeal to the courts may be had, but only after the warrant ordering deportation has been issued, this appeal taking the form of *habeas corpus* proceedings. The court check upon the action of the administrative department, however, is imperfect, because the court's review of the case is not held to determine whether the decision was just or unjust, but only whether the department did or did not have jurisdiction.

In the deportation proceedings we find an interesting parallel with the court proceedings of continental Europe. As in the preliminary procedure of the modern continental court, we find a combination of powers in one body, and one official, who is investigator and prosecutor and judge. The examining inspector resembles the *juge d'instruction*, holding secret sessions, invaded only by counsel, with limited rights. We find a disregard of the rules of evidence which characterizes the preliminary proceedings of the continental court, and the pressure upon the person under charges to incriminate himself.

THE IMMIGRATION LAW

But, in the modern continental court, after the preliminary examination, a public trial is held in a trial court, in which greater safeguards to the person on trial are afforded. No such subsequent proceeding guards the hearing before the examining inspector in a deportation case. As in the ancient unreformed court of continental Europe the first inquiry is also the last. The inspector, like the judge in the ancient French court, is practically the final arbiter, making his decision without a public trial, without a jury, without confrontation of witnesses by the accused, without a re-examination of witnesses under the rules of evidence, and without a cross-examination by the accused person or his representative.

All of this is excused on the ground that deportation is not a criminal proceeding. It is not, technically; but is it not, substantially? In these proceedings are certainly to be found the essential features of a criminal proceeding. The deportee is charged with some disqualification, he is arrested, held forcibly in detention, if found guilty of the disqualification he is subjected to a penalty, which is not, it is true, fine or imprisonment or loss of life, but may amount to any one of the three or perhaps all, through the loss of money, of liberty, and the possibility of losing his life if he is deported under dangerous conditions or to a country where he may be subjected to peril. Some of these things have happened. Deportees have died on board ship, or in detention stations, or in foreign countries to which they have been sent, who might have been alive and well if they had not been involved in deportation proceedings.

Finally, if the deported alien ever attempts to return to this country he will be distinctly classed as a criminal and subjected to punishment.

THE IMMIGRANT'S DAY IN COURT

What can actually happen to the immigrant under these laws and these rules of procedure is seen in the numerous deportation proceedings carried through under the anarchy clause in the years 1919 and 1920, to be described in the following chapter.

X

THE DEPORTATIONS OF 1919–20

A GREATLY increased activity in deportation proceedings under the "anarchy clause" of the immigration law marked the years following the entry of this country into the World War. This was due to the same causes which occasioned severity in the handling of labor cases in the courts, as shown in a previous chapter—war excitement turning into fear of political and economic revolution.

Deportation had, indeed, been thought of as a means of dealing with labor disturbances. In the handling of troubles arising from strikes, judges and city authorities were found threatening deportation as an additional penalty to be imposed on strikers who could be shown to fall under the provisions of the law. In various places in which labor difficulties had arisen, governmental agents were on the watch for evidence of deportability under the anarchy clause against the strikers and their leaders, but with little result. The mayor of Lawrence told an investigator for this study, during the strike of 1919, that the city was then swarming with Federal agents looking for revolutionary manifestations which would render the aliens engaging in them deportable, but were unable to find anything. The same scrutiny was given to the strikers in the steel strike of 1919, but without effect in finding deportable persons.

Direct proceedings against groups and organizations considered revolutionary, however, which were undertaken by the Department of Labor in coöperation with the Department of Justice and citizens' organizations such as the American Protective League, netted large numbers of persons adjudged liable to deportation.

THE "RED SPECIAL"

The first incident in that campaign to attract widespread public attention was the journey across the continent of a train bringing a load of aliens to the port of New York for deportation, and popularly dubbed the "Red Special" because the larger part of its passengers were persons ordered deported under the anarchy clause.

Of the 54 persons in this trainload, landed at Ellis Island February 11, 1919, 39 had been arrested in the course of a program of activities undertaken against the Industrial Workers of the World in the far West; the remaining 15 were not connected with any radical movement.

The I. W. W. group, although small, was of widely diversified nationality. The list was made up of 13 Scandinavians, 9 from the British Islands, 7 Russians, 4 Finns, a Pole, a Czech, a Hollander, a German, an "Austrian," unspecified, and one man called a Swiss by the government, but he himself claiming to be of native birth. They had been arrested at different dates, many months previous to their arrival in New York, most of them in the winter of 1917-18.

The cases against all these persons had been closed, warrants for their deportation had been issued, and they had been sent to New York for immediate shipment from the country. But after their arrival at the port their presence was discovered by one of the counsels for the I. W. W. who happened to be in New York at the time, and efforts were made to secure a reopening of their cases, through direct application to the Secretary of Labor at Washington and through *habeas corpus* proceedings in the Federal district court.

As a result of these efforts, about a month later, 12 men, and about a week after that, 2 more men were released on their own recognizance by the Department of Labor. Meanwhile, 6 of the men had preferred not to make an appeal, 5 of these had been deported; the sixth, a German, was deported some months later.

For the remaining 19, writs of *habeas corpus* were secured, and in April the cases were argued before Judge Augustus Hand, with the result that in one case the writ was sustained (meaning that the proceedings so far taken by the Department of Labor were nullified and the man discharged, leaving the department, however, free to initiate new proceedings if it wished to do so). In 11 cases the writs were withdrawn and the cases returned to the department for reconsideration by mutual consent, and of these, 3 men were released on parole, and in 3 additional cases the warrants of deportation were canceled.[1]

In the 33 cases, then, for which rehearings were secured, 21, or just short of two-thirds, were either released on parole or discharged outright. And of the men held for deportation, seven were released on bond because of difficulty in arranging for deportation to the home country. In two cases the fact of birth in the country to which it was proposed to send the deportee could not be established, because he had left at so early an age, that the country in question refused to receive him.

[1] For action on these cases see, "I. W. W. Deportation Cases," *Hearings before a Subcommittee of the Committee of Immigration and Naturalization, House of Representatives, Sixty-sixth Congress, Second Session*, p. 56.

The bare fact that the department altered its decision in two-thirds of the cases, after many months of imprisonment, and a long and costly journey across the continent, reveals a state of affairs confusing to the alien, to say the least, and involving much hardship. This is certainly not the speedy and sure process of justice to which the client is entitled according to the spirit of our law, even when he is guilty, and it is certainly an injustice to hold the innocent through so long a period.

What was the trouble? Searching for an answer in a review of the history of the proceedings and in the records of the cases, we find some interesting illustrations of the difficulties which may arise from indefinitely framed provisions of law and from the administration of law without the safeguards provided in regular court procedure—our much cherished due process of law.

The campaign against the I. W. W. in the far West which resulted in these cases for deportation was an incident in a running warfare with that organization, carried on by the large industries, with the support of influential elements in the community. This campaign was definitely directed toward the deportation of alien members of the I. W. W. in the fall of 1917, following a strike in the lumber industry of the previous summer. The expressed purpose of this campaign was to remove hindrances to the production of war materials, but behind it was the fear of revolutionary action on the part of the organization.

But as in the case of other labor troubles already discussed, the expressed demands of the lumber strikers were entirely economic. In the strike instructions of the Lumber Workers' Industrial Union No. 5500, I. W. W., it is stated:

338

THE DEPORTATIONS OF 1919-20

Owing to the comparative scarcity of men and the large amounts of orders the lumber companies have on hand, we have now an opportunity such as we have never had before to shorten hours, raise wages, and improve conditions. . . . The paramount issue in this strike is the eight-hour day. . . . We hereby call upon you to strike. . . . Strike against the tyranny of the lumber trust, against the long hours, the low wages, the rotten grub, and the filthy, louse-infested, unsanitary bunkhouses. Strike against the robbery of the employment shark and the graft of the hospital fee. The rise in the cost of living has made the present wages insufficient to maintain a man in decency. There is only one thing to do about it. Strike, and force the greedy lumber barons to give us living wages and human conditions.

And as in the labor troubles already reviewed, I. W. W. members suffered from open lawlessness at the hands of citizens and of town officials. They were deprived of the rights of free speech, they were expelled forcibly from localities where their presence was not wanted, some were even done to death by hostile mobs, without interference or punishment by government. Such actions certainly would not predispose alien members of the organization to a respect for the law.

The movement for the deportation of these aliens was started through coöperative action by the Department of Labor, the Department of Justice, and unofficial bodies of citizens, such as the Minute Men of Seattle, and other groups affiliated with the American Protective League.

They began operations under the law of 1917, which permitted deportation under the "anarchy clause" only for personally advocating or teaching the doctrines forbidden, not for belief in anarchy or membership in an organization unless such belief or membership was held prior to entry and the discovery was made within five years after entry. It did not provide for deportation for membership in an organization joined after arrival of the alien. However, the proceedings were planned to prove deportability through connection with an organization advocating and teaching things that would be forbidden to the person, regardless of time of entry or place of joining the organization and on the assumption that the I. W. W. was such an organization.

The weaknesses of the law as it stood, to sustain this view, were recognized,[1] and the Department of Labor, in May, 1918, sent a recommendation to Congress for the passage of an amendment to the immigration law to remedy these difficulties. These recommendations were embodied in the law of October, 1918, already described.[2]

Meanwhile, from the first of the year 1917 on, arrests were made and hearings before the examining inspectors were held, in accordance with a policy of the department to separate the sheep from the goats in the I. W. W. ranks—the passive followers, and the active agitators and leaders—and deal only with the latter class, under rulings of which we may undoubtedly take a memorandum dated July 26, 1918, as a substantially accurate formulation. In this memorandum it is stated that at a conference held by Acting Secretary Abercrombie, the Commissioner General, the law officer of the bureau and two other officials, it was agreed:

That membership in the I. W. W. together with evidence of knowledge on the part of the alien as to the nature of the propaganda and aims of the organization, as contained in its official literature, sympathy with and approval of such propaganda and aims, financial support by purchasing such literature or through paying membership dues into the

[1] *Report of the Commissioner General of Immigration, 1918*, p. 40.

[2] *Ibid.*, p. 41, and p. 316, the present work.

general fund of the organization, to which fund the expense of publishing such literature is charged, voluntary contributions to the general defense fund for the members of the I. W. W. now under arrest or indictment, or in prison, and active support by distributing literature or acting as delegate or organizer, and soliciting membership, collecting and transmitting dues, etc., shall be considered good grounds for deportation on the charge of advocating and teaching the unlawful destruction of property.[1]

A memorandum of the Bureau of Immigration[2] dated December 2, 1918, after most of the arrests had been made, and after the law of 1918 which they had themselves asked for had been passed, expresses fear that Federal district judges would not sustain the department in the *habeas corpus* proceedings which were likely to be undertaken. It goes on to say that appeal from such decisions would be inadvisable because, if the higher court sustained the lower court, the department would be worse off than before, while if the lower court was overruled it would probably be on the ground that "advocacy of unlawful destruction of property" is proved simply through membership in an organization, and this "would amount to doing the very thing the department had been attempting to avoid— the deporting of aliens because they belonged to the I. W. W." "In other words, if the department is going to be forced eventually to handle the I. W. W. cases under the new law, it might as well handle them under that law immediately."

The bureau urged, therefore, that the cases of persons under arrest be taken up again, and that against the

[1] "I. W. W. Deportation Cases," *Hearings before a Subcommittee of the Committee on Immigration and Naturalization, House of Representatives, Sixty-sixth Congress, Second Session*, p. 79.

[2] *Ibid.*, p. 69.

aliens shown by the records in their cases to be "active and dangerous advocates and teachers" of the unlawful doctrines, warrants be issued under the new Act, for membership in an organization that teaches the unlawful destruction of property, and that in cases showing the aliens to be, "while members of the organization, rather inactive in connection therewith and not dangerous advocates or teachers," "the records be filed without further action."

Appended to this memorandum is a list of 108 cases of the latter class, in regard to which it is stated that they "were accordingly left open and they were as a rule paroled for one year, generally with the condition that they report periodically to the immigration officer at Seattle concerning their whereabouts and occupation."

Among the 39 deportees sent to New York were 11 men who evidently were considered as belonging to the class of active and dangerous advocates, since they had been rearrested under the law of 1918, for membership in the I. W. W. One of these men was among those who took no appeal and was deported; one of them was among those for whom writs were obtained, and was discharged by Judge Hand; the nine remaining were among those released on parole by the department, after withdrawal of *habeas corpus* writs.

Rearresting men already held in confinement under one law, for violation of another law passed since their first arrest—passed, in fact, to enable the government to deal with cases like theirs which could not be carried through under the old provision, looks like that punishment under *ex post facto* legislation which is also against the spirit of our laws. But technical reasons may be brought forward to show that this was not strictly *ex post facto* action, and although the department's decision to release all these men looks like a recognition and a repudiation of *ex post facto* action, no such reasons are given in the memorandum in the cases released on parole.

In the case of James Lund, on the basis of which seven of the other cases were paroled as "substantially similar," it is noted in the memorandum of Acting Secretary Abercrombie, recommending deportation, that the old warrant of arrest charged the alien with advocating or teaching the unlawful destruction of property, and

while the record showed that there was some evidence upon which to base this charge, the facts brought out did not appear to be sufficient to justify deportation on that ground. On the other hand, it was not considered advisable to cancel the warrant proceedings outright, but to release the man on probation for a period of one year on his promise to report to the Commissioner of Immigration at Seattle, at regular intervals of three months, as to his whereabouts and occupation. This he refused to do. The new Immigration Act having come into effect, it was then decided, in view of his refusal to comply with the department's terms and the fact that he seemed to fall within its scope, to rearrest him under the new Act.[1]

The memorandum goes on to state that the man admits he is a member of the I. W. W., and that "in the opinion of this Bureau . . . the I. W. W. is an organization teaching and advocating the unlawful destruction of property." This memorandum is signed by the Commissioner General and indorsed "approved" by the Acting Secretary, Mr. Abercrombie.

A memorandum of March 8th recommending the

[1] "I. W. W. Deportation Cases," *Hearings before a Subcommittee of the Committee on Immigration and Naturalization, House of Representatives, Sixty-sixth Congress, Second Session,* p. 7.

release of the man on parole at New York, however, says:

There is only a little evidence in the record that can be pointed to as justification for holding that the man has, either as a member of the organization or independently, distributed literature or otherwise advocated the unlawful destruction of property, and the bureau is satisfied from the statements made by the attorney that in his instance the previous decision is not as fully or as substantially supported as is desirable under the policy which is being followed in these cases generally.

It is hard to see how this man, who became a member of the "dangerous" class by refusing parole the first time, became a harmless, inactive member three months later. Perhaps we may look ahead in time a bit to get some further and more definite information on the "policy that is being followed in these cases." On November 15, 1919, the Commissioner General, in a memorandum, referring to requests for information from the Chamber of Commerce at Spokane and the Commissioner at Seattle, says:

The bureau is of the opinion that in the replies to said Chamber of Commerce and to the Commissioner at Seattle they should be advised that proceedings against members of the I. W. W. organization will be ordered, just as the department is now and for some time past has been proceeding against the Russian Workers' Union. It is apparent that the former constitutes the same menace in the West that the latter does in the East, and the question arises at this time, should not the same treatment under the anarchistic provisions of the immigration laws follow as to the I. W. W.?

The bureau has heretofore, in memoranda on the subject, expressed its views and made recommendations in relation to the matter of the prosecution of persons who hold membership in the I. W. W. organization. It continues in the opinion that the organization is anarchistic and revolutionary in its teachings.[1]

On November 19, 1919, Assistant Secretary Post, to whom this memorandum was addressed, informed the Commissioner at Seattle that the "department adheres to previous decisions that under the I. W. W. constitution mere membership in that organization does not bring aliens within the scope of the Act of October, 1918.[2]

It seems then, that so far as the I. W. W. was concerned, the passage of the new law had little effect, and the literal wording of either law had little to do with decisions. The policy followed rested upon interpretations of department and of bureau officials which changed from time to time and from official to official.

First we find the officials troubled because the law is not adequate to hold aliens for deportation without some provision for exclusion for membership, and they urge the passage of such an act. Then, while the new law is in process, we see them framing a definition of personal advocacy which is based on membership in the organization—that is, "active" membership. Then, when the law has been passed we find a division of opinion in the department as to proceedings under it. The Commissioner General states definitely that the I. W. W. is an organization teaching unlawful destruction of property, and membership in it is a cause for deportation, and warrants of deportation are issued for that reason by the Secretary of Labor. Later, the Secretary of Labor regards membership as a cause of deportation only when the alien is found engaged in

[1] "I. W. W. Deportation Cases," *Hearings before a Subcommittee of the Committee on Immigration and Naturalization, House of Representatives, Sixty-sixth Congress, Second Session,* p. 82.

[2] *Ibid.,* p. 82.

345

some personal activity—a complete reversal of the first position, which proved personal activity by "active" membership.

If, then, the examining inspectors could not be sure who was personally guilty of "advocacy of unlawful destruction of property," or when a "member of an organization" is deportable under the law, unless they had detailed instructions from headquarters, and if headquarters was not always at one on these matters, how could the alien know when or whether he was rendering himself subject to deportation. Apparently the only working information on that point was contained in departmental memoranda which were not given publicity.

What was done in these cases really amounted to the making of a law by an executive department, and a law which is not publicly promulgated, which again is contrary to the spirit of our law. At the hearings, one and another alien would say he was not aware that the I. W. W. was an illegal organization; if he had known it he would not have belonged.

The interpretation of active membership is so vague that in reading the records of the cases one cannot find any sharp lines marking off the "active" from the "inactive" member, as finally decided by the granting of parole in the latter case or reaffirming the order of deportation in the former. One man admitted membership in the organization, admitted securing other members, but denied circulating literature; another admitted circulating literature, but said he knew nothing about its contents; another admitted various activities in connection with the I. W. W., but denied absolutely any belief in the "unlawful destruction of property." Could this man, then, be "advocating" that belief in distributing the literature if he did not hold the belief? Another claimed that the literature he distributed did not preach the unlawful destruction of property, although it was official literature of the I. W. W. Some of these men were paroled, others held for deportation. We cannot see just why. Since the distinctions in these cases are so fine that they are matters for dispute by lawyers and judges, the lay reader of intelligence can hardly distinguish them. They certainly must be invisible to the untrained mind of the immigrant I. W. W.

These cases also show the difficulty of securing adequate proof for charges of this character, under the wording of the law and under the methods of examination. To show the actual commission of the acts of "advocacy of unlawful destruction of property," the examining inspector has before him only the complaint, with such testimony as has been gathered, and the testimony of the alien himself, at the hearing, while he is "showing cause why he should not be deported." The acts are indefinite, and the testimony is inconclusive, because witnesses are not brought in for examination and cross-examination, for confrontation by the accused person, so that the evidence adduced on one side may be checked up by the other. The fact that the evidence presented at the hearing, aside from the written complaint, is that of the accused person, who will naturally try to make out the best case for himself, may naturally influence the inspector to go a little beyond the evidence in making his recommendation. This is certainly not in accord with the safeguards of ordinary court procedure. In the Nelson case, for example, the one case in which the writ was sustained and the man directly released by the Court, Judge Hand says:

In this case the relator explicitly denies that he advocates the destruction of property. Such a denial, of course, may be expected in cases where a relator in fact does advocate active sabotage; but in the face of his denials, which are uniform, some other evidence must appear substantiating the charge for which he is being deported.[1]

In the opinion of the court, in this case, the examining inspector has, as a matter of fact, gone beyond the evidence in recommending deportation.

To give an idea of the methods of procedure in these cases and to show the difference between a case released and a case held, let us briefly compare two of them, on the basis of the records.

Martin de Wal, the Hollander, was arrested in May, 1918, at an I. W. W. meeting, together with all the other members present at the time, and was held thirteen days before he was released. He was again arrested in July, 1918, and after a hearing before the examining inspector was recommended for deportation. The warrant of arrest was issued on the ground that he had been found advocating the unlawful destruction of property and was a person liable to become a public charge at time of entry. But the latter charge was abandoned. The warrant of deportation was issued on the former ground only.

The trend of questioning, the statements of the examining inspector, the final recommendation of the Commissioner General, seemed to show that both belief and connection with the organization weighed heavily in the matter, although technically, neither was involved in the charges. And the reason stated for the arrest was even more remote from the final charge. "He was brought to this office," says the examining officer, "by an officer of the Army Intelligence Service, having been

[1] "I. W. W. Deportation Cases," *Hearings before a Subcommittee of the Committee on Immigration and Naturalization, House of Representatives, Sixty-sixth Congress, Second Session*, p. 4.

arrested on account of his activities in organizing men in logging camps who were doing government work and handling government contracts."

These "activities" are thus described by De Wal himself. "We made the bosses stick to the eight-hour day with no overtime, and made them raise wages, keep the linen clean, and give us coffee instead of bootleg chicory."

The examining inspector in ordering deportation states that "he has been found advocating and teaching the unlawful destruction of property . . . by reason of his activities in, and the support he has given to, the I. W. W. organization."

The summary of the case by the Commissioner General stated, "He has been a member of the I. W. W. since September, 1917, and was a delegate and organizer at time of arrest. He acknowledges that he has initiated new members, collected money, and distributed literature. It is apparent that he has been quite active in spreading the doctrine of unlawful destruction of property, especially by distributing books teaching such doctrine. The inspector read to him excerpts from the official literature of the order dealing with sabotage. He insisted, though, that he had not talked sabotage or distributed books dealing with that subject among new members, because of the fear that they would not understand the matter and would lose their heads and do something which would be to the disadvantage of the government or of the organization."

There is nothing in the record, so far as the reader can see, to substantiate the charge of advocating the unlawful destruction of property even through the distribution of literature, for he denied distributing the only literature adduced which could be interpreted as advocating this, giving as his reason that it might hinder the progress of the war, as the statement of the Commissioner General himself shows.

In his case, the order of deportation was sustained. Compare the case of John Morgan, who was arrested, January, 1918, under the charges of advocating anarchy and liability to become a public charge. Both of these charges were abandoned, and he was ordered deported on the alleged ground that he advocated the unlawful destruction of property.

The line of questioning was the same as in the case of De Wal, and before the same inspector, and his answers were similar to those of De Wal, except that he denied somewhat more circumstantially the beliefs with which he was charged. He admitted distributing literature. As stated in the memorandum of the Commissioner General, which seems to be borne out by the record, "He denied his belief in the tenets of the I. W. W. organization and the fact that he had read or was in any way familiar with the literature published by it.

"He admitted, however, when confronted with positive proofs, that he had distributed I. W. W. literature at various times. Receipts and copies of letters in the file will show that he has been in correspondence with prominent I. W. W. members." In his case, the writ of *habeas corpus* was withdrawn at the request of the department for reconsideration, and he was released on parole.

Among the aliens arrested in connection with I. W. W. activities were a number who were charged, in addition to advocacy of unlawful destruction of property or membership in an organization advocating this doctrine, with liability to become a public charge upon entry into the United States, and a number against whom this was the only charge. This charge was dropped in some of the cases; in those where it was the only charge it seems to have been used as a means of getting rid of a person objectionable because of I. W. W. membership, but against whom the evidence on that point was weak.

Five of the deportees brought to New York under warrant of deportation for liability to become a public charge at time of entry were arrested in connection with I. W. W. activities, and in the examination, as shown by the records in their cases, the line of questioning was mainly directed toward showing participation in I. W. W. activities and little toward establishing "liability to become a public charge" as contemplated by the law. One of these men wished to be deported and was deported, and one, by the time he reached New York, was found to be mentally unstable, and consequently subject to deportation on that ground. In the other three cases the evidence was such that apparently the charge of dependence would not have been brought except to bolster up a weak case under the "anarchy clause." One of these men was among the first fourteen paroled in New York. He was sufficiently able bodied to have served in the Canadian army. Another, a Czecho-Slovak of working age, had earned his living in this country through the statutory five years, but admitted that once he had been obliged to ask a night's lodging in a police station. It is not the general custom of the Immigration Bureau to recommend deportation for such a slight degree of dependency as that.

In the third case, the man against whom this charge was laid had $100 cash in his pocket at the time of arrest, over $700 in a Canadian bank, and was the owner of real estate in that country. He was ordered deported on this charge alone, but after reconsideration at Washington the warrant of deportation was canceled. This case also shows the limited application of a remedy through *habeas corpus* proceedings. Under these proceedings the judge is not required to retry the case—merely to rule whether proceedings from which the appeal is taken were regular and under due authority. This man had been refused a writ of *habeas corpus* in the state of Washington, on the ground that whether the decision was just or unjust, he had had a fair hearing. The Federal judge in New York, on the other hand, granted a writ, and in the course of the hearing made some severe remarks about the failure of the evidence to substantiate the charge, but he did not discharge the man; this was among the cases in which the writ was withdrawn by consent and the department discharged him after reconsideration of the case.

Another matter to note is the use of "parole" in these cases. The immigration law itself makes no provision for the parole of persons liable to be deported. The law says that "any alien" falling under the classes specified "shall, upon the warrant of the Secretary of Labor, be taken into custody and deported." The administrative rules (Rule 17-A) provide for the temporary release of aliens, "whose prompt deportation cannot be accomplished," to accept self-supporting employment, and subdivision 6 provides for applying the provision of this rule to aliens "who have heretofore been released upon personal recognizance or parole," but no reference is found in the regulations to the terms on which this latter may be secured. Nor can they be learned on application to the department.

In answer to a request made by the writer to the department for laws or rulings under which parole might be granted, the Assistant Commissioner General replied that the information requested "cannot be furnished, as to do so would be in violation of a departmental order."[1]

Turning back to such bits of evidence as are available in the cases themselves, it would appear that parole, as a technical matter, is a method of relieving the person under charges from the hardships of confinement while his case is pending; as a practical matter, it seems to have been used as a species of probation—a means of testing continued good behavior.

It would seem that here is another feature of the immigration procedure as carried out in these cases which is not in accord with the spirit of our law. A man is entitled to a speedy decision in his case, whether he is innocent or guilty. If the former he is entitled to a complete discharge; if the latter, to such punishments as the law provides. In the case of the men offered parole at Seattle, and afterward arrested and brought to New York under the membership charge, the departmental memorandum distinctly states that "the facts brought out did not appear sufficient to justify deportation under the charges brought." Why were the men not cleared? One reason given was that if the men could be held, further facts might develop which would warrant deportation. But the fact that as a rule the cases were paroled for the definite period of one year, during which time the final decision was held in abeyance,[2] together with the condition of a periodical report on whereabouts and occupation to the Commissioner at Seattle would seem to show that the probation idea was in mind. But the courts do not hold a man on probation until it has been definitely established that he has committed the offense with which he

[1] Under date, September 14, 1921.
[2] *Hearings*, p. 70.

was charged, nor can they do so unless the law has provided probation as a means of treatment for the convicted offender.

Because of the very nature of the procedure, it is impossible to prove whether the aliens brought before the examining inspectors had had a fair hearing or not. Members of the I. W. W. group freely charged that the hearings were most unfair and that the records in their cases were incorrect and incomplete. As these records are the only material upon which the Secretary of Labor can base his warrant of deportation, it is important that they should not only be correct, but be known to be so. Under the present system this cannot be the case.

The benefit of counsel was certainly considerably restricted. At the time these cases were heard, when the original warrant of deportation was issued, the rule was in force that the alien could not have counsel until after the beginning of proceedings. And it was difficult in any event to find attorneys willing to undertake these cases, in the far West where proceedings were started, owing to the local prejudice against the I. W. W. This prejudice, indeed, was not confined to the far West. It is generally supposed that even the worst criminal is entitled to the services of counsel to secure such rights as he has under the law. But the New York *Law Journal*, commenting on two of the very cases we have been discussing, says that they "bring to the light of day the revolting principles and practices of the I. W. W. organization. Information in regard to its purposes should be spread far and wide so that all lovers of our country may be roused for the overthrow of such a great evil. *Lawyers especially may well consider most seriously whether they should give legal aid to such dangerous ad-*

*versaries of our government and of our fundamental rights
and liberties.*"[1]

The poverty of the aliens arrested on these charges
also stood in the way of securing legal services. One
instance among the cases we are now considering is
pathetic enough. At the hearing the poor fellow persisted in saying that he wanted a lawyer, but he didn't
know any in the town. He thought perhaps there
might be some one connected with the immigrant
station who would help him. But he had only three
dollars in his pocket. "How can you get a lawyer for
three dollars?" asked the inspector. After some more
questions and answers, in which the man kept insisting
on his desire for a lawyer, and the inspector kept re-
minding him of his poverty and helplessness, the record
stated, "alien puts his hand to his head and begins to
cry." The next entry states that "alien waives his
right to an attorney" and the examination proceeds.
Perhaps in other cases in which right to counsel was
"waived" the waiver was equally under constraint.

The procedure followed in the disposition of these
cases involved many hardships to the aliens. Most of
them had been under arrest for over a year, and many
of them had been in confinement from the time of
arrest.

According to circumstantial accounts given by the
men themselves, their experiences in the places of
confinement were worse than those to which ordinary
criminals are subjected. The immigration regulations
provide (Rule 22, subdivision 6) that aliens who are
not able to give bail shall be held in jail only in case no
other secure place of detention can be found, as has
been noted. In the Washington cases many of the men.

[1] New York *Law Journal*, Friday, April 18, 1919, p. 224.

were thrown into jails where the conditions as described by them were unbearable, from crowding and filth. The immigration station itself, according to their statements, was not much better.

Martin De Wal describes the immigration detention quarters in which he was confined as a 45 by 40 foot room on the water front, in which 125 men were confined night and day. The bunks were arranged in triple tiers and shut off ventilation from the four windows of the room. The place was infested with vermin, he says, and the group of I. W. W.'s were herded in with Chinese and Japanese held for deportation on account of contagious diseases. In this place the men were held strictly incomunicado, but by some means they did succeed in effecting connection with friends outside, and an agitation was started that hurried up the deportation proceedings.

Finally, the men who were released in New York found themselves thousands of miles from home, with no money and no job, some of them in broken health, and were obliged to depend upon the charity of friends until they could reëstablish themselves.

This group well illustrates how far the present law of deportation has departed from its original purpose, to return undesirable human products to the countries which produced them.

Only 7 out of the group of 39 had been here five years or less, 11 had been here from six to ten years, 3 between eleven and fifteen years, 5 between sixteen and twenty, 7 between twenty and thirty, the supposed "Scotchman," a man sixty-five years old, had been here so long that he did not know where he was born, but his first recollection, as a child, was of selling papers on the streets of New York City, about sixty years ago; and, of course, the man who claimed birth in this country, if his claim was true, had lived here all his life and was not subject to deportation. Information is not available for the other 4.

Many of the men, even those who had been here comparatively few years, had come in early youth, when the character is still unformed, some as small children. Besides the "Scotchman" already mentioned, two of the Scandinavians had come here at the age of eight, the Pole at the age of two.

Surely the beliefs and activities of persons who had spent so large a proportion of their lives in this country would be determined much more by what they had learned and experienced here than from their surroundings and experiences in the country of birth to which, under the law, they were deportable.

And the I. W. W. itself, in connection with which they were arrested, is a genuinely American product. It is not, as is frequently supposed, merely a copy or translation of French syndicalism. It has had an independent development in this country, is an outgrowth of American conditions, and its more prominent leaders, from the beginning, have been mainly Americans, of old American stock.[1]

THE "SOVIET ARK"

In December, 1919, a ship set sail from the port of New York which attracted as much popular interest as had the "Red Special—the United States transport *Buford*, nicknamed the "Soviet Ark," because it was laden with Russians, under warrant of deportation to their country under the anarchy clause of the immigration law.

[1] *The I. W. W.*, by Paul Frederick Brissenden, Columbia University Studies in History, Economics and Public Law, pp. 53, 231, 274.

Most of these Russians had been arrested in comprehensive raids made by the Department of Justice in November, 1919.

What authority had the Department of Justice to take part in carrying out the deportation provisions of the immigration law? None beyond that belonging to any citizen to report suspected cases of violations to the immigration authorities. The immigration law expressly provides for the administration of the deportation clauses by the Department of Labor, and the constant insistence by the government that deportation proceedings are not criminal in their nature would seem still further to shut out the Department of Justice from any hand in them, so far as the immigrant himself is concerned. That department may properly act in the criminal proceedings provided for in the immigration law, against shipmasters or persons assisting in the violation of the law, but not in proceedings against the immigrant.

THE RADICAL DIVISION OF THE DEPARTMENT OF JUSTICE

How, then, did the Department of Justice come to take part in such proceedings? In the beginning of the campaign against radicals before the armistice, we find turned against them the machinery already employed against alien enemies. In various localities the American Protective League, by whatever special name it was known in a given place, took an active part in running down radicals and reporting them to the Department of Labor. The Minute Men, who had been active in Seattle and were responsible for the arrest of some of the passengers of the "Red Special," were an organization of this sort.

During the same period, and also after the armistice, when the American Protective League had been disbanded, local police officials busied themselves in the search for radicals. In certain places special measures were taken by the state or municipal governments, to run down radicals, as in New York State and city, by the Lusk Committee and by the city police. Large numbers of arrests were made by local authorities in many places, but in many of the localities only a small proportion of the persons arrested were held for deportation, as the suspicions of these local officers far outran any stock of evidence that could be mustered against the arrested persons.

But the general alarms of the spring and summer of 1919, which we have noted as inspiring severity toward the foreign born in labor troubles, increased by the bomb explosions of May and June, 1919, led certain officials of the Federal government to feel that the means taken so far to check radicalism were insufficient. In consequence, a "radical division" was organized in the Department of Justice, a large amount of money was appropriated for its use, and it set to work in the summer of 1919.[1]

The primary purpose of this division was to collect information about revolutionary and radical movements in this country and elsewhere. Early in the fall, of 1919, however, a conference was held by the Department of Justice with the Department of Labor, ending in an agreement for the participation of the radical division in carrying out the deportation provisions of the immigration law.

RAIDS OF NOVEMBER, 1919

Their first considerable proceeding was directed against a Russian organization, known as the "Union of Russian

[1] *Hearings before Committee on Rules, House of Representatives, Sixty-sixth Congress, Second Session*, part i, pp. 156–166.

Workers," an organization which had attracted the attention of the Bureau of Immigration at the time of the arrests of the I. W. W. members making up the passenger list of the "Red Special," and two or three of the passengers on that train were members of the union.

At the time the I. W. W. men from the West were held at Ellis Island, a handful of members of the Russian Workers' Union from another part of the country were also there under order of deportation and had also been arrested in the winter of 1917–18.

The persons gathered in the course of the proceedings undertaken by the Department of Justice were largely taken in raids made during November, 1919, or early in December upon meeting places of Russians, known by some such name as "People's House" or "House of the Masses."

In these raids the Department of Justice assumed much of the authority of local police forces, and of the Department of Labor itself, and were charged even with exceeding the lawful powers of any agency of government. Their agents entered private property, broke into meeting places, made forcible searches and seizures, made arrests without warrant, held arrested persons in detention for indefinite periods before turning them over to the Department of Labor, without access to friends or privilege of counsel, subjected them to examination prior to the hearing before the immigration inspector, and in the course of these examinations resorted to "third-degree" methods of threats and violence, according to affidavits of the injured persons.[1]

[1] See C. M. Panunzio, *The Deportations of 1919*, published by the Commission on the Church and Social Service of the Federal Council of Churches, and the *Report on the Illegal Practices of the U. S. Department of Justice*, published by the National Popular Government League.

THE DEPORTATIONS OF 1919-20

The November raids were made in eleven industrial cities and towns.[1] The passenger list of the *Buford*, including persons arrested at other times, showed 59 deportees from New York City, 52 from Hartford, 23 from Youngstown and East Youngstown, 18 from Fairmont, West Virginia, 14 from Greensburg, Pennsylvania, 10 from Cleveland, 9 from Buffalo, 9 from Pittsburgh, 2 from Bethlehem, and the remainder scattering.

Of the 249 passengers deported on the *Buford*, 13 were charged with deportation offenses outside of the "anarchy clause." But 6 of these were arrested as radicals, and while 5 were deported for "liability to become a public charge," and 1 for entry as a contract laborer, notes on the cases[2] state, of 1, that he was charged with "I. W. W. and other radical connections and activities"; of another, that he was in the penitentiary for refusing to serve in the army and "had radical ideas—in favor of Russian Soviet government"; of another, "evidence indicated but did not clearly prove anarchistic beliefs"; and of the remaining three, "evidence indicated but did not clearly establish radical beliefs and activities." Here, then, is another instance of the use of charges not relating to anarchy to get rid of agitators.

Of the remaining 236 deportees, only 52 were charged with some personal belief and activity which the law makes a cause for deportation, while 181 were charged

---

[1] *Hearings before the Committee on Rules, House of Representatives, Sixty-sixth Congress, Second Session,* part i, p. 168.

[2] *Hearings before a Subcommittee of the Committee on Immigration and Naturalization, House of Representatives, Sixty-sixth Congress, Second Session,* pp. 157–158.

only with "membership or affiliation" and 3 with only affiliation with an organization of a kind defined in the anarchy clause. So that against nearly four-fifths of the number deported on charges of radicalism, no charge of personal belief or activity could be laid, for in cases where such a charge would stand it was added to the charge of membership or affiliation.

In view of the fact that so large a proportion of the *Buford* passengers were deported for membership in a forbidden organization, it would appear that the Union of Russian Workers had been adjudged by the Department of Labor to be an organization of the kind forbidden by law.

In the preparation of the cases for action by the department, a standard form of evidence used in all of them consists of extracts from the statement of principles issued by the Russian workers, and from literature advertised in their newspaper, and the recommendations of the examining inspectors are based upon the supposition that the organization is of the forbidden kind. Furthermore, according to the bureau memorandum of July 26, 1918, quoted in the account of the I. W. W. cases, it was agreed at the conference described in the memorandum that "membership in the order of Russian Workers, whose constitution and policies are distinctly anarchistic, is sufficient to justify deportation."

But nowhere in the printed reports of the activities of the Department of Labor in deportation cases is to be found any general decision of the Secretary of Labor that the Union of Russian Workers is an anarchistic organization.

The only approach to the establishment of a general ruling is to be found in the fact that Mr. Abercrombie, who was present at the conference just mentioned, and presumably agreed in its conclusions, was at the time vested with the powers of Acting Secretary of the Department, with full authority to issue warrants of deportation and in other respects exercise the powers of the Secretary.

What was this Union of Russian Workers and what were the People's Houses in which so many of the deportees were arrested?

These People's Houses were interesting institutions. The Slavic peoples generally have a primitive habit of group life, and a strong love for it; they cannot content themselves with the isolation that satisfied the Anglo-Saxon or Scandinavian pioneer. And there are some peculiarities about the Russian-Slavic immigration in particular that call for special provision for satisfying the social need. The Russians had but newly started to migrate to this country, which means that the Russian immigration contained a relatively large proportion of young men who were either unmarried or had left wives and families at home. And rather more than some other types of Slavic immigrants, the Russians came intending to return to the old home to live, so that the wives and children were not sent for so soon after arrival or in so large a number of cases. Nor did they marry here so freely as the Poles, for instance.

One reason for their intention to return was that the Russian, even under the oppressions of the Tsar's government, felt himself a citizen of a dominant state in which he had some share, and to which he took some pride in belonging, so that he was unwilling to leave his country permanently. The Pole, the Croatian, the Slovak, on the other hand, were members of subject states, and were the more ready, on that account, to leave them for good and all. These peoples, then, were more inclined to set up a family life here. In consequence, the social instinct could be gratified through the family by the married and through the colony by the single, since the single man could find lodging with a family group and enjoy some social life with them.

For the Russian immigrant groups, made up so largely of single men intending to return to their own country, such resources were less available. The great opportunity of social life had to be found in some general meeting place where large numbers could gather.

This need was at first met by the Russian Orthodox church, backed by the Russian government, which established houses where immigrants could find shelter, companionship, and sometimes employment. One purpose of these centers was to keep the immigrant a Russian, to maintain his allegiance to the Russian Church and the Russian government. On the industrial side, these houses had the reputation of being used at times as strike-breaking agencies.

As the revolutionary movement developed in Russia, however, in the first decade of the century, the Russian immigration to this country was more and more numerously recruited from those who were dissatisfied with the government and the church in Russia, and in this country more and more of the immigrants kept away from the church houses and established meeting places of their own. With the Slavic talent for coöperation, societies formed for different purposes would unite in renting a house, in which all had quarters.

Such centers sprang up and flourished in many places where Russian colonies were established.

Groups of various kinds were housed in these centers. In any one of them might be found societies for the propagation of political doctrine, benevolent societies, social clubs, musical clubs, dramatic societies, classes, newspaper offices, offices of other businesses and enterprises meeting the especial needs of Russians.

Many of the Russian workingmen attracted to these places came there not because they were especially interested in any one society or activity, but simply to be where they could meet other Russians, speak the Russian language, find Russian books and newspapers to read if they were able to read, get some one to write letters for them if they were not able to write, drink tea served in the Russian style, play games to while away the long evenings after work was over, and to have an opportunity to study. Very noticeable was the eager desire for education shown by these illiterate peasant workers, especially after the Russian revolution, which opened up to them an opportunity for using an education in the home country.

Why should the Russian workingman turn to such places as the People's Houses for education rather than to the public schools? For various reasons. One is that the public schools do not give instruction in the Russian language, which the Russian workingman is anxious to have. This is a natural desire. The illiterate peasant finds it hard to learn a new language and a new means of expression at the same time. He can already speak Russian. It will be easier for him with his work-stiffened brain to learn to read and write the language he already knows the meaning of. And naturally, it interests him more, for around it cluster all the associations of home. He already is familiar with the scenes and situations depicted in the Russian literature and with the Russian method of expressing the ideas set forth in their literature. And there are other reasons.

Says Professor Alexander Petrunkevitch in a report on the education of Russian workmen in the United States:

Refugees of the Old World and of a time-honored system of exploitation, frequently illiterate in their own language, constantly on their guard against things unaccustomed lest some harm befall them, well aware of their own lack of training, class conscious, suspicious of the motives of men with better education, greater financial resources or authority, confused in their minds by events in Russia—the Russian workmen can be handled neither as normal adults nor as other foreigners. A few among them manage, indeed, to acquire some knowledge of English in the public evening schools, but the majority become quickly discouraged and drop out or continue to study in their own poorly equipped schools supported by some local Russian organizations. Any attempt to induce them to study at an American school meets with the suspicion that behind the outward desire to give them education may lurk the disguised intention to "Americanize." The workmen are willing enough and even anxious to study, provided the knowledge is imparted to them in a manner allowing easy assimilation, but even those among them who will eventually seek admission to citizenship resent the conjunction of education with Americanization.

Moreover, the Russian workmen need not only a knowledge of English which shall benefit them in their particular trade or work; they need knowledge of all subjects regularly studied in schools, especially mathematics, and that knowledge must be imparted to them simultaneously with the English language if it is to be of use to them while they remain in this country. Prolonged postponement of the acquisition of such knowledge is apt to produce an unfavorable reaction, to discourage them, to make them acquiesce in

366

their status quo. But how can the knowledge be imparted in a language which in itself forms a subject of hard study?[1]

One of the political societies, growing and flourishing, became the leading group in some of these houses, and started other houses of its own, in which it held the dominating influence. This was the society, or rather, federation of societies, known as the Union of Russian Workers. But the methods followed in the use of the social centers were the same as before. The different activities of the houses were carried on independently. It was not necessary to be a member of this society in order to take advantage of the clubs and classes, and in the houses quarters could be rented by independent organizations. In the People's Houses in New York, for example, the Union of Russian Workers occupied only two rooms in the building. Other tenants were two Russian newspapers (one the organ of the Union of Russian Workers), a steamship office, two other Russian societies, the Russian Dock Workers' School, giving instruction in Russian, classes in mathematics, classes in mechanical trades, musical and literary clubs. In this house was also a clubroom, open to Russians generally.

THE UNION OF RUSSIAN WORKERS

What was the Union of Russian Workers? As described by Attorney General Palmer:

The Union of Russian Workers is even more radical than the Bolsheviki. It was organized in 1907, by a group of eleven men, led by William Shatoff, at present the chief of police at Petrograd. The purpose of the society was to amalgamate all of the Russian groups in the United States into one organization. With the aid of newspaper and other

[1] *Report of the Board of Officers of the Russian Collegiate Institute of New York, 1919-20,* p. 3.

propaganda the membership of the Union of Russian Workers grew until at the present time its membership is about 7,000, and its branches number more than 100, located in the principal cities of the country.

The various locals are organized for the sole purpose of spreading the doctrine of the organization among the Russian immigrants working in the mines, shops, factories, logging camps and sawmills, and other centers of labor, and the propaganda is conducted by means of literature and lectures as well as through the radical newspapers. Lecturers are sent out by the executive committee of the group and cover all parts of the country. Funds of the organization are derived from dues, lectures, and concerts, and the sale of radical literature.[1]

The founders of the organization drew up a statement of fundamental principles and a members' contract of union, showing what the organization stood for and required of its members. This statement is the substance of the "Little Red Book," seized by the Department of Justice in the raids and used in framing the charges. This statement and contract, as translated by the Department of Justice, are as follows:

FEDERATION OF UNIONS OF RUSSIAN WORKERS OF THE UNITED STATES AND CANADA

FUNDAMENTAL PRINCIPLES OF THE FEDERATION

Modern society is divided into two opposed classes. On the one hand are the disinterested workers and peasants who, by their labor, create the entire wealth, and, on the other hand, the rich, who have taken possession of all this wealth.

The class of the disinherited race are repeatedly in revolt against the parasitic rich and against their handmaiden and protector the state (alternative translation "the governments") for the purpose of fully emancipating themselves from the yoke of capitalistic authority.

[1] New York *Post*, November 8, 1919.

But every time they suffered defeat because of not knowing the necessary revolutionary ways and means through which to gain their liberty. The unfortunate classes have been instruments in the hands of their enemies.

The struggle between these classes continues up to now, and will only terminate when the toiling masses organized as a class, will understand their true interest, and will, by means of a forcible social revolution, take possession of the entire wealth of the world.

Having accomplished such an upheaval and having destroyed at the same time all the institutions of the state and authority, the class of the disinherited will have to proclaim a society of free producers, who will be compelled to give satisfaction to the demands of every separate person who give their knowledge and labor to this society.

In furtherance of which aim we place in the front the necessity to create a wide revolutionary class organization of the toilers, who will conduct an immediate combat with all institutions of government and ownership.

We must teach the working class to take the initiative of self-activeness in order to bring about the necessary and inevitable strike to abolish government and proclaim the success of the social revolution.

Therefore, we organize in Unions of Russian Workers. We are the laborers of the world, and will lead in all our future work, so that the principles laid down in our federation will be as a directing string for us in the affairs of a large organized mass of Russian immigrants in the United States and Canada for a quicker liberation of Russia and enslaved humanity in all countries.

MEMBERS CONTRACT OF UNION OF RUSSIAN WORKERS OF
ALL THE UNITED STATES AND CANADA
UNIFIED INTO FEDERATION

PURPOSE OF FEDERATION

1. Unification of the organizations of Russian Workers of the United States and Canada for the struggle with capitalism and government.

2. To support the liberation movement in Russia.

3. To support the revolutionary elements of workers in America.

4. Moral and material support of the organs of the Federation, whether they be anarchistic or otherwise.

5. To create organizations where there are none and support those already created.

BY-LAWS OF THE ORGANIZATION

Members of the Union are qualified members of every other Union in the Federation.

All organizations entering into the Federation benefit themselves with full autonomy, giving one another a large material and moral support.

SUBSTANCE OF THE FEDERATION

All resources of the Federation are composed of 10 per cent deductions from the monthly dues of the members of the organization and voluntary contributions.

ADMINISTRATION OF THE FEDERATION

For carrying on the business of the Federation, a secretary-treasurer is elected, who handles all correspondence of the business of the Federation.

FOR THE INFORMATION OF MEMBERS OF THE FEDERATION

From the dues of every member of the organization is deducted monthly as follows: Into fund of printing machine, 5 cents. Into fund of Federation, 10 cents.

The declaration of principles contains some violent expressions couched in the language of agitation familiar in revolutionary propaganda in Russia, but the practical bearing of the whole movement, as expressed in the members' contract, is seen to center specifically in support of the liberation movement in Russia, and, more generally, in carrying on the class struggle, recognized as a common conception of many groups not under the ban of government, who are working for the betterment of the working class.

The articles of federation leave to every organization entering it full autonomy, do not prescribe any form of belief from anyone, demand no pledge further than to give general "support" to the liberation movement in Russia and the class struggle in the United States and "support" to the organs of the federation.

This granting of local and individual freedom is indeed the secret of the wonderful success of the founders of the Federation of Unions of Russian Workers in gathering in so many societies and individuals. While other political societies were laying down hard and fast principles for members to subscribe to, difficult for the untaught peasant to understand, and while they were trying to establish a discipline foreign to the easy-going Russian temperament, the founders of the union were leaving their members free to think as they pleased, or not to think at all, and were making provision for the plain human needs of sociability and for the simple education that these peasants wanted. The activities of the federation were, in fact, primarily educational, and they provided not only the literature of propaganda, but the classes in elementary and trade subjects that would fit the worker to be self-helpful.

In practice the union became a loosely knit group of locally self-determining bodies, of varying policies and beliefs. This became even more the case after the Russian revolution, for the founders of the union, the guiding minds in propaganda, all went back to Russia, leaving the work here to be carried on by a more heterogeneous group. In fact, leaders of any kind were few, and the local bodies had to depend more and more upon their own resources.

371

The members of these local bodies were not asked to subscribe to any doctrine or to take any pledge of obedience to orders of the organization. They were not even required to read the principles of the organization, and many of them had not read them or seen them, according to repeated testimony given in the hearings on deportation cases.

And gathered around the group of persons who had actually become members of the union were to be found persons coming to the houses just for education and sociability.

In any "People's House" run by the Union of Russian Workers, then, would be found a few persons of education and active interest in propaganda, who would endeavor to instruct the membership, and any others who might frequent the building, in radical views, but the rank and file of the attendants at the houses were peasant workers, illiterate, but not unintelligent, who were honestly trying to find out what life meant for them and for the world.

As the happy social life going on in these places is revealed in glimpses from the records of deportation cases, one must regret that such an opportunity was lost by other agencies. While settlement houses were trying to think up means to attract Russians into their clubs and classes, while the American schools were painfully gathering in small handfuls of them, while more orthodox political groups were trying to force on these Russian peasant workers a serious program of political action that they could not understand, the peasants themselves were flocking to the centers that gave them a home, and a chance to express themselves in any way that they desired, which was, for the most part, in tea drinking, talking, and studying.

After all, among these groups, the revolutionary

propaganda had little effect in action. It is a note-worthy circumstance that no disorder, no crime, no preparation for crime, even, has been traced to any group of the Union of Russian Workers. Their sin, such as it is, has consisted in talk only.

And is it not strange that authority does not recognize the value of talk as a safety valve, and a pressure gauge as well? The foreign workingman, outraged at some form of exploitation, some individual hardship, rails violently against the government or the society that permits such things to occur, and then sits down to his game of chess relieved and happy. If he is per-mitted to talk, not only is he relieved, but authority may know what is in his mind and take measures to cure the trouble. If he is shut up, the banked-up energy may gain force, the additional grievance of not even being allowed to complain is added, and no one knows what is brewing in his mind and what will be the outcome.

RUSSIAN WORKER DEPORTEES

Turning now to the deportation cases, we find the records indicating that of the large numbers of Russians gathered in the houses of the Russian workers and seized in raids, an exceedingly small proportion were under-standing followers of anarchist doctrine, still fewer were leaders and propagandists. The men arrested were, in general, in sympathy with the Russian revolution, be-cause they remembered the oppressions of an autocratic government. Most of them were illiterate peasants, of Slavic race, in large proportion from White Russia—on the western border of Russia, where they had lived min-gled with Lithuanians and Poles, and from them caught the stimulus to emigration. As shown in the records of their cases, they are, however, far from unintelligent.

373

Some of them had made remarkable progress in education and understanding, after a few years in this country, and many times as a direct outcome of the instruction thay had received in a house of the Union of Russian Workers.

The first four names on the *Buford* list[1] are of men arrested at Akron, Ohio, in December, 1917, two years previously.

Attention had been attracted to Akron, and its large numbers of Russians employed in the tire factories and elsewhere, because of what seemed to be disproportionately small registration for the draft.[2] An agent of the Department of Justice was sent to that place and started a branch of the American Protective League, in which the manager of a local manufacturing company took the position of chief.

Here, apparently, existed the same close connection between the industrial companies and the governmental authorities already noted in the steel towns during the steel strike. In this town at least one of the big companies paid the salaries of the stenographers employed by the Department of Justice, and reinforced the salary of the local agent of the department who, after the armistice, entered the employ of the company.

The four men deported on the *Buford* were arrested in a raid on a meeting, with two others, one of whom was finally released on parole, after the order of deportation had been issued,[3] the other turned out to be an

[1] Immigration Bureau number, 54248/20, Naum Stepanuk; No. 54235/151, John Tarasyk; No. 54235/158, Paul Krechin; No. 54235/159, Leo Haskevich.

[2] Emerson Hough, *The Web*, p. 393.

[3] No. 54235/160, Mike Elick.

"under-cover man," who had been stationed in one of the plants to spy upon the workers.[1]

All were originally charged with advocating anarchy and the unlawful destruction of property, and, with the exception of Stepanuk, of liability to become a public charge.

The men were not notified of their right to counsel until after a long day of grilling examination before the immigration inspector. Not until the second day's brief hearing, at which nothing material was added to the testimony of the first day, were they told they could have counsel. At this second day's hearing the record notes that representatives of the Department of Justice and of the American Protective League were present.

All of the men explicitly denied any intention of doing anything unlawful.

Mike Elick said:

In view of the fact that it is free to organize in this country, we were under the impression that the literature that was found on us and other evidences that were against us were not forbidden by the law. Should we have found out that such is the case . . . we would never have engaged ourselves in organizing or distributing or propagating or advocating such.

Naum Stepanuk:

We were never disposed to engage in any direct action of destruction, so that we didn't do anything contrary to law. . . . If I had anything against the American government I would not have bought Liberty Bonds.

Leo Haskevich:

We were having our meetings openly, we were not carrying any weapons, we were doing nothing that would make us subject to the charges which were against us. We never

[1] No. 54235/156, Daniel Kuts.

had any intention of killing or destroying, but only to speak and advocate by mere words, as it was permitted until the United States went into the war.

Paul Krechin:

We do not believe in labor disputes; we are Russians and, secondly, we hang together, and the Russian cause is the cause that mostly concerns us, and mutual help and education, because many of our people are illiterate. I myself was illiterate.

A memorandum of July, 1918, filed with these cases, says: "The only evidence, in addition to matter of membership in the Russian Workers' Union which supports any of the warrant charges, is the admission by some of the aliens that they have passed out literature or handbills which have reference to the subject of anarchy," and, "The allegations that aliens were persons likely to become a public charge at time of entry is not reasonably established," but their deportation is recommended because "clearly by their acts in subscribing to the principles and aiding by paying dues and otherwise furthering the spread of a radical anarchistic organization such as the Russian Union Workers" they "are clearly guilty of advocating and teaching anarchy and the unlawful destruction of property." This is in accordance with the conference decision of July 26th, already referred to,[1] making membership in the order of Russian workers a sufficient ground for deportation, although no law authorizing deportation for membership only had as yet been passed.[2]

The warrant of deportation in these cases was finally

[1] P. 362 above.
[2] "The I. W. W. Deportation Cases," *Hearings before a Subcommittee of the Committee on Immigration and Naturalization, House of Representatives, Sixty-sixth Congress, Second Session,* p. 79.

issued in November, 1918, and the five men transferred to Ellis Island. At a rehearing secured for them by counsel in New York, the charge of membership in an organization was added to charges of personal activities, and the four men on the *Buford* were finally deported on the charge of membership alone. The action of the department in paroling the fifth man (Mike Elick) was taken because "some parts of his testimony" "make a very good impression," and because he had a sick wife.[1]

Evidence of the four men deported as given in the records of the hearings also makes a good impression, both as to beliefs and as to personal character.

Naum Stepanuk, the secretary of the local at Akron, was a White Russian, thirty-five years old. He had been in the country since 1909 and had been a farm worker in Russia, on a farm that belonged to his parents. He had gone to elementary school in Russia, where he had learned to read and to write and to draw. In Russia he had never read any scientific or philosophical books and read newspapers very seldom.

After he came to this country he had worked as a laborer in various places—steel works, coal mines, in a smelter, in the Kansas harvest field in the summer time. There was nothing in his record to show that he had ever been in trouble of any kind. His last employment was with a rubber company in Akron, where his average wages had been $24 a week. He considered this and his working conditions satisfactory, and thought that the Russians generally were satisfied with their work and working conditions in this country. If this was the case,

---

[1] "The I. W. W. Deportation Cases," *Hearings before a Subcommittee of the Committee on Immigration and Naturalization, House of Representatives, Sixty-sixth Congress, Second Session*, p. 62.

he was asked, why did he belong to a revolutionary organization?

He explained that the purpose of the union was in general to educate the members through the reading of pamphlets and literature, and the study of school subjects, including the reading and writing of English and Russian. The inspector asking him what good he thought the study and reading of Russian literature would do a working man in the United States, he replied that it would help him "to understand life—their own lives."

He admitted that the organization was "revolutionary," but insisted that the revolutionary doctrines applied to Russia only. Individuals in the organization may have had something against other governments, but not so far as he knew. The Russians in this organization are not familiar with conditions in this country, and did not have anything against the government of the United States, and, he goes on to say, "I do not know that they have anything against the government of the United States now," referring evidently to the effect that the hunting down of Russians by our government might be supposed to have. In the union they carried on no propaganda except getting in members, and helping them to understand their condition and improve it.

As to his personal beliefs, he states that he believes in some of the things in the statement of principles of the Union of Russian Workers, and in some he does not believe. He thinks force has never done any good in changing conditions and he does not believe in force. He understands anarchy to mean, not assassination and destruction, but love, equality, and construction. He does not believe in sabotage, never participated in a strike, and never saw a bomb. He believes in change

378

in a peaceful way, through majority control. Personally he is not opposed to government if it is created and maintained by the people, and he thinks the United States government is of that type. Violence is not needed in this country.

He has no plans for change in this country because he does not understand conditions here, but for Russia he wanted to substitute for Tsarism the rule of the people, and therefore the great necessity was to enlighten the people so that they could find out for themselves what government they wanted, whether to elect a president or any other government.

He never thought about the immigration from Russia creating a revolution in this country. That was a matter for the American workers, and if they should start a revolutionary movement the Russian workers would of course be with them, but they would first have to consider whether this movement was just or unjust. He understands by a revolution a movement or change that is just. Asked how he would accomplish this revolution, he said that if the people were sufficiently enlightened and understood what they were about, and had the majority, they certainly could bring about any change they cared for. The ideal government, he thinks, is that where everyone understands its form and is interested enough to support it. But although he thinks that no such government actually exists now, he does not believe any change in the government could take place as long as the people do not understand the nature of such a change. He had never taught the destruction of property or the assassination of public officials. He believes in the private ownership of land, wants to inherit his father's property in Russia, own the land and work it, and would defend his rights to that property by force if necessary.

Asked why he remained a member of an organization advocating things he did not believe, he explained that in joining the union no one was required to subscribe to any belief or to undergo examination for fitness for membership, or even to read the principles in the preamble. The only requirement was to pay dues, and he thought that "anyone may be a member of an organization and think for himself if he does not hurt somebody else."

The experiences of Stepanuk after his first arrest gave him some lessons in the practical workings of this free government which were not of a nature to strengthen his confidence in it.

Some time after reaching Ellis Island he was released on bond and he turned naturally to the People's House in New York City as a home in a strange place. On the 1st of May, 1919, he was present at the new building of the New York *Call*, when that place was raided by a mob, without effective interference by the police, and records his impressions as follows in a letter to *Bread and Freedom* (May 15, 1919), the organ of the Russian Workers:

In a country where law and order are so honored and protected, a band of hooligans, in the form of soldiers and sailors carried on a series of pogroms against the gatherings and demonstrations of the workers of New York on May 1st. Peaceful private gatherings were beaten up without distinction of sex and age.

In one of these places, in the new premises of the *Call* newspaper, I had the misfortune to be present. Like myself, hundreds of others present at the opening of the new building were cruelly beaten. The panic arising in the building filled with women and children was indescribable.

The importance and interest of these pogroms rests in the fact that some one of the powerful in the community stood behind this and carried it out through these poor pawns, who were changed into wild beasts at orders from outside.

It is time for the workers to think seriously about this, it is time for them to speak their word.

Later, taking part in a parade organized to protest against the blockade of Russia, in which unresisting marchers were beaten up by the police, his own head was broken.

Finally taken back to Ellis Island, he shared the opinion of fellow deportees that they were suffering under unendurable restrictions and deprivations, and joined in a hunger strike, in which he suffered seriously.

Leo Haskevich was a young fellow of twenty-one when first arrested, had come to the United States in 1913, was from Grodno, and was presumably a White Russian by race. Since coming to this country he had been working steadily, at first in a meat market, then in a chain shop, then in the rubber works at Akron. He had gone to evening school and learned English. He had been a farm worker in Russia and would like to go back there, own the land, and live on it. He has no interest in any country but Russia; he came here to work because opportunities were better than in Russia and so he is not a citizen of this country and does not mean to be one.

He joined the U. R. W. to "help the working people," although he himself was satisfied with his treatment by his employers. The object of that organization he understood to be "education, civilization," and its activities were "reading, holding meetings, educational schooling." The union was also active in "getting ready as an organized body to go back to Russia and they were also in opposition to the monarch in Russia." He said the question was never raised of opposition to other governments. When he attended meetings of this organization he never heard force or violence advocated for the United States, nor did he ever hear such things in any other organizations. "At the meetings speakers would come and tell them that our people are ignorant and need teaching and study and organization." Speakers did not mention this government in his hearing nor were they in the habit of condemning all organized governments as they exist in civilized countries to-day.

His understanding of the term anarchy is "love, equality, fraternity," and its objects are that people should live according to the desires of the majority of the people, not according to the desires of one or two men. He thinks that by embracing anarchistic doctrines such a condition could be brought about. This would hold good for this country only in case the American people see it, want it, and bring it about; he has nothing in common with them. He has never advocated such a thing in this community or distributed anarchistic literature. He never made efforts to bring others to his way of thinking in this matter; he would only say what he thought and let others draw their own conclusions. He stands for majority rule and changes without force and violence, unless the majority decide that violence is necessary, in which case he would stand with the majority. His own opinion is that the objects desired should be brought about without force.

John Tarasyk, also from Grodno, was twenty years old at the time of his first arrest, came to this country also in 1913, worked in Youngstown about two years, in steel works and in a fireproofing company, then came to Akron, where he was working in a tire factory. He had worked steadily except for a vacation of a month and a half when he was taking little trips around.

He says that he subscribed to the principles laid down in the membership book of the U. R. W., but does not know that he would advocate all of the things named therein as the purposes of the organization. His purpose in joining the local union was to go to Russia because his people are there.

Books and papers found in a suitcase in his possession he said were left by a friend who went into the army. Among other books, one copy each of a botany, zoology, physics, geology, a few classics, and detective stories were found. Asked if he agreed with the revolutionary sentiments contained in the bundle of books presented in evidence, he said he did: "It was necessary for everyone in Russia to read such books while the Tsar was ruling." As far as reading such books in the United States is concerned, he understands that "it is free to organize in this country and to read books and to publish them." He has nothing against the capital and government of this country.

Paul Krechin, twenty-seven years old in 1917, came from farther East, from the Volga neighborhood, in the province of Saratov, in 1912, leaving a wife behind in Russia, but no children. He had worked all the time since his arrival, first in a soda ash shop, two and a half years with no lay off; "working Sundays and every day, pushing big chunks of caustic." Every two weeks he got $30 or $35. Then he came to Akron, and had been working in a tire concern, getting "nice money," from $25 to $45 a week, flattening rims. He spent only about $20 a month for his upkeep, sending the rest home to his wife in Russia.

At home he did not belong to any organization or political party, but in this country he joined the U. R. W. because, "as a Russian I joined the other Russians so that we might help each other." He could not read or write when he entered the organization, and joined because he wanted to learn. The main work of the organization was the school, and at meetings somebody would talk about the necessity of continuing school work and going back to Russia knowing how to read and write. Occasionally they would talk about getting rid of the Tsar. In response to his statement that the program of the Russian workers, after they had built up a strong organization, would be to "study books and learn how to read and write," the inspector somewhat baselessly asserts "as a matter of fact, you would strike and burn property, and all that sort of thing— strikes and labor disturbances all over the country," to which the arrested man replied, "Here? No, sir. our efforts are centered to Russia, not here."

Asked if he and the other members of the organization entertain the beliefs expressed in the literature which they distribute, he said: "No, gentlemen, we read everything, but we do not accept everything. What we do not like we reject, and what is good we retain." But they have to depend on other people to tell them what is good or not good, because he and the rest of the members "do not understand many things." He himself has had a little education, but cannot understand difficult literature. On the whole he believes that the program of the organization is good, "but maybe in the last moment I will throw it away and not accept it." In joining the organization he did not have to take a pledge, and did not even know what the program was. He was led to join the organization by what was told him and what he had read, but as to being governed by the rules of the organization and the instructions of its officers, "nobody shall dictate to me what I shall do, not even the officers of the organization, if I don't like it."

384

As to his own beliefs he said that he had not studied anarchy, but thinks it is the theory of loving everyone and not killing anyone. He does not believe in sabotage —"Why should good things be broken?"—and does not believe in violence. He was never arrested and was never in a strike. He has nothing against the American government and nothing against any Russian party except the Tsar. He would like to go back to Russia to help Russia, now that the Tsar is overthrown and now that Russia is free as America is free. His father owns a farm in Russia, and he would like to go back and work it. He believes in the private ownership of land. If anyone wanted to take the land away he would not want to give it up.

Mike Elick, the man paroled, was a Russian Pole, from Wilna, twenty-seven years old in 1917, who had come to this country in 1910, and had worked ever since, in a car shop, in a tin mill, in a match factory, and for four years in a rubber concern in Akron. Before his arrest he was making $20 or $21 a week. It cost him over $40 a month to live, and he could not save much because he "wears nice clothes" and it costs him a lot! He has sent money home to a friend and to his family in Russia. He had been a member of the U. R. W. he said, but did not know whether he was any longer a member or not, as he had stopped going to meetings. Being reminded that he was at a meeting when arrested in November, he said it was not really a meeting, but just a school session.

The purpose of the organization, he says, is to educate all the members "because the Russian people when they come to this country spend their time going to saloons and drinking beer." He does not believe in the doctrines contained in the preamble—only the educational part of the organization. It is a matter of individual preference with the members what part of the organization activities they support. One likes one thing and one likes another; for his part, he likes the educational features of this organization more than the rest of the program, and he "didn't print those booklets."

As to his political ideas, he believes "in the people's rule"—"I like this country; I don't like it like the Kaiser or the Russian Tsar." His opinion as to factory conditions is that they were very good; if his opinion were bad, he "would not have stuck there and worked for four years," and would not have become an inspector there.

He expressly disclaims belief in anarchism, thinks a government a necessity, thinks this country is better than Russia, and intended to take out first papers as soon as he learned the language.

This man had been reading the literature of the U. R. W., including works on anarchistic communism, but very plainly and definitely objected to their doctrine that government is unnecessary. We are to note that, although he was finally paroled, in the first instance he was ordered deported, and spent months under that charge.

Through the records in these cases we see these men as intelligent, industrious workers, anxious to learn something about the world they live in, and to take part in its improvement. And from them and also from what we know about Russian immigrants of the working class, it is seen to be the height of absurdity even to enter a charge of "liability to become a public charge" against them.

BETHLEHEM CASES

On the list of 181 persons deported for membership in the Union of Russian Workers, next after the four men from Akron in chronological order of arrest come two men from Bethlehem, Pennsylvania.

In this town, as in others in Pennsylvania, described in an earlier chapter, a large foreign population is preyed upon by runners and lawyers, and by unscrupulous police officials, constables, and the burgesses or aldermen themselves, who are also justices.

Here, as in other places, members of the police force often work in connection with certain of the aldermen. An investigator for this study learned that one alderman had several cousins on the police force, and gave a percentage on a rough-sliding scale of the fees and fines to policemen who brought him cases. This alderman secures most of the police business and many of the police were to all intents and purposes acting as constables for him.

Abuses in connection with enforcing the law which forbids aliens to have firearms were frequent. In one case two policemen broke into the home of an aged immigrant late at night, drove the man and his wife out of bed, and proceeded on a search for firearms, without any search warrant. Finally a rusty and useless revolver was found, by reason of which the man was taken to jail and kept there overnight. While the man was conferring with his attorney next morning at the attorney's office, an officer came in and arrested him, and it developed that the man had been held in the jail all night without any warrant of arrest, so that the superintendent of police could present information against the man, and get the half of the fine which goes to the informant in such cases.

Certain of the aldermen in this town were inclined to take advantage of the foreign born, and one of them, who had made use of all the common methods of extortion, had been known to go so far as to issue separation papers for $50 each, and other papers which he had no legal right to issue, for correspondingly extortionate amounts.

In this city, as in the other steel towns described in the account of labor troubles in the courts, the relations between the town government and the industry are close. The mayor of the city at this time was one of the vice presidents of the company, and at least nine-tenths of the city officials and persons having any municipal authority were either direct employees of the company or were dominated by that organization. And the population over which this city government rules is largely dependent on this same company for a livelihood; perhaps 60 or 70 per cent are in this situation. The company can, then, control both officials and population.

In this city there had been comparatively little open agitation of a radical character, but the steel company had insisted that the police be particularly stringent in dealing with any manifestation of it. The captain of police of this job had been a member of the state constabulary, had then joined the police force of Bethlehem, and later was chief of company police of one division of the company, where he became known as a fearless enemy of lawbreakers, but a bullying, brutal roughneck in his methods. He had been appointed from this post to the city police again, as chief, in order to clean up vice conditions in the city, and he showed considerable activity in this work, but he was accused of accepting graft from certain favored persons, and was brought up for investigation before the Borough Council. The evidence as reported in the daily press seems weighty,[1] but the captain was acquitted.

[1] The *Globe*, Bethlehem, Pennsylvania, May 28, 30, 1919.

In proceeding against radicals he inaugurated a veritable reign of terror among the foreign born, especially against the Russians. He and his first officer would walk around the town, and when they met a Russian who seemed to them suspicious, would arrest him, keep him overnight in the police station, and let him go next day. One outrageous action for which he himself was arrested and fined was entering the house of an orthodox Russian family while they were entertaining guests at an Easter dinner, and attempting to arrest the husband. The wife, protesting, was struck by the captain, although she was pregnant. He then beat up everybody in the house. The wife secured a certificate of injury later from a physician in another town.

The two men whose names appear on the passenger list of the *Buford* were arrested with three others at a meeting held on private property by several foreign societies in town, the purpose of which, according to accounts given by persons present and according to handbills announcing the meeting, was to discuss conditions in Russia and Poland, and ways of getting back there. One of the societies represented was the local branch of the U. R. W.; others were the Polish Socialist party and the Lithuanian Group of Workers. The group thus assembled was called the "Soviet of Workers' Deputies of Bethlehem."

The arrests were made so shortly after the opening of the meeting that nothing incriminating or significant could have been done or said. The men were taken to jail, held overnight, and some time the next day turned over to the immigration authorities, who sent them forthwith to the nearest immigration station, at Gloucester City, New Jersey, out of reach of friends.

Of the five men, two were members of the Union of

Russian Workers, two were representatives at the meeting of the Polish Socialist party, and for the fifth no party affiliations could be established; he had come he said, to address the meeting with regard to conditions in Poland at the request of one of the Polish Socialists. At the hearing before the examining inspector of the Bureau of Immigration, none of the five men had the benefit of counsel, and all were recommended for deportation.

Two months later they succeeded in obtaining a rehearing, with the aid of counsel, and as a result only the two whose names appear on the *Buford* list were finally held for deportation—the two representatives of the Union of Russian Workers, as "members of an organization" of the character forbidden by the law. All five were originally charged with being anarchists at the time of entering the country, to which was added, at the rehearing, the charge of advocating and teaching anarchy. Nothing in the record of the cases would seem to justify these charges, and on rehearing they were not pressed.

One of the men ordered deported[1] was a Pole living in Easton, Pennsylvania. He had spent three years in Denmark as a loom fixer, and was then a silk weaver at Phillipsburg, New Jersey. He was one of the men invited to speak at the meeting and said his topic was present conditions in Poland. He said he did not know it was a meeting of a "Soviet"—he thought it was the Polish Sick and Benefit Society—and he did not intend to speak about the condition of the Polish people in America. He was speaking when the police raided the place, but had been only about four minutes on the platform.

[1] Warrant No. 54616/96, Reinhold Rudner.

Asked about his beliefs, he said he was against the Tsar and with Kerensky, did not believe in the overthrow of capital or in socialism, and decidedly not in anarchy. He himself was a weaver on three looms, which is against even union rules. He did not want to return to Russia, as he was settled down here and was satisfied.

Evidence produced against him consisted in a notebook which seemed to contain nothing more harmful than some notes on casualties in the Great War and some fragmentary meditations such as, "I loved and was so happy and never knew the sweet pain," and a newspaper clipping referring to a conference of the Soviet of Russian Workers in America, made up, as there stated, of delegates from various parties, the object of which was the discussion and advancement of the various interests of Russian immigrants in the United States, as well as to look into the situation in Russia. He had never participated in a strike, he said, and if dissatisfied with a job would look for other work. This was one of the men released as a result of a rehearing.

Of the two representatives of the Polish Socialist party, one, Joseph Dyiak,[1] according to the record in his case, came to this country in 1913, had worked as fireman in zinc mines, then as blacksmith for the Lehigh Valley Railroad three years. For the past two years he had worked as blacksmith for the Bethlehem Steel Company, getting 44 cents an hour for a twelve-and-three-quarter-hour day. He had been arrested twice since coming to the United States—once for not paying his board, once for getting into a fight.

He did not approve of the sentiments in the an-

[1] Warrant No. 54616/96.

archistic papers he had read, although the inspector seemed to think that "the fact that you read those papers would show that you agree with what they set forth." He was willing to be returned to Russia. "All I have to say is that I came here, I was never out of work for a day, but I came here to learn, and I am satisfied to go back." But he strenuously denied being an anarchist.

Like the others, he said he would like to own land in Russia, and if the government interfered he would not like that government. He was never in a strike and if not satisfied with the job he had would ask the boss to pay him more, and if he would not, he would quit and look for another job.

The other delegate of the Socialist Party arrested[1] was chairman of the meeting, and, like Joseph Dyiak, utterly denied the charge of anarchy, nor is there anything in the record to show that he was an anarchist. Both of these men, however, were ordered deported by the inspector and afterwards released on rehearing.

Of the two members of the Union of Russian Workers, finally deported, one was an invited speaker from New York, a young Jewish student[2] born in Kiev, who came from Russia by way of England in December, 1914. From the record we learn that he had left Russia the previous April. In Russia he had got into trouble while at school, as he and his friends were issuing a paper "after the model of Alexander Pushkin," and he was expelled for that offense.

The inspector, suspicious at once, asked, "What teaching did this Alexander Pushkin advocate?" thinking, no doubt, that he was on the trail of another anarchist author. Asked why it was necessary for him

[1] Adam Czerwinsky.
[2] Fedor Kushnarev (or, Alexander Dalny), No. 54709/522.

to leave Russia after his expulsion from school, he replied that it was very hard for a Russian Jew to enter school in any case, and he had just got in because he had protection from relatives who had influence. When he was expelled from that school he saw no chance of getting into any other. When he came to the United States he had intended to study engineering, but when the break in communication came he was left without resources from home and had to go to work. He took all sorts of jobs, as dishwasher, porter, newsdealer. He had no home, used to sleep at Russian bath places, but used the People's House as a mailing address. They had a library and he studied there. He wrote poetry, but it was never printed. Being known in general as an educated person, he was sometimes invited to speak, and in this way was invited to South Bethlehem. What he intended to speak about was self-enlightenment for the sake of creating better citizens for Russia.

He admitted that he was a member of the Union of Russian Workers, but said he believed in organized government, and was not an anarchist. And he said he did respect authority, although the inspector intimated that his publishing the magazine in Russia when forbidden to do so showed a lack of respect for authority.

He described the Union of Russian Workers as an organization for self-enlightenment and its purpose to further cordial mutual aid among Russians. The literature they distributed, he said, is "the whole Russian literature." He had found at headquarters the works of Pushkin, Lermontov, Tolstoy, Turgenieff, books on literature and history, and Bernard Shaw's plays in Russian. He had not read any book or paper that called for violence, nor had he heard of anyone in the union who had done so.

Asked if he believed in violence, he said violence was a very broad word—"violence" was used in setting up the United States of America.

This young man was evidently one of the small number of the educated who were endeavoring to act as leaders in the Union of Russian Workers, taking the places of the original leaders, who had gone home.

The other man held was of a different type—the uneducated workman of inquiring mind. This man,[1] according to the record, was secretary of the meeting at which the arrests were made. He was born in Grodno, was thirty-one years of age, and could read and write.

He came to this country in May, 1914, went directly to Bethlehem, and had been there ever since, at first working for the steel company as a laborer, then in the ammunition works. In his leisure times he went to school—a "self-education school," he explained, where he studied "botany and forestry and where coal comes from and how it is formed." This instruction is carried on, he says, "because our Russians are illiterates and don't know very much, so we are getting together and reading books."

He denied most emphatically that he was an anarchist. Asked if he wished an attorney, he said that he had no means to pay one.

He could not speak or write the English language, could not read American newspapers, so had no knowledge of conditions in this country.

He was dissatisfied with conditions in Russia when he lived there, but never got into trouble on account of agitation. He was put under arrest for ten days once when in the army, for failing to perform some of his

[1] Im. No. 54709/696, Nicolai Volosuk.

duties. At that time he said he had no intelligent understanding about the government.

Asked whether he was a believer in Bolshevism, he said he did not recognize any of those parties: "I am not a Bolshevik. I only believe that if I go back to Russia I would have some land. That is the reason why I left, and that is the reason why I would want to go back." But now he could not buy the land if he went home—he has no money, "because I bought some land in this country, and now it is pretty cheap, and no one wants to give me the money that I paid for it." He paid $350 for two lots, each 120 feet by 40 feet. From his account we may infer that the suspected "red" had shared the common lot of the immigrant and been caught in a land deal, which did not turn to his profit. When he was told that he might be released on a bond of $1,000 he remarked that $1,000 was "quite a lot of money."

After this hearing the man was released under bond, but about a month later was arrested at Bethlehem for "condemning the government and making inflammatory remarks," by the police, who referred the case to the Bureau of Immigration for further action.

The first witness against him on this charge was a worker who boarded in the same house with him, and testified that the man had frequently talked against the government, but aside from general accusations of revolutionary talk, unsubstantiated by any quotations or dates, the specific offense reported of him was "condemning the Bethlehem Steel Company because the men whom he was addressing had worked there a number of years and had no money saved,"—hardly an attack on the government.

The next witness was the police officer making the arrest, an officer known as the right-hand man of the notorious chief. Asked to state what the man was saying before the arrest, the officer said:

"He says, 'What have you got in this country of this government? This government is no good. You only earn a couple of dollars and that is all.'"

Asked whether the man said anything about overthrowing the present government, the officer said:

"We were not there long enough to hear all. Just as soon as I heard him say the government was no good I placed him under arrest."

He had never seen the man before, and had not seen him selling any anarchist papers.

The testimony of the chief of police himself was equally fragmentary and inconclusive. He said he had had his eye on this man for some time, and had gone to the supposed headquarters of the Union of Russian Workers, "where he had like a school and scholars were sitting around," and (it is worthy of note) "we searched them for guns and did not find any." On another occasion a man came running to him to say that he "was reading a foreign American paper and it had Charley Schwab's picture in it, and one of these Bolsheviks took a match and lighted it and said it was no good, and I run down there with this man to point him out to me. This Volosuk was there and they all beat it away; in fact, I was not able to get the man that burned this paper." This chief of police had evidently lost the power of distinguishing between an insult to the government and an insult to an employer.

At a rehearing secured for Volosuk in May, 1919, in which he finally secured counsel, he told a circumstantial story of rough treatment by the police at the time of his arrest. He said the policeman took him into a separate room and told him that he was a "Russian

Bolshevik," and "he tore my cap off of me and gave me a smack in the face and then in many other ways has insulted me, and then he took me down before the judge and I could not understand all they were saying."

This man was not, however, deported because of anything done or said at the time of his second arrest, but as a member of the Union of Russian Workers, of which organization he admitted he was a delegate at the meeting of the "Soviet."

One whole year after the arrest of the two men from South Bethlehem deported on the *Buford*, we find the chief of police still at his work in a case throwing further light on the methods used in that city in dealing with immigrants.

One Sam Fidenco, a White Russian from Grodno, who had been in the United States since 1913, was arrested at his rooms in South Bethlehem, on February 26, 1920, for "sedition and slander against the United States government," under orders of the chief of police. Fidenco claimed, and it was admitted by the chief, that he was arrested without warrant and locked up in the police station. The chief asserted that this was done by the order of the division superintendent of the Department of Justice at Philadelphia, and that the telegraphic warrant of arrest from the Department of Labor came within forty-eight hours of the arrest by the police. The date on the warrant, itself, however, was March 8th, while the arrest was made February 26th, and as to the orders of the division superintendent, that officer stated that he had known nothing about the case and had given no orders. He said, however, that it was "only a little violation of the law," but that "the man's rights were infringed without question."

The chief testified that he thought he was under obligation to take orders from the Department of

Justice to hold a man for an indefinite period if he was charged with a crime against the government.

Back of the chief we find a private detective, a Pinkerton man, with whom, according to the chief's testimony, he "had conferred regarding the activities of this man and we had made arrangements with Mr. Daniel [the local officer of the Department of Justice at Philadelphia who denied any such 'arrangements'] to have a man up here and we would proceed to arrest that man." He said he conferred with the Pinkerton man because "he and I have been working together in connection with these Bolshevik activities in this section."

After the man was arrested, a representative of the Department of Justice did appear on the scene, to search the premises occupied by Fidenco and act as interpreter in the hearing.

The testimony against Fidenco as given in the record is flimsy. His landlady had filed an affidavit charging that the man was a "Bolshevist" and had held Bolshevist meetings in his room. But the affidavit gave every evidence of being dictated by some one else and was written on the letterhead of the Police Department. When the landlady was called personally to the stand she testified that she could not say whether the meetings were Bolshevist meetings or not. "But in this affidavit you say that upstairs they had Bolshevist meetings," she was reminded. To which she replied: "How could I say what I don't know? I don't understand English." According to her account, the affidavit was secured by threatening her at the police station.

She said that she could not read the affidavit herself, because she could not read English, but it was read to her word by word in English, and she signed it because "they asked me and made me swear if I saw Sam Fidenco there, and I swore I saw him." When they confronted her with the man at the hearing and asked her if she had seen him coming from a Bolshevist meeting she said she did not know. "But you have sworn that you heard Sam Fidenco here say things and address the crowd," the examiner said. To which she answers: "What do I know? They had a meeting somewhere; a man from New York talked to them. They wanted to open the blockade." On further questioning it appeared that she did not know what a Bolshevik was.

The chief of police testified that he had arrested Fidenco because he was a member of the Union of Russian Workers, and he thought he was that because he had seen him at their headquarters, or a place he believed to be their headquarters, where, according to statements of persons attending meetings, speakers called for the overthrow of government. He said he had no written records of the statements, and he did not present the men who had made them, but he "remembered" that such statements had been made. Another piece of evidence satisfactory to him was that Fidenco had received letters from a man held for deportation for whom he had deposited bail, and had associated with a Russian who had been deported and who had literature in his house of an anarchistic nature. He also saw Fidenco carrying foreign papers which he thought proved that he was an anarchist, but he did not arrest the man for it. He could not think of the names of these papers, but decided that they were prohibited.

The local agent of the Department of Justice, who had come to South Bethlehem to gather evidence on which to ask for a warrant, searched Fidenco's room, finding books and papers, and a key which he claimed was a key to the headquarters of the Union of Russian Workers. He could not remember whether Fidenco did or did not admit membership in the union—"he [Fidenco] did not want to admit anything"—but he believed he was a member, from the books and papers found in his room. Other evidence he secured from the chief of police and the Pinkerton man. As a result of all this Fidenco was recommended for deportation by the inspector in charge of the district.

At a rehearing held in May, some additional facts came to light. Fidenco claimed that he was not the man wanted, after all, and six witnesses were brought to show that he really was one Semion Kwedenco, who had nothing to do with the Union of Russian Workers and had been arrested by mistake for one Sergei Fidenco who was a member. It seems that "Sam" is used as a nickname for both Sergei and Semion, and in a community of the type where the foreign born are identified by numbers, for the most part, and where their names are looked upon as a peculiar manifestation of foreign humor and of no real consequence to anybody, it is hardly any wonder that it was a matter of indifference whether Sergei or Semion was nabbed—they were both Russians, and presumably both Bolsheviks.

The key, upon which so much stress was laid turned out to be a key to some social club that Semion belonged to, and on July 14th, nearly five months after the man's arrest, his case was dismissed by the Department of Labor on account of insufficient evidence.

But in this last hearing some further interesting testimony was given about the methods of the chief of police. "Fidenco" had charged at the first hearing that the local agent of the Department of Justice, who had acted as interpreter, was interpreting erroneously, so that the record may not contain what he really said on that occasion, but in the last hearing, held in Philadelphia, another interpreter was on hand and Fidenco then had a chance to tell some things he had on his mind.

One thing was that he was maltreated at the time of his arrest. Another was about the grafting engaged in by the chief of police. It seems that at the time Fidenco was arrested two other men, Daneluk and Ulchik, were taken. This is the story in which they as well as Fidenco were concerned, as told by Fidenco.

When I was taken to Easton I personally paid the fare. When S—— [the chief] took me back again I paid the fare, but it seems S—— had made a charge for that. Then, when I was arrested S—— came to me several times and he said to me, "buy a fur coat from me, because it will be cold for you to stay here," I asked him, "Why am I not sent to another prison?" and he replied, "Give me fifty dollars and I will help you and you will get out entirely, just as Jack Daneluk. He paid me and got out, and he is not any Bolshevik."

Also Ulchik was arrested together with me. He promised to pay $15 and was immediately released. The chief and the superintendent of police went to his home three times to collect the promised money, but he ran away to another place.

He also said that the police were taking abusive advantage of the house where he was arrested, which they had raided repeatedly as Bolshevist headquarters, collecting to his knowledge as much as $82 to let victims go after a raid.

Perhaps these charges of Fidenco are baseless. But it is not hard to believe that a chief of police with the record and the reputation of this one, who finds a profitable source of income in laying and withdrawing charges of vicious conduct, might naturally turn the same methods to account in red hunting, to the further instruction of the foreign born in the justice of our government. And as these general methods are not confined to one town, but may be seen in operation in various parts of the country, who knows how many ignorant immigrant workers whose cases have never come to public notice, have been victimized as "radicals" like Fidenĉo, Daneluk, and Ulchik of South Bethlehem?

CASES FROM THE STEEL AND COAL REGIONS

The cases of persons listed on the *Buford* from the steel and coal regions of Pennsylvania and Ohio, in addition to those already described from Bethlehem, open up other aspects of the methods used by the Departments of Justice and of Labor, and their relations to local authorities and to industrial companies.

It has been noted that the proceedings against steel strikers for activities in the strike yielded few or no candidates for deportation. The companies, however, busied themselves in the general hunt for radicals, whether they were to be found openly engaged in strike activities or not, and in the Pittsburgh district the companies rendered substantial financial aid to the Department of Justice by reinforcing the salaries of the local agents and by providing clerical service for the prosecution of cases. And under-cover men, recruited in part from the police force, by the companies, passed back and forth from the company to the Federal service.

A Federal officer of long official experience stated at a hearing in Pittsburgh before the Commission of Inquiry of the Interchurch World Movement:

Ninety per cent of all the radicals arrested and taken into custody were reported by one of the large corporations, either of the steel or coal industry. I mean by that that these corporations are loaded up with what they call "under-cover men" who must earn their salaries, and they go around and get into these organizations and report the cases to the detectives of the large companies. The detectives in turn report to the chief of police of the city. Generally the chiefs of police in these small cities around Pittsburgh were placed there by the corporations.

The corporation orders an organization raided by the police department, the members are taken into custody, thrown into the police station, and the Department of Justice is notified. They send a man to examine them to see if there are any extreme radicals or anarchists among them. They usually let all but a few go.[1]

One such raid was made at McKees Rocks in May, 1919, upon a meeting at which seventy-five men were arrested, and thrown into four cells in the police station, where they were so thickly crowded that they could not lie down. Many of these men were citizens, and against most of the aliens nothing could be found. The Department of Justice turned over eight or ten of these to the Department of Labor, which decided to hold only two. Of these one was released for lack of evidence, leaving one solitary name on the *Buford's* passenger list to show for the discomfort and disgrace of seventy-five arrests.[2]

It is to the credit of the immigration officer in this district that he refused to be stampeded by the corporations and the Department of Justice and insisted upon substantial evidence of breach of the law before he would recommend deportation. Had he been a more pliable officer, undoubtedly the deportations from his district would have been more numerous. Eighteen names on the *Buford* list, credited to Fairmont, West

[1] *Interchurch World Movement Report on the Steel Strike of 1919,* p. 225.
[2] Im. No. 54616/221, David Eelak.

Virginia, are the result of arrests made in connection with the coal strike in that region. An immigration officer sent to take charge of deportation cases in the late fall of 1919 found 80 men lying in jail, held by the sheriff, without even a commitment by a justice. All of these men had been reported by the superintendent of the mines. The immigration officer ordered the release of all against whom there was not positive evidence of membership in the Union of Russian Workers. This set free about 40 of them immediately. Of the remainder, some 4 or 5 were married, and the immigration officer refused on that account to recommend deportation. Of the rest, reasonable doubt as to membership subsequently shown occasioned the release of some more. One man had been in jail twenty-eight days, and was "lost," in the sense that no one knew anything about him. The immigration officer found him by accident and ordered his immediate release.

The fourteen cases on the *Buford* reported from Greensburg involve an interesting tale of spying. The men worked and were arrested at Monessen, Pennsylvania. This is the town in which investigators for the Interchurch World Movement turned up such striking evidence of the use of industrial espionage by the steel companies of the place.[1]

The records in the cases show the following facts. In June, 1919, there came to Monessen a member of the state constabulary on secret-service duty, whom we will designate as "Y." He had entered the service of the state constabulary on the previous January. On examination during a hearing of deportation cases

[1] "Public Opinion and the Steel Strike of 1919," *Supplementary Reports of the Commission of Inquiry, Interchurch World Movement*, pp. 2, 7, 9–11.

he testified that he "worked for the state of Pennsylvania, and also for the Pittsburgh Steel Products Company," whether simultaneously or successively does not make much difference, as either would tend to give him the point of view of the industry rather than of the worker.

The specific duty he undertook was to watch over the doings of the Union of Russian Workers, which organization he joined, as a member, in July. He attended meetings there for a while, then went away to another steel town. While in Monessen it had been his habit to frequent a pool room which was a favorite gathering place for Russians, and to make friends with the men who considered him a fellow member of their organization.

When the November raids of the Department of Justice were made, Y. had resumed his uniform, as the secret-service activities of the state police had been discontinued, and was ready to come out in the open and testify against his late companions. A raid, accordingly, was staged against the pool room and the pool-room crowd, wherever they might be found, depending on Y.'s identification and testimony for evidence.

Y. was sent for, went to the pool room, where the men were all "glad to see him" and asked where he had been for so long. He then slipped away and telephoned that about twenty members of the U. R. W. among them the secretary of the organization, were in the pool room and could be arrested. The sergeant of state police sent seven men, surrounded the place, entered, and arrested the men pointed out by Y. "much to the surprise of the foreigners," in the words of the report. These were then placed under arrest and their houses searched. Apparently only four of

them were found to have anything in the nature of
due books or membership books. Among these was
the owner of the pool room, a certain E——, but we
do not find his name on the list of those deported on
the *Buford,* nor does he seem to have been held for a
hearing before the Department of Immigration. The
testimony of Y. further states that "Mrs. E—— [his
wife] also had a blue book, but, as she had a six-months-
old baby, I did not deem it advisable to arrest her. I
also wish to state that she is an American girl and was
born in Monessen." We wonder at the hazy state of
mind of the agent, putting first the baby, and second,
as a slight makeweight to the first excuse, the fact of
native birth.

Others supposed to belong to the Union were picked
up at their houses. All told, 20 men were arrested in
the November raid in Monessen, and 14 were finally
deported. At the hearings in the cases of the 14, Y.
was the principal witness against them.

His general testimony as to the character of the
U. R. W. itself is of interest, as he had attended meetings and would naturally desire to make their record
as black as possible . In testifying as to the character
of the organization he made the general statement that
the purpose of the "organization was to establish communism in the United States," and that every member
of the organization understood himself to be an anarchist—he was told so when he joined." But he produced no proof of these statements, which are moreover
somewhat contradictory, as an anarchist is not a communist. And when he proceeded to details, these seemed
rather remote from the general statements he had made.
He denied that he was told when he joined that the
policy of the organization was to assist men to go to
Russia, but said their "principal interest was trying to

help the workers," which sounds harmless enough. He admitted that they were not told that the organization was opposed to the United States government, and testified that he had never heard anything in the meeting against the United States government, but at most, the proposition that the workers should take over the factories. In answer to a question whether it was the general belief of the majority of the members that they should take over the industries, he says members were "told" by "some of the speakers" that by organizing they would be able to do so. When asked to give some example of inciting to violence he said he had heard expressions like "we must fight our way through, and the only way we can do this is to follow the red flag of Bolshevism"—which might be interpreted in any number of ways. In the case of one of the deportees he testified that he "heard him speak, advocating anarchy." The man, however, "did not say directly that they must overthrow this government, yet he did say that only by following the example of Bolshevism would the country be fit to live in." In this case he testified that the speaker said that "to accomplish our end we may have to suffer a lot and rot in jails," which sounds rather like looking for violence at the hands of the other party than inciting to it. This, in fact, seemed to be the trend of many of the talks at the Russian meetings—as in another case, when Y. was asked whether a man who, as he testified, had spoken of seizing the mills and factories by following the red flag of Bolshevism, had spoken of violence, he answered, "Well, he spoke about going to jail!"

Of the 14 men deported, 5 admitted membership in the union, 3 said they had been members but were so no longer, and 6 denied membership. As to the evidence on which the men were held for deportation, it appears that the "blue books" to which reference is made as the membership books, contained no statement of principles, like the older "red book" found in the possession of some members arrested earlier.

Some illustrative cases indicate the nature of the evidence on which they were deported and what sort of men they were.

Frank Nikolaeff,[1] a white Russian, could not read or write. He denied that he was a member of the U.R.W. He had attended two meetings, but did not understand what was said. He denied holding any radical beliefs, and said what they talked about at the meetings was "mutual help." Asked why he attended the meetings, he said: "I was lonesome and had no place to go. I just went to spend the time where I could hear the Russian language." Asked whether he had been on strike, he said he had not. He had not been working for four weeks, because he had been sick.

Of course the men under charges who claimed that they were not working for some other reason than the strike might have been afraid to admit the strike as a reason, fearing that it would affect their cases unfavorably. Y. testified that he had known the man two months, had roomed with him, and had seen him at meetings eight or nine times. But he said that the man took no active part in the meetings; the only thing he heard him say was to object to the increase of dues from fifteen cents to one dollar. The object of this increase was to cover the cost of the literature, but the man said he could not read and did not propose to pay for the literature. The secret agent had never heard him speak against the government.

[1] Im. No. 54709/520.

Mike Yanish,[1] working in the wire mill, had been on strike. He also denied membership, but had been at three meetings. He testified that they had talked about money for a ship at the meeting. He denied all radical beliefs and said this was the first time he had been arrested. He did not know anything about any societies; he went to the meeting because he was on the street and saw others going. The secret agent testified that he had seen Mike Yanish at fifteen or twenty meetings, and thinks he was a member, because only members were admitted. But he had never seen him pay any dues or heard him make speeches.

Thomas Zayats[2] denied membership also. He was employed in the Pittsburgh Steel Products Company. He was not on strike, but was not working, because he had sore arms. He had attended one open meeting, but did not understand anything, because he was a Slovak. The secret agent said he knew him as a member, but all that he had heard him say was to object to the raising of the dues. The examining inspector reports on him that he is "too ignorant to become a real menace to the country." But out he went, on the ground of membership in a forbidden organization.

Leon Chrikolnik[3] was a laborer in a tool mill, had worked steadily until the strike, when he struck with the others. He denied membership and radical beliefs. His testimony indicated that the secret agent, Y., had acted as provocateur, because when the man was asked, "Who else asked you to join the U. R. W. besides Mr. Y.," he said, "Nobody." Y. denied this, but said he met Chrikolnik at the pool room, as he

[1] Im. No. 54709/521.
[2] Im. No. 54709/518.
[3] Im. No. 54709/516.

did the others, and was present when he joined the society.

Andrew Geray,[1] out on strike, denied membership in the U. R. W. but admitted that he belonged to a workman's organization, "the same as the rest of the boys in jail." The examining inspector did not consider him of a type that could possibly injure the United States, but he also was deported on the ground of membership.

Andy Prauka,[2] on strike when arrested, also admitted membership, but said he had attended only one meeting. He was a miner at Donora. He did not believe in the principles of the union and his only reason for joining was to "collect money and divide it so all could go to Russia," and also, "I had no other place to spend my time and had to go to a place where they spoke Russian, because I did not understand English." He would like to remain in this country and bring his wife over. He had shown his interest in the country by buying Liberty Bonds. The secret agent would not consider him an active member, and the examining inspector did not consider him dangerous to the country, but he too was deported, on the ground of membership.

Antony Lovonetsky[3] admitted membership in the organization and he was deported, not only for membership, but for anarchistic beliefs. He was a Russian Pole from Mohilev, had been in the country six years, was employed in the wire works and had gone on strike. He had already been arrested once before, in May, as a member of the Union of Russian Workers. He stated that his purpose in becoming a member was to get a ship to go home. This is the man whom Y., the

[1] Im. No. 54709/477.
[2] Im. No. 54709/475.
[3] Im. No. 54709/474.

secret agent, had seen in the chair at the meeting and heard advocating anarchy, and saying that the members would have to "suffer a lot." There seemed to be no evidence in the record of anarchistic belief on his part further than Y.'s report of hearing him "advocate anarchy" in this general way.

George Goroshkov,[1] from Mohilev, a stone mason, had been a member, but was not any more. He said he joined because he was told they were going to get ready to go to the old country. He denied that he had been secretary as the secret agent said he was. He was another about whom Y. told the story that his speaking about violence consisted in speaking about going to jail.

Jacob Zboromirsky,[2] a laborer in a bake shop, said he had been a member of the U. R. W., but was not now —he "got out the last time he was arrested." If the government means to discourage membership in an organization, it seems unwise to punish people after they have withdrawn from it. Why should one withdraw from membership in a forbidden organization and sever his connection if he is always to be suspected of membership or charged with it? A belief that "once a member, always a member," will certainly hold the membership together, not break it up.

He denied holding the beliefs with which he was charged, and said he joined the organization because he thought its purpose was to help Russians get back to Russia. The examining inspector thought he was a leader, however, and he was deported.

Efrem Potemkin,[3] a discharged soldier, had been lying in jail forgotten for some six weeks when the

[1] Im. No. 54709/214.
[2] Im. No. 54709/223.
[3] Im. No. 54709/579.

examining inspector of the Immigration Bureau came upon him in looking up some other cases, and promptly ordered him released. It appeared that he had been at a dance when the police came and chased them out because they had no license. Asked about his beliefs, he expressed quite correct and orthodox views. He had worked for the Pittsburgh Steel Products Company, but had quit work before the strike. Nothing connected him with the Union of Russian Workers but the statement of the secret agent that he had seen him at a closed meeting. The agent admitted that he had never heard Potemkin talk against the government of the United States nor speak nor talk like an anarchist. Potemkin himself denied that he was a member and said that "once Mr. Y. asked me if I belonged to it, and I said there was lots of time in the future when I might join it."

The examining inspector recommended cancellation of the warrant of arrest in this case, but the Department at Washington, although not sustaining the "membership" charge, deported him for "affiliation" with the organization.

The same Y., it appears, was the interpreter in the preliminary hearing before the agent of the Department of Justice, with the attendant opportunity of prejudicing the cases of the accused. When the cases reached the immigrant inspector, this official took pains to secure from the International Institute of the Y. W. C. A. an interpreter who was known to be intelligent and who could be counted on to give an unbiased report of the testimony. This Y., however, protested against her employment as interpreter, on the ground that she was biased through her sympathies, and the agent of the Department of Justice backed him up, forcing the immigration officer to displace her for a man who had the reputation of being a crook.

THE DEPORTATIONS OF 1919–20

Youngstown, where Y. was employed for the summer when the men at Monessen missed him, apparently made vigorous use of the spy system. The man Kuts, arrested with the other five men from Akron, went to Youngstown, where, in August, 1919, a raid was made on a meeting of the Union of Russian Workers—a convention of members from three states—and 118 men and women were arrested. Of these only two were held for deportation. In November and December other raids were made, which netted 24 passengers for the *Buford*.

RUSSIANS PROTESTING

How the Russians felt about this reign of terror in Youngstown is seen from the following extracts from Russian newspapers:

YOUNGSTOWN, OHIO.

DEAR FRIENDS:—The black hands of this land of liberty have laid an iron grip on our local society of the Union of Russian Workers. On the night of August 19th the police have raided our clubs during the progress of a lecture which was going on at the time. The angels of the police stick broke into the rooms and have destroyed everything in sight. They have also arrested 118 men. They took away our seal, all record books, and about $300 worth of Russian literature. The local jail was soon filled and it was necessary to place two men in a cell. Those that were jailed soon began singing Russian songs of freedom, and were thrown into the dungeons and tortured. The next day all of us were freed. A mass of people were in front of the jail. The police drove into and charged the crowds with sticks and rifles. This is the treatment given to us foreigners in the land of the free and the home of the brave.

Under the guise of "freedom" everything is permitted. It is allowed to torture us; keep us in jails without any charges, etc.

One thing they cannot do—and that is to kill in us our love for freedom.   Yours

A—— C—— *Bread and Freedom.*

413

THE IMMIGRANT'S DAY IN COURT

YOUNGSTOWN, OHIO.

We Russian workingmen of Youngstown and vicinity, temporarily residing in this country, having assembled under the open sky this 22d of September, and about 3,000 strong, have adopted the following resolution:

We protest against the violence, mockery, and rascality which are at present taking place in this city. We demand the lifting of the blockade of Soviet Russia. I wish to explain the motives which guide us in adopting the above resolution. Life for us in this damned city is unbearable. We are being persecuted, hounded, beaten up, fined, thrown into jails, horrible dungeons, etc., and without any visible reasons smashed up on any occasion.

All this is done by the police with help of bayonets and spies. On the 19th of August detectives have raided the Russian School in E. Youngstown. They destroyed everything, confiscated the books in the library, arrested 118 men, of whom only 2 are held for trial, and the rest of them were released after spending five days in the jail without any charges being preferred against them, except being crowned with epithet of "anarchists and Bolsheviki." Then all of us Russians were discharged from all factories.

Why do the employers refuse to give us work? Why do they force us to starve in this land of "freedom"? Is this in accordance with the law and justice to drive us alive into the graves? But we want to live. Why do you destroy us? We honest workmen are against such dastardly treatment. We protest against such abuse and DECLARE THAT AGAINST YOU AND YOUR GOVERNMENT WE HAVE NOTHING. WE DO NOT WANT TO HAVE ANYTHING AGAINST IT AND WE DO NOT CARE ANYTHING ABOUT IT. Those who wish to rule, let them rule; Carnegie, Morgan, Rockefeller; theirs is not our affair, and you may behave as you wish.

If you think that we are of such a great disadvantage to you, then why do you forcibly keep us here? We want home; we have fathers, mothers, wives, and children in our homes in Russia. Lift the blockade, recall your troops, and we will go there where we came from. Withdraw your bayonets, machine guns, tanks, and dirty paws of allies. We are not in need of a bayonet freedom. We will go from here and decide for ourselves who is more democratic, Kolchak, Denikin, Semenoff, or Sukin or the workmen's and peasants' government—the Soviets.

We do not need war—we are not going to fight.

What we need is liberty. We are hungry, cold, and ruined. Do not interfere with us with your lead.

We want bread and freedom.

Lift the blockade and do not torture us any longer.

> F. DMITRENKO, *The Workman and Peasant.*

October 16, 1919.

YOUNGSTOWN, OHIO.

Since our union (Russian Workmen Union) was first raided, 118 Russians were arrested. They were consequently all released. Two were in jail for a month and then released on $1,000 bail each.

Early last winter the raids again began. At first 13 and then 35 were arrested. They were caught everywhere—on the street, at the post office, in homes and barber shops. On one Russian was found a powder which he used to heal up a sore after an operation. This looked very suspicious to the detectives.

The Russians here are frightened on account of the raids and beatings. They cannot meet any longer. They are even afraid to talk to each other when they meet on the street.

March 8, 1920.   *Russky Golos.*

THE MARCH RAIDS IN NEW YORK CITY

Fifty-eight persons on the passenger list of the *Buford* were recorded as from New York, and were arrested in New York City or in the suburban districts. Forty-three of them were charged only with membership in an organization forbidden by law, 15 with personal beliefs and activities. Three men of the 15 charged with personal belief were the fruits of a raid made March 12, 1919, by the city police on their own initiative, without the participation of the Federal Department of Justice, on the People's House of New York, in which was established the headquarters of the Union of Russian Workers.

The police department, it was said, had been preparing for this raid for the previous two months. On the appointed night the police descended upon the building, arrested everybody in it, and carried them all off—164 in number—to the police station for examination. One hundred and thirty were freed at once, 34 were held overnight in the police station for further examination, and of the latter only 4 were finally held under warrant of arrest for deportation.

In this raid apparently little violence was used. The men arrested were treated with some humanity in the process of arrest and in the court next day. They all, however, had to undergo the ordeal of examination and suffer the fear of possible consequences, and, as the New York *World* remarked in editorial comment:

. . . to break up meetings and subject scores of people to inquisition, search and detention upon nothing more than conjecture is an intolerable abuse of police power.[1]

That conjecture was almost the only basis is shown by the fact that so few were held for examination out of the 164 arrests. That only four were finally held for deportation was due in part to the fact that the department at Washington ordered the release of all who did not themselves admit belief in anarchy, which by this time (March, 1919) would have made them deportable, under the law of 1918. Presumably some of the others might have believed in anarchy, but did not admit it.

[1] March 13, 1919.

THE DEPORTATIONS OF 1919–20

And none were held on the ground of membership in an organization.

Newspaper accounts drew a dark picture of the place at which arrests were made and of the crowds found there. The New York *Times* said:

> When Gegan and his men rushed the headquarters, they found that every effort had been made to disguise its real nature. In one room was a disassembled automobile used to give the place the aspect of a trade school, and a number of those present carried musical instruments and pretended to be there for rehearsal.[1]

Naturally this sort of description was calculated to inflame public sentiment against these Russian workers. It is a fact, however, that the activities were genuinely what they pretended to be, and that the New York People's House was one of those social centers described in previous pages as characteristic of the Russian colonies all over the country.

The New York *Times* wanted to know,[2] as an indication of the true character of the men arrested:

> Just what and how much of a relation exists between the peasant class and the foreigners who were arrested. If they are Bolsheviki, they almost certainly were never workers on the land, in Russia or elsewhere, and the leaders are not real proletarians, but intellectuals of the sort that have failed in all intellectual activities and have turned to exploitation of the masses as a last resort—a means of escaping the harsh alternative of going to work.

Had the government adopted this criterion, few of the rank and file would have been deported, for they had been almost without exception, as shown in the records, peasant workers on the land, in their home

[1] March 14, 1921.
[2] Editorial note of March 14, 1919.

country. And many of the leaders had arisen out of that class.

The four people held for deportation after the March raid were one woman and three men—Mollie Steimer, a young Russian girl already under a sentence, under the Espionage Act, of fifteen years' imprisonment, who was at the time out on bail, and was held in this country to serve her sentence, and Bianki, Oradovski, and Ketzes, three of the newer leaders, who were deported on the *Buford*. All three admitted a belief in anarchy, but of a nonviolent type. Bianki expressly repudiated the use of terror, which he considered futile, and said he had nothing against the United States government. And he would not admit that the Union of Russian Workers held any purpose of overthrowing the government of the United States.

Oradovski said: "If the authorities use force, then the people will have to use force. I did believe in the laws, but since the government violated the law on every step, it seems to me that the law lost effect."

THE NOVEMBER RAID IN NEW YORK CITY

The greater number of the men and women from New York and vicinity on the passenger list of the *Buford* were taken in the November raid, conducted by the Department of Justice in co-operation with the New York police. In New York City itself, the People's House was again the center of attack, and this time force and violence were unsparingly used by the police. This was the fourth time that the police had visited this center. A brief account of this raid, with affidavits of the victims of ill treatment, is given in the *Report on the Illegal Practices of the United States Department of Justice*, published by the National Popular Government League, and the general story of violence is

418

abundantly confirmed by reports in the city papers the next morning, even those which were most unfriendly to radicals. This report states:

At the time of the raid the department agents had a few warrants for the arrest of supposed offenders. They went through the building and broke up and destroyed most of the furniture in the place, including desks and typewriting machines. They beat up the persons in the place, amounting to several hundred, with blackjacks and stair rails; broke up all the classes then in session, and herded the students to the stairways, beating them as they went, shoving them from the landing on the stairway so that many fell and rolled down the stairs and were trampled upon by those who were shoved after them.[1]

The raid was made in all parts of the building, whether occupied by the Union of Russian Workers or not. On the top floor a class in algebra was entered, the students and the teacher were lined up against the wall and searched. They were then ordered downstairs, and on the way down had to run the gauntlet of a line of police officers, who beat them as they ran, with clubs improvised from banisters torn from the stairway. The teacher, a man of fifty, who had no connection with the union otherwise than by conducting classes in the building in which the union was a tenant, was not only beaten, but thrown down the stairs, getting his head broken in the process, as well as his left shoulder, left foot, and right side. The Attorney-General claimed that the damage and destruction committed in the building was done by "boys" after the raid, but he advanced no proof of this.

Perhaps 200 persons were taken in this raid, bundled into patrol wagons, and carried off to the New York

[1] *Report on the Illegal Practices of the U. S. Department of Justice*, pp. 17-18.

office of the Department of Justice, where the night was spent in the examination of the prisoners. The examinations, it is charged, were conducted according to the methods of the police "third degree," leaving many of the prisoners wounded and terrified. Of the 200, only 39 were finally held for hearings in deportation proceedings.

Other men credited to New York in the *Buford* list were taken in Newark, New Jersey, and one or two other New Jersey towns, and in Greenpoint and Maspeth, Long Island. The Greenpoint and Maspeth men, taken to the New York office of the Department of Justice, shared the rough treatment of the men taken at the New York People's House. The men taken in Newark seemed not to have been treated so badly in the New Jersey office.

Of the entire number from all these places recommended for deportation at the New York immigration station, some were afterward released on their own recognizance, some were released under bond for deportation at a future time, and the remainder were among the 58 assigned to the New York district on the *Buford* passenger list.

Yet all, whether finally adjudged innocent or guilty, had undergone some punishment—those from the New York People's House who were let off after examination at the Department of Justice had been through the raid, and many of them had undergone a beating at the hands of the arresting agents, and those who were held by the Department of Justice and the Bureau of Immigration, but finally released on their own recognizance, had been obliged either to raise bail in heavy amounts—the amount was increased from $1,000 to $10,000 for these cases—or to spend an indefinite period of confinement at Ellis Island.

THE DEPORTATIONS OF 1919–20

What was the general character of the persons sent from the New York district? In the group of 15 charged with some form of personal belief or personal activity against the government, 10 or 11 were known as leaders in radical propaganda and admitted belief in anarchistic doctrines. Most of them disclaimed any belief in violence, like Bianki, already cited. Ivan Duboff,[1] another of the 15, however, said, yes, he was an anarchist, and believed in the overthrow of government by force and violence, "such as was used in the American Revolution of 1776 when the American people liberated themselves from England." But as for a revolution here and now, he was not interested; he would leave that to the American working people. "How can I sympathize with America," he said "when they oppress me so much and beat me?" When he started for America this country appealed to him as a country of freedom, he said, but after he got here he lost his sympathy when he had to go to the factories and was driven here and there. He changed his opinion, he said, from the first day of his arrival, when he tried to get work and could not find any, and could not find a piece of bread, and was driven from place to place. Then he learned there is no freedom here. He was arrested at the People's House in the November raid while taking an automobile lesson. As he describes the circumstances:

About seven big men came with clubs or some weapons, came in and lined us up and searched every one of us without any resistance on our part. Every one of us got a blow under the chin or in the abdomen. I received one in the abdomen.

[1] Immigration No. 54709/97.

Then when we got downstairs I saw so much beating and so much blood spilled that this compared to the bloodshed in Russia in 1905 which I witnessed. This amounted to nothing compared to the bloodshed I witnessed at our beating. Then again I was hit with a blackjack going downstairs, but I bent myself down and my head wasn't split. I just received a blow. The beating continued when we were driven out until the time when they put us in the patrol wagons. Blood was all around, and the public, seeing these things, shouted, "Stop that beating!" On account of all this I am not willing to stay here and I would like to be sent back as soon as possible.

Those admitting a belief in anarchy were technically under the law and deportable. But in the three following cases of deportation for personal belief, it seems as if some mistake had been made.

Tom Turka,[1] who had been a member of an organization in South Bethlehem called the society of mutual aid, the purpose of which was to help members in case of sickness and to provide books for members to read, came to Newark and joined the Union of Russian Workers there, but had withdrawn three months before his arrest. The reason he gave was that he wanted to study at home evenings, and also to take up a course "in the automobile trade, so that when I went back to Russia I would have a good trade," and he could not get that course at the Newark union. He did not know the principles of the U. R. W. No principles were read to him, and no man was bound by any principles on entering the school.

As to his own opinions, he said he was not in sympathy with violence. He believed in change of form of government if it was desired by the majority of the people. He understood by "revolution" a revolution

[1] Im. No. 54709/341.

in the minds of people, and he thought that revolution was going on. He thought there would never be any need of armed revolution. He would not believe in overthrowing and destroying all institutions of government and organization to bring about his ideas. He said that "our ideas will some day be realized, but not by force of arms. And at any rate we are not in possession of force or violence, as in the case of our arrest, we were peaceful, the force of violence being used against us." He believed in the doctrine of the class struggle, but disclaimed belief in anarchy. He was not learned enough to understand what that was, but "I did lose confidence in the government of Russia when on one occasion . . . I saw a pogrom against Jews instigated by the government." (This man came from Grodno and is of Russian race, not a Jew himself.) He denied, in reply to the question put in three different ways, that he believed in overthrowing the government of the United States by force. The nearest he came to admitting anything like "anarchy" was when he said, "I believe that when the people will get more education they may not need any government." Or perhaps when he said, when asked whether he was in sympathy with the principles of anarchy as far as he understood them, "I sympathize with whatever is good for the working class." Or perhaps when he said that if the government should be destroyed by the people's minds being educated, he would be in sympathy, and would take part in it, but by force, no. He had read Kropotkin's works but did not fully understand them, and when asked whether, if Kropotkin should advocate the abolition of organized government, he would accept that doctrine, he said, "Kropotkin may be a great man, but I do not take any man's ideas for my own. I would read one great man's writings and then another great

423

man's writings, and would try to find my bearings, and by my own experience would form my conclusions.

Asked whether he was dissatisfied with the government of the United States, he said:

"Yes, I am dissatisfied with the treatment I received. I was beaten. All my money, which amounted to $49 and a book, were taken away from me. I asked for it several times. I ask you now if I cannot get back my property. I have no money to buy anything, and I consider that I have been mistreated."

He said that the money was taken at police headquarters in Newark, also an arithmetic book, also a flashlight. The money was in the book. The money was taken from his pocket at the time of his arrest and placed in the book and shown him. This is the last time he saw it. Asked whether at the time of his arrest the money and the book were all that were found on him he replied, "Yes, and the flashlight."

He was deported under the charge "that he is an alien anarchist, that he disbelieves in all organized government, and that he is an opponent of all organized government." A number of those deported for membership alone expressed views as radical.

Another man, Alfons Hajduk,[1] deported for membership in the U. R. W. and also for belief in the overthrow by force or violence of the government of the United States, had been in the country for six years, and "has nothing against this government." He was a window cleaner and was arrested while walking along the street. He had just left a restaurant and had no special place to go. There had just been a raid on that street, he understood. He admitted membership in the Union of Russian Workers, and was deportable on that

[1] Im. No. 54709/357.

424

ground, according to the letter of the law (if this organization actually is of the kind coming under the ban). But one cannot discover in the hearing anything relating to the overthrow of this government to substantiate the personal charge, except one statement that he "would be with the majority if the majority armed itself to change the government." He believed the majority should change the government the way they want it in any country. He said he had nothing against organized government, did not know what anarchy means. The government of the United States "is good for me. I am working and getting my money. The only trouble is that I cannot bring my wife here on account of the war." He had not read the principles of the U. R. W. because he could not read Russian well—he is of Polish race—and he joined the union to attend the school; they promised that there would be a school in automobiling and also reading.

When the principles were read to him he did not understand them. "I am almost an illiterate man," he said. When he came to this country he could not sign his name, but he can now. He had gone to public night school for about six weeks in Newark.

Fedor Antonchick,[1] deported on the charge "that he advocated the overthrow by force or violence of the government of the United States," did not belong to the Union of Russian Workers. He was a member of the Longshoreman's Union, A. F. of L., and was arrested during a strike for distributing handbills, which he could not read, as he did not understand English. A policeman's affidavit was produced, with a copy of a circular to longshoremen—a proclamation

[1] Im. No. 54709/94.

issued by the Communist party of America, which the examining inspector said advocated violence. The alien could not identify the circular, because it was in English, which he did not understand, and said he would not have distributed it if he had known it advocated violence. He thought it was a call to strikers to attend a meeting. He is not interested in the government of the United States, only in his own government. He has read some of the writings of Marx, but "can't understand a thing he says."

The only evidence against this man was the distribution of the circulars. Nothing was found on him at the time of his arrest but the circulars and a copy of the Russian *Voice*, a Socialist paper.

NEW YORK DEPORTEES UNDER CHARGE OF MEMBERSHIP

Only about one-fourth of the forty-three persons deported from New York for membership in the Union of Russian Workers admitted that they were members at the present time. The rest said either that they had formerly been members, but were not now, or that they were merely attendants at the school in the building occupied by the Russian Workers. The evidence used to show that they were members was in many cases a card, which was claimed by its possessor to be a school card only. As described in the record, it appears to have been such.

Possibly these men who denied membership really were members. But how could this be proved? An organization finding itself under the ban of the law might easily cease to issue membership cards, or to keep lists showing membership, and if members deny that they are such, what is there to show the contrary? But it would obviously be an injustice, because of this difficulty in determining membership, to take for granted that everyone found around the union headquarters was a member, and deport him accordingly, without positive evidence of membership. As a matter of fact, some who denied membership were released, and some were held for deportation. It is hard to see, from the evidence given in the records of the hearings, why differences were made in these cases.

One particularly baseless case was that of Harry Wadner,[1] a Jewish boy of twenty-five who had been in the automobile class in the New York People's House, learning to be a chauffeur, when he was arrested. The card found on him was for his school course. He did not speak Russian. He disavowed the principles of the U. R. W. when read to him, and said he was a Socialist—he believed in evolution, not revolution. He was satisfied in the United States and would like to stay here. He had registered for the draft. There is nothing in the record to show any connection with the U. R. W. or any anarchistic belief. Yet this young man was deported.

In the records of the hearings of the men deported for membership as well as in cases of the men deported for personal belief as just cited we find many of the men claiming that violence was used toward them, describing it circumstantially, and expressing an opinion unfavorable to this country as a result of the treatment received, as, for example:

Nikita Safronoff,[2] from Maspeth, who, when asked about his attitude to the American government, said he did not believe in any government that used violence. "I cannot think anything else about the government by whose orders we were taken from our bed, beaten up,

[1] Im. No. 54709/461.
[2] Im. No. 54709/284.

427

blackjacked, and imprisoned." He was "not questioned at all, only beaten." He was not against the American government before his arrest and the violence used against him. He had lived in Russia under the Tsar, but he said:

. . . I never saw the brutality that was committed on the Russian people here in this case. When I was arrested, four men came to my room in the evening when I was partly dressed and was doing exercises in arithmetic, and asked me my name and told me to go along with them. They showed me a badge, but would not tell me the reason for my arrest. When I left the house and at the time I was traveling in the automobile, they were beating me in the sides with their handcuffs, and this continued all the way until they brought me to the Park Row Building [Office of Department of Justice]. In a room where they took me and asked my name they were beating me again without any explanations.

As a result of his beatings he is not in sympathy with the United States, and would be glad to leave the country.

NEW YORK MEN PAROLED

The group of men released on their own recognizance and not shipped on the *Buford* had all paid some share of the penalty exacted for violation of the anarchy clause of the immigration law, in their arrest and detention—some for long periods—with such incidental hardships, not provided for in the law, as threats and violence, during the proceedings, and difficulty in getting work if out on bail. Yet the evidence against them, judging from the records was too slight in a large number of the cases to warrant a recommendation of deportation by the examining inspector in the first place.

One of these men, Demian Kravchuk, was on his way home from a bath, and had stopped in the neighborhood of the People's House at the time of the raid to ask what the excitement was. An officer asked him whether he was a Russian, and when he said yes, he was arrested. This man had served in the army and had his discharge papers on him at the time. No evidence was produced against him, but he was held, and, as he could not furnish the $10,000 bail, he was kept in confinement.

Mike Bratko[1] was a bus boy at a restaurant on Fourteenth Street, and had dropped into the People's House to ask about a Russian entertainment when he was arrested. He used to drop in there occasionally, he said, but anyone could go the People's Houses; they did not have to be members. He went to meetings occasionally, but did not understand their teachings— he was not literate enough. Asked about his beliefs, he said:

I am a laborer and do not know anything about governments; I do not know anything about the tsarists or governments in Russia. How the Tsar was chosen and for how long I never knew.

He denied that he was an anarchist, and did not believe in violence. He was also asked whether he believed in God, which was certainly beside the point. He would like to go back to Russia because:

Since my arrival in this country I found an unfriendly attitude toward me by the people of this country. They call me Polack, they say I cannot have everything they have, and I am treated in a manner that I feel I would do better in returning to my native country, where my relatives are. I cannot make a living here. Whatever factory you go to and they hear that I am a Russian, I am discriminated against. I am opposed to violence, but they use violence against me in beating me up, so I do not care to remain in this country.

[1] Warrant No. 98759/309.

THE IMMIGRANT'S DAY IN COURT

There seemed to be nothing against this man except the claim that anarchist literature was found in his room, but it took three hearings at three different dates to secure his release, under surveillance.

Gregory Melnikoff[1] was arrested at the school in the People's House in New York, where he was studying. He had been attending for about six weeks, studying the Russian language and arithmetic. Asked why he preferred that to a public school, he said that he could not study the Russian language at a public evening school.

No evidence was produced against him except that the agent of the Department of Justice had on a "finance list" a name that looked like his. The man had a card, but it was a school card only. He also had three hearings before he was released on parole.

Adam Chalof,[2] a Pole, went to the People's House in New York to get a glass of tea, and ten minutes later he could not get out because the police had come and blocked all the doors, and they took him for one of the Russian workers, which he says he was not.

He was a photographer and belonged to the Photo-engravers' Union. He belonged to no other organization, he said, and was opposed to Bolshevism and to the Union of Russian Workers. He knew that the Union of Russian Workers were radicals. He did not believe in anarchy, which he had heard was something frightful and destructive, but to what extent he did not know. He went to their place because he wanted tea in the Russian style, and the place was convenient to his lodgings. He had never been arrested, except once last summer for lying on newspapers in the Park. Up to the time of his arrest he was quite satisfied with con-

[1] Warrant No. 98759/312.
[2] Warrant No. 98759/302.

ditions in the United States, he said. He also had three hearings before he was given his liberty.

Ilia Shinkevich[1] claimed not to be a member of the U. R. W. or the I.W.W. and denied belief in anarchy. He had been a member of the Socialist party, but had left it because he had work to do and no time to belong to parties. He was arrested at the People's House in New York, where he had gone to meet a friend and get books about tractors, a subject he was studying at the Y. M. C. A. He was not attending the school there because he did not care for it. He was attending the Y. M. C. A. school, because it was a regular school and had regular studies, which the Russian school had not.

At the third hearing the agent of the Department of Justice could not identify the man, and all he could say in the matter was that "I believe he was thought to be a member of the Union of Russian Workers." There was nothing to prefer against him except the fact that he was taken into custody, so at last he was released "on probation."

Max Stocky[2] was arrested on Fifth Street, New York, on November 17th, why, it is impossible to determine from the record. He lived in Hartford and said he had attended some of the lectures of the U. R. W. there, but was not a member of the organization. He had attended a couple of large meetings in a theater in Hartford, where a Y. M. C. A. man recently from Russia had told about conditions in that country. He denied membership in various radical organizations, and had to repeat his denials so often that he became impatient. The only union he belonged to was the Union of Farm Instructors, and through it he went to Ithaca and took

[1] Warrant No. 98759/308.
[2] Warrant No. 98759/432.

a course in soil culture. By December 9th the agent of the Department of Justice was unable to identify this man, so he also was released on probation.

Fedosy Kutovich,[1] one of the men arrested in Newark, had an unfortunate experience. He was arrested at his lodging place, apparently because he was rooming with a man suspected of being a member of the U. R. W. He denied all the beliefs and affiliations he was asked about, and said he was satisfied with this government. He explained that he was with the other man who was arrested because his own things were stolen and he went home with this man because he was a Russian. In his possession was found a bag full of counterfeit money, which looked pretty bad for him, aside from the supposed radicalism, but he told a tale of how it happened, which was the familiar story of the confidence man who gives his victim a bag or a parcel to guarantee the safety of some money or other valuables that the victim is induced to hand over for some ostensibly good purpose. In the present instance the pledge was a bag containing counterfeit money and material for making it. The victim in this case did not go to the police, because he thought he would try to find the man himself, but he himself was found by the police and picked up as an anarchist. But after three hearings it was determined that he was neither an anarchist nor a counterfeiter, and he was allowed to go, although the agent of the Department of Justice was "sure" he was a member of the Union of Russian Workers, though, as far as he knew (he admitted), the man might have been in Newark only a day or two; he did not have him under surveillance.

Nick Melnick[2] also arrested in Newark, was taking

[1] Warrant No. 98759/322.
[2] Warrant No. 98759/337.

a walk one evening on the street in which the head-quarters of the U. R. W. were situated, because his health was not good and he had been told to take out-door exercise. Four men stopped him and asked him whether he was a Russian. When he said, "Yes," the men said, "Good boy. Come along!" He says he had nothing to do with the U. R. W. He came to this country to work a couple of years and then go back. He wanted to go home a good while ago, because "wherever I go to look for work they ask me if I am a Russian. When I say yes, they have no job for me and call me Bolshevik. I don't want to stay here any longer." Asked if it was because of anything he said that they called him a Bolshevik, he said, "No, they call every Russian a Bolshevik." But this man did not get his wish to return to Russia, for, after three hearings, he was discharged, to look for work again, and again be turned away as a Bolshevik.

Steven Uschenna[1] had read an advertisement in a Russian paper that the U. R. W. had a class for trans-lating Russian into English, so he went there to visit the class the evening of his arrest, but had not registered or enrolled in the school. It was the first time he had been there. He does not believe in the principles of the union as they were read to him at the hearing, and did not attend meetings. He spent his spare time going to movies and theaters.

He was finally released, but not until he had had three hearings and had been held on Ellis Island for some time.

Ignatz Bogdanoff,[2] arrested in Newark, had gone to the premises of the U. R. W. to take a bath, as there was a bathhouse at the rear of the building, and had

[1] Warrant No. 54709/346.
[2] No. 18759/342.

afterward gone to the front building to talk to some Russians there. This was his first visit to the place, he said. There were no lectures going on that night. Only four people were in the room, all drinking tea. He does not know why he was arrested except that all the people in the place and the people around in the street were arrested at the same time.

He said he was not an I. W. W., a communist, a Socialist, or an anarchist. He tried to become a citizen five years ago, but was told he must be able to read and write English. Now he would like to go back to Russia, not because he does not like the government of the United States, but "because I am branded as a criminal and I cannot get work." Although an illiterate man, he was charged by the agent at the office of the Department of Justice with being a teacher at the school. The agent had to admit, finally, that all he knew about it was that he recalled that at the time of the arrest one of his men said "here is the teacher," and asked him what he taught, and he said arithmetic and spelling.

Nikolai Besaroff[1] also lived in Newark and had gone to the U. R. W. headquarters for tea, when he was arrested. He had gone to the U. R. W. school thinking he would take a course in Russian and arithmetic. He could not read and write; he could only sign his name. He denied belief in any of the doctrines. He was taken to Ellis Island, where he participated in the hunger strike because he was not able to talk to his landlady, his only friend in this country, through the wire netting which had been put up in the detention room at the island to shut off close access to the deportees. And he, too, after all the unpleasant experiences, was found not guilty of the charges.

[1] No. 54079/355.

Misha Antonoff[1] was not a member of the U. R. W. and had not attended school at the headquarters in Newark, but was arrested apparently because his address was the former address of two people who were wanted. The agents looked over the house and did not find anything incriminating, then asked him if he was a Russian and took him along. This was at two o'clock in the morning. He was in jail a day and then taken to Ellis Island. He denied belief in any of the radical doctrines he was asked about, and said his object in coming to the United States was, "I heard of this country being free, and I came over here." Nothing was proved against him, for he also was released.

An unfortunate mistake was made in the case of another Russian, in New York City this time. He was arrested at the People's House, where he was attending school, taking a lesson in Russian grammar. As he described the scene "some men came in the class room and ordered us to rise, and then put us up against the wall, and, after searching us, told us to walk downstairs. While walking down the stairs they beat me and others with clubs and I still bear the marks of it." When he was taken to the Department of Justice offices he was cleared of blame and released, he said, at which the question was naturally asked, at the hearing before the immigrant inspector, how do you happen to be here now? His reply was:

"Waiting for the elevator, I was directed from the group I was in to stand with another group, and while the first group left as released, the second group in which I was ordered to stand were taken to jail."

The attorney for the men held for hearings learned of this man's predicament quite by accident, and he was soon released.

[1] Warrant No. 98759/348.

435

THE IMMIGRANT'S DAY IN COURT

The *Buford* set sail on December 21, 1919, under circumstances causing much suffering to families left behind. It is claimed by officials of the immigration service that due consideration was given to prevent the separation of families, and the possible dependence and destitution of wives and children if the deportee was married, and Secretary of Labor Wilson stated that instructions had been given not to include in the *Buford* sailing aliens having wives or families residing in the United States.[1] But according to his statement the telegram was dated December 19th, and, although the Secretary had given orders that the officers in charge of immigration stations should be called on the telephone and informed of the contents of the message, confirmation to follow by wire, "through some unaccountable oversight the confirmation did not go to New York."

At any rate, no provision was made to postpone the departure of the married members of the Russian workers with wives and families here, who had already been gathered on Ellis Island, nor was any provision made to send wives and children with them or after them. Nor were the wives even notified of the sailing of the *Buford*, so that they might have an opportunity to bid their husbands good-by, or to provide clothing or other necessaries for the voyage. Nor could the husbands arrange for the transfer of funds to their families in some cases. In more than one instance a wife was left behind with no power to draw on a bank account in her husband's name. Nor were the lawyers of the deportees notified of the sailing. The immigration officials claimed that advance notice had been

---

[1] *Survey*, January 17, 1920.

given, but this was apparently of so indefinite a nature that neither the deportees nor their counsel was able to make the necessary preparations for departure.

The deportees were informed, as they were at supper one night after all means of communication out of Ellis Island were cut off, that they were to sail in two or three hours. They gathered their belongings together, and the exodus from the island began about two o'clock in the morning. The *Buford* sailed at six. The relatives of the deportees knew of their departure only on going to the Barge Office to get passes to visit them, or on reading the newspaper accounts of the sailing. Several wives, finding at the pier that the *Buford* had sailed, and that there was no further opportunity to see their husbands, were excited and distracted by the unexpected event. One of them made a disturbance, was arrested by the police, found guilty in a magistrate's court of disorderly conduct and committed to the Tombs. As her story is given in *The Survey* of January 10, 1920:

Mrs. B—— read of her husband's arrest in the newspapers, and went to work to buy him some clothes. On Monday morning she called at the Barge Office at South Ferry, hoping to be allowed to take the clothes to him herself. The official then told her that her husband had sailed on the *Buford* the day before. The official, she said, laughed at her. Angered by her own loss and his unconcern, she broke a window in the Barge Office. This act, committed in the presence of some of the other wives, was distorted by the newspapers into a large-sized raid on the Barge Office. Mrs. B—— was arrested and spent five days in jail. There, she says, the other women prisoners—prostitutes, pickpockets, and so forth—jeered at her, calling her the wife of a "Bolshevik." She cried while she was telling this part of her story. . . . "I can't express my feelings so good in English," said Mrs. B——, "but maybe it ain't necessary. You understand. Anybody would feel terrible to have a friend taken away without saying good-by, but I am his wife."

DETROIT CASES

A large group of Russians were arrested in Detroit as members of the Union of Russian Workers in the raids of November, but none of them sailed on the *Buford*. Thirty-five or six were sent to Ellis Island early in January, too late to be included in the *Buford* list; the others were held in Detroit. Both sets of men were held in confinement, either in the immigration station or in jails in Detroit or vicinity for months. The men sent to Ellis Island were mainly the single men. Men with wives and families were kept in Detroit, or near by.

The conditions of confinement in the Detroit jails, and the prisons to which deportees were transferred, acquired evil notoriety through accounts of the sufferings of the Russian workers, and of the Communists, arrested in later raids.[1]

The Detroit cases are interesting as showing a change of attitude in final decisions on the part of the government and in the courts in practically the same type of cases as those deported on the *Buford*.

The circumstances of arrest were about the same as in other places, and the crowd gathered of about the same character. Eighteen or twenty men were taken at a meeting place known to the police as the headquarters of the local branch of the Union of Russian

---

[1] Charges of terrible conditions will be found, with affidavits, in *the Report upon the Illegal Practices of the United States Department of Justice*, pp. 22–29, a statement in rebuttal by the Attorney General in *Hearings before the Committee on Rules, House of Representatives, Sixty-sixth Congress, Second Session*, part i, p. 60, fol., and a report of an independent investigation in *The Deportation Cases of 1919–20*, Constantine M. Panunzio, pp. 81–82.

Workers. Others were taken at a dance and entertainment, at which everybody present was arrested, and perhaps twenty-five detained.

The records in the cases of the men taken at the meeting show the methods followed at the Detroit station. Here the agents of the Department of Justice were especially rough in their handling of the men, and especially active in directing the work of the inspector in charge of the Immigrant Station. One of the agents of the Department of Justice, a Polish Jew, who interpreted in the preliminary examinations and conducted some of them, had been an under-cover man who had joined the Socialist party and the Communist party as a spy. He carried on the examinations, apparently, with the most rigorous third-degree methods. Let us see what happened to the man who was arrested as the secretary of the branch.

This man was one Makarevich, a White Russian from Grodno, fifty years old, able to read and write Russian. According to the statement of the special agent of the Department of Justice, in his possession were found literature and tickets to a theatrical performance advertised by the Union of Russian Workers. He was advertised in *Bread and Freedom* as secretary, and an I. W. W. publication in Russian announced his acceptance of the office of secretary.

But no membership book was found in his possession, and no manifesto. At the hearing before the agent of the Department of Justice the record states that he at first denied that he was secretary—he was only a member. Asked about the meeting, he said they were preparing to open a school for the Russian workers. A question found in the record is significant "Tell him," said the agent, "if he doesn't tell the truth in the matter it is going mighty hard with him. Tell him we got all the books, his stamps, his cards, and everything and that there is no need of him lying." After this the record gives his answer, "I am the secretary," and then he proceeded to identify one man after another, of those taken in the raid, as members of the union.

At the reopening of his case, some seven months later, during which time he had been confined in various jails, and at Ellis Island, he testified in detail as to the circumstances of that first hearing. He was arrested, he said, at a school session while instructing some Russians in reading and writing Russian, at about ten o'clock in the evening. This was an evening school, "as we were all working in the daytime." The hearings took all night, from ten o'clock to four in the morning. Describing the first hearing in the rehearing of his case he said:

"They were engaged more in beating me up than in questioning. . . . I had two of my front teeth knocked out by a blow with the butt of a revolver, and I was badly beaten in my side, the effect of which beating I still feel now."

The records add that the alien showed one of the teeth which had been knocked out. He further states: "At the time of hearing one of the Department of Justice men, planting his legs between my legs and beating me, ordered me to answer questions that he asked; in fact, at the second hearing before the Department of Justice, after another beating, they brought me a tea tumbler full of whisky and told me to drink it, which I refused to do because I never touched whisky. Under these circumstances I gave the answers as they appear in Exhibit C" (the record of hearing before the agent). At one time, he said, he was unconscious as a result of the beating. He had no attorney. He was charged

440

with anarchy, but does not know what this is. He told them that he was an instructor, but they insisted he must also be a secretary, and after the severe beating he may have said, "I am secretary." He says that Exhibit C is not correct, anyway—he did not say the men were members of the Union of Russian Workers, but of the school only.

As to his own personal record, he said that he had been in the United States and Canada seven years, and during the war had worked three years and seven months at an ammunition factory in Canada, contributing a day's work without pay every month to help the war. He said that he "could never conceive that the United States government, with which I always sympathized, would permit practices of the kind as applied in my case." His only reason for not becoming a citizen was that he wanted to go back to Russia to his family.

He denied all the radical beliefs with which he was charged. Not only he, but the men he identified, were granted a rehearing in June and were discharged.

The examining inspector recommended deportation on about the same sort of evidence as the inspector in New York. One of the men identified by Makarevich, Michael Romanoff, had been in the Canadian army for two years, and no papers were found on him but his discharge papers from the army. He had been fighting for eighteen months, and had no sickness when he came to this country, except that he had been in the army hospital after being gassed. He said he was not a member of the Union of Russian Workers, but had attended some meetings, trying to find a mechanical school. He had been only twice in the place. He did not know what anarchy meant, but had heard that I. W. W. meant, " I don't want to work." He did not

441

think the workingman was able to run the country;
he thought the people were all one class and a capitalist
government was all right. He denied that he ever told
the agent of the Department of Justice that he was
a member of the Union of Russian Workers. He was
a farmer in Russia and had had three years' schooling.
He came over to earn a living, and thought if he joined
the-army he was "as good as a citizen." He intended
to become a citizen if he stayed in the United States.

Although this man had fought and suffered in the
World War, and had $400 when he entered the country,
the additional charge that he was in the country
unlawfully, because liable to become a public charge
when he entered, was brought against him.

Another man identified was Sam Waschuk,[1] a
Ukrainian, who had $125 when he entered the country,
had been working at the Ford plant steadily, eleven
hours a day, but he also was charged with liability to
dependency, in addition to the original charge, also of
entering with a contagious disease, although he insisted
that he had acquired that in this country. He denied
all radical beliefs and membership in the union, and
said he was at the meeting because he wanted schooling.
There was apparently no evidence against him but
the secretary's identification.

Against the men arrested at the dance the evidence
was mainly indirect. No identifications were made
of any of them as members of the union. One man
had sold tickets for the ball. Another, to whom a
membership book was attributed, said it wasn't his.
The book gave only the last name, and as the name was
a fairly common one there was no reason for charging
him with the ownership of it. Against another it was

[1] No. 54709/466.

alleged that radical literature was found in his house, that he had been seen at meetings, that a notice in the paper had instructed the turning in of money to him for some suspicious purpose. Another man admitted membership, but said he only attended meetings. Another man was seen at meetings. Another man was arrested at a table where literature was being distributed.

These men were all recommended for deportation, but as they were too late for the *Buford* there was more time and opportunity for a further review of their cases than in those of the men sent on that ship.

In the case of the man who admitted membership but said he only attended meetings, the warrant was canceled as the result of a rehearing in the department itself. The reasons leading to cancellation in this case would apply to a large number of the others. The man who was found at the table where literature was distributed was released as a result of *habeas corpus* proceedings before Judge Learned Hand in the New York Federal Court. Judge Hand's decision in this case (the Tolsky case) and the departmental decision in the other case (Omelinow) established principles which would have freed perhaps three-fourths of the cargo of the *Buford*, as guiltless of membership in an anarchist organization, or of affiliation with it.

The essence of these decisions is that proof of membership in a proscribed organization must be direct and positive, not inferential, from school attendance for example as in some of the New York and Newark cases, or from attendance at meetings, as in some of the Monessen cases, or from the possession of literature, as in many other cases noted, or even from its distribution and sale.

An important feature of Judge Hand's decision is

his ruling on the term "affiliation" in the law, which was charged in two cases on the *Buford*, where membership could not be proved. "Affiliation," according to Judge Hand, "involves a mutual recognition of permanent co-operation between the organization and the person affiliated, and not a spasmodic or casual assistance. Mere sympathy with the aims of a society, even accompanied by efforts to further its aims, does not fall within that word."[1]

As a result of these decisions about two-thirds of the group of men brought from Detroit to Ellis Island under warrant of deportation were freed.

THE COMMUNISTS

Soon after the sailing of the *Buford* occurred wholesale raids against Communists and members of the Communist Labor party on January 3, 1920. At that time it was assumed by the Department of Justice that both of these parties were organizations of the kind proscribed in the immigration law, although no decision to this effect had at the time been rendered by the Secretary of Labor. This assumption was later sustained by the Secretary for the Communist party in his decision in the Preis case, rendered January 23, 1920. The status of the Communist Labor party was not settled, however, until May 5, 1920, when the Secretary rendered a decision in the Miller case, that the Communist Labor party was not an illegal organization.

The raids were made in thirty-three cities and towns, according to a statement made by the Attorney General. According to the report of the Commissioner of Immigration,[2] five thousand warrants of arrests were issued,

[1] *Opinion* handed down, June 22, 1920.
[2] *Report of the Commissioner General of Immigration for the fiscal year ending June 30, 1920*, p. 32.

of which approximately three thousand were served. But according to Francis Fisher Kane, Assistant Attorney General,[1] "the total number of arrests in the January raids may never be known . . . for persons were taken into custody for whom no warrants were obtained, either before arrest or afterward." And the number of arrested persons released for lack of evidence, after the examination held by the agents of the Department of Justice and after confinement in a police station or elsewhere for hours or even days, may also never be known, but it must have been considerable, judging from chance instances reported in the newspapers and elsewhere.

In Lynn, Massachusetts, 39 persons were arrested at a meeting called to discuss the establishment of a co-operative bakery, and 38 were discharged, after being held in jail all night. It may be worth noticing, in passing, to illustrate the perils the alien incurs when under the jurisdiction of officers who do not understand any language but their own, that these arrests were made because, according to the affidavit of the special agent in charge, the hall in which they were meeting was well known as the meeting place of a Communist local and "in view of the fact that the records of the meeting then in progress were in a foreign tongue with which" he was "unacquainted."[2] It was found later that 14 of those arrested were American citizens.

The assistant division superintendent of the Department of Justice in charge of the raids in the Massachusetts district testified at a court hearing that he had taken into custody about 600 persons, of whom about

[1] *The Survey,* April 24, 1920.
[2] *Hearings before the Committee on Rules, House of Representatives, Sixty-sixth Congress, Second Session, June 1 and 2, 1920,* p. 110.

160 were released, and that 440 were sent to Deer Island, the immigration station, for about 100 of whom there were no warrants.[1]

An agent of the Department of Justice testified that in a raid in which he had taken part 16 Labor Department warrants were in his possession, but none of them were used in the arrest of the 29 persons taken. These were locked up overnight. In the morning, those who were citizens were released, and the other 22 forwarded to Deer Island. At Worcester, 100 persons were arrested at a mass meeting, were imprisoned all night, and next morning 84 were discharged.[2] It is estimated that of all the persons arrested in the Massachusetts raids, from one-third to one-half were released after the preliminary examination.[3]

In New York City it was stated that 650 were arrested, of whom 201 were being held.[4] In Buffalo 130 were arrested and 82 held. In Philadelphia about 200 were arrested at a concert of the Lithuanian Socialist Chorus. Out of that concert audience presumably the larger part were released after arrest. In the Philadelphia district as a whole, including Scranton and Wilkes-Barre, Trenton and Camden, it was reported that of 700 arrested, about 350 proved their American citizenship and were released. The agent of the Department of Justice in this district estimated that about 150 were subject to deportation.[5] In Detroit, of about 800 arrested, perhaps one-half, after periods of detention ranging from a day or two

[1] *Report upon the Illegal Practices of the United States Department of Justice*, p. 49.

[2] *Survey*, July 14, 1920.

[3] *Ibid.*

[4] New York *Evening Post*, January 3, 1920.

[5] *Ibid.*

to a week, were discharged.[1]   Among those arrested were many American citizens.   In Cleveland, 41 out of 90 arrested were held.[2]

The people taken in these raids were largely Slavic, Russians, and Poles, with some Lithuanians, some Jews, and a scattering of other nationalities.   Of the 41 taken in Cleveland, as an instance of the racial varieties, 15 were Russians, 14 "Austrians," 7 Hungarians, 3 Germans, 1 Rumanian, 1 Greek.

It is difficult to tell how much violence was used in the process of arrest and examination in the different places.   Confidential instructions from the Assistant Director of the Bureau of Investigations, relating to these raids, expressly ordered that "violence toward any aliens should be scrupulously avoided."   It is noticeable also that the affidavits gathered by outside investigators from persons arrested, showing violence in the way of actual beating up and general third-degree methods, are mainly from victims of the November raids.   On the other hand, circumstantial stories of beatings, and some of a really horrible nature, were told their attorneys by one and another Communist arrested in January.

In the preliminary hearings before the agents of the Department of Justice the aliens did not have the benefit of counsel, for this examination is in the nature of a preliminary inquiry by the police officers, which is secret.   And after they had been brought before the immigration inspector they were not permitted to have counsel until the immigrant inspector was ready to allow it, for meanwhile Rule 22 of the Immigration Rules, governing the procedure with regard to counsel,

[1] New York *Times*, January 4, 1920.
[2] *Hearings before the Committee on Rules, House of Representatives, Second Session, Sixty-sixth Congress, April 27–May 8, 1920,* p. 42.

which had been revised to provide that the alien should be allowed counsel from the very beginning of the hearing, had been changed, a day or two before the raid took place, back to its earlier form, not allowing counsel until the hearing has proceeded sufficiently to protect the government's interests.[1]

Instances of unfairness in these hearings were brought out in the reopening of cases by the Department of Labor, together with other irregularities of procedure.[2]

The mere mass of persons arrested taxed the accommodations for detention far beyond their capacity, both before the hearings for all those arrested and after the hearings for those held for deportation, and resulted in terrible conditions in a number of the detention places. In Detroit, Communist prisoners were poured in upon the congestion already resulting from the arrests of Russian Workers.[3]

Conditions at the Hartford jail,[4] where both Russian Workers and Communists were confined, became notorious. The jail was badly overcrowded, the cells arranged in such a way that ventilation was bad in all of them, and some were so horribly overheated by

[1] *Hearings before a Subcommittee of the Committee on Immigration and Naturalization, House of Representatives, April 21–24, 1920, Communist and Anarchist Deportation Cases, Sixty-sixth Congress, Second Session*, p. 41, fol.

[2] *Hearings before Subcommittee of the Committee on Immigration and Naturalization, House of Representatives, Sixty-sixth Congress, Second Session, on House Res. 522; Hearings before same committee, June 1, 1920*, and following dates, *passim* for instances.

[3] Constantine M. Panunzio, *The Deportation Cases of 1919–20*, pp. 81–82.

[4] *Report upon the Illegal Practices of the United States Department of Justice; Hearings before the Committee on Rules, House of Representatives, Sixty-sixth Congress, Second Session, part I*, June 2, p. 75, C. M. Panunzio, *The Deportation Cases of 1919–20*, p. 79.

their neighborhood to steam pipes that the temperature was unendurable. The charge was made that there were "steam rooms" in the jail, used for the punishment of refractory inmates, but Mr. Panunzio, who made the independent investigation referred to, was of the opinion, after careful inquiry, that the cells overheated through bad planning of the structure were the "steam rooms" referred to. He found men confined in these cells, however, while there were vacant cells at a distance from the steam pipes, affording better ventilation, which might indicate that the hot cells were used for disciplinary purposes. When this condition was brought to the attention of the prison official, he said that a transfer to the better cells would involve too much trouble and red tape and would not be worth while. This investigator found that the men here had been held incomunicado for a long period. They had not seen a newspaper, nor received letters from relatives and friends, and had not been permitted visits from their friends until the latter part of January. In April, 1920, Mr. Panunzio found that 14 men were then held incomunicado in the upper cells because they had not had their first hearing. They had been there for three weeks, without a hearing and without knowledge on the part of the authorities as to whether or not they were members of a proscribed organization.[1]

In New York, accommodations at the immigration station were overcrowded at once. In a news account of the raids, it was said:

Great congestion will result at Ellis Island, Byron H. Uhl, Acting Commissioner of Immigration declared this morning. The acting commissioner was plainly not pleased with the

[1] C. M. Panunzio, *The Deportation Cases of 1919–20.*

prospect of incoming guests, maintaining that there are not proper facilities on the island for the detention of so many in addition to those already held there. He said that he had warned both the Department of Justice and the Bureau of Immigration not to make raids at this time, owing to the crowded conditions of the government institutions on the island.[1]

Many complaints were made of the sudden seizure of men in these raids, some being dragged from their beds and hurried off with insufficient clothing to Ellis Island, where they fell ill of pneumonia and more than one died. Serious charges of neglect in the hospital were made by friends of the deportees, but, making all allowance for possible exaggeration and falsification, the haste with which arrests were made, the crowding on Ellis Island, must have brought an especially high risk of disease and death.

And the congestion was not relieved by the prompt deportation of those declared deportable. After catching and judging its horde of "radicals" the government did not know what to do with them, for the number of those under orders of deportation by immigrant inspectors in the raids of November and January amounted to about as many as the deportations for all causes through a normal year.

Owing to the number of cases to be heard, the speedy deportation of those found guilty is an impossibility, John W. Abercrombie, Solicitor of the Department of Labor, said to-night. About 3,000 aliens a year were deported normally, he said, and to arrange for the sailing of the *Buford* with 249 deportees all the other work of the Bureau of Immigration had to be suspended. The task of deporting over 2,000 aliens in one group would tax the Bureau to the utmost.[2]

[1] New York *Evening Post*, January 3, 1920.
[2] New York *Times*, January 4, 1920.

In some of the Communist cases, as in the cases of some of the Union of Russian Workers, rehearings were secured at the Department of Labor, and hearings were held before Federal judges in *habeas corpus* proceedings which established interesting precedents.

An important point under the clause of the law making membership in an organization of a certain character a reason for deportation, is to determine what is membership. In the Russian Workers cases attendance at meetings, the possession of literature, membership in a school, were ruled out in Judge Hand's decision, and decisions of the Department of Labor, as criteria of membership. In the Communist cases, many of those recommended for deportation by the immigration officer were found to have acquired "membership" in the Communist party without knowledge of what that membership implied, or even without knowledge that they had become members of that party, through the practice of automatic transfer of membership by the secretary of a Socialist local, authorized by a vote of the national organization of which individual members might know nothing.

Assistant Secretary Post, who took charge of the deportation proceedings in the Department of Labor early in March, 1920, and to whom the country owes a debt for bringing back to the enforcement of the immigration law the principles and practices of justice, which are apt to be forgotten in times of excitement, ruled that automatic membership of this sort was not membership as contemplated by the law and canceled a large number of warrants on this account. A large number of others were canceled by him on the ground of insufficient evidence, or irregularities in the procedure.[1]

[1] For details of the controversy between Mr. Post and the Attorney General, over these proceedings, see the *Hearings* already referred to.

THE IMMIGRANT'S DAY IN COURT

Federal District Judge George W. Anderson, in *habeas corpus* proceedings brought before him in Boston, sustained the writs on two grounds—one, that the Communist party was not an organization falling under the ban of the immigration law; the other, that in the majority of the cases brought before the court due process of law was lacking from the beginning of the raids until the conclusion of the hearings on Deer Island. He pointed out that in four cases due process had been carried out to a great extent, because the four persons in question were capable and intelligent people, who understood their rights well enough to insist on due process. The other cases (the bulk of the group before the court) in which due process was lacking, were of aliens unable to speak English well, or at all, and ignorant of their rights.

It is worthy of note that the Department of Labor evidently accepted Judge Anderson's decision as to due process of law, by announcing that it would appeal only in the four cases where the procedure was apparently regular and where the persons admitted membership.

LATER DEPORTATIONS

Of the 3,000 or more cases of Communists and members of the Communist Labor party in which deportation was recommended by immigration officers, about 300 were Communist Labor cases, and were canceled, because of the decision of the Secretary of Labor that the Communist Labor party was not an unlawful organization, 2,200 others were canceled before the close of the fiscal year 1920 for other reasons, and only 556 were ordered deported up to that time. The number of deportations effected, of Communists apart from others as a distinct group among the "anarchists" reported in the annual statement of the Commissioner General, is not given there, but we may infer that it was very small, since the *Buford* cargo, practically all Russian Workers, account for 242 of the 314 deported for anarchy in that year,[1] leaving 72 at most for all cases of anarchy—Italian, Spanish, anarchist, Communist, and everything else—deported in that year aside from the Russian Workers.

On January 22, 1921, 71 persons were deported, mostly Russian Workers whose cases had not been decided at the time of the sailing of the *Buford*, or who had been out on bail. Only a scattering two or three were Communists.

The circumstances of this sailing indicate how little reason there was for the harshness and secrecy of the deportations on the *Buford*. Sixty-three of the Russian Workers paroled in the custody of their counsel on bail and scattered about in all parts of the country came to New York at their own expense and assisted in every way in the task of securing the final papers necessary for deportation and of making other arrangements. Those of the deportees who wished it were able to take their wives along. On the sailing list were three men accompanied by wives, and three by wives and children.

None of the men were forced to go unprepared for the voyage. If a man was sick, he was permitted to remain behind from this sailing. If he had a wife, and no money for her transportation, he was allowed to wait here until he could secure the necessary funds. The counsel for the deportees worked in harmony with the department to make preparations for the deportations, and the men were glad to go. The general feeling among them, as among the Russian

[1] *Annual Report of the Commissioner General of Immigration, 1920,* pp. 201, 203.

colonists generally, was that if this country did not want them they did not want to stay, and they were all eager to be back in a freed Russia, to take part in the building up of the new scheme of things. The hard feelings that arise when men are roughly or, as they think, unjustly treated, were not awakened under these circumstances, and the smoothness and lack of disorder with which the deportation was made seem to indicate that the method of co-operation is the more effective.

No further mass raids were made after January, 1920, and with the deportations for anarchy on January 22, 1921, we may consider the deportation campaign substantially at an end.

FAIRNESS OF THE PROCEEDINGS

Summing up, what may be said as to the actual working out in practice of the possibilities for uncertainty in the application of the law and for misuse of the broad discretionary powers given to the Immigration Department in deportation proceedings?

It must be plain, from a survey of the cases, how difficult it is to prove belief, to prove " advocacy," to prove "membership." If the accused person chose to deny any or all of these charges, the other available evidence was so scanty and uncertain that the department found itself obliged to choose between discharging persons because they denied belonging to prohibited classes, and no definite proof to the contrary could be brought forward, or when the department was morally certain they did come under the law, deporting them on this moral certainty, which is not a legal certainty, and deprives the person so treated of the due process of law to which he is entitled.

It seems also plain that the possibilities for unfair treatment in the procedure itself were realized.

In the account of the individual cases we have noted various instances of what seemed to be very clear injustice to the alien, and failure to give him a fair hearing and a fair opportunity for defense. The congressional hearings referred to give other instances. A study of the complete records of 200 deportation cases in the Bureau of Immigration at Washington, chosen to give a representative cross section of the cases as they ran, of Russian Workers and of Communists, from all parts of the country,[1] showed various irregularities. Beginning with the arrests by the Department of Justice, it was found that of the 200 persons involved in the cases, 89 were arrested from 1 to 57 days before the warrant of arrest was issued; in 48 cases no date of arrest is recorded; in 2 the date of issue of the warrant is not recorded. In one case no warrant was ever issued. Thirteen persons were arrested on the date of issue of the warrant, and in only 47 cases is it shown definitely that the arrest was made on a date subsequent to the issue of the warrant. This means that for the cases in which information is given, 60 per cent were arrested prior to the issue of the warrant of arrest.

As to the use of interpreters, according to this investigation, in one city where 27 of the arrests in the 200 cases had been made, for 17 of the cases the interpreter was an employee of the prosecuting department of the government, and in 3 of these he was also the witness against the alien; in 2 he had furnished the original affidavit of probable cause. In the remaining 10 of the 27 cases, 5 of the aliens could speak

[1] C. M. Panunzio, *The Deportation Cases of 1919-20*, p. 27.

English and did not need an interpreter, and 5 had an interpreter not connected with the case.[1]

In the 200 cases studied, somewhat less than two-thirds of the men had counsel at some stage of the proceedings, but not necessarily at the beginning, and somewhat over a third waived their right to counsel.[2] This waiving of right to counsel, as shown by individual cases we have studied, is not the free-will giving up of unnecessary privilege that it would seem on the face of it. The man might have been deprived of the services of counsel until the case had proceeded so far that he thought counsel would be of no use, or he might be too poor to employ a lawyer. In many places, also, as we have noted in relation to the I. W. W. cases, lawyers refused to serve as counsel for "anarchists," although presumably any of them in criminal practice would have felt it a moral duty to see that even a murderer had his rights of defense before the court. The men who were willing to undertake such cases were so few in number that they had to travel far and wide, and, while busy in one spot, would be unavailable in another where their services were needed.

How far does this special study agree with what has been seen in the cases presented in previous pages as to the adequacy of the evidence on which deportation was ordered by the immigration officers? In 124 cases taken at random by Mr. Panunzio and studied with particular reference to the types of evidence submitted, he found that in 8 no evidence whatsoever was presented. In 14 cases the only evidence was the affidavit of the special agent of the Department of Justice, in mimeographed form (standardized for every case) in which the agent states that he "is informed and verily

[1] *The Deportation Cases of 1919–20*, p. 36.
[2] *Ibid.*, p. 38.

believes" that the alien is an anarchist or member of a proscribed organization, without further detail. In 6 cases the record of the preliminary examination before the agent of the Department of Justice is the only evidence submitted.

These records [says Mr. Panunzio] frequently did not bear the signature of the alien or of the officer making the examination, and often were extracted under threats and varying forms of compulsion. The absence of the interpreter also gave rise to all kinds of possibilities in the way of misunderstanding, as an examination of the records reveals.

Again, the records of the hearings frequently revealed the fact that the agent making the original charge was asked to produce the evidence or to disclose the source of his information. Invariably he refused to do this.

When questioned concerning his information that the alien was a member of a proscribed organization, the agent would frequently state that his information was derived from confidential sources the disclosure of which he considered would be inimical to the interests of the government.[1]

In 36 of the 124 cases membership cards were submitted as evidence, but 10 of them showed membership in the Socialist or Communist Labor party, neither of which was a proscribed organization. From some of the cards for proscribed organizations, it was clear that no dues had been paid to the organization. This certainly bears out the impression given by the cases presented in previous pages, as does the remainder of the description of the character of the evidence.

Other forms of evidence consisted of tickets to meetings and social gatherings given under the auspices of the Socialist or Communist party; subscription lists containing names of those who had contributed to funds to help the wives of men arrested or for purposes of like character. In the cases of

[1] *The Deportation Cases of 1919-20*, p. 40.

two men there were photographs showing the alien with a copy of a Russian paper called *Bread and Freedom* in his hand. In two other cases, group pictures were submitted purporting to show the members of a local branch of the Communist party. Post cards and letters were also frequently found among the exhibits, and when signed "yours for Communism" were considered particularly strong evidence.[1]

In one case no other evidence was introduced than a red flag, on which was printed "Good Luck to Soviet Russia." This case was finally canceled, but not until three months after the date of arrest.

A detailed study of all facts given in the record of the 200 cases, all under warrant of deportation, went to show that 47 were distinctly not members of proscribed organizations, 56 of them admitted membership in the organization or there was sufficient evidence to show membership, and 74 were members by automatic transfer (presumably Communists), of whom 29 did not know that they had been transferred, while the remainder did not understand what it meant. Eight were members only of a school attached to a proscribed organization (presumably Russian Workers), while 15 cases were doubtful.[2]

This study confirms the showing of the cases given on previous pages as to the motives for joining organizations.

By far the greater number [says Mr. Panunzio] give as their reason for belonging to a proscribed organization their desire for knowledge of one kind and another.[3] Some belong to the organization for political reasons, declaring that their interest was

---

[1] *The Deportation Cases of 1919-20*, p. 41.

[2] *Ibid.*, pp. 52–65. The numbers given by Mr. Panunzio total 199. We are not told the status of the two-hundredth man.

[3] *Ibid.*, p. 66.

confined to Russian politics; others had an idea of improving their economic status by joining the organization; and others joined for sociability and mutual aid in sickness.

NUMERICAL RESULTS OF THE DEPORTATION CAMPAIGN

As a result of the year's campaign, how far did the government actually clear the country of elements considered dangerous? The estimates of the number of "dangerous radicals" made by government agents both at the beginning and in the course of the campaign were alarmingly large. A record of the activities of the Department of Justice, presented by the Attorney General at the hearings of June 1 and 2, 1920,[1] estimated the number of radicals as follows: Industrial Workers of the World, 300,000; Communists, 40,000; Communist Labor party, 10,000; Union of Russian Workers, 4,000; and two small anarchist groups of Spaniards and Italians. Leaving out the Industrial Workers of the World, who are by no means all foreign born, and the Communist Labor party, who are also not made up so largely of the foreign born as the Communist party, we have estimated here at least fifty thousand people considered dangerous by government agents, most of them aliens and therefore subject to deportation, if falling within the classes proscribed by the immigration law.

In New York state, Senator Lusk estimated that there were 20,000 "alien enemies" (meaning radicals) in that state alone. Other estimates refer to 60,000 dangerous aliens in the country.

The number of warrants served in the raids, although large, was, then, a mere fraction of the number needed

[1] *Hearings before the Committee on Rules, House of Representatives, Sixty-sixth Congress, Second Session,* p. 156, fol.

to clear the country of the danger as estimated by the investigators of radical activities for the government. The Attorney General, defending his mass raids in a letter, says:

. . . To have arrested an individual member would have been as useless as to endeavor to curb a great epidemic by merely isolating one case of the disease.[1]

But his procedure had practically the same effect, as far as segregating all the "infected" was concerned.

Then when we note that the entire number actually deported for anarchy for the fiscal year ending June 30, 1920, the year covering the raids, was only 314, and for the fiscal year of 1921, the year in which most of the cases were disposed of, was only 446, it is seen how ineffective, even from the government's point of view, was the long and expensive and terrifying campaign against the reds.

If there were so many people in the country dangerous to it, how little was effected by sending out less than 1 per cent of them. If the original numbers were exaggerated, why could not the pursuit of the comparatively few lawbreakers have been conducted with the care and judgment and the adherence to long-standing principles of justice that are required in ordinary criminal cases brought before the courts of the land?

Did these proceedings even stop such manifestations of violence as occasioned some of the impetus on the part of governmental authorities to make the raids?

The bomb plots of May and June, 1919, if they were plots, were never explained, nor were any persons brought to justice on account of them. After a year of terror, which, it was calculated, would frighten evildoers, even if only a few of them were actually

[2] *The Survey,* January 31, 1920.

apprehended, occurred the explosion in Wall Street, New York City, in September, 1920, which, if it was the work of anarchists, the reign of terror did not prevent.

REACTION OF THE FOREIGN BORN

What can be the effect on the immigrant who has gone through these raids and arrests? One effect, as has been pointed out, must be intellectual confusion, resulting from the different decisions of different government officials as to the meaning of the anarchy clauses of the immigration law. In the records of the cases the persons arrested frequently said that they did not know that they were doing anything unlawful. The fact that on one day the Communist Labor party was considered a proscribed organization, and the next day it was not, that it took deep and detailed and subtle discussion of terms to show the difference between it and the Communist party, which was declared unlawful by the Department of Labor, must have made it impossible for the average immigrant to decide whether he could belong to that organization or not. And when the line between it and a proscribed organization was so faint, how could the proscribed organization itself be so harmful, especially when a Federal judge (Anderson, in the Boston case) decided that it also was lawful.

The Industrial Workers of the World was never declared an unlawful organization by the Secretary of Labor, but in the deportation cases it was plainly to be seen that the real cause of offense was membership and leadership in that organization. And in the case of the I. W. W. that confusion was added to by the fact that under some state laws it was penalized as an unlawful organization; under others it was not.

461

THE IMMIGRANT'S DAY IN COURT

From the methods followed in the raids and arrests, how can the alien but be reminded of the autocratic governments of Europe? How can he believe in the freedom and justice of this country?

Judge George Anderson said, in his decision on the Communist cases brought before him in Boston: "A mob is a mob, whether made up of government officials acting under instructions from the Department of Justice, or of criminals, loafers, and the vicious classes."

We have seen, in the study of the cases presented here, how some of these people felt about it, and it is to be remembered that for one person actually arrested and ordered deported, whose case we may read, there are perhaps hundreds of foreign born who have been the object of attack by local authorities, who were not ordered deported, who remain here, but who are learning an unfortunate lesson in government and citizenship, as in the following instance:

ARRESTED AND FREED

NEWARK, NEW JERSEY.

Not quite two months have passed since the arrests and persecutions of Russian Workers, and again we are being arrested.

This time it happened in the Ukrainian People's Home, 57 Bacon Street, on Saturday, February 28th. A ball was to be given at that hall to help the families of those that were arrested and in jail. At the proper time the people filled the hall and the concert began. At 9 P.M., one of the Secret Service men appeared on the stage and demanded that the concert end immediately. At the same time forty other agents placed themselves at all exits. The detectives ordered all women to leave the hall. The women protested and did not want to leave their husbands, but were thrown out from the hall. After this began the questioning and the arrests.

As a result thirty-four were held. They were taken to the Department of Justice and examined again by officials. Part of those arrested were freed. Twelve were detained for twenty-four hours, at the station. The next day they were all freed. No charges were preferred against any one.

VINOGRADOFF.

Russky Golos, New York, March 9, 1920.

If we want the alien to respect government and the orderly processes of the law, we certainly do not want to give him examples of mob rule and lynch law, or law mixed with loot, as in the following instance:

ROBBED AND ARRESTED

On January 31st, at midnight, nine men broke into our house. They were apparently detectives armed with clubs and revolvers. Upon entering the house they asked, "Where are the Bolsheviki?" and were told that there are none here; that only workmen live here. In spite of this answer, they threatened us and handcuffed us, then searched our pockets. In one of my pockets they found a copy of *Golos Truzhenika*, and in the other $62 in cash. The paper they threw to the floor and the money they pocketed. Then I realized that they were not looking for Bolsheviks, but for money.

In this manner the robbers visited six houses and took with them over $2,000. The next day, about 6 P.M., six detectives came around and asked from whom the money was taken. Then they asked who of us is a Russian, locked me and my friend in a room and searched us. They turned everything upside down and found my membership book. As soon as they noticed the three initials I. W. W., they grabbed us in a car and put us in jail, where we were left in the hands of destiny.

Three days later we were told that if we put up $1,000 as bail we will be released, but we said that if they want they can keep us here even three more years. We have not even enough to buy bread. In half an hour we were released and

told that all that were robbed should come next to Union
Town.

I decided to leave town and get away from the robbers.

This is how things are in our locality. First robbed—and
then arrested.

P. Karol.

Golos Truzhenika (I. W. W.), February 28, 1920.

The following story told by a man who came to an
information office for immigrants to ask aid, is interesting as giving an instance of the troubles of the discharged deportee when he drops back into ordinary life,
and how he feels about it.

Early in 1920, Stepan Ivanov was arrested in his lodgings
by three policemen. He was taken to the police station,
where he was searched and deprived of his belongings. No
damning evidence being discovered, he was taken to the
Broad Street Post Office, Newark, where he was examined
further. The method employed was to lead him to a table
covered with literature and point out one pile at a time, asking
him if he belonged to the organization indicated. He was
told by an interpreter that he could have a lawyer to help
him answer the questions, but his reply was that he did not
need one—he "did not do anything bad." These attempts
to gain an admission that he belonged to an anarchistic or a
Communistic organization having failed, he was sent the
next day to Ellis Island, where on February 5th he was tried
by an immigration inspector, who, Ivanov said, remarked,
after the proceedings were over, "They were fools to have
sent you here." His case was referred to Washington, and
on February 26th he was released. For two weeks he was
too ill from the insufficient food and unsanitary conditions
at Ellis Island even to look for work. Finally he found a job,
but was driven from it after two months, unable to bear any
longer the treatment of his fellow workers, who taunted him
with being a Bolshevik. He went the rounds of New Bruns-
wick plants, but found that no one would employ a Russian,
all of whom are considered to be dangerous characters.

THE DEPORTATIONS OF 1919-20

Finally a letter from his family in Minsk, of whom he had had no news for five years, decided him to return to them. They were in need and had not received the money he had sent them through a banker five months before.

He went to the banker and asked for a Russian passport,[1] for which he paid $10. On arriving at the Customs House, where everyone, alien or citizen, leaving the country, must satisfy the authorities that all income-tax requirements have been met, he was told that his tax would be $57 from 1919 and 1920, although his earnings for that time were only about $640.

In despair he appealed to a Russian paper, which referred him to an organization which he was assured would help him. Here he learned that he had been taxed as a Ukrainian, to whom the $1,000 exemption applicable to Russians does not apply. Further, he was told that the Ukrainian passport would not take him beyond the seaports of Europe. The Province of Minsk, to which he wished to return, was under Polish control (though still disputed by Russia), and consequently any passport required the visé of the Polish consulate. The consulate refused to visé Ukrainian or Russian passports. Ivanov's only chance of joining his family is to get a Polish passport, which would make him liable to being drafted into the Polish army, to fight against his countrymen in Minsk. Denied the means of a livelihood here, he can return to his home only by taking up arms against his people.

When the full realization of his plight was borne in upon him, Ivanov's first idea was to give up—"to throw himself from the fifth story." "All these things make me nervous all the time. . . . I cannot work; I cannot do anything. . . . It does not matter." Then other impulses again became uppermost, and he reiterated that somehow he "must leave this country, where they accuse innocent people."

Palmer's name apparently meant nothing to Ivanov. "I do not blame the government for arresting me; it was the

[1] Russian and Ukrainian passports are, strictly speaking, the affidavits of nationality which are authorized by the State Department for use in lieu of passports, by persons of doubtful nationality.

465

policeman on the corner." He has a vague idea that he was arrested because he boarded with a man who belonged to "Nauka" ("Science"), an educational organization where he studied arithmetic. (This friend was also arrested, and released after long detention at Ellis Island.) Ivanov was shown no warrant for his arrest, but understood that he was thought to be a Bolshevist. "Then I was not," he said, "but *now* I am Bolshevik."

It would appear, from all the evidence available, that the deportation proceedings of 1919-20 realized many of the possibilities for oppression and lawlessness in the discretionary powers of the immigration officials and in the indefiniteness of the immigration law, and that, in justice to the alien, both law and procedure should be changed to afford the substantial justice that it is the aim of our legal system to secure.

It may be said that the special troubles recounted in this chapter were due to an exceptional set of circumstances—to a state of popular excitement following the nerve-racking experiences of a period of warfare, and that under ordinary circumstances such troubles will not arise. But it is not so sure that such events may not be repeated. Times of excitement against the alien may recur, for other reasons than a state of warfare. It is for that reason especially necessary that the bulwarks of a strictly secured legal procedure be firmly established in a time of calm to prevent wholesale injustice against individuals in times of excitement.

Just what changes should be made in the laws and their administration would have to be made the matter of special, detailed study, but it would seem that the main line of improvement should be in the direction of adjusting law and procedure to the general principles of the law as laid down in our codes and the rules governing our courts.

THE DEPORTATIONS OF 1919–20

In the immigration law, provisions which are indefinite, or of a nature to make proof of violation difficult if not impossible, should be replaced by definite provisions, violations of which are susceptible of proof. The anarchy provisions are certainly of the former nature.

And in the law a return should be made to the principle that deportation is merely an extension of the exclusion provisions, and this country should accept responsibility for its residents after they have been here for a reasonable time.

The administration of the law should be changed to afford more completely the safeguards of regular court procedure, especially in cases of deportation. Publicity, the right to counsel, opportunity for a court review which should be a review of the facts in the case, not merely to determine jurisdiction, as in *habeas corpus* proceedings, are some of the obvious remedies.

Certainly the immigrant cannot feel that he is being given due process of law as long as the present secret, changeable, irresponsible method is followed.

XI

MEANS OF ADJUSTMENT

WHAT is being done to remedy such imperfect adjustments between the immigrant and our legal system as have been noted in the course of this study? For getting him in relation with the courts various private and public agencies are available to give legal advice, and to afford such general instruction and protection as will make appearance before a court unnecessary.

THE LEGAL-AID SOCIETIES

Mainly in possession of this field are the organizations known in general as legal-aid societies. These societies trace their origin historically to a society established in New York City for the protection of a certain class of poor immigrants from exploitation at the time of their arrival, and in many of the cities where legal-aid societies are established a large proportion of the clients of these societies to-day are of foreign birth. The opportunities of such societies for promoting good citizenship among the immigrant population have been seen and expressed by many familiar with their work. The long-time president of the New York Legal Aid Society, Mr. Arthur von Briesen, to whom the legal-aid movement owes so much, emphasized this function of a legal-aid society as follows:

"The society's work makes good citizens and arouses a sentiment of respect for the laws, and also, I may say, a sentiment of patriotism. Many of our clients are of foreign birth—people, often, who are ignorant of the laws, and of how to set the machinery of the law in motion. They have some vague idea that there is law for the redress of wrongs, but they have heard that it is too costly a luxury for the poor; that it is law for the rich and not for the poor. They know that they have been defrauded and wronged, but redress may seem to them hopeless. They have no money to secure it, and therefore think it is not for them. The consequence is that they become bitter, not only against the particular person who has wronged them, but against society in general, against the country which permits society to be organized on so unjust a basis. Such persons— and these need not be confined to persons of foreign birth by any means—are ripe to listen to those social agitators and disturbers who are only too prevalent. They are ripe for enlistment in the ranks of those who are regarded as dangerous to the security of law and order."

A later president, Mr. Charles E. Hughes,[1] urges that "the importance of this service among the alien population should be emphasized, as it only not brings relief to those in need, but promotes respect for American justice among those who are least familiar with our institutions."

As these societies have developed, however, certain theories of the nature of the work have also developed which seem to lead a little away from the line of the closest adaptation to the needs of the immigrant population.

A legal-aid society is naturally under the influence of lawyers. Any society of this type has a staff of lawyers to afford the "legal aid" which, as the name applies, it

---

[1] *Report of the New York Legal Aid Society, 1917*, p. 1.

is the primary purpose of the society to provide. Some of the societies are under the direct management of lawyers also, in contrast to others, under nonprofessional control. The legal mind, trained in analyzing technical distinctions in laws, and in deciding how far certain acts may be defined as in conformity with or in violation of the law, tends to regard legal protection as the task of fitting a given law to a set of circumstances shown in a given case, without reference to the personality of the client, or to any service to be rendered him other than that of securing the technical right involved.[1]

And in accordance with that earlier conception of equality of justice as a refusal to recognize differences in the people to whom the law should be applied, under which our courts were in theory operated until the more modern idea of varying treatment to correspond with personal differences found entrance to the court system, the "legalistic" legal-aid society prides itself upon not recognizing differences in clients, beyond one fundamental distinction between the "poor" and the "rich," and in treating everybody alike.[2]

Some of the societies, and among them some of the most important, require in addition that the client be "worthy" or "deserving," but many of them make no requirement of the sort, beyond that which

[1] The scope of the work is confined to legal action. The societies are engaged in the practice of law and not in social-service work as that phrase is generally used.—REGINALD HEBER SMITH, *Justice and the Poor*, p. 152.

[2] The fundamental object of our society . . . is to see that all, no matter how poor or how oppressed, shall get justice. We care nothing for race, sex, color, or creed, or previous condition of servitude; we do believe that the laws mean something and our work is to see that they mean the same for the poor as for the rich.—*No. 38, New York Legal Aid Review*, p. 152.

would be made by any reputable lawyer in accepting a case.[1]

And, according to this legalistic theory of the function of a legal-aid society, development along class or group lines is deprecated. A criticism brought against a specialized legal-aid work for labor unions, organized in New York City, is that it has done this.[2]

The legal-aid society is, then, according to this theory, primarily a means of service for the poor.[3]

Another principle of operation is to avoid competition with the regular practitioners at the bar. This is one reason for the general rule of these societies not to take as clients persons who could afford to pay for legal services at the usual rates. Such a rule excludes many an immigrant who can afford to pay a reasonable fee, but does not know where to go for disinterested legal advice. The same principle of operation hampers the legal-aid society in trying to meet this need by recommending

[1] Realizing that their work was in the field of the law and that they were taking a part in the administration of justice, the organizations have wisely refrained from erecting any moral standard which applicants must satisfy before being entitled to assistance. The only test is the intrinsic merit of the claim, plus a due regard for those restrictions which good ethics impose on all members of the bar. Suits for reasons of spite, vexatious proceedings taken for delay, technical defenses for just claims, will not be undertaken. . . . If the worst man in the world was actually owed ten dollars by the best man, the society would undertake the collection for the former, provided he was too poor to engage his own attorney.—REGINALD HEBER SMITH, *Justice and the Poor,* p. 162.

[2] The secretariat plan was never formally extended beyond New York, and it is perhaps fortunate, for if legal-aid work had developed along class or group lines, its real position in the administration of justice, the essentially public nature of its service, would have been obscured.—*Ibid.,* p. 14.

[3] The function of the legal-aid society is to furnish counsel to poor persons; to undertake their cases where no other assistance is elsewhere available.—*Ibid.,* p. 129.

some reliable attorney. Different societies meet this situation in different ways. Some may refer clients, whom they will not accept themselves, to a list of attorneys prepared by the local bar association, from which the names are taken in alphabetical order. According to this plan, the client has no choice and must take the attorney thus indicated, whether he is the best to deal with the special class of case in hand or not. Other societies prepare lists of outside attorneys, known to be reliable, who will work in co-operation with the society. This plan lays the society more open to charges of favoritism, in assigning cases. Other societies refer cases to attorneys formerly on their own staff.[1]

This rule shutting out from the service of the legal-aid society the immigrant who can afford to pay a reasonable fee, but does not know where to go for disinterested advice, and the difficulties placed in the way of recommending attorneys to whom such persons may go without fear of being defrauded, bring it about that a large and important branch of immigrant need is not met by the legal-aid societies generally, for it is especially the immigrant who has accumulated a little stock of money who is the prey of the exploiter. Failing the help of the legal-aid society, he may have recourse to the swindling lawyer, and his feelings are as keen at being swindled, his idea of the country to which he has come is as greatly lowered, as would be the case with the poverty-stricken immigrant—perhaps more so, as the poorer man has so much less to lose and to feel grieved about.

A failure to take account in the treatment of clients of differences in nationality may lead to the same hindrances to justice as we have noted in connection with

---

[1] Reginal Heber Smith, *Justice and the Poor*, p. 163.

court action. The legal-aid society follows the modern court in laying emphasis on conciliation and arbitration. But how can these be effected if the personal peculiarities of clients and their opponents are not taken into account? Conciliation and arbitration depend upon persuasion, upon the voluntary co-operation of the parties in interest, not upon the sanctions of the law. The parties must be approached on the basis of their own feelings and prejudices about the matter in hand. How can this be done if the differences are not thought important and are not seen?

Certain discriminations are made in the classes of cases accepted by different legal-aid societies, and in the point of view from which the cases are treated, which may reduce the possibilities of help for the immigrant. Among the economic troubles, personal injury cases are refused by perhaps three-fourths of the legal-aid societies, on the ground that, under the contingent-fee system, undertaking such cases would mean competition with the bar.[1]

[1] The chief point of contention among the organizations is with regard to accepting personal-injury cases. . . . The majority position is that to do such work is to enter into competition with the bar. . . . The minority hold to the proposition that a poor man does not cease to be entitled to the services of a legal-aid organization because he has suffered a serious injury. They regard the contingent fee, as it is used in practice, as an exploitation of the unfortunate position of the injured person, and not as the method of giving him proper relief. The organizations which decline personal-injury cases are forced into a most uncomfortable position. An injured poor person applies for assistance, which is refused; he then asks to whom he should go, and this information cannot be given him. . . . The result of the double refusal . . . is disastrous. The injured party may not know anywhere to go and so fail of relief altogether, or, what is more likely, will fall into the hands of a "runner" or a lawyer's agent, and will then pay the larger proportion of any settlement or recovery in fees.— REGINALD HEBER SMITH, *Justice and the Poor*, p. 156.

Another reason for refusing such cases where the injury is industrial, in states where a Workman's Compensation Act does away with the contingent fee, is that legal service is not needed. Experience indicates that under any system legal service may be needed, and the absence of it may be a handicap in enforcing a claim.[1]

A few of the societies refuse all bankruptcy cases. This is a hardship to the poor man who is harassed by a vindictive creditor, to such an extent that he cannot keep a job or support his family, or pay another creditor.[2]

A few societies refuse to take complaints against attorneys. Where such complaints are received the usual procedure is to refer them to the local bar association for action.

In domestic difficulties, the immigrant usually finds that the legal-aid society will refuse to institute divorce proceedings, because of a general sentiment against the breaking up of a home. The same reason, however, leads the society to accept the defense in cases of divorce. But the peculiar circumstances accompanying the domestic life of the immigrant may sometimes make the institution of divorce proceedings the one best way out.

The legal-aid societies almost entirely fail the immi-

---

[1] Thus the rule tends to enforce the too common opinion that attorneys are unnecessary under the compensation acts, so that the legal-aid societies are keeping out of a field where their services are sorely needed. Not all, but many of them, are making their original mistake over again. An injured workman, receiving one-half or two-thirds of his former pay, is not in a position to pay largely for lawyer's services. . . . With the passage of time there will inevitably be an increasing necessity on the part of injured workmen for representation at hearings in all contested cases.—REGINALD HEBER SMITH, *Justice and the Poor*, p. 158.

[2] *Ibid.*, p. 153.

grant in criminal cases. Nearly all of the societies refuse criminal cases, and the few which accept them do little work along that line.[1]

This is not the result of theoretical objection to such cases, but of limitation of resources. Quite recently, a society organized in New York City, to fill this gap, undertaking the defense of criminals unable to secure counsel, has been affiliated with the New York Legal Aid Society, becoming part of its system of legal aid. This society concerned itself only with the more serious charges, leaving the defense of those charged with smaller crimes and misdemeanors unprovided for.

Societies may not make any definite discrimination against certain types of cases, but may differ in the emphasis laid upon certain classes of cases, so that the immigrant who is in trouble of a particular kind may find that the nearest legal-aid society is not in the habit of paying much attention to cases of that sort. A tabulation of cases analyzed according to the nature of the legal question involved, for seven of the older and more important legal-aid societies in 1915, showed varying proportions of the different classes of cases. Part of these differences are due to difference in other facilities for securing legal assistance in the community in question; part are due to the differences in classification of services, so that for some, "advice" is included in one sense; for some, another meaning is attached; and some omit it altogether, to the confusion of the percentages. But omitting "advice" is a classification, and taking all cases handled and classified according to their nature as a basis of percentage, we find that Philadelphia,

[1] Of the thirty-one organizations having any clear policies or rules, twenty-one refuse criminal cases, and those which have no rule do very little, if any, such work.—REGINALD HEBER SMITH, *Justice and the Poor*, p. 156.

Boston, and Chicago, in the order named, show larger percentages of domestic-relations cases than the other cities; that St. Louis, Kansas City, and New York show larger percentages of three main classes, taken together, of cases involving money—personal property, wages, and contract, debt, and money claims; and that the same order is shown for wage claims taken separately. Other differences will be noted in the table following:

PERCENTAGE OF CASES WHICH ARE[1]

Domestic-relations cases		Contract, debt, and money claims alone		Cases involving economic difficulty, personal property, contract, and money claims, and wages, taken together.	
Philadelphia	23.8	Boston	28.6	St. Louis	74.0
Boston	19.5	St. Louis	22.1	Kansas City	70.4
Chicago	16.9	New York	17.1	New York	67.1
Cleveland	16.0	Chicago	16.8	Boston	52.3
Kansas City	13.0	Kansas City	15.7	Chicago	47.1
New York	10.9	Philadelphia	9.7	Philadelphia	37.0
St. Louis	8.5	Cleveland	7.7	Cleveland	25.5

Personal property alone		Loan shark cases		Wages alone	
Kansas City	10.6	Cleveland	25.5	St. Louis	45.2
Boston	10.5	Chicago	8.3	Kansas City	44.1
New York	9.6	St. Louis	8.2	New York	40.4
St. Louis	6.7	Kansas City	7.7	Chicago	26.3
Philadelphia	6.0	Other cities		Philadelphia	21.3
Chicago	4.0	negligible		Cleveland	15.5
Cleveland	2.3			Boston	13.2

Landlord and tenant	
Cleveland	14.0
Philadelphia	8.2
Boston	2.8
Chicago	2.8
Others, 2% or less	

[1] Reginald Heber Smith, *Justice and the Poor*, p. 154.

476

Turning to some of the special difficulties encountered by the immigrant, noted in previous pages, it was not found in any of the cases studied here that in labor troubles or deportation cases any legal-aid society had interested itself in the immigrant's need.

It has been learned by the writer, however, that the Legal Aid Bureau of the United Charities of Chicago did undertake legal aid for some cases of communists arrested for deportation. This was apparently due to the fact that certain cases of arrests were referred to the United Charities for family relief. When these cases were taken up for consideration it seemed that legal aid in the nature of arranging for bonds was needed rather than relief, and also assistance in presenting cases at the hearings. These cases were handled in conference with the Bar Association, and in full coöperation with the Departments of Justice and Labor.

That labor and deportation cases are not touched by the legal-aid societies generally may be explained quite naturally by the fact that the proceedings in such labor cases as we have been discussing are of a criminal nature, a type of cases which the legal-aid societies do not deal with. The Voluntary Defenders' committee, the society organized for defense of criminals in New York, does not undertake minor cases, in which class most of the labor cases fall. Deportation cases are not counted as criminal cases; on the other hand, they are not of the nature of the civil proceedings which the legal societies are most accustomed to handle.

Whatever may be the reasons, however, the fact remains that the legal-aid societies do not help the immigrant in these types of cases. Nor do any of them seem to undertake as a regular function the preparation and presenting of cases for criminal prosecution. It is supposed that private counsel for the prosecution of criminals is unnecessary, because of the fact that prosecution is provided for by the state, through the state or city prosecuting attorney. But it is found desirable in practice, if punishment of the criminal is involved in a case in which an individual has been wronged, to give assistance to the public attorney in preparing the case, so that he can put it through successfully. When an immigrant, for example, is swindled, even when he cannot recover his property through civil proceedings, it satisfies his sense of justice to have the offender brought to punishment. But if the case is left to the ordinary routine of an overburdened prosecuting office, perhaps it will not be carefully attended to. This is not a part of the stated function of the legal-aid society, although some of them undertake such work as this, incidentally, especially in connection with cases of domestic relations.

If the legal-aid societies are to meet fully the needs of the non-English-speaking immigrant, it would seem that the same equipment of knowledge of the language, knowledge of the customs of the different kinds of immigrants with whom they have to deal, is necessary for them as for officers of the courts, probation officers, and other public officials.

But in the one comprehensive account which we have of the legal-aid societies[1] no mention is made of the presence or absence of any such equipment. This is in accordance with the theory that the client's only need is that of technical legal service. We cannot even tell from that report to what extent the clients served are of foreign birth. None of the statistics given bear upon that point.

---

[1] Reginald Heber Smith, *Justice and the Poor.*

MEANS OF ADJUSTMENT

That the societies do not meet the need fully may be inferred from the comparatively small total of cases handled. In the year 1916, for example, 41 societies in 37 cities, most of which contain a large foreign-born population, and in which exploitation runs riot, handled 117,201 cases. This includes all cases, whether of the native or foreign born. Obviously, only a fragment of the needed work for the foreign born was done by these societies in that year.

It is acknowledged that the work of these societies is not extensive enough to meet the general need, owing to lack of sufficient endowment. They cannot undertake publicity campaigns for the purpose of reaching all who need their services, because they could not provide for the flood of business that such a publicity campaign would bring. Furthermore, it is again a violation of professional ethics to advertise in the ordinary way. They must content themselves with attending to such cases as come to them through the passing of information from one client to another, or through the recommendation of social agencies who have cases needing legal advice. Naturally the new immigrant, knowing less about the social resources of the country than the older immigrant and the native, is the last to learn of the legal-aid society, and is the one for whom a campaign of publicity is most needed. This is perhaps one reason why, in some cities with a large foreign-born population, the clientele of the legal-aid society, as shown by its annual report, will be almost entirely native, or of the older, English-speaking immigration.

To get a more concrete picture of the legal-aid societies and a clearer idea of their possibilities for meeting immigrant needs, let us look at two or three of them, as observed at their work.

THE IMMIGRANT'S DAY IN COURT

THE NEW YORK LEGAL-AID SOCIETY

Of the cases handled by the New York Legal-Aid Society in a recent year, 41 per cent were alien foreign born, 18 per cent naturalized foreign born, showing the extent of the work of this society with the foreign born. But the attorney in chief thinks that there is no "immigrant problem" in legal-aid work; the problem is practically the same for all the clients, whether foreign born or native. It is essentially the work of giving adequate and honest access to the methods and institutions of justice, and the fact that many of the cases are those of immigrants is due only to the fact that such a large proportion of the poor and ignorant population of the country is composed of immigrants. As the attorney in chief describes their policy, the society makes no special provision for dealing with foreign-speaking clients, but in choosing attorneys for the office an effort is made to get men and women with a knowledge of some language in addition to English. At the time this study was made he mentioned French and German as the languages spoken by attorneys, but one of his assistants informed the investigator that the society at that time had no foreign-speaking attorneys. This was not considered necessary by the officials, as usually some one could be found to interpret—a friend or relative accompanying the client, perhaps.

The attorneys attached to this society have all been admitted to the bar, and during the summer a few law students from leading universities give assistance. Two women are on the staff at the main office, a small proportion compared with the number of men, but the attorney in chief thinks that the clients prefer to tell their troubles to a man, the Europeans especially

MEANS OF ADJUSTMENT

feeling greater respect and confidence in a man in regard
to legal matters.

A few years ago a special branch for immigrants was
opened to which all foreign-born clients were to be
referred, but after eight months of operation it was
closed, on the ground that the work was identical with
that done in the regular office, and a special provision
for the foreign born was an unnecessary duplication.
Apparently the methods used were the same.

In the work of this society claims for wages form the
largest single class of cases. The society tries to avoid
taking wage-claim cases for less than five dollars,
regarding the time and effort and money spent on such
small cases as disproportionate. One member of the
staff, however, thought that, on the other hand, if the applicant had a claim for a considerable amount the
society would not take the case, as a person who could
get along and manage to live without his wages through
the long period necessary to make the claim come to a
large amount was not an object of charity. It is hardly
necessary to point out the social value of giving redress
even for small money losses, while the larger claims may
come from those having some savings, and not poverty-
stricken, who really need the service of some one to
secure redress for them, because of their ignorance.

A member of the staff said that when an answer was
received from an employer, the society was disposed to
favor his side of the case, but if he failed to answer the
first and second letters sent him, a summons was issued
for court appearance. While the investigator was in the
office a young woman of Irish birth came in to get help
in collecting a wage claim. She had been employed in a
restaurant, and because she had refused to work nine
hours a day and on Sunday, she had been dismissed and
her pay docked. She was advised to accept the amount

481

for five days' work which had been paid her and make no effort to collect more. The attorney was apparently not interested in the laws regarding the hours of women's labor. While the investigator was there, a German was present who had claimed pay for forty-five hours overtime. On receipt of a letter from the employer, however, this attorney decided the employer was right and the client a liar, and told the man so in plain terms. This made the client angry and he went away abusing the society. "You can't trust the workingman," said the attorney; "they are out to beat you every time."

Among the persons applying for assistance in collecting wages are many domestic servants. The attorney in chief thinks the fault is often with the employees in these cases, as they are undisciplined and irresponsible.

In domestic-servant claims, if the servant leaves without giving reasonable notice, and without giving the employer a reasonable opportunity to engage other help, regardless as to whether the contract of hiring is for a definite, or an indefinite period, her case is refused. The present policy of unwillingness to take a case in which the employee leaves without notice was adopted in response to complaints from the contributing clientele of the society, that this was encouraging servants to leave without notice and distinctly undermining the character of the working classes. In fairness it should be stated that the society takes an equally firm stand against unannounced dismissals on the part of the employers.

The society does not take bankruptcy cases, nor does it accept accident cases, both because it has no facilities for handling the work, and for the usual reason that other lawyers will take such cases on a percentage basis, and it is the policy of the society not to compete with the legal profession. It will, however, do what it can to handle such cases out of court and try to secure a settlement. The society is active in assisting in the probate of wills. They will not contest a will, but will defend clients against other contestants. They also help in proceedings for adoption.

This society does not take divorce cases for men, but will handle them for women with children. An outside agency is employed to make the investigation in domestic cases, and a member of the staff spoke with admiration to the investigator of the information that a woman social worker had secured in relation to one of the cases. A man could never have got to the bottom of this case, he thought. This leads to the reflection that possibly a woman employing the methods of the social worker rather than those of the lawyer, might be equally effective in getting at the heart of the trouble in the original interview, which the attorney in chief would reserve to the man lawyer.

In cases of separation the society will interfere when the complainant is a woman with children. Cases arise in which a woman secures a separation or divorce through a private lawyer, who will then refuse to collect the alimony for her, but this society will not take the collection of alimony unless it has had the case from the start.

This society sets up a personal qualification for clients, in addition to poverty. It assists "only those who are worthy" (to quote an annual report) "and who cannot afford to pay for the services of a private attorney. . . . It is not our object to compete with the outside profession, but to relieve it in so far as charity cases are concerned."

Occasionally the society refers cases to other agencies, to that extent recognizing a social side to its work. Questions of support are sent to the Court of Domestic

Relations, cases of great need are referred to the Charity Organization Society.

When a case is taken to court this society is not able to prepare it as carefully as cases of important law firms are prepared. The amount of work handled and the nature of the cases make it necessary to hurry through them in a more superficial way. The society is not able to make exhaustive investigations or employ expensive expert witnesses, and its workers must judge as nearly as they can of the merits of cases by talking with the applicants. Occasionally they find that they have undertaken an unmerited claim. When this is found to be so they are ready to admit their mistake. It must also happen, however, that under this system of procedure they may reject a good claim and leave an applicant without the redress to which he was entitled.

No definite program for educating the immigrant in legal or civic affairs is undertaken by the society. It is the opinion of the attorney in chief that the best education along those lines comes from actual experience. The occasion when the immigrant comes into direct contact with the law is an excellent opportunity for him to be instructed in its operations on that particular point. This is the typical legal attitude, corresponding to the principle of law that the criminal judge is not to rule upon anything but a specific act, which has been committed. While this is a sound principle so far as it prevents punishment for something which has not yet been done and perhaps never will be, it is not so sound when it stands in the way of taking measures against some harm which may or may not happen.

The attorney in chief has, however, a real sense of the value of the legal-aid societies' function in assimilating the foreign born. He has found that the newly arrived European immigrant has a wholesome and profound respect for the law, above that of most native Americans, and he considers it the task of the legal-aid society to preserve this by seeing that the foreign-born person gets justice when he has a grievance. Many of the clients of the office have been embittered and alienated in their loyalty to the country because of their experiences of exploitation. He says that when the immigrant goes to court he is often heard by an unsympathetic, if not corrupt judge, and comes out of the experience with his faith in the democratic ideals of America broken, and with the conviction that in this country, as in all others, the rich thrive on the misery of the poor. If the legal-aid society can assist him in getting justice when he first comes in contact with the courts and the law, it is doing much to preserve and strengthen the loyalty and idealism of the coming citizens of the country.

BOSTON LEGAL-AID SOCIETY

In Boston the legal-aid society does no specialized work for the foreign born, although this is a city of large immigrant population. The attorney in charge said that it was of no interest to an attorney to know the nationality of his client, consequently the matter of nationality has no significance for the legal-aid society. They do not even keep a record of it. He estimated that perhaps 10 per cent of the cases coming to them were Jewish, and the society employs two Jewish lawyers, but these attorneys do not specialize on Jewish cases unless the client cannot speak English. A stenographer who speaks Italian is called in to interpret when necessary. When clients cannot speak English they are told to bring a friend to interpret for them, or are sent to a state office for the aid of immigrants for an interpreter.

Wage-claim cases have decreased because a state bureau has undertaken to collect wages, and all wage claims are now referred to it. The society handles many cases of domestic relations, in co-operation with the local charity organization society, which makes the investigation and recommends action to the legal-aid society. They do not take cases of divorce, because they have not time and also because it would probably not meet with the approval of their contributors. The society also refuses all criminal cases, with the idea that its contributors would object to aiding in the defense of a criminal. To the suggestion made by the investigator that a person charged with crime was not necessarily a criminal, and that according to the Anglo-Saxon principles of justice even a criminal is entitled to protection in his rights before the court, the attorney replied that "most of them are guilty." In the state in which this society is operating, no provision is made for the defense of a criminal unable to employ counsel, except that which is provided by a state bureau of immigrant aid. Consequently, many of the poor men charged with crime go undefended or fall a prey to unscrupulous lawyers.

A view of this office at work shows the attorneys most courteous and considerate in their treatment of the foreign born. Clients are received in private rooms so that their affairs are not exposed to others. The attorneys are young men recently out of law school and they are well versed on points of law, but not always so keen to note the social aspect of the cases. At one time this society employed a social worker, but the experiment was not considered successful and was discontinued.

MEANS OF ADJUSTMENT

Cases come to this society largely from American social agencies. Of the foreign born who need its aid, many have never heard of such a society, and many have money enough to hire lawyers for themselves, frequently, however, only to be defrauded by them.

Some of the foreign-born leaders in that city do not know that there is such a society. Some of the foreign born object to going to the society because they look upon it as a charity. They prefer to have a private lawyer because they feel that he will take a greater interest in the case. The fact that insufficient provision is made for the interpreting of different languages discourages some of the foreign born from making use of this society. They complain that they cannot make their cases clear to the society, and that it in turn cannot explain matters to them. It cannot be said that this society is meeting fully the need of the foreign born for legal aid in that city.

CHICAGO LEGAL-AID BUREAU

The Chicago Legal-Aid Society at the time this study was begun was under the direction of a social worker, and the staff was made up of social workers and lawyers, in the proportion, in 1918, of about two social workers to one lawyer. The first interviews were made by social workers, and the work was carried on with regard to the social as well as the legal factors involved. Much interest was taken in the immigrant cases, and unending patience was shown in dealing with them. About one-half of the applicants were foreign born, in many cases entirely ignorant of our language, yet no interpreters were attached to the office staff.

And no special effort was made to secure foreign-speaking social workers, but often the workers did speak some foreign language. Usually several were able to speak German, and at times one or two could speak French or Polish. As a rule, the person who did not speak English came to the office with a child or a friend to interpret. If not, some one was found in the office among the clients. The disadvantages of this latter practice are obvious.

The superintendent of this society felt that the disadvantage of the trained American worker in not understanding the language was counterbalanced by a greater efficiency in the work itself over that shown by the foreign-born worker. In her opinion the trained American worker assisted by an interpreter is more effective than a less well trained foreign-speaking worker. She thought that a foreigner could not Americanize foreigners; that an intelligent American could interpret America to the immigrant far better than a foreigner could do it.

At various times a judge in that city has asked that a Legal-Aid worker be assigned to his court, not as an attorney, but as a social worker, and at various times a woman has been kept in court in answer to this appeal. The experiment was considered a success, but the funds secured to maintain it were inadequate and the plan had to be given up.

This society would accept the classes of cases usually taken by a legal-aid society, and would even institute proceedings for divorce, but very sparingly. Every case in which divorce was asked was considered carefully, and was taken if social interests would be subserved thereby, if the wife or the family were in physical danger from the man, or property rights, civil rights, or protection for the children was involved. This society was one of those most active in domestic cases generally.

No effort was made to educate the foreign born to a better understanding of the laws nor in the usages and customs of the courts, but the society was active in promoting useful legislation and helping to defeat harmful measures. Among the laws promoted by this society are a law relating to seduction, a law of crimes against children, and an antiloan-shark law.

This society was greatly pressed for funds and was, consequently, restricted in expanding its work to meet the needs of the immigrant population more adequately. It was barely able to care for the cases sent to it from the settlements, the foreign consuls, the newspapers, old clients, friends, attorneys and judges and court employees. Campaigns for publicity several years ago resulted in a large increase in the number of clients without a corresponding increase in the number of subscribers, so that this method of reaching the foreign born had to be discontinued. The society was finally taken over by the United Charities of the city, and is now conducted as a bureau of that agency. Under the new plan, social workers specially trained in legal aid are assigned to district offices to receive applications, discuss cases, and settle them without legal action if possible. In the year before the transfer of the work, while the Legal-Aid Society was a separate organization, 96.3 per cent of the cases were settled without litigation. Such cases can now be handled entirely in the districts. Cases in which court action is necessary are sent to a central office, in which are found four attorneys and two social workers. Assigning workers to districts makes the bureau much more easy of access to clients, and in this way extends the service it renders.

Under the new plan domestic cases are transferred to the social-case-work department of the Charity Organization Society, on the theory that domestic cases involve social rather than legal questions, and that no case of divorce, of nonsupport, or of annulment of marriage should be taken to a legal-aid bureau unless social treatment has failed. If legal action is seen to be a social necessity the case is then referred to the legal-aid bureau. The necessary technical standard is maintained by the organization of the bureau as a separate department of the United Charities, under a legal-aid committee, in which five of the seven members are lawyers, and by the provision of a separate director of legal aid, and of a staff of trained lawyers to do the necessary court work. A professor from a law school has been assigned to act as advisory attorney.

AKRON LEGAL-AID BUREAU

The Akron Legal-Aid Society is also organized as a department of an organized charity. This bureau does not seem to be very well known in its neighborhood and the work is never advertised because the directors think that if it were it would grow so fast that the business could not be handled.

The legal-aid bureau consists of a committee of three attorneys who give advice to clients and sometimes represent clients in courts. They devote only a small part of their time to this work.

The head of the charitable organization looks after the legal problems until it is necessary to call in the help of the attorneys, which is more often to advise the social workers in regard to the treatment of cases than to take over the care of the cases personally.

BUFFALO LEGAL-AID SOCIETY

In Buffalo, a city having an especially large proportion of foreign born in the population, the legal-aid society shows a clientele only a little more than one-third foreign. Large colonies of Italians and Poles are found in the city and there is much defrauding of the foreign born. It cannot be thought that this society comes anywhere near to meeting the needs of the immigrant population in its community.

Their theory of legal aid is giving help to the "worthy poor." Aside from poverty, all clients are regarded as equal, as stated in a report:

Class, creed, or political influence never interferes in the bureau's decision or determination of any matter. The legal-aid bureau exists so that legal aid may be given gratuitously if necessary, to all who may be worthy thereof, and who through poverty cannot procure legal assistance elsewhere.

This society recognizes, however, the possibilities before it of helping the foreign born. In a report, is said:

Not infrequently the alien lacking knowledge of our language seeks legal aid. In these cases it is our prerogative to describe to him the advantages of citizenship and to assist him in communicating with those who will aid in his becoming better acquainted with our language, customs, and ideals.

But at the time of this study not one interpreter was found connected with this society, nor any employee who spoke any language but English, When a non-English-speaking person applies, he is asked to bring in an interpreter of his own. This naturally goes far toward accounting for the small proportion of foreign born served in a city with so large a population of non-English-speaking peoples.

The society employs no social workers, and perhaps connected with this is the fact that out of a total of about 2,000 cases in 1918, only 130 were domestic cases. The social worker is apt to pay more attention to cases of domestic relations, which are so largely social in nature; the lawyer to cases of economic relations, such as wage claims or breach of contract, and so on.

This society will undertake the collection of alimony for a woman if she will bring a letter from an outside attorney asking it to do this. The defense of criminals is not undertaken by the bureau because the judges have power to appoint an attorney to defend an accused person who cannot afford a lawyer. This service is rendered by members of the bar association, who have volunteered to donate a certain amount of time to the defense of persons accused of crime.

When this society finds it necessary to refer a client to an outside attorney, the client is referred to the president of the bar association, who chooses a lawyer. This prevents any appearance of favoritism on the part of the society.

LEGAL-AID BUREAU OF DETROIT

In Detroit a legal-aid bureau is maintained by the local bar association. The work has been carried on by one man, who has brought unflagging energy, industry, and zeal to the task, and has accomplished an almost incredible amount of work.

This man is himself a Czech, and understands Polish, but no interpreter is attached to the office. This office can, however, call upon the information bureau of the Board of Commerce, which affords interpreters for seventeen immigrant languages.

But in this city, which contains a large immigrant population, the legal-aid bureau hardly touches the foreign born. Out of a large population of Poles, at the time of this study, only five Polish cases were listed in the bureau; out of a large Italian colony, only four Italian cases were recorded. Of all of its clients, however, in a given year, from 30 to 45 per cent will be foreign born.

MEANS OF ADJUSTMENT

This bureau is open only to "deserving" applicants, who are unable to procure legal assistance because of their poverty. This legal-aid bureau does not start divorce proceedings, but will defend in any case where the client cannot afford to pay an attorney. So many cases where divorce seemed the only remedy came to them in a recent year that they kept a list of attorneys to whom divorce cases could be referred. Arrangements were made with these lawyers to charge only nominal fees, and it was even possible to pay on the installment plan. The bureau feels that divorce is a luxury and should be paid for.

In this bureau, entirely under the control of the legal profession, with a great expansion of the number of cases each year, those involving domestic relations have not grown. The actual number of cases remains about the same, but, while these amounted to a little over one-fifth of the total number of cases in 1913, in the year 1917-18 they amounted to a little less than 7 per cent.

This society, however, takes cases of failure to pay alimony, and also cases of nonsupport. In these we find a considerable increase. Nonsupport cases had increased from less than one-fourth the number of the cases classed as domestic relations in 1913 to one-and-one-third times as many in 1917-18. Cases of failure to pay alimony amounted in 1913 to about one-third the number of those classed as domestic relations, while in 1917-18 they amounted to one-and-two-thirds times as many. So that the proportion of the three classes to total cases dropped only from 34 per cent in 1913 to 26 per cent in 1917-18.

Criminal cases are not taken, partly because of limitation of resources, partly because the bureau considers that the work is well done by the attorneys appointed by the judges. In the state of Michigan a fund is set aside for the payment of attorneys for the defense of persons accused of crime who are too poor to pay a lawyer.

CLEVELAND LEGAL-AID SOCIETY

In Cleveland, a city with a large foreign-born population, the staff of the legal-aid society is composed entirely of attorneys. But in the office affairs are conducted with the patience and interest in the social aspect of cases that does or should characterize the method of the social workers. The head of this bureau is interested in the possibilities of social work in his office, and would like to try the experiment of introducing social workers to interview clients when they first come, leaving to the lawyers the purely legal work. This attorney is unusual among legal-aid attorneys in showing an interest in the number of foreign born who are reached. In 1918 the society registered clients of 42 different nationalities, and 41 per cent of all of their clients were nonnaturalized immigrants.

The society has co-operated with the Americanization Bureau of the city in urging the alien to take out citizenship papers and to go to night school and learn English, for his own protection. And there are no interpreters in the employ of this office, on the theory that their absence is an incentive to the foreign born to learn English, since it is difficult for him to get an interpreter himself, and it costs him time and money to make himself understood if he has to provide his own interpreter. It is the policy of this society to avoid litigation where possible, and settle difficulties through arbitration and adjustment without court action.

This society accepts divorce cases more freely than some of the other societies are in the habit of doing.

MEANS OF ADJUSTMENT

The board of directors leaves it to the discretion of the attorneys to institute divorce proceedings where they think it necessary.

It also takes criminal cases, the record for 1917-18 showing somewhat over 2 per cent of its cases to be of that nature. In 1914, over 5 per cent of the cases were criminal, a larger proportion than was shown for any of the large cities in the cases studied in *Justice and the Poor*.[1]

The society has been active in securing the passage of legislation, notably an act making it a felony for a husband to desert a pregnant wife.

Like other legal-aid societies, this society takes no publicity measures because of the lack of means to carry on a larger business, and of it, as of other societies, it can be said that it is not fully meeting the need of the foreign population.

LEGAL AID IN CALIFORNIA

A legal-aid society in San Francisco was organized at the initiative of the State Immigration Commission, in co-operation with the bench and bar association and the organized charities of the city. Contributions come entirely from the bar of the city. Unlike most of the other societies, the bulk of their cases involve domestic relations. This is probably because the state Department of Labor relieves them of the handling of wage claims, a class of cases which makes up a large part of the work of a legal-aid society in states where no such state action is taken.

This society is not very well known, and does not wish to be, as it could not handle any more work than comes to it now, mainly through the Immigration

---

[1] *Justice and the Poor*, p. 155.

Commission, the consulates, and the charitable organizations. Few non-English-speaking clients are on its roll and it keeps no record of nationalities, notwithstanding the fact that the state contains considerable colonies of Italians, Russians, and Mexicans, to say nothing of other nationalities. It has refrained from asking about nationalities since the war, because it feels that people are sensitive on this matter.

LEGAL AID GIVEN BY SOCIAL AGENCIES

Social agencies dealing with one and another phase of the social problem, encounter the need for legal aid among their clients and try to meet it in one way and another, in connection with their primary functions. Charity-organization societies and social settlements refer cases to the nearest legal-aid society or try to afford help directly, perhaps by enlisting volunteer legal service from the ranks of their supporters, or by establishing legal bureaus of their own. Some of the charity-organization societies have established or acquired (as in the case already noted) separate bureaus for the giving of legal aid.

The Salvation Army in this country has not made a regular business of giving legal aid, but so many persons go to them, asking for advice on business and legal matters, that they have for some years had a practicing attorney connected with their staff at national headquarters. Few of their clients, however, are non-English-speaking immigrants.

LEGAL AID SPECIFICALLY FOR THE FOREIGN BORN

The legal-aid societies so far considered render service only incidentally to the foreign born, so far as he is among the "poor" whom it is their purpose to serve.

The foreign-born client is, however, primarily in mind in another group of societies giving legal aid.

A strong group devote themselves to the legal problems arising from Jewish immigration. The Educational Alliance, of New York, an institution established for the Americanization of the immigrant, conducts an active legal-aid bureau. This bureau does not shut out any applicant on the basis of race or religion, but its work is chiefly with Jewish immigrants. The director of the alliance, Dr. Fleishman, describes its purposes, and its qualifications to carry these out, as follows:

The lands from which the Jewish immigrants come have for the greater part deprived them of any standing in the courts and to a very large extent have failed to offer them an opportunity to participate in the civic life of the community. Because of its thorough knowledge of the Jewish immigrant and through the specialized and concentrated efforts made by the Alliance in his behalf, the institution is peculiarly fitted to aid the immigrant in matters requiring the intervention of the legal authorities. It is also especially fitted to carry out the more important policy of preventing resort to the courts through arbitration and adjustment. Only a comparatively small percentage of the cases that come to the bureau reach the courts. Many of the claims are the result of misunderstanding, ignorance of commercial procedure, ignorance of the language, and the immigrant because of these deficiencies readily falls a prey to those who are ever ready to reap whatever profit they may at his expense.

In this bureau we are to note that the aim reaches beyond the purely legal help to the broader forms of social work.

It would be a mistake to assume that the only function of the legal-aid bureau is the untangling of the legal difficulties of the immigrant. Our knowledge of the people enables us to make the bureau a far-reaching activity. Those presenting legal claims are urged to join many of its other activities [the Alliance]. Mothers are made members of the Mothers' Clubs, and are invited to the various lectures and gatherings. The children are enrolled in the Club Department and in the various classes. Very often a legal difficulty brought to the bureau results in the active participation in the work of the Alliance of the entire family of the client.

In many respects the legal work of this bureau differs from that of other associations devoted to legal aid. The customs and the traditions of the Jewish immigrant in the home lands are of talmudic and rabbinic origin. In the Jewish communities of Eastern Europe the ancient biblical laws are still those by which the Jewish community guides itself and the administrations of these codes in the hands of the rabbinical authorities. It is not difficult to understand what complications arise on the arrival of the immigrant in America. All the ancient laws and customs, particularly those of marriage and divorce must be thrown aside.

The Educational Alliance was instrumental many years ago in doing away with what was known as the "Ghet" evil[1] and it has been responsible for much legislation for the benefit and protection of the immigrant. Much of the work of the bureau is of a propaganda nature. This work can be effectively done only by those who possess a thorough knowledge of the psychology of the Jew, his social and economic life, his traditions, his customs, and his language. It must not be inferred from this that the Jew is not a law-abiding or law-loving individual. The contrary is the truth, but his lack of recognition on the part of the governments of eastern Europe makes necessary a certain preparation for participation in American civic life, and it is the endeavor of the Legal Aid Bureau to aid in the process. This broader educa-

---

[1] The rabbinical divorce accepted as lawful in some eastern European countries, by which a rabbi may grant divorce on the simple request of the husband to be freed from his wife. This practice, although not recognized by law in this country, was carried on until stopped as described, causing many distressing domestic situations.

tional field we consider fully as important as a solution of the immigrant's legal difficulties.

This bureau, like other legal-aid bureaus, makes every effort to settle by conciliation and arbitration the matters referred to it, avoiding litigation as far as possible. On the average, fewer than 1 per cent of the cases coming to them go to court. Special arrangements are made to secure the personal appearance of parties to a dispute before representatives of the bureau, so that matters may be cleared up through discussion.

In claims against employers, if the person against whom complaint is made fails to answer a letter, the possibility that this is owing to inability to understand English is taken into account, and if he has failed to call at the office, as requested, the possibility that if he is a small employer he may be unable to call without closing up his place of business is realized. To meet these difficulties an assistant is assigned to visit employers who fail to answer letters. Many cases are thus settled in the employer's office which would otherwise have to be taken to court for adjudication.

Another means of making the bureau accessible to complainants and those complained of is to keep it open evenings and Sundays. By such methods the society has succeeded in winning the respect and friendliness of employers, and a considerable degree of coöperation, from them. It is able to get the employer to the office and into relations of conference in a surprising number of cases, and with surprisingly little effort.

Another admirable feature of its method is to leave clients free to decide matters for themselves, after they have received full information, without urging one or another course of action.

The visitor to the office of this society, however, notes that the cases are handled so rapidly that the explanations made do not fully enlighten the clients. The attorneys use technical terms, which the clients do not understand, and often they seem puzzled to know what action they are supposed to take. At this point the equipment of racial psychology seems to break down, for the typical client of this bureau is accustomed in his own country to endless discussion in the settlement of the simplest affairs, and cannot understand much without it.

This bureau, although recognizing the social worker's point of view in attempting to give something to clients beyond legal aid, in attempting to understand them as social beings, does not employ social workers in its office.

In general, the service is intended for poor people, but no maximum income is set above which an applicant may not receive attention. The fact that a man is earning $25 or $30 a week is not considered a bar to receiving the services of the society, for it is considered that the wages he is then receiving may be temporary, that he has to lose time in making his claim, and that the ordinary lawyer's fee in addition would be too heavy a burden upon him.

If an applicant is so well-to-do that he is not considered a proper client for the bureau, he is not turned away to fall a victim to some unscrupulous lawyer, but is given a list of reputable attorneys personally known to the bureau as trustworthy from which he can choose counsel. Giving a list from which the client may make his own choice relieves the society of the charge on the part of members of the legal profession of favoring certain lawyers, and relieves it of responsibility for the outcome of the case, in the estimation of the client.

The bureau undertakes the classes of cases usually received by a legal-aid society. In contrast to some of the societies, however, it will undertake the collection of any claim no matter how small, if it is considered just. No difficulty is found in securing service of summons for the smallest claims—one of 94 cents is noted among the cases—and the society is ready to take them to court if necessary.

THE BUREAU OF PERSONAL SERVICE

A bureau for the service of Jewish people in Chicago is listed as a legal aid in *Justice and the Poor*, but it seems to be in fact rather a bureau of advice and relief, as the society employs no attorneys. Every effort is made to keep cases out of court, but when court action is necessary, the clients are accompanied to court by members of the staff who are not attorneys. All the workers speak Yiddish or German, or both—an adequate equipment for the cases they handle.

THE NATIONAL DESERTION BUREAU

The National Desertion Bureau is an agency doing legal work in Jewish cases, which is widely known throughout the country. This society came into existence through the efforts of Jewish social agencies which were endeavoring to find some adequate solution of the problem of desertion—a problem accentuated by the newer immigration. The purpose of the bureau is to apprehend husbands and wives who have left their families unprovided for, and to make the best arrangement possible for the support and welfare of the family. The methods and technique of finding and prosecuting the offender have, so far, received more attention than those of family rehabilitation. The policy of the bureau as stated, however, is to effect amicable adjustments and reconciliations in every instance where this can be done.

They feel that the home is the bulwark of society and should be kept intact.

The central office employs attorneys who do court and legal work, and investigators who do social work. The attorneys on the staff must have passed the bar examination, but the investigators are not required to have training in the methods of social work. All of the workers are Jewish, and must be able to speak Yiddish. In addition, most of them speak German, and some of them Russian. The bureau also secures the services of volunteer lawyers in cities throughout the country, and of the Jewish welfare agencies in the various communities for legal and social work.

One of the best-known features of the desertion bureau is the "Gallery of Missing Husbands" consisting of photographs of the missing men, published in the leading Jewish newspapers. The "gallery" is a vital interest of the Jewish reading public, and many people buy the papers in which it appears for the sole purpose of studying it. And replies to the appeals for information about these culprits are received from all over the country.

In its court work the bureau is not inclined to be lenient with offenders and does not hesitate to use drastic measures. It insists upon a decided attitude on the part of the wife also. It will not take a case unless the woman is willing to prosecute.

The organization is just beginning to develop the social side of its work. Effective first visits are made to families, but follow-up visits are not recognized as a necessary element in treatment. There is no developed treatment of the problems allied to the desertion problem, in the cases which the bureau handles. When there is evidence of ill health the client is referred to a dispensary. If the applicant is in need of support, she is turned over to the United Hebrew Charities. The destitute, the homeless, the sick are referred to appropriate agencies. At one time the bureau employed a psychiatrist, but this work has been discontinued.

The greater number of the applicants at the bureau are women of foreign birth, mostly from Russia and Poland. Aside from the language requirement for workers, there is little evidence of an attempt to formulate and meet racial or national peculiarities in the problem, and members of the staff are not unanimous in recognizing such differences. The director is of the opinion that there are none. He is inclined to think that the causes for desertion are the same for all groups of people, and that under certain given circumstances anyone will desert, whatever his race or nationality. There is no opposition from private attorneys to the work of the bureau, as the sort of case attended to by them is not sufficiently profitable to attract the private lawyer.

As the woman in the family is usually the applicant, the men are inclined to look upon this bureau as a woman's institution, but the investigators try to remove this misunderstanding wherever possible, and point out to the man that the welfare and happiness of all members of the family is desired.

INTERNATIONAL INSTITUTES, Y. W. C. A.

The Young Women's Christian Association has organized a Division for Foreign-born Women which directs local branches, called international institutes, in various cities throughout the country. The purpose of these institutes is to give such aid as seems to be necessary to foreign-speaking women in the communities in which they are located.

In the course of the work many problems arise which call for legal aid, and although the institutes have no specialized legal-aid department, they try to meet the need by giving such help as the nonlegal worker can render, by advice and information and efforts toward adjustment and conciliation, or by referring cases to the nearest legal-aid society or to some private attorney who will volunteer to help.

Typical cases are those involving nonpayment of wages, which the workers settle wherever possible by an agreement between the two parties. The workers are also often called on to help in the court proceedings incident to obtaining support and the adjustment of family difficulties.

The institutes are notable among American agencies working with the foreign born in being well equipped with workers of the nationality and speaking the language of the people with whom they are to deal. In Cleveland, for example, of twelve workers, three spoke English only; the remaining nine, among them, spoke, in addition to English, Czech, German, Polish, Serbian, Croatian, Slovenian, Hungarian, Finnish, Italian, French, Spanish, Bulgarian, and Lithuanian.

In other places, Russians, Armenians, Greeks, and other representatives of our newer immigration are found as workers in these institutes. This equipment of foreign-speaking workers affords the opportunity for a particularly valuable service in legal aid, the supplying of interpreters, in court, or at departmental hearings, or at the offices of other social agencies, like the legal-aid societies, which are not equipped with foreign-speaking workers, and where the peculiar problems of the foreign born are not understood.

The demand for this service, in fact, has been so great that the institutes have been obliged to restrict it. Interpreting from one language to another is only an incident in a broader social work of the institute worker, and the national leaders do not wish this broader work to be obscured in the public mind by the smaller task of interpretation, aside from the fact that the demands upon the time of the worker are excessive. The national headquarters has established a policy that the institute workers may be used in cases of emergency, and in cases where it seems desirable to demonstrate the necessity for a provision of adequate interpreters. If the institute is called upon too frequently the agency making the demand is urged to provide the necessary persons to do the work.

In court cases workers have been a wholesome check upon the official interpreter, and in some communities have been able to impress upon the courts the necessity for providing adequate interpreters.

In contrast to some other organizations giving legal aid to the foreign born, the Y. W. C. A. institutes have been found, in the course of this study, standing by the immigrant not only in the ordinary complications of life requiring legal aid, but in labor and political troubles. In Pittsburgh, as has been noted, an interpreter from the institute called in by the immigrant inspector in charge, courageously protested against false interpretations and mishandling of cases of Russians in deportation proceedings. In Lawrence, in Passaic, institute workers were found observing the handling of labor cases by courts and police, and protesting against unfair treatment. Each institute office visited in the course of this study has shown a true sympathy with the foreign born, and it is probably true of them in general, as it is true of the Cleveland institute, as expressed by its head, that they "try to think in terms of the foreign-born people."

The director of the Division of Foreign-born Women feels that they have made one important contribution to work with the foreign born—they have demonstrated the necessity of using foreign-language workers for work among non-English-speaking women. The national leaders are fully convinced that for direct work among the foreign-born women only foreign-speaking women are efficient, and that the workers should not only speak the language of those with whom they work, but should have the same cultural background. For peoples from parts of Europe where national or racial differences are keenly felt, this must be carefully considered in choosing a worker.

It is, however, difficult to find women with the necessary knowledge of languages who have the necessary social training. The American worker is needed, it is thought, in addition to the foreign-speaking workers, to correlate the work of the foreign-language secretaries, and to win the confidence and co-operation of various groups in the community.

Protection of the newly arrived immigrant is a considerable part of the work of the international institutes. The secretaries try to come in contact with immigrant women on their first arrival in the community, and make known the services they are prepared to render. They meet boats and trains and call upon girls in lodging houses. Some institutes have accommodations for housing girls.

Under the Division for Foreign-born Women a bureau of information is organized. Part of its work is to give to the foreign peoples the information about the laws and the courts which they are likely to need. Excellent pamphlets have been prepared, framed in simple language that the immigrant can understand on the nature and function of the courts, the provisions of laws likely to affect the immigrant most directly. These pamphlets are printed in all the important foreign languages and are used in connection with classes held by the institutes.

Not every organization attempting to instruct the foreign born in our laws and customs appreciates the difficulties in the way of making such collections of information really useful. Sometimes a young attorney prepares a bald statement of legal provisions and the organization of courts that even a native-born American, with some acquaintance with the subject cannot read with interest or understanding. After the subject matter has been expressed in English in the clear and concrete way necessary to impress the untrained mind of the immigrant, it is difficult to secure satisfactory translations into the different foreign languages. An intimate knowledge of both languages—English and that into which the translation is to be made—and facility in idiomatic expression are essential. It is also necessary that the translator appreciate the cultural background of the nationality for which the pamphlet is intended, in order that just the right meaning shall be conveyed by the translation. The bureau of information has appreciated all of these necessities, and has to a great extent succeeded in meeting them.

LEGAL AID PROVIDED BY THE FOREIGN BORN

Apparently little provision for legal aid is made among the foreign groups themselves, or for any single foreign group apart from the others, except for the Jewish immigrants. The legal aid afforded to Jewish immigrants is provided for by established residents of the community, who, although Jewish, are primarily Americans. Aliens of certain nationalities find legal aid in the offices of their respective consuls. This is especially true of the Italians. Italian consulates in large cities, in accordance with the general policy of the Italian government to follow their nationals to foreign countries, do a fairly active legal-aid work. In Chicago a practicing lawyer at the head of the legal-aid division not only prepares cases, but goes to court with them. In important cases, the suit is turned over to a firm that represents the consulate. The office will accept wage claims, personal injury or bankrupt cases, but will not touch criminal cases unless under exceptional circumstances. The staff of the consulate has no sympathy for the Italian criminal, and thinks that the Americans are not sufficiently severe with them. They say that the Italian criminal knows better than to go to the consulate for help.

Among the many societies for mutual aid, or national propaganda among the immigration groups, little or no organized provision for legal aid is found. A Polish leader explained, for his people, that although legal protection for the Poles was badly needed here, because the American courts did not understand the Pole, especially in providing Jewish interpreters who are prejudiced against the Polish people, the Polish organizations do little or nothing to help the situation. The organization with which he was connected does not send men to court to check up interpreters because of trouble and expense. He said that the Poles do not come to them with that kind of trouble. If they did, probably the organization would help them out.

The editor of a Polish newspaper confirmed this statement that the Poles do not ask for legal aid. In his opinion, they are too self-sufficient and prefer to suffer rather than to ask help from anyone. From the long list of Polish cases found at the legal-aid societies conducted by native Americans, it would seem that there must be some other reasons for their failure to appeal to their own national societies. Possibly the societies are not sufficiently interested in the life of the Pole in this country, possibly they embrace in their membership too many of the more prosperous nationals who make a living out of attending to the legal difficulties of the immigrant for pay.

As an exception may be noted the Polish Women's Alliance, with headquarters in Chicago, which gives indirect legal help to Polish women. Usually, however, only the more serious cases attract their attention, such as have been given publicity through the newspapers, and such legal help as is given is especially provided for each occasion.

In contrast to the general inactivity of the Polish societies, an investigator for this study found in Buffalo a little group of Polish lawyers banded together to protect their countrymen. The original intention of the group had been to conduct a campaign of education and warning through the foreign-language press. Members of the group were to write editorials, warning against business solicitors, urging against lending money without receipts and without security, and explaining the difference between the notary public in Europe and the same person in the United States. This part of the work, however, was neglected under pressure of the need that was immediately felt, as soon as they got to work, of unmasking and prosecuting persons practicing law without a license, and attorneys guilty of dishonest practices. They have recently sent one of these sharpers to the penitentiary, and brought two others before the bar association.

INDUSTRIAL LEGAL AID

Legal aid for the foreign born, not because they are members of some foreign group or are among the

509

"poor," but because they are workers, is provided in many large industrial establishments, as a logical development of "welfare work." This is an activity of recent development. Only one establishment giving such aid is noted in *Justice and the Poor*. At the time of this study, fourteen establishments were found and visited in only four cities, and reports were received from a number of others, which give legal aid in one form or another to their employees.

The fourteen establishments visited represented the metal, rubber, and clothing industries. Each employed a large number of workmen, the proportion of foreign born among them ranging from 25 to 50 per cent or over for the diffcrent establishments.

Legal aid was provided according to different methods in different establishments. Legal assistance might be given in a casual way when occasion arose. There might be some one person not a lawyer to whom the workers understood they might come for advice. In one establishment it was the purchasing agent; in another, the employment manager, or perhaps, if a workman got into serious difficulty, an attorney for the company might help him out. Or legal aid might be definitely arranged for, under some labor or welfare bureau, or in a separate legal-aid bureau. Nine of the establishments had such a bureau; in five of them the head was a social worker, in four, a lawyer.

When the legal-aid work of one of these establishments is in charge of a social worker without legal training, he usually may draw upon the legal knowledge of the attorneys of the firm to help him with his cases. The attorney of the firm does not, however, take cases of workers in the establishment he represents, to court.

The service rendered in these industrial legal-aid

bureaus is primarily advice, and the end sought is the prevention of trouble, rather than a remedy through court proceedings. This service involves the use of the social worker's method of conciliation and adjustment, which is followed even in bureaus where the head of the bureau is a lawyer.

The service given by these industrial bureaus is not restricted to the "poor," and the fact that so many well-paid workmen get into trouble from which it is necessary for some disinterested service to help them out, indicates the inadequacy of the conception held by the average legal-aid society, that poverty is the only basis of need for service.

Perhaps the greatest number of cases handled in these bureaus are those involving the purchase of real estate, in which the service of the industrial legal aid prevents them from being swindled. In some cases advice is given as to whether the property is worth the money asked. Another form of service consists in examining the contracts and helping to make out other legal papers. This is done perhaps more frequently than advising about the value of property.

Garnishment cases are also numerous. The industrial legal-aid service confers with credit houses, sees whether claims are well founded, and sometimes arranges for pro-rata payments so that the client can pay up without hardship. Some arrange for loans, so that the employee is not obliged to deal with loan sharks.

Domestic difficulties are referred to these bureaus, and are looked after by most of them. The legal-aid worker in one establishment, however, said that there were "no such cases"; the worker in another would not take them when presented. In this class of cases especially an effort is made to settle difficulties without recourse to the law, by advice, and sometimes by admonition and instruction to wife or husband, or both, on their duties and deficiencies.

If employees are charged with some minor offense, such as disorderly conduct, most of the establishments studied try to look after his interests, see that he has witnesses, and produce records showing character.

Most of the service rendered is outside the court, and if a court appearance is necessary, it is often that of a friend or a witness, rather than of a lawyer to see the case through a trial. In fact, most of the establishments do not, as a regular practice, see cases through a court trial—their appearances are largely to look after arrested or accused employees, to secure bail or to produce witnesses. Some of the establishments, however, will have nothing to do with this class of cases—if an employee gets into trouble of this kind, it is his own lookout.

It is a common practice among them, however, to refer the employee to an outside lawyer when a case comes up of such a nature that it has to be taken through the regular court procedure. This is a legitimate means of assistance to this class of workers, because they can, in most instances, afford to pay a moderate and reasonable lawyer's fee, and the company in recommending them to a lawyer, takes care to see that the character of the lawyer is good, and that his fee is not excessive, thus rescuing the workingman from the exploiting lawyer who is so great a source of trouble.

Many of the establishments give the ordinary notarial service free of charge, and write letters and attend to business as the "business agent" of unsavory reputation pretends to do but does not. Among the services rendered during the past years has been assistance in making out income-tax reports. One establishment assumed responsibility for any errors caused by confusing instructions of the government, which, if followed literally, would have resulted in loss to its employees.

Many of the establishments also took pains to instruct their employees in such matters of law as would be desirable for them to know about.

The equipment of these industrial legal-aid bureaus in knowledge of language and customs of foreign peoples seems to be somewhat above that of the average legal-aid society. In some of the establishments studied, the head of the legal-aid bureau was foreign born, understanding a number of languages and familiar with the psychology of the people. No regular force of interpreters can be detailed to such work, in the average establishment, but when interpretation is needed, some fellow workman or foreman is called in, with the same disadvantage found in other cases where the interpreter is a casual bystander or a friend—or enemy—of the client. One of the bureaus is careful to take an interpreter of its own to court hearings, to check up the accuracy of the court interpreter.

VALUE OF INDUSTRIAL LEGAL AID

Are any objections to be brought against this method of giving legal aid to the workman through the establishment that employs him? Does it fully meet the need of the foreign workman, and is he satisfied with it, and is it, for him, a means of making him better satisfied with the country to which he has come?

The usual objections to "welfare work" in general may be urged against this form of assistance. The suspicion may arise that the service rendered is not disinterested, but is given only as a means of pacifying the worker. And the worker may object to paternal interference in his affairs. The establishments studied differed in their attitude on this point. One of the establishments is strongly paternal, assuming charge of the worker's legal affairs, as it does of all the rest of his life. Another firm, on the contrary, feels the danger involved in this attitude so strongly that it tries to avoid the least appearance of paternalism. This establishment loans money to its employees, and when application is made the man is not asked why he wants the money, nor is the offer made to prepare papers for him. He is given full information and encouraged to transact the actual business for himself.

The full working of the principle of conciliation must be somewhat hampered by the relation in which the employee stands to the legal adviser, who is also his employer. He naturally feels a strong undercurrent of pressure to follow the course laid down by the employer's representative, if he wants to keep his job, even when nothing in the way of direct pressure is exerted, as it actually is in one plant, where employment depends upon home conditions and the family situation.

Perhaps the worker may contrast the attitude of protection taken by the establishment in real estate and domestic cases with the attitude of conflict in the labor cases that mean so much to the workman. When wholesale raids were made upon the foreign workingmen in the disturbances of 1919-20, the foreign-born workers did not find the industrial establishments sending representatives to the court to give testimony to their good character (although this could have been done quite properly in many of the cases). On the contrary, they found some of them maintaining a spy system calculated to land as many of them as possible in a legal trap.

Perhaps the instance of the Youngstown Sheet and Tube Company may be in point as indicating why industrial legal aid may not be an entire success.

MEANS OF ADJUSTMENT

That company, as stated by one of its representatives, in a description of the legal-aid work it carried on, is one of the largest employers of labor in the United States, employing 14,000 men, of whom about 12,000 are unskilled, and of these perhaps 70 per cent are foreign born. This company carried on legal-aid work in a legal bureau under an industrial relations department. The head of this bureau in an account of the work urges the value of the legal-aid service for reducing the labor turnover, saying that on this ground expenditure is justified in perfecting an efficient organization whose duty it shall be to render confidential legal aid and defense to employees, "whose troubles, though small, are legion."

This work is part of a general work in which, since "American ideals should be before the eyes of all employees, therefore, we find that the employer of to-day must be as it were a big brother, and assist him (the foreigner) in laying aside his European mode of life and thinking and adopt our own in their stead. . . . An employee who can be taught to live cleanly and truly thinks in terms of American principles, will most assuredly be a better employee, both for himself and others. In the above respect, our legal department supervises the taking out of first papers and perfecting naturalization."

A claim department acts to secure compensation for injured employees and their families in case of death. The legal department also assists the dependents of the deceased employees in a legal settlement of the property rights of the deceased, without expense. Other cases assisted are those in which an employee is injured outside of the employment of the company. Their activity is confined to efforts at adjustment. If court appearance is necessary, a competent attorney is secured at the expense of the employee. The department also concerns itself with wage-attachment cases. In these paternal help and advice are given to the workers who seem unable to manage their own affairs, and admonition and discipline to those who seem inclined to neglect their honest debts. The legal department feels other duties toward the employee. The account goes on:

Many times we find that in order to instil respect and order, as well as our righteousness, that we are often required to turn temporarily at least, our faces against our employees and assist our safety department in prosecuting them for petty thefts, etc. The employees must learn that their employer is only their friend and protector so long as they may be in the right.

Advice on all sorts of matters is given to employees. And the legal bureau holds itself open to give the same aid as a practicing attorney, except that it will not appear as attorney for employees in court cases, except in attachment cases. As a result of these activities the head of the bureau notes a growth

more marked as time passes, of the feeling of confidence that naturally arises between attorney and client. We endeavor to impress upon the employee that it is not the individual who may be in the legal department at the time who is his benefactor, but that it is his employer who, through such an organization and agency, stands ready to assist him in his difficulties, no matter how small, because experience teaches that to him they are all important.

In the account of the deportations it was noted that in the Akron cases one Dan Kutz, arrested with the four men on the *Buford*, disappeared from the group and was found afterward at Youngstown as a spy. In the account of the Monessen cases it was noted that one Yankevich, former member of the state constabulary, after winning the confidence of the Russian workers in that town, as a spy and suspected agent provocateur, went to Youngstown for the summer to ply his

trade further. Among the Communist cases, one Dmitri
Ivankow,[1] (or Iwankiw, as it was spelled in the official
record) who had been a writer for foreign-language
papers, and an interpreter, had been charged with em-
bezzlement in Pittsburgh, and with running an illicit
still in Youngstown. He became an employee in June,
1919, of a detective agency in Pittsburgh, which was
furnishing information to the Department of Justice,
and was detailed to the Youngstown Sheet and Tube
Company to find out about the activities of the Russian
anarchists. There he not only tried to find out things,
but acted as a true agent provocateur by establishing a
local of the Communist party and inducing men to join
it. This man was arrested with the Communists, and
had some difficulty in getting freed. Assistant Secretary Post, who uncovered so much of the irregularity in
deportation proceedings, charged that Ivankow furnished reports to the Youngstown Sheet and Tube
Company, which were in turn transmitted to the agent
of the Department of Justice, and that the bond under
which Ivankow was released was furnished by the
company.

It is of interest to note that this is the only case that
has come to the writer's attention in which a workman
under charge of deportation was bailed out by his
employer.

Secretary Post thought this man deportable, and
issued a warrant on June 12, 1920, for his deportation
for committing a crime involving moral turpitude. On
June 26, 1920, *The Survey* notes that

The Youngstown Sheet and Tube Company, which for
five years has been one of the leaders in welfare work in the

[1] For details of this case, see C. M. Panunzio, *The Deportation
Cases of 1919–20*, p. 31.

country, has come to the conclusion that some phases of welfare work are a waste of time and effort, that they serve to antagonize the workers rather than to make them more friendly, and that it is the part of wisdom to curtail an expenditure which is not producing desirable results. . . . Schools for foreign-born workers' legal-aid and visiting nursing have been altogether abandoned by the company. . . . The company is now convinced that the workers are distrustful of all these services, and that they would prefer to act for themselves and to have the cost of the services added to their wages.

WORKINGMEN'S LEGAL AID

An organization through which workingmen as a group provide legal aid to individual workingmen is the Labor Secretariat of New York City. This agency is conducted for the benefit of members of trade unions which contribute to the plan in proportion to their regular membership. It is under the direction of a board of delegates representing various unions, and a board of directors elected by the board of delegates. The office retains the services of an attorney.

The general purpose of the secretariat is to protect the legal rights of the unions and their members. A large proportion of the cases presented in monthly reports are cases of accident, coming under the compensation law, but apparently all sorts of cases are taken. The secretariat will defend in criminal cases, small and large. Monthly reports show cases in which advice was given or action taken involving the behavior of pickets, defense for reckless driving, for violation of the excise law, for disorderly conduct (probably picketing), for assault. Wage claims and other money claims are taken. One is amusingly entitled, "Claim of $65 for damaged overcoat caused by attack on him on account of argument." One is for breach of contract of employment, one for payment of railroad fare promised when a job was given.

The advantage of this plan for the worker is that it is run according to his own ideas. The persons for whom the work is done are setting the standard, so that there is no question of one class superimposing its standard of limitation of cases taken, or methods of handling them, as may arise in connection with the work of the general legal-aid societies and the industrial legal aid given by employers.

For workers in strike difficulties, the labor union to which they belong provides counsel, free of charge, to the individual member, and for the foreign born held in deportation proceedings for connection with some organization, attorneys are found to represent the organization and defend the accused person at the hearings and before the courts. But as has been pointed out, the legal service available for persons under charges of deportation for political causes in the past two years has been narrowly limited. Practicing lawyers have been afraid to take these cases, because of the general popular sentiment against them. An attorney who ventured to defend such cases, in some communities had to face a social and business ostracism which he could not afford.

PROTECTION OF THE IMMIGRANT

Three state bureaus and one active private society undertake the general task of protecting the immigrant, so that he shall not need the services of lawyers, and of helping him to get legal service, when that is found necessary. An important function of these bureaus and societies is to push the prosecution of exploiters and others who mistreat the immigrant; another is to frame and urge legislation to check these evils.

THE IMMIGRANT'S DAY IN COURT

The first state bureau to be established was the Bureau of Industries and Immigration, in New York—naturally—as the evils of exploitation at that great gateway of immigration forced themselves upon public attention as they did nowhere else. The bureau was created, as a division of the New York State Department of Labor, under a law passed in 1910, which gave to the new bureau broad general powers of investigation, research, and coöperation with other departments in enforcing the laws affecting the immigrant.

In its first year of activity the New York bureau concerned itself with the distribution of labor, the regulation of distributing agencies such as the employment bureaus, with the protection of the unemployed, with transportation, including baggage transfer, with labor camps and colonies, with industrial calamities, personal injuries, child labor.

The bureau was especially active in pursuit of the irresponsible private banks and other agencies of exploitation, such as the real estate dealers, fraudulent benevolent and fraternal societies, raffles, and stock companies. It interested itself besides in the notaries public and information bureaus and collection agencies which had been exploiting the immigrant. The bureau was also directed by the law to assist in education and naturalization. To carry out this purpose it undertook the registration of names of children, on first arrival, so that they could be reached by school officers.

In the bureau a division of complaints and adjustment was opened for the benefit of individual immigrants. The plan of action of this division is outlined in the first report of the bureau.[1]

[1] *First Annual Report of the Bureau of Industries and Immigration, 1911*, p. 123.

MEANS OF ADJUSTMENT

The experience of the bureau in the first few months of its existence has demonstrated that the alien has peculiar problems of language and adjustment in a new country which, while often properly matters for a court, can be settled or adjusted before an impartial state referee who can secure for him a hearing and can bring the aggrieved parties together. The chief difficulty is that the alien, being so often friendless, unemployed, without money, and unable to make himself heard, cannot reach his employer or associate to state his case, or cannot get into court or afford the cost or delay incident to a hearing there. While the bureau has no legal power to enforce its decisions, it can, in criminal cases, through duly constituted authorities, prepare the case and appear with the district attorney in behalf of the friendless, helpless alien. It can investigate and assure itself and such authorities of the facts in the case, thereby simplifying the procedure or preventing unnecessary litigation. It can urge voluntary settlements on the part of aggrieved parties, and can advise terms of settlement after due investigation.

It is seen, then, that the bureau has the function of a legal-aid bureau so far as conciliation and adjustment, the major part of the work of a legal-aid bureau, is concerned, with additional privileges of coöperation with the district attorney in the prosecution of exploiters.

The work outlined, however, was too heavy for the bureau as organized, and became more so as time went on. The official service possible under an exceedingly small initial appropriation had to be supplemented by the volunteer service of public-spirited individuals. But the staff, small as it was, always included foreign-speaking workers. During the first years of its existence the bureau did bring about valuable additions to the banking legislation, conducted some effective campaigns against swindlers, and was able to attend to a moderate number of individual complaints. In the first year, 515 complaints were received and taken care of; the following year, 1,112; the next year, 2,121; 3,482 in 1914; 2,357 in 1915; 1,044 in nine months of 1916; and 1,040 in 1917. Since that year no statistical report has been printed.

During these years the management of the bureau has been changed, and the staff, too small even at first for the work which had to be done, has been reduced. The work seemed to be losing its vitality, and the Governor's Reconstruction Commission of 1919 recommended that the bureau be abolished as ineffective.

CALIFORNIA COMMISSION OF IMMIGRATION

In 1913 California established a Commission of Immigration and Housing to protect and aid immigrants within the state, under a law giving it powers similar to those of the New York bureau, with some important additional functions. The California commission, however, unlike the New York bureau, is an independent body, under no existing bureau. The theory underlying the work of the commission is outlined in the annual report for the year 1918 as follows:

This commission was built upon the conviction that all the problems which touch the immigrant take on a distinct aspect peculiar to no problem of the native born. It was built upon the conviction that the foreign born suffer great hardships because from the moment of his arrival, he is placed at a disadvantage, and that, in order that he may be placed upon an equal footing with his native-born neighbor, definite constructive aid must be given him in overcoming his handicaps. Furthermore, it was built on the conviction that as the immigrant suffers from his shortcomings, so does the community in which he lives suffer with him. . . . And then came the war, came war work, came the cry for Americanization. . . . From the start, in the scheme of the commission, these tasks outlined themselves, following the belief that before a man should be asked to become a good American by being worthy of his surroundings, those surroundings should be made worthy of a good American.

The work of the commission directly applicable to the adjustment of the immigrant to the law is done through a bureau of complaints similar to that of the New York bureau. The fruitful principle was adopted from the start "not to theorize concerning the problems and difficulties met with by newly arrived immigrants, but to find out from the immigrants themselves what those facts and problems were."[1]

In the first two years of operation about five thousand complaints were received; in the following three years about 8,500, an average of about 2,750 a year. Considering the higher percentage of foreign born in the population of New York and the fact that New York City is the gateway of the main port of entry to this country, the complaints received in the California bureau indicate a more adequate service than practically the same number of complaints in the New York bureau.

The California complaint bureau, like that in New York, is largely a bureau of adjustment and conciliation, and of advice and information. The California commission has also been active in securing the passage of preventive and remedial legislation.

On the staff of the commission are to be found a full equipment of foreign-speaking workers, and we may note in the work of the commission a policy as to the use of foreign languages opposed to popular sentiment. In times of disturbance and unrest it was the conviction of the commission that foreign languages should be used not less, but more, in order that the foreign born could

[1] *Report for 1918*, p. 13.

be reached by the American. Consequently, in the face of an agitation for the suppression of the foreign-language press in California, the commission installed more foreign-speaking agents in its various offices and made more frequent use of the foreign-language press as a medium of communication with the immigrant population.

The war program carried out in this way won the interest and co-operation of immigrants in California for each Federal order, and a good mutual understanding was established.

The commission has published from time to time information useful to the public as well as to the immigrant. A recent pamphlet of special importance for the immigrant is a *Bulletin of Information for Immigrants*, compiled after a study of the complaint register for the years in which the bureau has been in operation, to learn what matters most frequently cause trouble for the foreign-born people. The way to avoid such difficulties is explained in the bulletin in an exceedingly clear and simple way, in terms that the immigrant can understand, and applied to the special matters in which he has been found to need help. This commission is still in active and successful operation.

MASSACHUSETTS BUREAU OF IMMIGRATION

In Massachusetts a Bureau of Immigration was created as an independent bureau, responsible to no other board or department, by an Act of Legislature in 1917, under the direction of a board of five members. It was required that at least one member of the board should be a woman, and at least two members should, by nativity or descent, be of the races most largely represented in the immigration to Massachusetts during the ten years preceding their appointment. The duties of the bureau, as set forth in the law, were to take such measures as would tend to bring into sympathetic and mutually helpful relations the commonwealth and its residents of foreign origin, to protect immigrants from exploitation and abuse, to stimulate their acquisition of the English language, to develop their understanding of American government, institutions and ideals, and generally to promote their assimilation and naturalization. In the first year of operation special attention was paid to abuses in connection with immigrant banks, cases of exploitation in factories were heard by the bureau, resulting in a remedying of the condition complained of, and a campaign was carried on against "runners" in the city courts.

An interesting feature of the work of this bureau was the recognition of the foreign born as a partner in the enterprise, not only in the requirement that two of the board should be of the same stock as newer immigrants, but in the plan of organizing advisory co-operative committees of American citizens of foreign origin or descent, for stimulating the acquirement of English and citizenship by their alien fellow countrymen. Committees of Italians, Lithuanians, and Greeks were formed in the year 1919.

The bureau also held the idea that an Americanization program should include an effort to educate Americans to a sympathetic understanding of later comers, and as a feature of that effort planned a series of racial monographs, to inform the public of the contribution made by newcomers to the civic and industrial life of America, and issued and circulated broadcast a leaflet urging Americans to make the strangers in a strange land feel "at home," and to show them courtesy and patience. In 1919, in the course of a reorganization of state bureaus, this bureau lost its independent existence, its functions being transferred to the Division of Education of Aliens in the State Department of Education.[1]

The directors of the bureau felt that through this transfer the bureau was likely to lose much of its effectiveness and influence with the immigrant groups. The criticism is made by them that the transfer brings under one responsibility activities which have nothing in common. The Department of Education is not concerned with the abuse and exploitation of the foreign born, which frequently carries the Bureau of Immigration into the criminal courts. It has not within its scope the banking experiences of the foreign born, or conditions affecting their landing and safe conduct to immediate destination, or conditions affecting housing, their naturalization, their problems of employment, or of domestic life.

And they feel that the effect upon the foreign born will be unfortunate. The new title "Education of Aliens" will be distasteful to the very people whom it is designed to attract, and discards the name under which the bureau had become favorably known to the foreign born throughout the state. In their opinion a falling off in applications for service will result from this transfer.

IMMIGRANTS' PROTECTIVE LEAGUE OF CHICAGO

The Immigrants' Protective League of Chicago is a private society doing a work substantially the same as that of the New York, California, and Massachusetts state bureaus of immigration. The league, established in a city which is practically, if not technically, a port

[1] *Second Annual Report of the Bureau of Immigration, Boston, 1920*, p. 11.

of entry, and at the same time unprovided with the official safeguards against exploitation of a port of entry, has done a most valuable and effective work in the protection of newly arrived immigrants, especially of women and girls, who run the danger of being lost in the great city and thrown into the hands of white slavers. Like the bureaus of immigration, the league receives complaints, gives advice and information, and refers cases to the appropriate agency for attending to their needs. The league also does social service work with individuals. It is well equipped with foreign-language workers. On the staff are found persons speaking Italian, Russian, German, Lithuanian, Polish, Croatian, Hungarian, Greek, Turkish, French, and Czech. All of the case workers are foreign speaking. Not one native American is employed.

The league is greatly handicapped by lack of money, and for that reason, perhaps, has never conducted a publicity campaign to advertise its work among the immigrant population.

FOREIGN LANGUAGE INFORMATION SERVICE

An agency doing valuable service in the adjustment of the immigrant to the law in the course of a more general work is the Foreign Language Information Service, which was organized as a division of the United States Committee on Public Information in March, 1918, to meet the emergency needs of the war. Its purpose was to inform the foreign born and non-English-speaking population of the nation's purposes and needs. This society is now operating as an independent service. Part of its work is to disseminate through the foreign-language press such information about the laws as will help the foreign-born person to understand and obey them. And through a personal

THE IMMIGRANT'S DAY IN COURT

service, advice and instruction are given to persons bringing to them individual difficulties. An especially important and extensive help was rendered by them in explaining the alien income-tax provisions to bewildered aliens, and instructing them how to secure their rights.

PRESENT NEEDS

From a survey of the field of immigrant aid in matters involving the law it is evident that much remains to be done. Certain limitations in the different types of agencies now in the field show themselves plainly. The public agencies cannot hope to work under a continuous policy. Changes in administration bring in directing heads and staff members of varying capacity for the work, and with varying conceptions of its nature. And financial support of public undertakings varies from administration to administration.

The private agency can count upon a greater uniformity of policy, can perhaps count upon a higher standard of efficiency year in and year out, and can be independent in framing a policy. But the private agency is usually limited in resources and has no authority to carry on activities further than will be permitted by voluntary coöperation. Perhaps this is, after all, not a drawback, if we accept the principle that the voluntary response is the one most valuable. The private agency also may represent too strongly some private interest, and try to put into effect the private views of its members and directors.

The agency purposing to adjust the immigrant to the legal institutions of our country should not only represent our community as a whole, but should also represent the best in the thought and life of the immigrant peoples. It should include both the foreign born and the native element in relations of mutual sympathy and coöperation, it should fit its aims and purposes to real needs of the immigrant people rather than to any preconceived idea of those needs, and should encourage the abolition of itself as rapidly as possible by working for modifications in our legal system, for education of the immigrant, and also for the education of American sentiment about the immigrant, so that an intermediary between him and the law will no longer be needed.

INDEX

531

INDEX

INDEX

Courts (continued)
  Duties, 102
  European, 149, 151–153, 156
  Relation to immigrant, 102–
      144, 145, 243, 255, 261
  Treatment, 164–166, 172, 190,
      196, 233
  Types
    Appeal, 154
    Federal
      Appeal to in deportation
        cases, 332
      Cases in, 319–322
    Minor, 153–155, 178, 181, 239–
      243
      Aldermanic, 174–177
      Criminal, 196–197
      District courts, 178
      Domestic Relations, 182–
        189
      In Chicago, 207–210
      In Massachusetts, 189–207
      In Philadelphia, 234–239
    Justice, 178, 210, 215
      Constable, 166–168
      Lawyers, 173
      Practice, 158–164, 168–
        174
      "Runners," 173
      Theory, 155–158
    Juvenile, 193, 215
    Magistrates, 178
    Municipal, 207–210, 210– 217,
      234–239
      Boys', 207
      Domestic Relations, 207,
        215, 239
      Moral, 207
      Small claim, 207, 210
    Police, 178, 187–189
Crimes
  Larceny and burglary, 117–
    120
  Liquor cases
    "Runners'" aid, 129–130
  Violence, 105–117
Criminality (foreign born)
  Cause, 105, 192

Statistics
  Adjustment, 103
  By nativity, 102–105
Croatian, 250
  In steel industry, 288
Czech
  Crimes
    Larceny, 117
    On "Red Special,"336, 351

D

Davis, Jerome, 274
Davis, Michael M., 63
Defendant
  Immigrant, 128–132
Denaturalization
  Cases, 319–322
Department of Labor, 305, 322,
    328–330
  Deportation, 335–467
Department of Justice
  Deportation, 335–467
  Illegal procedure
    Report, 419, 438, 445
Deportation
  1919–1920, 335–467
  Anarchy clause, 339–346
  Effect on immigrant, 461–467
  Later, 452–454
  Laws, 315–318
  Numerical result, 459–461
  Proceedings, 339–356
  Procedure, 328–334
  Russian workers, 373–435
Detroit
  Board of Commerce, 60
  Communist attests, 446
  Deportation cases, 437–444
  Legal-Aid Society
    Case record, 14, 75, 83, 86,
      493
    Clients' nationalities, 492
Dialect
  Need for interpreters, 229
District of Columbia
  Legislation
    Workmen's compensation,20
DuBesse, Attillio Stanislav

INDEX

537

THE IMMIGRANT'S DAY IN COURT

INDEX

THE IMMIGRANT'S DAY IN COURT

540

INDEX

INDEX

543

THE IMMIGRANT'S DAY IN COURT

INDEX

545